Characteristics of Children's Behavior Disorders

Second Edition

James M. Kauffman

University of Virginia

Charles E. Merrill Publishing Company
A Bell & Howell Company
Columbus   Toronto   London   Sydney

Published by Charles E. Merrill Publishing Co.
A Bell & Howell Company
Columbus, Ohio 43216

For Tim and Missy

This book was set in Times Roman.
Production Coordination: Judith Rose Sacks
Cover Design Coordination: Will Chenoweth

Photo Credits

pp. 3, 182—Harvey Phillips   *p. 31*—Ohio Historical Society   *p. 85*—Jerry Bushey   *p. 105*—Rohn Engh   *p. 219*—Rick Smolan   *p. 264*—Edgar Bernstein   *p. 283*—Myron Cunningham

Library of Congress Catalog Card Number: 80-82607
International Standard Book Number: 0-675-08055-X
Printed in the United States of America
1 2 3 4 5 6 7 8 9 10–86 85 84 83 82 81

preface

This book, like its first edition, is intended primarily as a text for an introductory course in special education for emotionally disturbed children. Because behavior disorders are commonly observed in the children who populate special education classes and schools regardless of their designated categories, the book should be of value in other special education areas as well, particularly the areas of learning disabilities and mental retardation. Students in developmental, abnormal, educational, or school psychology may also find the book to be useful reading.

The organization of this book differs noticeably from that of most earlier texts. The emphasis is on clear description of disordered behavior, research of factors implicated in its development, and assessment of methods for its amelioration. Although there are no chapters devoted to "diagnostic" categories, such as *normal, psychoneurotic, juvenile delinquent,* and *autistic,* there are chapters dealing with the contributions of family, school, and biological status to disordered behavior and chapters focusing on specific types of disordered behavior, such as aggression, hyperactivity, and distractibility. The titles and the organization of these chapters reflect my belief that children's behaviors can be more easily and productively classified than children themselves. Discussion of traditional categories is thus subsumed under the more generic behavior disorders that cut across diagnostic classifications.

The book is organized in four major sections. Part One is an introduction to some of the major concepts and historical antecedents of contemporary special education for disturbed children. The first chapter begins with vignettes selected to orient the reader to the characteristics of emotionally disturbed children and the emotions they disturb in others. Definition and prevalence of behavior disorders are then presented from a conceptual problem-solving approach rather than as an exercise in memory of facts and figures. Chapter 2 is a brief account of how the field grew out of the disciplines of psychology, psychiatry, and public education. Chapter 3 presents major considerations for assessment—screening, identification, and evaluation for intervention purposes. In Part Two, the origins of disordered behavior are discussed. Research on the role of the family, biophysical factors, and the school is reviewed, and implications of the research for special educators are summarized. The four chapters comprising Part Three deal with salient types of disordered behavior. For each type of behavior there is discussion of definition, measurement, etiology, and methods of control. I have attempted to maintain an empirical, research-based perspective in each chapter and to emphasize issues germane to special education. Part Four, containing only the last chapter, represents my attempt to synthesize the preceding material and formulate a rationale for educational intervention.

Several additional comments should clarify my intent in this volume. First, developmental processes are an important concern. I have tried to integrate relevant parts of the vast and scattered literature on child development and relate the findings to children's behavior disorders. My intention in struggling with this task was not only to outline what we know about how and why disordered behavior develops, but also to suggest how children's behavioral development can be changed for the better. Second, in trying to give attention primarily to research and theory grounded in replicable experimental data, I have shown bias toward a behavioral viewpoint. I believe that when one examines the literature with the intention of being swayed by empirical evidence rather than by devotion to humanistic ideology alone—as I believe one must if truly humane treatment of children is to become a reality—then a behavioral bias is understandable. Third, this book was not intended to be comprehensive in its treatment of the subject. An introductory book must leave much unsaid and many loose ends which need to be tied up. Unquestionably, the easiest thing about writing this book was to let it fall short of saying it all and to hope that its readers will pursue what is said by those whose work is cited in the references. Finally, this is not a "how-to-do-it" methods book. Although examples of how disordered behavior can be controlled are found in several chapters, the book is meant only to introduce students to the field and to provide background.

I am grateful to my colleagues who provided helpful comments on various drafts of the manuscript: Norrie Haring, Mary Margaret Kerr, Rick Neel, Mike Nelson, Lou Polsgrove, Dick Shores, Phil Strain, and Dick Whelan. Their perceptive suggestions improved the book considerably. I also thank two graduate students who were particularly helpful in tracking down references, proofreading, and indexing: Jim Krouse and Joanna Szymczyk.

contents _____

prologue

The boy was small but with tough, stringy muscles standing out on his neck and forearms. Childhood lingered in his features, but when he paused to rest, his fingers went hopefully to the silky beginnings of sideburns and a mustache. He mopped like a robot, jerkily, brainlessly, but took pains not to splash suds over the toes of his black boots.

"That boy," said Helmholtz, "I've seen him around school, but I never knew his name."

Quinn laughed cheerlessly. "Billy the Kid? The storm trooper? Rudolph Valentino? Flash Gordon?" He called the boy. . . . "Hey, Jim! Come here a minute."

Helmholtz was appalled to see that the boy's eyes were as expressionless as oysters.

"This is my brother-in-law's kid by another marriage—before he married my sister," said Quinn. "His name's Jim Donnini, and he's from the south side of Chicago, and he's very tough."

Jim Donnini's hands tightened on the mop handle.

"How do you do?" said Helmholtz.

"Hi," said Jim emptily.

"He's living with me now," said Quinn. "He's my baby now."

"You want a lift to school, Jim?"

"Yeah, he wants a lift to school," said Quinn. "See what you make of him. He won't talk to me." He turned to Jim. "Go on, kid, wash up and shave."

Robotlike, Jim marched away.

"Where are his parents?"

"His mother's dead. His old man married my sister, walked out on her, and stuck her with him. Then the court didn't like the way she was raising him, and put him in foster homes for a while. Then they decided to get him clear out of Chicago, so they stuck me with him." He shook his head. "Life's a funny thing, Helmholtz."

"Not very funny, sometimes," said Helmholtz.

"Like some whole new race of people coming up," said Quinn

wonderingly. "Nothing like the kids we got around here. Those boots, the black jacket—and he won't talk. He won't run around with the other kids. Won't study. I don't think he can even read and write very good."

"Does he like music at all? Or drawing? Or animals?" said Helmholtz. "Does he collect anything?"

"You know what he likes?" said Quinn. "He likes to polish those boots—get off by himself and polish those boots. And when he's really in heaven is when he can get off by himself, spread comic books all around him on the floor; polish his boots, and watch television." He smiled ruefully. "Yeah, he had a collection too. And I took it away from him and threw it in the river."

"Threw it in the river?" said Helmholtz.

"Yeah," said Quinn. "Eight knives—some with blades as long as your hand."

Helmholtz paled. "Oh." A prickling sensation spread over the back of his neck. "This is a new problem at Lincoln High. I hardly know what to think about it. It's a kind of sickness, isn't it? That's the way to look at it?"

"Sick?" said Quinn. He slapped the table. "You can say that again!" He tapped his chest. "And Doctor Quinn is just the man to give him what's good for what ails him."

"What's that?" said Helmholtz.

"No more talk about the poor little sick boy," said Quinn grimly. "That's all he's heard from the social workers and the juvenile court, and God knows who all. From now on, he's the no-good bum of a man. I'll ride his tail till he straightens up and flies right or winds up in the can for life. One way or the other."

"I see," said Helmholtz.

part one

The Problem, Its History,
and Its Assessment

chapter 1

Definition, Prevalence, and Conceptual Models

This book is about children who arouse negative feelings and induce negative behaviors in others. These children are not typically popular among or leaders of their classmates and playmates. They usually experience both social and academic failure at school. Most of the adults in their environment would choose to avoid them if they could. Their behavior is so persistently irritating to authority figures that they seem to invite punishment or rebuke. Even in their own eyes these children are usually failures, obtaining little gratification from life and chronically falling short of their own aspirations. They are handicapped children—not limited by diseased or crippled bodies but by behaviors that are discordant with their social and interpersonal contexts.

Some of the behaviors that handicap children are recognized as abnormal in nearly every cultural group and social stratum. Muteness at age 10, self-injurious behavior, and eating of feces, as examples, are seldom considered culture-specific or socially determined problems. Such disorders represent discrepancies from universally accepted developmental norms. On the other hand, many behaviors handicap children because they violate standards peculiar to their culture or the social institutions in their environment. Academic achievement, types of aggression, moral behavior, sexual responses, language patterns, and so on will be judged as normal or disordered depending on the prevailing attitudes in the child's ethnic and religious group, family, and school. For example, failing to read, hitting other children, taking the belongings of others, masturbating, and swearing are evaluated according to the standards of the child's community. Thus, a given behavior may be considered disordered in one situation or context and not in another simply because of differences in the expectancies of the people around the child. The majority of most children's behavior disorders in this book are defined by such sociocultural expectations.

Many behavior disorders develop from social interactions through the ubiquitous learning processes of modeling, reinforcement, extinction, and punishment that produce and maintain human behavior. Adults and other children in the youngster's environment, then, may inadvertently arrange conditions that develop and support undesirable or inappropriate responses. Ironically, the same adults who unwittingly shape inappropriate behavior may then initiate action to have the child labeled *disturbed* or *disordered*. The child might behave quite differently if these adults changed their own behavior in relation to the child's, or if the child was placed in a different environment. The locus of the problem in these cases may be as much in the child's caretakers or peers as in the child; the child may be as disturbed by others as he or she is disturbing to others.

Children's behavior influences the actions of their parents, their teachers, and others who interact with them. Children "teach" their parents and teachers how to behave toward them as surely as they are taught by these adults (Bell & Harper, 1977; Rosenberg & Graubard, 1975; Sameroff & Chandler, 1975). Teaching and learning are mutually interactive processes in which teacher and learner frequently and often subtly exchange roles. When a child has difficulty with teachers, parents, or peers, it is as important to consider *their* responses to the behavior as it is to evaluate the child's reactions. It is not surprising, therefore, that an ecological perspective on the problem of disordered behavior is gaining popularity.

An ecological perspective takes into account the interrelationships between the child and the various aspects of the environment. The problem of disturbed behavior is not viewed simply as actions of the child that are inappropriate but rather as undesirable interactions and transactions between the child and other people. For example, a child's temper tantrums in school could indeed be a problem and a focal point of concern, but an ecological perspective would demand that the behavior of the child's teachers, peers, and parents—their expectations, demands, and reactions to the child's tantrums—be taken into consideration to explain and deal with the problem.

The specific behaviors of children that can induce negative feelings and reactions in others are as varied as any human characteristic. Children's disordered behavior may be described according to two primary dimensions: aggressive acting out, and immature withdrawal. Behavioral excesses and deficiencies along these dimensions—too much or too little of behaviors that would be considered normal in an appropriate quantity—are the essential characteristics of *disturbed* children.[1] The following vignettes illustrate the variety of behavioral excesses and deficiencies that can plague children and those around them.

vignettes

1 Henry's incessant talking and loud outbursts made it almost impossible for the teacher to carry out her routine. His misbehavior was all the more salient as the class was in general well behaved. Some of Henry's deviant behaviors were smearing and spraying paint on desks and floors, unraveling roles of tape, destroying a pegboard with a hammer, chipping away at the sidewalk outside the classroom with a screwdriver and hammer, throwing temper tantrums during which he turned over desks and chairs, not returning to the classroom after recess, sometimes from morning recess not until lunch-time. This caused considerable consternation among school personnel since they are responsible for students' well-being throughout the school day. When asked what Henry liked to do, the teacher included "swearing" and "tipping over his chair." When we came upon the scene, Henry's mother was about to take him to a child psychiatrist, and school administrators were considering a plan to place him on a half-day schedule or possibly even to remove him from the public school and place him in a special class for emotionally handicapped children. (Kubany, Weiss, & Sloggett, 1971, p. 174)

2 I remember Joey, one of our first students, and the destruction resulting from his acts of aggression and hostility. There were days

---

[1] The terms *emotionally disturbed* and *behavior disordered* are used interchangeably in this book. Although *behavior disorder* may be a more accurate descriptor of most children's socialization difficulties (Ross, 1974), *emotionally disturbed* is also recognized by most individuals as a label signifying that the child exhibits behavior that is perceived as a problem. The terms *emotionally handicapped* and *behaviorally handicapped* also are used to signify the same population of children.

when everything within his reach was either thrown, torn, or smashed. Even with one teacher assigned exclusively to him, he created chaos. Here is a typical school day as described in excerpts from the teacher's anecdotal records:

> Joey threw a tray with snacks on the floor . . . spilt the orange juice . . . upset two jars of paint . . . threw a pail at the window and broke a pane . . . swept food and dishes off the dining room table . . . kicked his heels through a wall. . . . (Fenichel, 1974, p. 64)

3 N.B., aged 16, was described to me by his father, who came to consult me, in regard to his management, as a boy of singularly unruly and untractable character, selfish, wayward, violent without ground or motive, and liable under the paroxysm of his moodiness to do personal mischief to others; not, however, of a physically bold character. He is of a fair understanding, and exhibits considerable acuteness in sophistical apologies for his wayward conduct. He has made little progress in any kind of study. His fancy is vivid, supplying him profusely with sarcastic imagery. He has been subjected at different times, and equally without effect, to a firmly mild and to a rigid discipline. In the course of these measures, solitary confinement has been tried; but to this he was impassive. It produced no effect.

He was last in a very good seminary in a town in _____, where he drew a knife upon one of the officers of the establishment, while admonishing him; and produced a deep feeling of aversion in the minds of his companions, by the undisguised pleasure which he showed at some bloodshed which took place in this town during the disturbance of 18____.

He has not appeared to be sensually disposed, and he is careful of property. His bodily health is good, and he has never had any cerebral affection. This boy was further described to me as progressively becoming worse in his conduct, and more savagely violent to his relatives. Still I easily discovered that he was unfavourably situated; for his relations appeared to be at once irritable and affectionate; and the total failure of various plans of education was throwing him entirely upon their hands.

As an instance of the miserable pleasure which he took in exciting disgust and pain, I was told, that when 13 years old, he stripped himself naked and exposed himself to his sisters. (Mayo, 1839, pp. 68–69)

4 Rodney's personal care habits were atrocious. He seemed to attract dirt, grease, and filth. His vocabulary was also foul, and he was generally just plain obnoxious. Not always, though—for he could be very likeable. However, most of the time he found ways of mak-

ing people want to get away from him as fast as possible and stay away for as long as possible. It is hard to imagine a more repulsive twelve year old, and it is no wonder that he found his way into the psychiatric hospital where I was teaching.

In school, the work Rodney handed in reflected his personality. He picked his nose until it bled and wiped the blood and mucus on the papers. He picked his ears and wiped the wax on his papers. He picked his acne and wiped the blood and pus on his papers. He spit on his papers and smeared the saliva over his answers to try to erase them. When he did use an eraser, he made holes. He wrote answers at the wrong place and then circled them and drew arrows, often to another wrong place. He wrote four-lettered words and drew lewd pictures and swastikas on his papers. He punched holes in his papers, tore them, wadded them, taped them together, ripped them apart again, and retaped them. All the while, he muttered curses — he couldn't do the damned work because it was too babyish or too hard or too stupid or too crazy and "what kind of a stupid goddamned bastard was I to give him such crap?"

Rodney made himself the bane of everyone's existence. He teased and bullied smaller children unmercifully. He baited teachers and threatened other adults. Cleanliness and pleasantness seemed completely foreign to him. He referred to his former teacher most often as "f—— stick."

My first confrontation with Rodney was the first minute of the first day I tried to teach him. He sauntered into the classroom, took one look at me, and said, "If you're going to be in here, then I'm getting the hell out!" In an instant, he was out the door, around the corner, up two flights of stairs, and out of the building. It did not take me long to realize that I had to go after him and bring him back, even if it meant dragging him. I caught up with him about twenty feet outside the building. I fully expected that we would have a physical struggle and I would end up dragging him back to the classroom. Instead, when I reached out to grab him, he stopped, looked at me for a moment, and said, "Well, hell! I guess I might as well go back." He got back to the classroom before I did and never tried to run again.

But that was not our last confrontation. Rodney did not like homework. We teachers assigned homework as a policy, and we expected that it would be done. Rodney said that if I gave him homework he would burn it. I replied matter-of-factly that I didn't think he would, since he wasn't allowed to have matches, and that even if he did it wouldn't get him anywhere because I had duplicate assignments I would give him. "Well, you son-of-a-bitch, just wait and see," he said. The next morning he was brought to the classroom by a child care worker (attendant). Triumphantly, he threw a tin can on my desk and sneered.

"Here's your goddamned homework!" I opened the can. It was full of ashes. (Payne, Kauffman, Patton, Brown, & DeMott, 1979, pp. 34-34)

5 If you could look back and focus on my most vivid memory, you might see me, now the teacher in Mrs. Wright's former classroom, futilely hovering over two hyperactive twelve-year-old girls who are fighting about which one should use the free half of an easel, while on the other side of this easel, a big, burly, belligerent boy is calmly painting, secure in the knowledge that no one would dare question his right to do so. Standing near the window is a small, thin-faced, pale, remote-looking boy who is staring at the fish tank, apparently just watching the fish swim around. Next to him, another boy is sitting on the rocker tickling himself under the chin with the mink tails he has just cut off the collar of the school secretary's new spring coat. Two children, a boy and a girl, perched on the old dining table, are playing a loud game of checkers, while another boy is silently resting, stretched out atop an old upright piano which I had enveigled into my room. Sporadically, in the midst of this magnificent atmosphere for learning, some child says to another, "Your mother," and the entire class seems to leap together and land in a football pile-up on the floor, while I stand helplessly by.

Of course I made many mistakes, but I hope I also learned something from each. Let me share just one of these early mistakes with you. I was doing my weekly planning when a brilliant idea occurred to me. I decided that the greatest contribution I could make that week would be to bring some culture into the lives of those poor, deprived, disturbed children at Bellevue. To start on this enriching experience, I elected to read to them a favorite poem from my own elementary school days, "The Owl and the Pussycat." Imagine my consternation at the chaos I caused when I reached the lines, "What a beautiful pussy you are, you are. What a beautiful pussy you are." The children actually tumbled out of my room with noisy screaming and guffawing. Within minutes, I was left alone in the classroom, bewildered and unaware of what had caused the difficulty. I had a lot to learn. (Berkowitz, 1974, pp. 30-31)

6 Looking back on those initial experiences with emotionally disturbed boys, I still wonder how the senior staff tolerated some of my naive behavior. For example, I remember encouraging an anxious, withdrawn boy to express his anger until he became so furious that he punched me in the nose. Then there was the time I overcontrolled my cabin group and intervened at the slightest ripple of trouble. While the other groups appeared chaotic, my group was

a perfect example of goodness. During the last week of camp, one of the boys baited me into a shouting match by refusing to do a simple task. At the outburst of my anger, the entire group exploded in grand style. They started fights, broke windows, and climbed on the roof of the cabin where they shouted obscenities and suggested that all adults perform impossible anatomical tricks. (Long, 1974, p. 173)

Up to this point, the vignettes have illustrated aggressive, disruptive behavior. Certainly these children's behavior is perceived rightfully as troublesome and in need of change. Yet it is obvious that the way these children were treated by their peers and adults may have added to the difficulty.

The following descriptions provide pictures of another dimension of disordered behavior—extreme withdrawal into a private fantasy world. In the case of "No. 210," consider how the abuse, here sarcastically referred to as *kind guardianship and protection*, might have added to the young woman's aberrant behavior.

vignettes

1 I was aware, of course, that emotionally disturbed children sometimes have wild fantasies, but I was not prepared for Wanda. Wanda was eleven years old when I met her. She had a tested IQ of about 160, but it didn't do her much good except, perhaps, to enrich her fantasy life. I was never able to find a topic of conversation, an area of the curriculum, a place, or a time that was free of her bizarre imaginings. She had fantasies about jeans—she "wore" special forty-pocket and hundred-pocket jeans with zippers in the front and drew stylized pictures of them. She had fantasies about the president and the governor and crucifixes and *The Pit and the Pendulum*, doctors, nurses, swimming pools, toilets, injections, physical examinations, Project Mercury (this was in 1962), moles (she had one on her arm that was a microphone into which she talked and one on her leg that was a thermostat controlling her body temperature) . . . there was no end.

When she engaged in her fantasies, Wanda got a peculiar, fixed grin on her face, her eyes became glazed, she giggled, and she talked (often apparently to herself) in a high-pitched squeaky voice. Frequently, she drew pictures with captions representing the fantasied object and activities. Sometimes she engaged in other bizarre behaviors, such as flattening herself on the floor or wall, kissing it, caressing it, and talking to it. It was impossible to teach Wanda or to have a rational conversation with her while she was fantasizing, and she was "in" fantasy most of the time. It was impossible to predict when, during times of lucidity and reality-oriented behavior, she would suddenly enter her fantasy world again.

Mostly, Wanda had fantasies about buildings. She carried on conversations with them, and they took on human characteristics. Certain parts of buildings—doors, floors, windows, chimneys, porches, and the like—sometimes became separate entities with lives of their own. At other times, these parts of buildings were body parts to be physically examined, injected, or manipulated. Custodians and engineers were, to Wanda, "building doctors." "Dr. Brady just sprayed some white stuff in Bonnie's ass" could be translated to mean that the chief building engineer had just sprayed some lubricant in the door locks in the residence hall.

Wanda had some very special building acquaintances: Elmer (the school building), the governor's mansion (it actually had a name—Cedar Crest), capitol buildings (it didn't really matter which one—they were all prized for their domes), certain churches (those with more than one steeple were special), and the White House (even though it had a peculiar and irreverent habit of "passing gas from under the South Portico"). Wanda also had some favorite building parts. A dome or cupola was, in her terms, a "Beulah Murphy." And a "Beulah Murphy" was a breast. A church steeple represented a penis. Buildings always cried from their windows and talked out of their doors. (Payne, Kauffman, Patton, Brown, & DeMott, 1974, pp. 31–32)

2 No. 210 is a young woman in the 19th year of her age, who although poor and uneducated, has been virtuously and genteelly raised; she was brought to us on the 21st day of last October, with her hands tied behind her, and her back most shamefully lacerated by the whip of a brute in human form, to whose *kind guardianship and protection* she had been confided for the journey by the law of the land. For several days after her arrival here, she continued in a state of uninterrupted phrenzy, insomuch that when her hands were not confined, they were employed mostly in tearing her clothes, pulling out her hair by the handful, or in plucking out her toe nails by the roots. She seemed indeed to be callous to violence of any character or degree inflicted upon her person. Although unmarried and in the absence of the slightest ground on which a suspicion could rest, prejudicial to her virtue, she conceived the singular delusion that she was pregnant; that the foetus stood erect, with its feet planted on the os-pubis, and that with outstretched arms and grasping hands it was striving to lay hold upon her heart and suppress its pulsations. Her screams were often most terrific, and her countenance indicated but too plainly the horrid apprehension and wretchedness which such a fact, could it have really existed, would have been so well calculated to produce. (Stribling, 1842, p. 54)

Not all withdrawals are so extreme. These were cases of psychotic detachment from the real world. Some children need special assistance in school because they lack social skills or because they are treated by others as social outcasts. These last two vignettes illustrate social-emotional withdrawal and provide a child's eye view of an environment that could reasonably be expected to foster withdrawn behavior. They reveal adult insensitivity to children's feelings and circumstances and highlight the fact that behavior problems do not reside simply or exclusively in the child.

vignettes

1 From the start, I hated school, deeply, irrevocably, and silently.
Kindergarten was anathema. Rather than take me to the doctor every other day with sore throats and stomach aches that were strictly school-induced, my mother finally capitulated and let me stay at home. First grade was no better, however, and as my sore "threats" would no longer work, and as the compulsory school laws prevented my mother from withdrawing me, I had no alternative but to start off for school daily and then divert myself to the rocks and crevices that then underlay the Hellsgate Bridge in the new and growing suburb of Queens, twenty minutes away by subway from the lower East Side where I was born.

I wonder if teachers really appreciate how overwhelmingly frightening it is to be a truant. Fear possessed me completely— fear of ridicule by school-loving seat-mates, each of whom was smarter than ten of me put together; fear of God, who was certainly going to punish me by striking my parents dead; but, most of all, fear of tongue lashings by arm-twisting teachers, who were going to debase me by "leaving me back." Which indeed they did. I was a "holdover." My teacher didn't bother to explain to my mother why I was left back, but she clearly told everyone else. I couldn't read. And I couldn't read because I played hookey—or so she said. The fact that I was already reading Hebrew and the exotic adventures of Dickie Dare in my friend Lilly's third-grade reader was totally unknown to my teacher, yet I am certain, even now, that if she had known it, she would not have altered her decision.

My teacher was what I knew she was—anti-Semitic—because my mother told me so. This was a word I learned very early in life, and I accepted it casually as I accepted being an alien, one of only four Jewish children in the entire school. I felt special—not a bad feeling, but not completely good either.

I was never permitted to hold the American flag in front of the class for our morning class salute—a sacrosanct ceremony in every classroom in the entire school. My shoes were never clean enough. Once I was told I had lice. Or sometimes I did not have a handkerchief safety-pinned to the lower left shoulder of my dress; this handkerchief always had to be in that exact same spot—never elsewhere. I never figured out how it was that we were supposed to blow our noses, and I never asked. I settled it myself. I had a handkerchief for showing and a handkerchief for blowing. And usually I forgot one or the other or both deliberately because I firmly believed that good little girls should never need to blow their noses at all. It was too crass. Instead, I stuffed pencil tip erasers up my nostrils. As for boys, I never even wondered what they did. Handkerchiefs were not within their generic classification.

These memories come flooding over me as I write—the hurt of being labeled a liar by a seventh-grade teacher who did not believe I had written a composition using the word chaos because I could not give him a definition of it. Did he never understand that I knew the word chaos down to my very toes because I felt it deeply every day of my life in school? Then there was the day my fifth-grade teacher threw into the garbage can the chocolate cake my mother had baked for a class party and which the children had voted to give to the teacher because it was the prettiest cake of all. And going farther back, I remember staring at the school map that hung—large, frightening, and overwhelming—from the border of the chalkboard and trying desperately to find New York State while not another child spoke—every eye, especially the teacher's, was glued to me. But worst of all was the indignity, fear, and humiliation of having to cheat on a test because I could not remember whether four-fifths equalled 80 percent. (Rothman, 1974, pp. 221–222)

2 That school day had been like all others—bright with the joy of being with children and blurred in a kaleidoscope of activity. But in late afternoon, there was something different in the way Miss Joseph asked us to take our seats. Her customary calm and warmth were missing. On top of that, she announced that the principal had come to talk to us. My stomach squinched "danger."

The principal, small, grayed, and austere, spoke in her usual clipped fashion about the importance of working hard in school. As her train of thought thundered by, I was aware only of its ominous roar. The meaning of her words did not come into focus until she made the pronouncement: "Those boys and girls who have frittered away their time, and as a consequence will not be pro-moted to second grade, will stand when I call their names." Then she called *my* name.

The shock and mortification staggered me, making it difficult to struggle out of my seat to stand beside my desk. Who stood when she called the other names, the faces of those who remained seated, and what further remarks she intoned all blurred into a macabre dance that encircled my shame. Breathing was painful and had, I was sure, a ridiculously loud rasp which was heard by everyone. My legs rebelled at supporting my weight, so my fingers, aching tripods of ice, shared the burden. In contrast to the cold of my numbed face were the hot tears that welled in my eyes and threatened to spill down my cheeks to complete my degradation.

The principal left. Class was over. Amid joyous shouts, children milled through the door that for them was the entrance to summer fun and freedom. Some may have spoken to me, to tease or to console, but I could not hear them. The warm and pretty Miss Joseph was there, speaking to me, but I could neither hear nor respond. The borders of my mind had constricted like a hand clutching my pain.

Daily I sat staring at a book that would not surrender to me its meaning. In my war with the book, now and again I was victorious over an isolated word, but the endless legion of pages ultimately defeated me. Repeatedly, I looked back over the unfriendly, un-yielding rows of print to find a word that I could recognize. In doing so, my failures amassed by the minute, like a swelling mob jeering at me. Finally, the fury rising within me burst from my fists, while from between clenched teeth I silently cursed the head I was pounding. To me, the immutable reality was that my head was bad. It caused my frustration. It sponsored my shame. I knew no alternative but to beat it into becoming a smarter head. That failed, too, adding daily to my feelings of frustration and worthlessness.

Daily terrors were walking the eight blocks to and from school and going into the school yard for recess. Being all flab and clumsi-ness *and* wearing thick glasses made me a ready target for any kid who needed to prove his prowess by beating me up. And the number who needed that were legion. Consequently, a rainy day became a reprieve. To awaken to a rainy morning was like an eleventh-hour stay of execution. It meant no recess outdoors. And nobody who wanted to fight. But even better than a rainy morning was being ill. Only then, in *my* bed, in *my* room, did I feel really secure. In the fall of third grade I missed twenty-two days of school. I was confined to bed with rheumatic fever, as I learned from the family doctor when I didn't have the desired wind for distance running while in college. Despite pains which I can still vividly recall, that confinement is the most peaceful of all my childhood memories.

The only outdoor activities I enjoyed were pretend ones. (The woman who lived in the next row house must have been sainted.) To get me out of the house, my mother put on the open porch the piano stool I played with. It became the steering wheel of a huge, power-ful truck (you know how loud *they* are), which I guided flawlessly along endless highways, gaining the admiration of all whom I passed. At other times, I ventured across the street where the vacant lot became a battlefield on which I, clothed in my father's army tunic and overseas cap, performed feats of heroism and distinction for which I received countless medals and accolades. Those fantasized moments of glory apparently nourished my thin strand of self-respect enough to enable it to withstand the daily siege on my pride.

At night, when the cannonade of derision was still and my imperiled pride temporarily safe, I implored God and the Christ, Jesus, to see to it that tomorrow would not hold for me the tortures of today. I offered all possible concessions and deals, but relentlessly the tomorrows of Monday to Friday were no better. (Rappaport, 1976, pp. 347–350)

Other vignettes involving disordered behavior and its treatment are scattered throughout this book. In each case it is important to consider not only the unpleasant or disturbing features of the child's behavior, but also the circumstances that may have contributed to the problem and the reaction of others (children and adults) to the child's behavior. Disturbed children cannot be considered merely as youngsters who cause others to experience anger, grief, anxiety, or other unpleasantness. They are troubled children in situations that may not be conducive to satisfactory interpersonal relations.

DEFINITION

Problems of Definition

The children who are the topic of this book typically etch pictures in one's memory that are not erased easily. The foregoing discussion and case descriptions provide an intuitive grasp of what a behavior disorder is. But the definition of emotional disturbance—the construction of guidelines that will foster valid and reliable judgments about who is and who is not disturbed—is anything but simple. The reasons it is difficult to arrive at a reliable definition have to do with the very essence of the problem of behavior disorder. Behavior disorder is not a *thing* that exists outside a social context but a label assigned according to cultural rules (Burbach, 1981). Perhaps there is a science of behavior, but the objective methods of natural science do not play an extremely important part in assigning the status of deviant to someone. Disordered behavior is whatever behavior the chosen authority figures in a culture designate as intolerable. Typically, it is behavior that is perceived as threatening the stability, security, or values of that society. For a further discussion of threat and deviance, see Rhodes and Paul (1978).

In the final analysis, the definition of behavior *disorder* or emotional *disturbance* is unavoidably a subjective matter. One can be very objective and precise in measuring specific responses of children and one can be painstakingly explicit in stating social norms or cultural rules for behavior. But ultimately one has to face the realization that the norms, the rules, and professional appraisal of the extent to which particular behaviors deviate from those norms, are matters of subjective judgment. As Rhodes and Paul (1978) have stated so succinctly:

The epiphenomenal problem of deviance is complex and the definitions that exist are many. Each time a group of special children gain social and professional attention, a plethora of definitions of the problems of these children follow. The inconsistency is not, as is typically thought, simply in the definitions, but rather in the primary view of the world from which the definition is derived.   (p. 137)

Differences in world views or conceptual models are but one factor contributing to the problem of defining behavior disorder. In addition, there are problems created by different purposes of definitions, by measurement of behavior, by the range and variability of normal behavior, by the relationship of behavior disorder to other types of deviance, by the transience of behavior problems in children, and by the problem of labeling. Each of these will be considered more closely.

Conceptual Models

Prior to 1950, virtually all intervention with disturbed children was derived from Freudian theory or variations of his psychodynamic model. Within the past two decades, however, a variety of alternative approaches, each associated with a distinctly different conceptual model, have been developed. In addition to the psychodynamic model, biological, sociological, behavioral, ecological, psychoeducational, and phenomenological models have been described (Kauffman & Lewis, 1974; Rhodes & Tracy, 1972a). Each of these conceptual models includes a set of assumptions about why children behave as they do and what must be done in order to correct disorders. The nature of the problem presented by disordered behavior in children is at the heart of controversy among proponents of divergent models. It is not surprising, then, that a definition derived from the tenets of one conceptual model does little but baffle or disappoint those who hold the assumptions of a different model. The task of writing a definition to which all can subscribe, regardless of their conceptual persuasion, may be impossible. An additional problem derives from the fact that many current concepts of childhood behavior disorders are rather crude adaptations of conceptual models of adult psychopathology (Phillips, Draguns, & Bartlett, 1975).

Conceptual models are discussed more fully in the final section of this chapter. Suffice to say here that people who disagree about what emotional disturbance represents at a theoretical or philosophical level are unlikely to agree on a practical definition. For example, proponents of a psychodynamic conceptual model start with the assumption that observable behavior is only symptomatic of an underlying problem of personality integration. To a behaviorist, the real problem is nothing more than the observable behavior itself. The basic assumptions of psychoanalysts and behaviorists are irreconcilable differences that simply preclude agreement about how behavior disorders are correctly or accurately defined.

Purpose of Definitions

Definitions must serve the purposes of the social agents who use them. Within the social structure, courts, schools, clinics and families rely on different criteria to define children's behavior disorders: courts give attention to law-violating behavior, schools to academic and social failure, clinics to reasons for referral, and families to behavior that violates their rules or strains their tolerance. It is difficult, perhaps impossible, to formulate a single definition that is maximally useful to all the social agents who are responsible for children's conduct.

According to Cullinan and Epstein (1979) and Epstein, Cullinan, and Sabatino (1977), a definition can be useful for one or more of several purposes: (a) to guide the delivery of services to children through administrative channels, (b) to reflect a particular theoretical position or to structure a discussion, or (c) to describe populations of children for research purposes. No authoritative definition used to structure discussion or to give apparent substance to a theory has been generally accepted as correct by most professionals working with disturbed children. Such definitions have had little or no influence beyond the covers of the books in which they have appeared. And, as Wood and Lakin (1979) found, definitions used in research studies have varied so widely from study to study that they have added to the confusion concerning the nature of disordered behavior.

Surveys of administrative definitions used by various states (Cullinan & Epstein, 1979; Epstein et al., 1977) showed that most of them contained several identifiable components, such as statements indicating that the child exhibits:

1. disorders of emotions and/or behavior
2. interpersonal problems
3. inability to learn or achieve at school
4. behavior differing from a norm or age-appropriate expectations
5. problems of long standing
6. problems that are severe
7. a need for special education

The same surveys revealed that governmental definitions often include statements regarding *causes* (often pointing to biological or family factors), requirements for *certification* of the child (often specifying who may legitimately make the decision to classify the child as disturbed), and *exclusions* (e.g., a statement that the child cannot be mentally retarded or have serious sensory or health impairments).

Epstein et al. (1979) found that administrative definitions varied so much between states that a child could be reclassified easily as disturbed or normal for educational purposes merely by moving across a state line. This problem was lessened somewhat when Public Law 94–142 (Education of All Handicapped Children Act) went into effect in 1978. The rules and regulations accompanying the law contain a definition of "serious emotional disturbance" which is to be used in judging compliance with the law's requirements of special education and related services for all handicapped children. Naturally, state definitions are now being aligned with the federal definition so that legal compliance with PL 94–142 is not an issue. But, as will be discussed, the federal definition will not resolve many of the problems mentioned here.

Measurement

There are no tests that measure personality, adjustment, anxiety, or other relevant psychological constructs precisely enough to provide a sound basis for definition of *emotionally disturbed*. The reliability and validity of psychometric tests are simply not adequate for purposes of dividing the disturbed from the nondisturbed. While the problems of reliability and validity are especially great in the case of projective tests constructed on the basis of psychodynamic theory, these problems also occur in personality inventories, behavior rating scales, and screening tests designed to sift out those children who *may* have behavior disorders.

Some of the difficulty in measurement is a result of attempts to assess supposed internal states or personality constructs that cannot be observed directly. Direct observation and measurement of children's behavior have in recent years reduced reliance on psychometric tests, but these newer techniques of assessment have not resolved the problem of definition. While it may be more useful to a teacher to know the frequency with which a child hits his classmates than to know that his test responses show him to have a low self-concept or poor ego control, there is no consensus among teachers or psychologists regarding the frequency of a given behavior (e.g., hitting a classmate) that indicates emotional disturbance.

If comparisons between children for purposes of classification as disturbed or nondisturbed are to be made, then behavior will have to be measured under specified environmental conditions. Even if environmental conditions are specified and behaviors of children are measured directly and reliably in that environment, however, it is not likely that a truly satisfactory definition can be constructed on the basis of such measurement. The reason is that given a single set of environmental circumstances, behavior disorder and social adaptation involve more than frequencies of certain behaviors. Adaptive and disordered behavior are defined by the child's ability or inability to modulate his behavior in his everyday environment in order to avoid the censure of others and obtain their approval. The problem of measurement here is somewhat analogous to that in the fields of vision and hearing. Central visual acuity and pure tone auditory thresholds can be measured rather precisely under carefully controlled conditions, but these measures do not indicate how efficiently one will see or hear in one's everyday environment (except within very broad limits). Two people with the same visual acuity, for example, may function quite differently, one as a sighted person and the other as blind. Visual and auditory efficiency must be assessed by observing how the individual adapts to the changing demands of his environment for seeing and hearing. Behavioral adaptation too must be judged by observation of how well one meets environmental demands that frequently and often subtly change. This judgment calls for experienced "clinical" appraisal which is based on precise measurement of behavior but goes beyond that appraisal.

Some researchers have observed normal and acting-out children in classrooms and described the relative frequencies with which disruptive children and well-behaved children exhibit certain types of behavior (Walker, 1979). Such observations could be used as one criterion to decide which children in a particular class or school fit the definition *disturbed* and therefore are in need of intervention.

Range and Variability of Normal Behavior

A wide range of behavior is considered normal. The difference between *normal* and *disordered* behavior is one of degree rather than kind, and there is no sharp line between the two. Normal children do nearly everything disturbed children do but they do not do them under the same conditions or at the same rate. Crying, throwing tantrums, fighting, whining, spitting, urinating, and so on are all behaviors that can be expected of normal as well as disturbed children. Only the situations in which disturbed children perform these acts or the intensity and the rate at which they do them can set them apart from normal children. Longitudinal studies and surveys of children's and parents' perceptions of problem behavior show clearly that a large number of children who are considered normal show disturbed behaviors, such as tantrums, destructiveness, fearfulness, and hyperactivity to *some* degree at times during their growing years. Most children are considered at some time by one of their teachers to be a behavior problem (Griffiths, 1952; Macfarlane, Allen, & Honzik, 1955; Rubin & Ballow, 1978; Thomas. Chess, & Birch, 1968). The problem of definition, then, involves comparison with a nebulous and constantly changing standard—for most behaviors there are no quantitative norms against which measurement of the disturbed child's behavior can be judged.

Relationship to Other Conditions

As Hallahan and Kauffman (1976) point out, there are more similarities than differences among educable mentally retarded, learning disabled, and mildly or moderately disturbed children. Severely retarded and severely disturbed children also share many common characteristics (Balthazaar & Stevens, 1975; Werry, 1979a). Not only is it difficult to distinguish between psychotic or autistic children and retarded children, but it is also difficult to separate the severely and profoundly disturbed from the deaf, blind, and brain damaged (J. K. Wing, 1966; L. Wing, 1972). There is, of course, the possibility that the child has more than one handicap. Disordered behavior may occur in combination with any other type of exceptionality. Indeed, it is possible that behavior disorders occur more frequently in combination with other problems than alone. Defining behavior disorders in a way that excludes other handicapping conditions, therefore, is completely unrealistic. A behavior disorder should be defined specifically enough to be of value in working with children but broadly enough to admit its coexistence with other difficulties.

Transience of Behavior Problems

Available evidence indicates that children's behavior problems often are transitory. Behavior problems evidenced by young children seem likely to disappear within a few years unless they are severe or include high levels of hostile aggression and destructiveness (McCaffrey & Cumming, 1969; Robins, 1979). Thus, definitions of behavior disorders must take into account age-specific and developmentally normal problems which do not persist over a long period of years (Cromwell, Blashfield, & Strauss, 1975). For this reason, among others, it seems prudent to some (e.g., Phillips, Draguns, & Bartlett, 1975; Quay, 1979) to define behavior rather than children as disturbed or disordered.

Pejorative Labels

A problem associated with the issue of definition is the practice of labeling—attaching a diagnostic or classifying label to the child or behavior. Assigning any label to a child is dangerous in that the label is likely to be stigmatizing and may significantly alter the child's opportunities for education, employment, and socialization (Cromwell, Blashfield, & Strauss, 1975). This seems to be true regardless of the conceptual foundation of the definition with which the label is associated or the semantics of the label. As Hobbs (1975b) observes, the terminology employed is often unrelated to the behavior characteristics of the child. Affecting the child's placement into a diagnostic category will be factors such as his social class, the professional group choosing his label, and official policies and legal restrictions at the time (White & Charry, 1966). Furthermore, once the child is labeled, it is very difficult to change his status. As others note, "Of special concern to many educators is the process of labeling. While the process of labeling is a formal procedure, that of removal of labels is not" (Goldstein, Arkell, Ashcroft, Hurley & Lilly, 1975, p. 36). Thus, the terminology as well as the conceptual bases of definitions is at issue. Definitions should be couched in language that will minimize the damage done to children when they are identified as members of a deviant group.

Importance of Definition

At first thought it may seem that the problem of definition is not a very serious one. If, as it appears, a child is disturbed *when we (adult authorities) say so*, then why not concern ourselves with the more important issue of effective intervention and leave the question of definition to those who enjoy semantic quibbles? Serious reflection leads ultimately to the conclusion that definition is too important to be left to chance or caprice. The definition one accepts will reflect how one conceptualizes the problem of disordered behavior and, therefore, will determine what intervention strategies one considers appropriate. A definition communicates succinctly a conceptual framework that has direct implications for practitioners. Medical definitions imply the need for medical interventions, educational definitions imply the need for educational solutions, and so on. Furthermore, a definition specifies the population to be served and, thereby, has a profound effect on *who* receives intervention as well as *how* they will be served. It follows that if a definition specifies the population, then it will provide the basis for estimates of prevalence. Finally, decisions of legislative bodies, government executives, and school administrators concerning the allocation of funds and the training and employment of personnel will be guided by the implications of working definitions. Vague or inappropriate definitions are likely to result in confused and inadequate legislation, foggy administrative policies, nonfunctional training, and ineffective intervention. Definition of behavior disorders is, then, a crucial as well as a difficult problem, and it behooves special educators to construct the soundest possible definition.

Current Definitions

During the past 20 years, numerous definitions of emotionally disturbed children have been constructed. Each has served the particular purposes of the writer, but none of the definitions resolve the problems of terminology that we have discussed. Only one has had a significant impact on public policy at the national level, namely, that of Eli M. Bower. Bower (1969), in what has become a classic treatise on definition and identification of disturbed children, defined emotionally handicapped children as those exhibiting one or more of five characteristics *to a marked extent* and *over a period of time*:

1. *An inability to learn which cannot be explained by intellectual, sensory, or health factors* . . .
2. *An inability to build or maintain satisfactory interpersonal relationships with peers and teachers* . . .
3. *Inappropriate types of behavior or feelings under normal conditions* . . .
4. *A general, pervasive mood of unhappiness or depression* . . .
5. *A tendency to develop physical symptoms, pains, or fears associated with personal or school problems.*   (pp. 22–23)

According to Bower, the first of these characteristics, problems in learning, is possibly the most significant school-related aspect of disturbed children's behavior. Another important feature of his definition of behavior disorder is the inclusion of degrees or levels of severity.

Emotional handicaps may be displayed in transient, temporary, pervasive, or intensive types of behavior. To complete the definition, it would be necessary to establish a continuum in which the degree of handicap can be perceived and perhaps estimated, especially as it relates to possible action by the school. One could begin such a continuum with (1) children who experience and demonstrate the normal problems of everyday living, growing, exploration, and reality testing. There are some, however, who can be observed as (2) children who develop a greater number and degree of symptoms of emotional problems as a result of normal crises or stressful experiences, such as death of father, birth of sibling, divorce of parents, brain or body injury, school entrance, junior high school entrance, or puberty. Some children move beyond this level of adjustment and may be described as (3) children in whom moderate symptoms of emotional maladjustment persist to some extent beyond normal expectations but who are able to manage an adequate school adjustment. The next group would include (4) children with fixed and recurring symptoms of emotional maladjustment who can with help profit by school attendance and maintain some positive relationships in the school setting. Beyond this are (5) children with fixed and recurring symptoms of emotional difficulties who are perhaps best educated in a residential school setting or temporarily in a home setting (Bower, 1969, p. 27).

Bower's definition has much to recommend it, particularly its specification of five characteristic types of behavior shown by disturbed children. Still, it is not a definition that easily enables one to determine if a particular child is or is not emotionally handicapped. There is much latitude in the interpretation of the terms *to a marked extent* and *over a period of time*. Furthermore, there is need for subjective judgment about each of the five characteristics. Consider the problems in answering the following questions:

Just what is an *inability* to learn? Is it evidenced by 1 year's lag in achievement, 6 month's, or 2 year's? Does it include inability to learn appropriate social behavior?

How do you establish that inability to learn is *definitely not* explainable by intellectual factors?

Exactly what are *satisfactory* interpersonal relationships with peers?

What behavior is *inappropriate*, and what are *normal* conditions?

When is unhappiness *pervasive*?

Even though Bower's definition is cited widely and may be the best one available, it obviously lacks the precision necessary to take much of the subjectivity out of decision-making about children.

The definition offered by Bower has had a tremendous impact on public policy not because of its accuracy, but primarily because it is included, with few changes, in the rules and regulations governing the implementation of PL 94–142. Section 121a.5 of the rules and regulations is reprinted below. The most significant differences between Bower's definition and the federal definition are italicized.

"Seriously emotionally disturbed" is defined as follows:

(i) The term means a condition exhibiting one or more of the following characteristics over a long period of time and to a marked degree, *which adversely affects educational performance*:

(A) An inability to learn which cannot be explained by intellectual, sensory, or health factors;

(B) An inability to build or maintain satisfactory relationships with peers and teachers;

(C) Inappropriate types of behavior or feelings under normal circumstances;

(D) A general pervasive mood of unhappiness or depression; or

(E) A tendency to develop physical symptoms or fears associated with personal or school problems.

(ii) *The term includes children who are schizophrenic or autistic. The term does not include children who are socially maladjusted, unless it is determined that they are seriously emotionally disturbed.* (from the *Federal Register*, Vol 42, No. 163—Tuesday, August 23, 1977, p. 42478)

As noted by the use of italics above, the federal rules and regulations contain three statements not found in Bower's original definition. These added statements do not make the definition clearer; in fact, they come close to making nonsense of it. The additional clause "which adversely affects educational performance" appears to be a *pro forma* statement that PL 94–142 is concerned with educational matters, for it is inconceivable that a child could exhibit any one of the five characteristics to a marked degree and over a long period of time without an adverse affect on educational performance. The statement specifically including "children who are schizophrenic or autistic" is unnecessary, since such children obviously would exhibit at least one of the five characteristics (especially items B and/or C) to a marked extent and over a long period of time. This clause merely fosters the mistaken notion that childhood schizophrenia and autism are unambiguously defined diagnostic entities. The statement excluding "children who are socially maladjusted, unless it is determined that they are seriously emotionally disturbed" is impenetrable in meaning. It is a logical impossibility for a child to be *socially maladjusted* but not *seriously emotionally disturbed* according to the characteristics specified in the definition (especially item B), unless social maladjustment is defined too narrowly.

In summary, the definition of behavior disorder or serious emotional disturbance remains largely subjective, even though it is possible to describe clearly several relevant characteristics of disturbed children's behavior. The definition of emotional disturbance eludes objectification for the same reasons that happiness and beauty defy objective definition, even though happy behaviors and dimensions of beauty can be described clearly. Thus, although the best possible definition should be earnestly sought, the clear description of behavioral characteristics appears to be a more productive goal.

The fact that behavior disorder only can be defined subjectively presents serious problems for a public policy that *mandates* special services for *all* disturbed children and exacts penalties for noncompliance. Mandatory services for children with behavior disorders, though a well intentioned humanitarian effort to meet the needs of exceptional children, may be a tragic public policy error (Kauffman, 1980, 1981; Magliocca & Stevens, 1980). The mandate is analogous to requiring that all "ugly" children be identified and provided special education and related services for their unique needs. The policy encourages intellectual dishonesty and professional malpractice because it contains the implicit assumption that professional judgment is precise, highly reliable, and prepotent over economic factors in the identification of emotional disturbance. When the law *demands* that money be spent to serve the "beautiful," the "ugly," or the "disturbed," then the beholder's eye will follow only the dictates of economic realities, a point elaborated upon in the discussion of prevalence.

PREVALENCE

Problems of Estimation

Prevalence estimates have little meaning for the classroom teacher of disturbed children. When your responsibility is to teach a class of difficult children and you know that there are many more such pupils whose teachers or parents are waiting anxiously for the day when their child can enter your class, what difference does it make whether 2% or 5% or 10% of the school's children are disturbed? However, for those who plan special education programs for a school district or a state or a nation, prevalence is of great importance.

Estimates of the prevalence of behavior disorders have varied from about .5% of the school population to 20% or more. It is easy to see why the estimates are varied and confused. First, since the definition of disordered behavior is an unsettled matter, it is understandable that the number of disturbed children cannot be determined accurately or reliably. It is difficult to count the instances of a phenomenon that has no precise definition. Second, there are numerous ways to estimate the number of disturbed children. Differences in methodology can produce drastically different results. Third, the number of children counted by any definition and methodology can be influenced more by powerful social policy and economic factors than by professional training or clinical judgment (Magliocca & Stevens, 1980). Judgments about who is and who is not disturbed are surely influenced by social consequences and their economic implications.

Lack of Standard Definition

The effect of differences in definitions on estimates of prevalence needs no more elaboration. But even when the same definition is used, estimates have been different. Consider that a survey of state directors of special education (Schultz, Hirshoren, Manton, & Henderson, 1971) found prevalence estimates ranging from .5% to 15% in various states.

The question most relevant to discussion here is, "What is a reasonable estimate of the percentage of school children whose behavior is so persistently troublesome that special educational treatment is desirable, assuming the adequacy of definitions on which estimates are based?" The best available evidence indicates that the estimate of 2% is too conservative although it has been used for over a decade by the Bureau of Education for the Handicapped (BEH) of the U.S. Department of Education. A more reasonable estimate is 6% to 10% (e.g., Glidewell & Swallow, 1968, Graham, 1979; and Rutter, Tizard, Yule, Graham, & Whitmore, 1976). Bower (1969), using his own definition and data from ratings by teachers, peers, and children themselves, estimated that 10% of school age children are emotionally handicapped. Perhaps the most important recent estimate of prevalence of emotional disturbance for educational personnel is a longitudinal study by Rubin and Balow (1978). Each year they asked teachers to report via questionnaire whether or not the children in their study sample had shown behavior problems. The decision as to what constituted a problem was left to the individual teacher. Over half of the children in their sample (n = 1,586) were at *some* time during their school years considered by at least *one* of their teachers to show a behavior problem. In any given year, about 20% to 30% of the children were considered by at least one teacher to be a problem. Most importantly, 7.4% of the children (11.3% of the boys and 3.5% of the girls) were considered a problem by *every* teacher who rated them over a period of three years.

The findings of Rubin and Balow (1978) are consistent with those of previous studies. They indicate that *most* children at some time exhibit troublesome behavior (e.g., Griffiths, 1952; Macfarlane et al., 1955; Thomas et al., 1968). Far more than 2% of school children, consistently and over a period of years, are considered by teachers and other adults to exhibit disordered behavior (e.g., Bower, 1969; Glidewell & Swallow, 1968; see also Report to the President from the President's Commission on Mental Health, 1978). Furthermore, the 7.4% of the child population found by Rubin and Balow to be consistently identified as behavior problems over a period of 3 years appear to fit the Bower/PL 94–142 definition. When compared with other children, they scored significantly lower on achievement tests in language, reading, spelling, and arithmetic. They scored significantly lower on tests of intelligence, showed significantly lower socioeconomic levels, totalled significantly higher numbers of grade retentions, and required more special services (e.g., remedial reading, speech therapy, psychological evaluation).

The Methodology and Terminology of Estimation

As Cooper and Shepherd (1973) point out, there are numerous ways to arrive at an index of disordered behavior in a given population. *Prevalence* refers to the total number of cases of X disorder existing in a population; *incidence* refers to the rate of *inception*, or the number of new cases of X disorder. *Cases* can refer to individuals *or* to episodes of disorder. While *incidence* necessarily refers to rate of inception over a given period of time, *prevalence* refers to the calculated number for a period or for a point in time. In the Rubin and Balow (1978) study, the results reflect prevalence of individuals over a period of time.

How data are taken and from whom they are taken make a difference in the resultant number of cases. Should teachers, parents, psychologists, children, or some combination of these be consulted? Should one rely on mailed questionnaires, personal interviews, referrals to social agencies, or direct observation? And how should the survey sample be selected? For reasons of economy, most prevalence surveys have relied on questionnaires. For purposes of identifying disordered behavior in the schools, teacher judgment is obviously relevant (Rubin & Balow, 1978) and has been shown to be effective and reliable as well (Bower, 1969; Nelson, 1971).

Social Policy and Economic Factors

At any given time 2% is a conservative estimate of the school population that needs special education because of behavior disorders. Because PL 94 – 142 requires that *all* handicapped children, including those seriously emotionally disturbed, be identified and given special education appropriate for their individual needs, it could be expected that at least 2% of the school population has been identified and is being served. However, in early 1980 only about .5% of the school age population was being served as seriously emotionally disturbed (Kauffman, 1980). Social policy (as embodied in PL 94–142) and economic factors are likely responsible for the discrepancy between reasonable prevalence estimates and prevalence statistics based on services provided. It seems highly probable that prevalence estimates will, in the future, be lowered to reflect the percentage of children being served by special education. The reason is simply this: the law *requires* that *all* seriously emotionally disturbed children be identified *and that all identified children be served.* Furthermore, the penalty for noncompliance is a cutoff of all federal education funds. As we have seen, the definition of emotional disturbance is so vague that one *can* include or exclude just about any child, so long as inclusion or exclusion serves a useful purpose. It is useful to school systems to maintain federal support of their programs. It is also useful for school systems to stay within their local budgets. Lowered prevalence statistics, and therefore lowered costs of services provided, become a convenient result.

Social policy and economic realities effectively preclude the public schools' identification and service of 2% of the school age population as seriously emotionally disturbed. Consider these figures for school year 1979-80 published in the *Newsletter of the Council for Children with Behavioral Disorders* in October, 1979 and noted by Grosenick & Huntze (1979):

estimated cost of regular education per pupil	$ 1,665
estimated cost of education per seriously emotionally disturbed child or youth	4,711
estimate of total school age population (5-17)	51,317,000
2% of school age population	1,026,340
number of seriously emotionally disturbed children and youth receiving special education	248,645
conservative estimate of number of seriously emotionally disturbed children and youth *not* receiving special education	741,000

Under the provisions of PL 94–142, the federal government will provide 40% of the *excess* costs of educating each handicapped child, or an estimated $1,218 per disturbed child per year using these figures. By 1982, then, the federal government would need to provide *over $900 million more per year* to meet the needs of disturbed children; and state and local governments would need to budget *nearly $1.4 billion additional dollars per year* for these children. In addition, the figures cited are based on a conservative prevalence estimate; and they do not include allowances for inflation or funds for training personnel. No one can seriously entertain the hope that governments will be able to spend such prodigious amounts of money for the education of disturbed children, especially when other categories of handicapped children are also in need of additional resources.

Faced with a shortage of adequately trained personnel and insurmountable budget problems, what can be expected of school officials? They cannot risk litigation and loss of federal funds by identifying disturbed children they cannot serve. It is reasonable to expect that they will identify as many disturbed children as they can find the resources to serve. The tragedy is that the social policy mandates the impossible and that the public, and even some professionals, are likely to change their perceptions to match the economic realities. The mandate changes the question, at least for those who manage budgets, from "How many disturbed children are there?" to "How many disturbed children can we afford?" And in order to save face and attempt to abide by the law, it is tempting to say that there are, indeed, just as many disturbed children as we are able to serve (Magliocca & Stephens, 1980).

Prevalence and Incidence of Specific Disorders

Up to this point behavior disorder in the general case has been considered. But there are many types of disordered behavior, and therefore it is possible to estimate the prevalence of more specific problems. Unfortunately, many of the same problems of estimation discussed for the general case present themselves when more specific disorders are discussed. The classification of behavior disorders is almost as problematic as definition. In addition, the methodology of estimation is at least as varied for specific disorders as it is for the general case. Consequently, prevalence and incidence estimates of specific disorders are typically varied and confused. For example, the annual incidence of anorexia nervosa—severe self-starvation and weight loss that may be life threatening—has been estimated at .24/100,000 (Theander, 1970), 1.60/100,000 (Kendall, Hall, Hailey, & Babigan, 1973), and 50 75/100,000 (Copeland, 1974).

Whenever possible, prevalence data for more specific types of disorders will be provided. Here it will be noted, however, that estimates of the prevalence of psychotic children, those considered autistic or schizophrenic, range from 2/10,000 to 4.5/10,000 (Hingtgen & Bryson, 1972). As in the case of nearly every type of behavior disorder, males outnumber females by a ratio range of 2:1 to 5:1.

In summary, it is difficult to make accurate estimates of the prevalence of behavior disorders in general or of the prevalence of most specific disorders. Nevertheless, it is a reasonable assertion, based on available evidence, that more than 2%—probably 6% to 10%—of the school age population is in need of special education services due to disordered behavior. Only about .5% of school children were identified as disturbed and received special services at the beginning of the 1980s. Prevalence estimates appear to conform to social policy and economic realities.

CONCEPTUAL MODELS

It is impossible to offer a coherent discussion of the remaining topics in this book without describing the conceptual models that underlie research and practice. Hence, capsule summaries of several models are presented along with a rationale for the way the models will be treated here.

Nearly every reader of this book will know that there are alternative theories of behavior (or schools of psychology), and each of these offers an explanation of behavior and suggests what can be done to change it. But the essential problem is not the number of alternative conceptual models from which to choose. Rather, the problem is to choose or construct a gnoseology, a theory or philosophy of knowledge about behavior, and to evaluate conceptual models accordingly. More simply, the problem is to decide what is believable and what is not believable.

Conceptual models and their implications have been analyzed by Rhodes and his colleagues (Rhodes & Head, 1974; Rhodes & Tracy, 1972a, 1972b). Based on their work, short descriptions of several categories of models will be provided as a backdrop for subsequent discussion.

Biogenic Models

Human behavior seems to involve neurophysiological mechanisms; that is, a person cannot act without the involvement of his/her anatomy and physiology. One set of conceptual models begins with the hypothesis that disordered behavior represents a genetic or biochemical defect. For example, it has been suggested by some that disorders such as autism, hyperactivity, or hyperaggression are manifestations of genetic damage, brain dysfunction, food additives, biochemical imbalance, or simply disorders most responsive to or most easily ameliorated by chemicals (Campbell & Small, 1978; DesLauriers & Carlson, 1969; Eyde & Fink, 1979; Finegold, 1975; Rimland, 1964; Rose, 1978; Sprague & Ullmann, 1981; Werry, 1979b). According to these models, successful treatment of behavior disorders must address the underlying biological problem; hence, interventions such as drug therapy, dietary control, exercise, surgery, or alteration of environmental factors that exacerbate the problem are suggested.

Psychodynamic Models

Dynamic psychiatry is concerned with hypothetical mental mechanisms and their interplay in the developmental process. Psychodynamic models, sometimes called psychoanalytic models because psychoanalytic theory provides so many of their tenets, rest on the assumption that the essence of behavior disorders is *not* the behavior itself but a "pathological" imbalance among the dynamic parts of one's personality (e.g., id, ego, superego). The behavior of a disturbed child is merely symptomatic of an underlying "mental illness." And the cause of mental illness usually is attributed to excessive restriction or excessive gratification of the child's instincts at a critical stage of development (see Axline, 1947; Berkowitz & Rothman,

1960; Bettleheim, 1970; Freud, 1965; Kornberg, 1955; Scharfman, 1978). Interventions based on a psychodynamic model typically stress the importance of individual psychotherapy for the child (often for the parents as well) and the necessity of a permissive, accepting classroom teacher.

Psychoeducational Models

Psychoeducational models show concern for unconscious motivations and underlying conflicts (hallmarks of psychodynamic models) yet stress the realistic demands of everyday functioning in school and home. There is an assumption that academic failure and misbehavior can be dealt with directly and therapeutically. There is reliance on *ego psychology*, an offshoot of psychodynamic models. There is an attempt to focus on ego tasks and self-control through self-understanding (Fagen, 1979; Fenichel, 1974; Long, 1974; Long, Morse, & Newman, 1976; Morse, 1974; Redl, 1966). Intervention based on a psychoeducational model is likely to consist primarily of therapeutic discussions or *life-space interviews* with children—attempts to get them to see that what they are doing is a problem, to understand their motivations for behaving as they do, to observe the consequences of their actions, and to plan alternative responses.

Humanistic Models

Humanistic models draw heavily from humanistic psychology, the counter-culture, counter-theory movement of the late 1960s and early 1970s, and the free school, open education, alternative school, and deschooling ideas of the same era. Self-direction, self-fulfillment, self-evaluation, and free choice of educational activities and goals are emphasized. But the theoretical underpinnings of humanistic models are hard to identify (see Burke, 1972; Dennison, 1969; Knoblock, 1970, 1973, 1979). A teacher who devises an education for disturbed children based on a humanistic model will be more a resource and catalyst for children's learning than a director of activities. The teacher is nonauthoritarian, and promotes a classroom atmosphere that can best be described as open, free, nontraditional, affectively charged, and personal.

Ecological Models

An ecological model is based on concepts in ecological psychology, community psychology, and the work of European *educateurs* who work with children in their homes and communities as well as their schools. The child is considered as an individual enmeshed in a complex social system, as both a giver and receiver (an excitor and responder) in social transactions with other children and adults in a variety of roles and settings. Emphasis is placed on study of the entire social system, and intervention is directed ideally toward all facets of the child's milieu (Hobbs, 1966, 1974; Rhodes, 1965, 1967, 1970; Swap, 1974, 1978).

Behavioral Models

Two major assumptions underlie a behavioral model: the essence of the problem is the behavior itself, and behavior is a function of environmental events. Maladaptive behavior is viewed as inappropriate learned responses; therefore, intervention should consist of rearranging stimuli and consequences to teach more adaptive behavior. Clearly, behavioral models are derived from the work of behavioral psychologists such as Thorndike, Pavlov, and Skinner. A behavioral model represents a natural science approach with its emphasis on precise definition and reliable measurement of behavior, careful control of the variables thought to maintain or change behavior, and establishment of replicable cause-effect relationships (Gelfand, 1978; Leitenberg, 1976; Lovaas, Young, & Newsom, 1978; Maloney, Fixsen, & Maloney, 1978). Interventions based on a behavioral model consist of choosing a target response, measuring its current level, analyzing probable controlling environmental events, and changing stimuli or consequences until the controlling events of the target response are found and behavioral changes have occurred.

There are two significant extensions of behavioral models. *Cognitive-behavior modification* represents an attempt to take self-perceptions and self-dialogue into account as a factor in behavioral change (Kauffman & Hallahan, 1979; Kneedler, 1980; Mahoney, 1974; Meichenbaum, 1977, 1979, 1980). A cognitive-behavior modification approach might include, for example, self-observation, self-recording, or self-instruction techniques. *Social learning theory* is an extension of a behavioral model to include observational learning and "person variables"—thoughts, feelings, and other internal states—in an analysis of behavior. The foremost proponents of social learning theory are Bandura (1977, 1978) and Mischel (1973, 1976). Kauffman (1979) and Kauffman and Kneedler (1981) have discussed the implications of social learning theory for special education. Interventions based on social learning theory could include any of the techniques used in a typical behavioral approach and cognitive-behavior modification strategies as well. Social learning theory obviously provides much of the rationale for cognitive-behavior modification.

Cognitive-behavior modification and social learning theory rely on measureable, overt behavioral change as the test of outcome of interventions. Nevertheless, their inclusion of cognitive or person variables in an analysis of behavior problems and in interventions is not without controversy among proponents of behaviorism (Ledwidge, 1978; Mahoney & Kazdin, 1979).

The Use of Conceptual Models

There are several distinct options for treating the issue of conceptual models. First, a single model can be adopted as an unvarying theme, as a template by which all hypotheses and research findings are judged. Although this option has the advantages of consistency and clarity, it is disconcerting to many careful thinkers; it rests on the questionable assumption that reality is encompassed sufficiently by one set of hypotheses about human behavior.

Second, a nonevaluative stance can be taken, a posture in which all concepts are treated as equal, deserving of the same attention and respect. This option has immediate appeal, for it carries an acknowledgement that every model has its limitations and allows the reader to choose from a fair treatment of all contestants. The drawbacks of this option, however, are considerable. Under the guise of eclecticism, the option rests on the implicit assumption that we have no sound reason to discriminate among ideas. This concept fosters the attitude that child behavior and education, like religion and political ideology, are matters better left to personal belief than to scientific scrutiny.

A third option, and the one chosen for this book, is to focus attention on hypotheses that can be supported or refuted by replicable and public empirical data—ideas that lend themselves to investigation by the methods of science. The result of this choice is that most of the discussion is consistent with behavioral conceptual models. Although biogenic models are discussed because they are open to empirical investigation, they are not treated extensively: They have comparatively little to offer educators and clinical psychologists insofar as their legitimate interventions are concerned. And psychodynamic, psychoeducational, and humanistic models are almost totally ignored because the scientific evidence supporting them, data that are replicable and open to public scrutiny, is meager. Ecological concepts are addressed because they, too, are compatible with an empirical approach.

The choice made for this book should not be interpreted to mean that there is only one "way of knowing." It means that there is a *best* (most reliable and most useful) way of knowing *for professionals who work with troubled children*, that there is a systematic approach to knowledge of behavior that is the firmest foundation for competent professional practice. The most useful knowledge is derived from experiments that can be repeated and that consistently produce similar results—in short, information obtained from investigations conducted according to well established rules of scientific inquiry.

SUMMARY

Definition of behavior disorders is a subjective matter. There is no standard definition that is accepted by all professionals. The problem of definition is heightened by differences in conceptual models, the differences in purposes served by definitions, problems in measurement, ranges and variabilities of normal behavior, the transience of disorders of behavior in childhood, and pejorative labels. The most common definition in current usage is one proposed originally by Bower. It is the one now used in the rules and regulations for PL 94-142 and specifies persistent child characteristics having to do with

1. school learning problems
2. unsatisfactory interpersonal relationships
3. inappropriate behavior and feelings
4. pervasive unhappiness or depression
5. physical symptoms or fears associated with school or personal problems

Inclusion and exclusion clauses that are of questionable meaning have been appended to these characteristics in the federal definition.

Estimates of the prevalence of behavior disorders vary widely. Prevalence is difficult to estimate because of the lack of a standard definition, differences in methodology and terminology in prevalence studies, and social policy and economic factors that influence the decision about who should be counted. A reasonable estimate, based on the best information available, is that 6% to 10% of the school age population needs special education services due to disordered behavior. In 1980, only about .5% of the school population were receiving special education as seriously emotionally disturbed. Social policy and economic factors may result in lower prevalence estimates than the 2% figure used for the past decade by the federal government.

Emotional disturbance has been described using a variety of conceptual models, including biogenic, psychodynamic, psychoeducational, humanistic, ecological, and behavioral models. Cognitive-behavior modification and social learning theory are significant variations of the behavioral model. Empirical data derived from scientific inquiry—primarily behavioral research—is the focus of this book.

chapter 2 _____

Historical Development Of the Field

There is no reason to doubt the fact that teachers in every era have faced the problem of disorderly and disturbing behavior. Throughout the recorded history of humankind one can find examples of children's behavior that angered and disappointed their parents or other adults and violated established codes of conduct. Furthermore, throughout history persons in every culture have sought to conceptualize unusual or disturbing human behavior in terms of causal factors and to draw implications of those factors for eliminating, controlling, and preventing deviant acts. Although a myriad of causes and remedies have been suggested over the centuries, several conceptual themes can be identified. These themes have remained remarkably consistent for thousands of years, and contemporary versions are merely elaborations and extensions of their ancient counterparts (Kauffman, 1974b). For purposes of explanation and control of behavior, humans have been variously conceptualized, for example, as spiritual beings, biological organisms, rational and feeling persons, and products of their environments. These and other conceptual bases for current approaches to intervention in children's behavior disorders will be implicit in this chapter and will be discussed explicitly throughout the remainder of the book.[2]

The historical roots of special education for children with behavior disorders are not easy to identify, for although behavior disorders in children have been recognized for thousands of years, it is only in relatively recent times that systematic special educational provisions for these children have been devised. As Lewis (1974) states:

> When charting the growth of this field, one must make an arbitrary decision concerning a starting point. No matter where one begins, examples of earlier programs or treatments probably can be identified. Tracing the history of the field presents great difficulty because these children have been subsumed under so many different labels and because labeling itself frequently has been determined by the sociological and scientific conditions of the moment. Thus, the beginning of the field of education for the disturbed child is difficult to find; it is lost not only in the confusions of sociological history but also in the myriad of disciplines that crisscross its development. (p. 5)

To the extent possible, this chapter focuses on the history of *education* for disturbed children and other interventions directly relevant to *educational* concerns. A purely educational emphasis is not possible, for the conceptual foundations of special education are found for the most part in the disciplines of psychology and psychiatry; and thus its historical origins are intertwined inseparably with the histories of other fields of study and practice. Over the years education has come to play a prominent role in the treatment of children's behavior disorders. As this historical sketch unfolds, therefore, it will become increasingly educational in its focus.

---

[2] The Conceptual Project in Emotional Disturbance under the directorship of Dr. William C. Rhodes had as its prime purpose the organization of the vast and scattered literature on behavior disorders and other types of variance in children. Three volumes published under the general title of *A Study of Child Variance* (Rhodes & Head, 1974; Rhodes & Tracy, 1972a, b) report the results of the project and provide in-depth discussion of various conceptual models and their implications. Discussion of the history of special education is also found in Kauffman (1981), Mann (1979), and Payne et al. (1979).

BEFORE 1800

In the years prior to 1800, handicapped children of any description were at best protected from abuse, and few, if any, systematic attempts to teach them are known. Behavior disorders were typically seen as evidence of Satan's power, and children and adolescents were often punished under the law as adults (Bremner, 1970; Despert, 1965). Abuse, neglect, cruel medical treatment (e.g., bleeding), and excessive punishment were common and often accepted matter-of-factly for children as well as adults who showed undesirable behavior. It was not until the period following the American and French revolutions in the closing years of the eighteenth century that kind and effective treatment of the *insane* and *idiots* (terms used then to designate the mentally ill and mentally retarded, adults and children alike) made their appearance. In that era of political and social revolution, emphasis on individual freedom, human dignity, philanthropy, and public education set the stage for humane treatment and education of the handicapped.

Immediately after the French revolution, Phillipe Pinel, a distinguished French physician and one of the earliest psychiatrists, unchained several chronic mental patients who had been confined and brutalized for years in the Bicetre Hospital in Paris. When treated with kindness and respect and with the expectation that they would behave appropriately, these formerly deranged and regressed patients showed dramatic improvement in their behavior. Pinel's revolutionary and humane methods were widely known and used in Europe and the United States during the first half of the nineteenth century. His approach, which was elaborated upon and extended by his students and admirers, became known as *moral treatment*.

One of Pinel's students was Jean Marc Gaspard Itard, another French physician, who in the late 1700s and 1800s attempted to teach the "wild boy of Aveyron" (Itard, 1962). This boy, named Victor, was found in the forest where he had apparently been abandoned at an early age. Pinel believed him to be profoundly retarded (idiotic), but it is clear from Itard's description that he exhibited many of the behaviors characteristic of severely and profoundly disturbed children. Itard was convinced that the boy could be taught practical skills, including speech, and he was remarkably successful although Victor never uttered more than a few words. Itard's work with the boy provided the basis for the teaching methods of Edward Seguin and other educators of idiots later in the nineteenth century. His book remains a fascinating and moving classic in the education of the handicapped. Contemporary educational methods for the retarded and disturbed are grounded in many of the principles expounded by Itard almost two centuries ago (Lane, 1976).

Besides the work of Pinel and Itard in Europe, there were developments in America in the late 1700s that provided a prelude to educating the disturbed. The most important development was the influential writing of Dr. Benjamin Rush of Philadelphia, often considered the father of American psychiatry. Following the American revolution, Dr. Rush became a strong proponent of public education and public support for schools for poor children.[3] In his writing he argues vehemently and eloquently for the abolition of corporal punishment and cruel discipline and

---

[3] For excerpts from the writings of Benjamin Rush see Bremner (1970) pp. 218–223, 249–251.

for kind and prudent methods of behavior control. His words, first published in 1790 in *The Universal Asylum and Columbian Magazine*, have the ring of present day child advocacy and current appeals for more caring relationships with children:

> I conceive corporal punishments, inflicted in an arbitrary manner, to be contrary to the spirit of liberty, and that they should not be tolerated in a free government. Why should not children be protected from violence and injuries, as well as white and black servants? Had I influence enough in our legislature to obtain only a single law, it should be to make the punishment for striking a school-boy, the same as for assaulting and beating an adult member of society.
>
> The world was created in love. It is sustained by love. Nations and families that are happy, are made so only by love. Let us extend this divine principle, to those little communities which we call schools. Children are capable of loving in a high degree. They may therefore be governed by love.   (Bremner, 1970, pp. 222–223)

In his writings, Rush does not advocate the abandonment of discipline. Mild forms of punishment in school are suggested: private admonition, confinement after school hours, and holding a small sign of disgrace of any kind in the presence of the other children. If the child does not respond to these methods, Rush recommends dismissing the child from school and turning the business of discipline over to the parents. His emphasis on education and love oriented methods of control had a profound influence on the early years of American psychiatry and the *moral therapy* employed in many American lunatic asylums during the first half of the nineteenth century.

THE 1800s[4]

Twentieth century descriptions of nineteenth century treatment of children with behavior disorders are typically brief and negative (e.g., Despert, 1965; Kanner, 1957, 1962; Lewis, 1974; Rubenstein, 1948). Only recently has the history of public education for such children been traced (Berkowitz & Rothman, 1967b; Hoffman, 1974, 1975). It is true that the literature of the nineteenth century is meager by current standards, that children in this literature often are looked upon and treated psychologically as miniature adults, and that bizarre ideas (such as the notions that insanity could be caused by masturbation, by studying too hard, or by watching someone have an epileptic seizure) are persistent. Nevertheless, it is now clear that most histories of childhood behavior disorders consistently contain certain inaccuracies and distortions that lead to an underestimation of the nineteenth century literature and its value for approaching present day problems (Kauffman, 1976).

Examination of the nineteenth century literature on insanity and idiocy, in which most of the literature on children's behavior disorders is found, leads to the conclusion that nearly every current issue of importance has been an issue for well over a century. It is a moot question whether the persistence of these issues is due to the intractability of the sociopsychological problems they represent or to the

[4] Section adapted from J. M. Kauffman, "Nineteenth Century Views of Children's Behavior Disorders; Historical Contributions and Continuing Issues," *Journal of Special Education*, 1976, *10*, 335–349. Used with permission.

ineptness with which potential solutions have been implemented. Regardless of which one believes to be the case, the study of historical contributions is of importance in assessing current problems: "History is the basic science. From history flows more than knowledge, more than prescription, more than how it was—how we might try to make it become" (Blatt, 1975, p. 402).

Mental Retardation and Behavior Disorder

One of the primary reasons the nineteenth century is not often seen as an era of importance for behavior disorders is because the relationship between behavior disorders and mental retardation has been overlooked. It is clear to many writers today that mentally retarded and emotionally disturbed children are not as different in their characteristics as had been assumed several decades ago. This is true regardless of whether one considers the mildly and moderately retarded and disturbed or the severely and profoundly handicapped (Balthazaar & Stevens, 1975; Crissey, 1975; DeMyer et al., 1974; Fenichel, 1974; Hallahan & Kauffman, 1976; Kanner, 1960; Menolascino, 1972). Nineteenth century writers also recognized the great similarity between the conditions of idiocy (retardation) and insanity (disturbance). It was not until 1886 that there was a legal separation between insanity and feeble-mindedness in England (Hayman, 1939).

Some nineteenth century descriptions of idiocy and its varieties present a picture of children who today might well be labeled *psychotic* or *autistic*. For example, Itard's (1962) description of Victor, written at the end of the eighteenth century, is important as a study of behavior disorder as well as a treatise on mental retardation. Esquirol (1845), a French physician, describes in considerable detail the physical and behavioral features of an 11-year-old "imbecile" admitted to the Salpetriere hospital. His description includes the following:

> R. usually sits with her knees crossed, her hands beneath her apron, and is almost constantly raising or depressing her shoulders. Her physical health is good, and she has a good appetite. She is a gourmand, worrying herself much about what she shall have to eat at her meals; and if she sees one of her companions eating, cries, and calls for something for herself. Whilst with her parents, she was accustomed to escape and run to the shop of a pastrycook who lived near, and devour the first pie that she saw. She was also in the habit of entering a grocer's shop, seizing upon the bottles of liquor, and if they attempted to prevent her from drinking, dashed them upon the ground. . . . She is cunning and conceited. On wetting the bed, as she sometimes does, she defends herself, and accuses the servant girl of it. She detests her room-mate, who is mute, and poorly clad. She has been caught thrusting needles into a blistered surface, which had been made upon the person of her wretched companion. (p. 450)

The description of Charles Emile, a 15-year-old idiot at the Bicetre, also contains reference to severely disordered behavior. Brigham (1845) summarized the observations of Voisin, a physician at the Bicetre, who said of Charles:

> He was wholly an animal. He was without attachment; overturned everything in his way, but without courage or intent; possessed no tact, intelligence, power of dissimulation, or sense of propriety; and was awkward to excess. His *moral sentiments* are described as *null*, except the love of approbation, and a noisy instinctive gaiety, independent of the external world. . . . Devouring everything, however disgusting, brutally sensual, pas-

sionate—breaking, tearing, and burning whatever he could lay his hand upon; and if prevented from doing so, pinching, biting, scratching, and tearing himself, until he was covered with blood. He had the particularity of being so attracted by the eyes of his brothers, sisters, and playfellows, as to make the most persevering efforts to push them out with his fingers. . . . When any attempt was made to associate him with the other patients, he would start away with a sharp cry, and then come back to them hastily.   (p. 336)

Dorothea Dix, the great reformer, reports in 1844 the shock of finding in an asylum "a little girl, about nine or ten years of age, who suffered the fourfold calamity of being blind, deaf, dumb, and insane. I can conceive of no condition so pitiable as that of this unfortunate little creature, the chief movements of whose broken mind, were exhibited in restlessness, and violent efforts to escape, and unnatural screams of terror" (Bremner, 1970, p. 777). Dix recognized that behavior disorder could occur in combination with other handicaps. There is little doubt that institutions for the deaf and blind, as well as the retarded, served children that would fall into the contemporary categories of *autistic* or *disturbed*.

The eminent American educator of the handicapped, Samuel Gridley Howe, understood the difficulty in separating the mildly disturbed from the mildly retarded. He uses the term *simulative idiocy* (Howe, 1852) to describe the problem that today would be termed *pseudoretardation*—the problem of knowing the difference between children who are *truly* retarded and those who only *appear to be* retarded.

In short, the close relationship between mental retardation and emotional disturbance in children (and in adults) was known in the nineteenth century, and the observations of many nineteenth century writers are surprisingly consonant with today's emphasis on the similarities and overlapping characteristics, etiologies, and interventions for these two handicapped groups.

As far as treatment is concerned, the recent historical reviews of Hoffman (1974, 1975) make it clear that the public schools of the late nineteenth century made provisions for inept and unruly students who today would comprise groups labeled *emotionally disturbed, learning disabled,* or *educable mentally retarded.* "Incorrigible," "defective," and non-English-speaking children were typically lumped together in special *ungraded* classes with little or no regard for their specific educational needs. Thus, early public education for children with behavior disorders must be viewed in the context of attempts to deal with the problem of mental retardation as well.

Theories of Etiology

By the end of the eighteenth century, it was no longer in vogue to believe that behavior disorders should be treated by religious means because they were caused by demon possession. It is undeniable, however, that nineteenth century writers were preoccupied with the relationship between masturbation and insanity, particularly insanity in children. The *prevailing* belief was that masturbation *caused* (or at least aggravated) insanity (Hare, 1962; Rie, 1971).[5] Nevertheless, there were those who

---

[5] The idea that masturbation was an intolerably horrible and debasing practice had not been laid to rest by the end of the nineteenth century. Castration and ovariotomy were still being used in the 1890s and

questioned the causal relationship between masturbation and insanity long before the beginning of the twentieth century. Stribling (1842), who refers to masturbation as a "detestable vice" and a "degrading habit," comments eloquently on associative and causal relationships:

> There is no subject connected with insanity of more interest than the causes from which it proceeds; and there is none certainly in regard to which the enquirer has more difficulty to ascertain the truth. The ignorance of some, and the aversion of others to disclosing the circumstances (which are often of a delicate character) connected with the origin of the patient's malady, are obstacles frequently to be encountered in such investigations —whilst even with the intelligent and communicative, it too often occurs that cause and effect are so confounded, as that the one is improperly made to, take the place of the other. . . .
>
> Masturbation . . . as a cause of insanity, we are induced to think is often much exaggerated. Intellect is the great regulator of the human passions and propensities; and as we possess the latter in common with and to as great a degree as other animals, it is only by the former that we are distinguished from and elevated above them. When therefore the mind is thrown into chaos, and man is no longer a rational creature, his animal nature acquires the ascendancy and directs his actions. In this state, too, he is almost invariably cut off from intercourse with his kind, and hence this detestable vice in too many instances becomes his daily habit. When, therefore, in this condition it is first observed, the beholder, forgetting the circumstances which preceded, at once imagines that as no other cause for the mental disorder had ever been assigned, he has made the important discovery; and thus, what in most cases was merely the result of reason dethroned, is chronicled as the monster which expelled her from her empire.   (pp. 22–23)

Many of the "causes" of mental illness listed by nineteenth century writers are laughable indeed: "idleness and ennui," "pecuniary embarrassment," "sedentary and studious habits," "inhaling tobacco fumes," "gold fever," "indulgence of tempor" (all of these causes among those named by Stribling, 1842); "suppression of hemorrhoids," "kick on the stomach," "bathing in cold water," "sleeping in a barn filled with new hay," "study of metaphysics," "reading vile books," "license question," "preaching sixteen days and nights," "celibacy," "sudden joy," "extatic admiration of works of art," "mortified pride," "Mormonism," "duel," "struggle between the religious principle and power of passion" (causes listed by Jarvis, 1852); *ad infinitum*. Nevertheless, writers of the day did question supposed cause-effect relationships, as evidenced by the previous quote from Stribling and Jarvis's comment that masturbation could not be evaluated as a factor in any increase of insanity because "we have no means of knowing whether masturbation increases or diminishes" (Jarvis, 1852, p. 354).

Some psychiatrists of the early nineteenth century identified etiological factors in children's behavior disorders that are today given very serious consideration. For example, Parkinson (1807) and West (1848) (in Hunter & Macalpine, 1963) point to the interaction of temperament and child rearing, overprotection, overindulgence, and inconsistency of discipline as factors in the development of troublesome behavior. In Parkinson's words:

---

early 1900s in attempts to stop masturbation and sexual interests in "idiotic," "imbecile," "feebleminded," and "epileptic" children and youth, many of whom exhibited other disturbing behaviors (Bremner, 1971, pp. 855–857).

> That children are born with various dispositions is undoubtedly true; but it is also true, that by due management, these may be so changed and meliorated by the attention of a parent, that not only little blemishes may be smoothed away, but even those circumstances which more offensively distinguish the child, may, by proper management become the characteristic ornaments of the man. . . . On the treatment the child receives from his parents, during the infantine stage of his life, will, perhaps, depend much of the misery or happiness he may experience, not only in his passage through this, but through the other stages of his existence. (Hunter & Macalpine, 1963, p. 616)

These observations of Parkinson, published in 1807, are not discordant with the more recent findings of Thomas, Chess, and Birch (1968), and his comments on the nefariousness of inconsistency in child rearing and discipline are not unlike those of Haring and Phillips (1962). Note Parkinson's modern ideas in the following:

> If, on the one hand, every little sally of passion and impatience is immediately controuled; if those things which are admissable are regularly permitted, and those which are improper are as regularly withheld, the wily little creature will soon learn to distinguish that which is allowed of, from that which is prohibited. He will, indeed, urge his claim, for that to which he has been taught he has a right, with manly boldness; but will not harrass himself and his attendants, with ceaseless whinings or ravings, to obtain that which uniform prohibition has placed beyond his expectance. But a melancholy reverse appears, if, on the other hand, no consistency is observed in his management; if, at one time, the slightest indulgence is refused, and at another the most extravagant, and even injurious cravings, are satisfied, just as the caprice of the parent may induce him to gratify his ill humor, by thwarting another; or to amuse his moments of *ennui*, by playing with his child as a monkey, and exciting it to those acts of mischief and audacity for which, in the next moment, it may suffer a severe correction. Continually undergoing either disappointment or punishment; or engaged in extorting gratifications, which he often triumphs at having gained by an artful display of passion; his time passes on, until at last the poor child frequently manifests ill nature sufficient to render him odious to all around him, and acquires pride and meanness sufficient to render him the little hated tyrant of his playfellows and inferiors. (Reprinted in Hunter & Macalpine, 1963, pp. 616-617)

Summary of Theories

While biological causes of retardation and behavior disorders were recognized during the first half of the century, the emphasis was on environmental factors, especially early discipline and training. It is not surprising, then, that interventions in that period center on environmental control—providing the proper sensory stimulation, discipline, and instruction.

As Hoffman (1974, 1975) notes, the impact of Darwinist thought in the late nineteenth century was profound. The British philosopher, Herbert Spencer, and the American spokesman for social Darwinism in the United States, William Graham Sumner, saw the seeds of social decay and destruction in the unchecked propagation of the lower classes and defective individuals, as did Dr. Walter E. Fernald (1893), the distinguished medical superintendent of the Massachusetts School for the Feeble-minded. The ideas of social evolution, survival of the fittest, and eugenics were to lead inevitably to the writing and influence of Henry H.

Goddard, an early twentieth century progenitor of special education (Balthazaar & Stevens, 1975; Smith, 1962). The favored position in the late nineteenth and early twentieth centuries was that undesirable behavioral traits represented inherited flaws. Intervention was limited to selective breeding.

Intervention

There can be no denial that many children, including those with behavior disorders and limited intellect, were neglected and abused in the nineteenth century. Bremner (1970, 1971), Hoffman (1974, 1975) and Rothman (1971) amply document the cruel discipline, forced labor, and other inhumanities suffered by children in the 1800s. Neither can there be any reasonable refutation of the assertion that in many cases nineteenth century attempts at education and treatment of handicapped children were primitive in comparison to the *best* that can be offered today. Nevertheless, it is also clear that the best care available for behavior disordered children in the nineteenth century was considerably better than the care received by many such children today. If one were to concentrate attention on the neglect and abuse of children in institutions, schools, detention centers, and homes in the twentieth century (Blatt & Kaplan, 1966; Deutsch, 1948; Harrington, 1962; James, 1969; Kozol, 1967; Rothman, 1971) one might be justified in concluding that the plight of children has not improved much in the last hundred years. When the best of contemporary thinking and treatment are contrasted with the least savory of the nineteenth century, a dark and distorted vision of the last century is created. Yet, historical comments on the 1800s tend toward emphasis on imprisonment, cruelty, punishment, neglect, ignorance, bizarre ideas (masturbatory insanity), and absence of effective education and treatment for the behavior disordered child (Despert, 1965; Kanner, 1962; Rie, 1971; Rubenstein, 1948).

Seldom has *moral treatment* been mentioned in connection with children. "Moral treatment, in modern technical jargon, is what we mean by resocialization by means of a growing list of therapies with prefaces such as recreational, occupational, industrial, music—with physical education thrown in for good measure" (Bockoven, 1956, p. 303). As Bockoven points out, these therapies do not add up to moral treatment, which implies an integrated total treatment program (see Brigham, 1847, for a succinct description of moral treatment).[6] Rie (1971) discusses moral treatment of the 1800s but largely discounts its relevance for child psychopathology because children were not admitted to institutions in great numbers. Yet it is very clear that children *did* find their way into institutions and did come under the care of moral therapists during the first half of the nineteenth century (*Annual Reports of the Court of Directors of the Western Lunatic Asylum*, 1836–1850, 1870; *American Journal of Insanity*, Vols. I–VI, 1844–1850; Esquirol, 1845; Mayo, 1839). For example, Francis Stribling, a prominent moral therapist of the

---

[6] The term *moral treatment* did not, as some have surmised, connote religious training. Originally, as translated from the work of Pinel, *moral treatment* meant *psychological* as opposed to *medical* treatment of insanity and included every therapeutic endeavor other than medication or surgery. For further discussion of moral treatment, see Bockoven (1972), Caplan (1969), Carlson and Dain (1960), Dain and Carlson (1960), Grob (1962), Menninger (1963), Rees (1957), and Ullmann and Krasner (1969).

early 1800s, reports that of 122 patients in Western Lunatic Asylum during the year 1841, nine were under the age of 20, two of these being under the age of 15 (Stribling, 1842). Thus, moral treatment should be included in any list of types of care offered to children in that era.

Moral therapists emphasized constructive activity, kindness, minimum restraint, structure, routine, and consistency in treatment. Furthermore, obedience to authority and conformity to rules were primary features of child-care institutions and child-rearing dogma in mid-nineteenth century America (Rothman, 1971). Rothman's account makes it clear that the emphasis on obedience and conformity was sometimes carried to a ridiculous or even harmful extreme, that some children still languished in jails or poorhouses, and that the concepts of structure, consistency, and re-education were sometimes distorted to include cruel and excessive punishment. Still, it is evident from the writing of moral therapists that humane, nonpunitive care was the goal. An example of the type of treatment afforded behavior disordered children by moral therapists is provided in a case report by Mayo (1839). The following is a continuation of his report on the case of the adolescent boy described in Chapter 1.

vignette

When I saw him, (December 8th, 18____) he received me courteously but suspiciously; his demeanor was soft, but there was a bad expression about his mouth; I believe his *eyes* gave him the appearance of softness; they were large and dark; his skin was smooth; he was small for his age, not having grown for some years. On my addressing him in regard to his peculiarities, he equivocated and became irritable; and he asserted that he was under impulses which he could not resist. He spoke unkindly of his father, and tried to snatch out of my hand a very wicked letter written by himself to one of his relatives, which I produced as an evidence of his misconduct. This peculiarity seemed to pervade his views of his own conduct,—that he contemplated past offenses, not only as what could not be recalled, but also, as what ought not to be remembered to his disadvantage.

Having satisfied my mind by careful observation, that the accounts given by his relatives were substantially correct, and that the ordinary principles of education, however skillfully applied, would here lead to no salutary result, I suggested the following line of treatment, as calculated to give him his best chance of moral improvement. Let him reside in the neighbourhood, or, if possible, in the family of some person competent to undertake this charge, under the attendance of two trustworthy men, who should be subject to the authority of the superior above alluded to; one of these persons should be in *constant* attendance upon him; but if coercion should be required in order to induce him to comply with reasonable requests, both should be employed so as not to make such violence necessary as should produce the slightest bodily pain. The object of this plan would be to accustom him to obedience, and by keeping him in a constant state of the exercise of this quality, for such a length of time as might form a habit, to adapt him to live in society afterwards, on terms of acquiescence in its rules.

Now the principle of management suggested here, is that ordinarily applied to insane patients alone; but this young man could not be considered insane in any accredited use of the term. He was totally free from false perception, or inconsequential thoughts; he was neat in his person, agreeable in his address, and of an intellect above rather than below par. Yet, education in its appeal to the moral principle had been tried on him in many various forms with total unsuccess: youth was advancing into manhood; and his chances of attaining a state, in which he might be a safe member of society, were becoming slender according to any of the usual methods of moral education.

The case seemed to warrant the application of the principle recommended; and after much thought, I determined to try it in the only way in which it was practicable *to me*, namely, in the walls of an establishment, a few miles from the place in which I resided, the proprietor of which was well known to me for excellent judgment and an amiable character.

I took him to this establishment, accompanied by his father and another relative, showed him at once into his apartment; and briefly told him why he was placed there; and how inflexible he would find his restraint there, until he should have gained habits of self-control. At the same time I pointed out to him the beautiful and wide grounds of the establishment, and the many comforts and enjoyments which he might command by strict obedience. This I stated to him in the presence of his two relatives, whom I then at once removed from the room. When I saw him about an hour afterwards, the nearest approach to surprise and annoyance which he made, was the expression, "that he never was in such a lurch before." He wished to see his father again before he left the house, not however, apparently from motives of feeling, but in order to address some persuasives to him against the scheme. I refused this interview.

For about a fortnight he behaved extremely well. He then lost his self-command, kicked his attendant, and struck him with a bottle of medicine. On this, I went over to see him; he vindicated himself with his usual ingenuity; but looked grave and somewhat frightened,—when I told him, that if he repeated this offence, he would be placed in a strait waistcoat, not indeed as a punishment, but as a means of supplying his deficiency of self-control. He expresses no kindly feeling towards his relatives; but confesses the fitness of his treatment and confinement. It appears to me, that he is tranquillised by his utter inability to resist.

January 16th, 18____. Visiting N.B. today, I told him, that he

might write letters to his father or uncle, but that he would at present receive none from them. To have refused him permission to
write letters would have been tyrannical; besides, they would afford
insight into his character; to have allowed him to *receive* letters,
would have been an interference with that principle of entire
separation from his family, which I wished to maintain, until he
should have learned the value of those ties to which he has been indifferent. He made complaints in very unimportant matters against
his servant, to which I paid attention, but gave no credence.
Great unfairness in these remarks. I have endeavoured to make
him understand, that in dealing with Mr. N____, the proprietor
of the establishment, and myself he can neither enjoy the pleasure
of making us angry, nor hope for advantage from sophistry. But
that strict justice will be done him, upon the terms originally
stated to him.

In a letter to his father about this time, I observe—"the plan evi-
dently works well. He is practising self-restraint successfully; not
indeed from conviction of its moral fitness, but from having
ascertained its necessity. He is aware of the state of entire subjec-
tion in which he is placed; and yet his spirits do not flag, neither
does his health suffer. It is curious, that he has ceased to use his old
argument in conversation with me, that past conduct ought not
to be taken into the account in regard to present proceedings."
From the time above alluded to, during his stay at the establishment, which I continued for fourteen months, no further out-
break against authority took place. He ceased to be violent, because
the indulgence of violence would imply risk of inconvenience to
himself, without the comfort which he had formerly derived from it
in exciting the anger of his friends or giving them pain. (Mayo,
1839, pp. 69–70)

By the middle of the nineteenth century, educators were providing programs for the
intellectually limited and behaviorally disordered. Schools in asylums for the insane
and the idiotic flourished for a time under the leadership of humanistic teachers who
developed explicit teaching methods (Brigham, 1845, 1847, 1848; Howe, 1851, 1852;
Ray, 1846). As Bockoven (1956) notes, education was a prominent part of moral
treatment. Teaching and learning were considered conducive to mental health—a
concept that can hardly be considered bizarre or antiquated.

Most of the education for severely and profoundly behavior disordered children and youth, aside from the academic instruction offered in asylums for the
insane, was provided under the rubric of education for idiots. The teaching techniques employed by leading educators of the retarded were amazingly modern in
many respects—they were based on individual assessment, were highly structured,
systematic, directive, and multisensory, emphasized training in self-help and daily
living skills for the severely handicapped, made frequent use of games and songs,
and were suffused with positive reinforcement (Brigham, 1848; Itard, 1962; Ray,

1846; Seguin, 1866). Despite the overenthusiasm and excessive claims of success by moral therapists and early educators of idiots, such as Howe, Itard, and Seguin, the basic soundness of their work and the changes they were able to produce in disturbed and retarded children remain impressive (Balthazaar & Stevens, 1975). At midcentury the prevailing attitude was one of hope and belief that every handicapped child could be helped. As Brigham (1845) states:

> The interesting question is, to what extent can careful and skillful instruction make up for these natural deficiencies [of idiotic children]; and, as already done for the deaf, the dumb, and the blind, reclaim for these unfinished creatures the powers and privileges of life. The exertions of future philanthropists will answer this question. Improvement must not be looked for beyond what is strictly relative to the imperfect individual in each case; but it would seem to be true of idiots, as of the insane in general, that there is no case incapable of some amendment; that every case may be improved or cured, up to a certain point,—a principle of great general importance in reference to treatment. (pp. 334–335)

In the nineteenth century there was considerable concern over children who were delinquent, vagrant, aggressive, disobedient, or disadvantaged (poor or orphaned), but not considered insane or idiotic (Bremner, 1970, 1971; Rothman, 1971). Many of these children, who today might be categorized as mildly or moderately handicapped (behavior disordered or retarded), found their way into jails and almshouses. However, there was in that era a strong movement to establish childcare institutions (orphan asylums, reformatories, houses of refuge, etc.) for the purpose of reforming and rehabilitating children. The intent was to protect wayward, handicapped, and poor children and to provide for their education and training in a humane, familial atmosphere. Concern for the futures of children exhibiting *acting-out* behavior was not entirely misguided. Contemporary longitudinal studies tend to confirm what nineteenth century writers suspected—aggressive, acting-out, delinquent behavior in children predicts misfortune for their later adjustment (Robins, 1966, 1979).

Intervention in the public schools became a reality only after the enactment of compulsory attendance laws in the closing decades of the century. One of the reasons for enactment of compulsory attendance laws, in fact, was the large number of non-English-speaking immigrant children who poured into the United States during this period. Immigrant children, it was felt, should be compelled to be socialized and Americanized by the schools. Once the attendance laws were enacted and enforced, it became obvious that there were many children who interfered with the education of the majority and benefited little from the regular class themselves. Before these children had been compelled to go to school they had merely dropped out, causing no problems except by roaming the streets and committing delinquent acts. Partly out of concern for such troublesome children and partly out of desire to be rid of such problems, the public schools established *ungraded* classes. In 1871, New Haven, Connecticut opened an ungraded class for truant, disobedient, and insubordinate children. Soon afterward, other cities followed suit, and classes for the socially maladjusted and "backward" (i.e., mentally retarded) children grew rapidly (Berkowitz & Rothman, 1967b; Hoffman, 1974). It soon became obvious that these special classes, as well as *corporate* schools and similar institutions were little more than dumping grounds for all manner of misfits. Whether the children or the public school administrators were the misfits is as pertinent a question for that era as for the present (Cruickshank, Paul, & Junkala, 1969).

Changes within the 1800s

The nineteenth century cannot be viewed as a unitary or homogeneous historical period. It is evident that in the years between 1850 and 1900, important changes took place in attitudes toward severe and profound behavior disorders and mental deficiency, and rather dramatic differences were seen in the type of care afforded in institutions. Optimism, pragmatism, inventiveness, and humane care, associated with moral treatment and model social programs in the first half of the century, gave way to pessimism, theorizing, rigidity, and dehumanizing institutionalization after the Civil War. The failure of private philanthropy and public programs to solve the problems of idiocy, insanity, and delinquency and to rectify the situations of the poor led to cynicism and disillusionment. More and larger asylums and houses of refuge turned out not to be the answers. The reasons for the retrogression after 1850 are many and complex and include economic, political, social, and professional factors analyzed by Bockoven (1956, 1972), Caplan (1969), Deutsch (1948), Grob (1973), Kanner (1964), Menninger (1963), Rothman (1971), and Ullmann and Krasner (1969).

Ironically, most historical comment on children's behavior disorders seems to favor the last decades of the century as more auspicious in the development of child psychiatry (Alexander & Selsnick, 1966; Harms, 1967; Kanner, 1973b; Rie, 1971; Walk, 1964). MacMillan's (1960) review of the literature suggests that the earlier decades provided a richer body of information, at least for the severely and profoundly disturbed:

> Examination of the 19th century literature relating to psychosis in childhood shows that the psychotic child was an object of study in the first part of the century, and that a substantial body of knowledge on the subject was accumulated in that period. Toward the latter part of the century, not only did the level of knowledge decline, but the psychotic child even seems to have ceased to have been an object of study. (p. 1091)

These observations seem to be borne out by examination of some of the literature published during the last decades of the century. Certainly, there is little or nothing to be found in the writings of Hammond (1891), Maudsley (1880) or Savage (1891) that improves upon earlier works insofar as treatment is concerned. The valuable and insightful work of late nineteenth century psychiatrists (such as Griesinger) reviewed by Harms (1967) is concerned with the theory and diagnosis of psychological disturbances in children and youth. After the demise of moral treatment about midcentury, psychiatry became increasingly engrossed in varieties of psychodynamic theory, and therapeutic action on behalf of patients gave way often to interest in diagnosis and classification. Educational and reform efforts with problem children and delinquents succumbed largely to social forces and to criticisms that they had failed; they increased in number and size, but not in quality or effectiveness. Hoffman (1974) notes that "in each case, what began as sincere, humanistic efforts toward change were turned into near caricatures of their original purposes" (p. 71). Before 1900 it was clear that institutionalization did not mean treatment and that special class placement meant marred identity.

Late 1800s

By the end of the nineteenth century, several textbooks had been published about the psychiatric disorders of children. These books deal primarily with etiology and classification and, as Kanner (1960) notes, tend toward fatalism. It was assumed that psychiatric disorders were the irreversible results of such widely varied causes as masturbation, overwork, hard study, religious preoccupation, heredity, degeneracy, or disease. The problems of obstreperous children and juvenile delinquents had not been solved, but new efforts were being made: Lightner Witmer established a psychoeducational clinic at the University of Pennsylvania in 1896; Chicago and Denver established the country's first juvenile courts in 1899. Events and trends during the first decades of the twentieth century represented a gradual increase in concern for the child with disordered behavior.

THE 1900s

1900 to 1910

Several important events occurred in the first years of the twentieth century that were to give direction and impetus to concern for children for many years to come. Ellen Key, the Swedish sociologist, awakened great interest with her prophecy that the twentieth century would be "the century of the child" (Key, 1909). Clifford W. Beers, a bright young man who experienced a nervous breakdown in 1900 and later recovered, recorded his experiences in a mental hospital. His autobiography, *A Mind that Found Itself* (Beers, 1908), had a profound influence on public opinion. Along with the psychiatrist Adolph Meyer and the philosopher and psychologist William James, Beers founded the National Committee for Mental Hygiene in 1909. The mental hygiene movement resulted in efforts at early detection and prevention, including the establishment of mental hygiene programs in schools and the opening of child guidance clinics.[7] Also, in the same year Dr. William Healy founded the Juvenile Psychopathic Institute for the psychological and sociological study of juvenile delinquents. Healy and his second wife, Augusta Bronner, along with Grace M. Fernald, Julia Lathrop, and others in Chicago began their systematic study of repeated juvenile offenders that influenced research and theory for many years.[8] These years were also the period in which Alfred Binet introduced an intelligence scale to measure the performance of children and to predict their success at school. It was at this time that Sigmund Freud and his contemporaries began writing widely on the topics of infant sexuality and human mental

---

[7] For descriptions of mental hygiene programs and special school provisions for maladjusted children during this era, see the historical account of Berkowitz & Rothman (1967b).

[8] See Healy (1915a, b, 1931) and Healy and Bronner (1926).

development. The work of Freud and other psychoanalysts was to have a profound effect on the way children's behavior was viewed and, eventually, on attempts to educate disturbed children. Finally, it was during these years that Drs. Henry Goddard and Walter Fernald forwarded the notion that mental retardation was inseparably linked to criminality and degeneracy (Doll, 1967; Hoffman, 1974; Smith, 1962).

1911 to 1930

Concern for the mental and physical health of children expanded greatly after 1910. In 1911, Dr. Arnold Gesell founded the Clinic for Child Development at Yale, and in 1912 Congress created the U.S. Children's Bureau "to investigate and report upon all matters pertaining to the welfare of children and child life among all classes of our people." The first teacher training program in special education began in Michigan in 1914. By 1918, all states had compulsory education laws, and in 1919 Ohio passed a law for state-wide care of handicapped children. By 1930, 16 states had enacted laws allowing local school districts to recover the excess costs of educating exceptional children (Henry, 1950). Educational and psychological testing were becoming widely used and school psychology, guidance, and counseling were emerging. Mental hygiene and child guidance clinics became relatively common by 1930, and by this time child psychiatry was a new discipline (Kanner, 1973b). According to Kanner, child guidance clinics of this era made three major innovations: (a) interdisciplinary collaboration, (b) treatment of any child whose behavior was annoying parents and teachers, not just the severe cases, and (c) attention to the effects of interpersonal relationships and adult attitudes on child behavior (Kanner, 1973b pp. 194–195).

In the 1920s there were calls for mental hygiene programs in the schools, and programs were established in some school systems. Thomas Haines, director of the Division of Mental Deficiency of the National Committee for Mental Hygiene, called for statutes governing the study and training of *all* exceptional children in the public schools, including the "psychopathic," the "psychoneurotic," and "those who exhibit behavior problems" (Haines, 1925). In an article in the *New Republic*, Dr. Smiley Blanton (1925), director of the Minneapolis Child Guidance Clinic and a practicing child psychiatrist, describes the operation of mental hygiene clinics in the public schools of Minneapolis.[9] The staff consisted of a psychologist, three psychiatric social workers (who had been teachers before they became social workers), 20 visiting teachers, and 10 corrective speech teachers. One of the functions of the clinic was to organize a course in mental hygiene for high school juniors and seniors. Another objective was to establish behavior clinics in kindergartens. The clinic took referrals from teachers and parents and also served preschool and juvenile court cases. After referral to the clinic, a child was studied carefully and a staff meeting was held to determine a course of action. Typically, the staff talked things over with the parents and teacher and tried to change their attitudes toward the child. Specific instructions were given on behavior

---

[9] See Bremner (1971) pp. 947–957, 1040–1057.

management, and a social worker would then go to the home or classroom to help carry out the program.

Two professional organizations that are particularly important to the education of disturbed children were founded in the 1920s. The Council for Exceptional Children, organized in 1922, was then made up primarily of educators but included other professionals and parents. The group was a powerful force for the appropriation of monies and the passage of legislation concerning the education of all handicapped children. The American Orthopsychiatric Association (AOA), dominated by the professions of child psychiatry, clinical psychology, and social work but including education and other disciplines as well, was founded in 1924. The AOA did much to encourage research and dissemination of information regarding therapeutic and educational endeavors with behavior disordered children.

1931 to 1945

The Depression and World War II necessarily diverted attention and funds from education of the handicapped. However, there were more handicapped children in special education in 1940 than in 1930, and by 1948 41 of the 48 states had enacted laws authorizing or requiring local school districts to make special educational provisions for at least one category of exceptional children (Henry, 1950). The vast majority of special classes were for the educable mentally retarded. Programs for children with behavior disorders were relatively few and were designed primarily for acting-out and delinquent children in large cities.

Hitler's rise to power in Europe provided several unanticipated benefits for the education of handicapped children in this country. Several people who later were to influence special education fled to the United States, including Bruno Bettelheim, Marianne Frostig, Alfred Strauss, and Heinz Werner.[10] The contributions of some of these individuals will be touched upon later in this chapter.

There were several significant developments in child psychiatry during this period. The first psychiatric hospital for children in the United States, the Bradley Home, was established in Rhode Island in 1931 (Davids, 1975). Leo Kanner of Johns Hopkins University contributed immeasurably to the field with the first edition of his textbook *Child Psychiatry* in 1935 and with his initial descriptions of early infantile autism (Kanner, 1943, 1973a, b, c). In the following he described his first experience with children who would later to be said to have "Kanner's syndrome."

> In October 1938, a 5-year-old boy was brought to my clinic from Forest, Mississippi. I was struck by the uniqueness of the peculiarities which Donald exhibited. He could, since the age of $2^1/_2$ years, tell the names of all the presidents and vice-presidents, recite the letters of the alphabet forwards and backwards, and flawlessly, with good enunciation, rattle off the Twenty-Third Psalm. Yet he was unable to carry on an ordinary conversation. He was out of contact with people, while he could handle objects skillfully. His memory was phenomenal. The few times when he addressed someone—largely to satisfy his wants—he referred to himself as "You" and to the person addressed as

---

[10] See Frostig (1976), Hallahan and Cruickshank (1973), and Hallahan and Kauffman (1976, 1977).

"I." He did not respond to any intelligence tests but manipulated intricate formboards adroitly. (Kanner, 1973a, p. 93)

During the 1930s, Despert (a 1968 collection of her papers) and Potter (1933), along with Kanner and others, tried to clarify the characteristics of various categories of severely and profoundly disturbed children. Dr. Lauretta Bender, also writing on the topic of childhood schizophrenia, pioneered the development of education for these children in the 1930s. Having organized the children's ward at Bellevue Psychiatric Hospital in New York City in 1934, she appealed in 1935 to the New York City Board of Education for teachers to staff special classrooms for severely disturbed children at Bellevue. The Board responded by assigning two substitute teachers to teach ungraded classes (the category used for mentally retarded children) at Bellevue under the administration of the school for the physically handicapped. In spite of inadequate facilities and a complete lack of instructional materials in the beginning, the program succeeded (Wright, 1967). The Bellevue school was to become a fertile training ground for future leaders in the education of disturbed children, notably Pearl Berkowitz and Esther Rothman (Berkowitz, 1974, and Rothman, 1974).

By the end of the 1930s, the literature on children's behavior disorders had grown to sizeable proportions (Baker & Stullken, 1938). Attempts had been made to define emotional disturbance and to delineate several sub-classifications. Surveys of children's behavior problems and teachers' attitudes toward misbehavior (Wickman, 1929) had been completed and attempts had been made to estimate the prevalence of behavior disorders. Various plans of special education for disturbed children, such as special rooms, schools, classes, and consultative help had been tried.

The Post-War Years and the 1950s

Following the Second World War, additional varieties of severely disturbed children were described by the psychiatric profession.[11] Mahler (1952) delineates a form which she calls *symbiotic infantile psychosis* (overattachment to the mother); Rank (1949) introduces the term *atypical child* (any severe disturbance of early development due to problems of relationship between mother and child); Bergman and Escalona (1949) describe children with unusual sensitivity to sensory stimulation; and Robinson and Vitale (1954) write about children with circumscribed interest patterns. All of these types of children with severe disorders fit under the general rubric of childhood psychosis.

The 1940s and 1950s saw a rising wave of interest in the education of disturbed children. In 1944, Bruno Bettelheim began his work with severely disturbed children at the Sonja Shankman Orthogenic School at the University of Chicago. His concept of a "therapeutic milieu" (Bettelheim, 1950; Bettelheim & Sylvester, 1948) continues to be used in educational methods based on psychoanalytic thought (Bettelheim, 1961, 1970; Redl, 1959b, 1966; Trieschman, Whittaker & Brendtro,

---

[11] For succinct summaries of the contributions of numerous individuals working in this era, see Haring and Phillips (1962).

1969). During the 1940s, Fritz Redl and David Wineman began their work with hyperaggressive youngsters in Detroit. Basing their strategies on the ideas of Bettleheim and others who were psychoanalytic in their thinking regarding delinquency (Aichhorn, 1935; Eissler, 1949; Freud, 1946), Redl and Wineman describe their use of a therapeutic milieu and a technique called the *life space interview* at Pioneer House, a residential setting for young aggressive and delinquent boys (Redl & Wineman, 1951, 1952). The efforts and thoughts of Redl and Wineman influenced an entire generation of educators of the disturbed (Long, 1974; Morse, 1974).

The New York City Board of Education organized its *600 schools* in 1946.[12] These schools, arbitrarily numbered from 600 to 699, were established specifically for the purpose of educating disturbed and maladjusted children. Some were day schools located in regular school buildings; others were located in residential diagnostic and treatment settings (Berkowitz & Rothman, 1967b).

One of the most important publications of the 1940s was a book by Alfred A. Strauss and Laura E. Lehtinen, *Psychopathology and Education of the Brain-Injured Child* (1947). This book summarizes the work of Strauss and his colleagues (especially Heinz Werner) and students at the Wayne County Training School in Northville, Michigan and the Cove Schools in Racine, Wisconsin. Although much of the work of Werner and Strauss was with the *exogenous* (i.e., brain-damaged post-natally) mentally retarded child, Strauss and Lehtinen recognized that learning problems exist in some children of normal intelligence. These learning difficulties they attributed to brain injury. However, they did recognize that emotional maladjustment is characteristic of such children:

> The response of the brain-injured child to the school situation is frequently inadequate, conspicuously disturbing, and persistently troublesome. The following excerpts from teacher's reports are illustrative.
>
> J.M., 7 years old: ". . . . doesn't pay attention to any directions. He is unaware of anything said, yet at times he surprises me by noticing things that others don't . . . ."
>
> D.J., 7 years old: ". . . attention hard to hold. Asks constantly: 'When can I go? Can I go now?' etc. No initiative. Little self-control. Seems high strung and nervous . . . ."
>
> D.H., 8 years old: ". . . has proven quite a serious problem in behavior. Has acquired the habit of throwing himself into tantrums at the slightest provocation . . . ."
>
> J.K., 8 years old: ". . . has made scarcely any social adjustments in relationships with other children, he loses all self-control, becoming wild and uncontrollable; he is extremely nervous and excitable; his attention span is very short and he is unable to concentrate for more than a few minutes. During work periods he jumps from one activity to another . . . ." (Strauss & Lehtinen, 1947, p. 127)*

For such children Strauss and Lehtinen recommended a highly structured educational approach and a highly consistent, distraction-free environment. Besides general educational principles, they describe special methods for teaching arithmetic, reading, and writing. Their work is particularly important because it pro-

---

[12] The designation "600" has now been dropped in favor of a random numbering system. This decision was made in 1965 after it became apparent that *600* was stigmatizing. For additional description of education in schools of this type, see Tobin (1971).

* From *Psychopathology and Education of the Brain-Injured Child* by A. A. Strauss and L. L. Lehtinen (now Rogan), 1947, p. 127, 129–130. Copyright 1947 by Grune & Stratton. Reprinted by permission.

vided the foundation for the later efforts of Cruickshank (Cruickshank, Bentzen, Ratzeburg, & Tannhauser, 1961) and Haring and Phillips (1962).

By the early 1950s interest in special education for children with behavior disorders gained considerable momentum. In fact, one could say that this area of special education came of age by the end of the 1950s, for one no longer had to be content with examining developments in psychiatry or with citing references in mental retardation. Education of the disturbed child had become a field of specialization in its own right. One early indication of the recognition by mental health professionals of the importance of education in dealing with the behavior disordered child was publication of a symposium on the education of emotionally disturbed children (Krugman, 1953). This article was one of the first attempts by the *American Journal of Orthopsychiatry* to devote an appreciable number of pages specifically to a collection of papers on the importance of schools and education. Included among the papers of the symposium are those of Louis Hay (1953) detailing the Junior Guidance Class Program in New York City and Dr. J. Cotter Hirschberg (1953) explaining the important roles of education in residential treatment of the severely disturbed child. It is worthy of note that the second part of *Forty-ninth Yearbook of the National Society for the Study of Education* on the education of exceptional children (the first in its history, published in 1950) includes a chapter on the education of socially maladjusted children (Stullken, 1950). Another landmark event of the early 1950s was the founding of the League School by Carl Fenichel in 1953 (Fenichel, 1974; Fenichel, Freedman, & Klapper, 1960). The League School was the first private day school for seriously emotionally disturbed children in the United States. Fenichel, who had training in psychoanalysis, began the school with a permissive, psychoanalytic orientation but soon gave this up in favor of a more directive *psychoeducational* approach (Fenichel, 1966, 1974).

In 1955 the first book describing classroom teaching of disturbed children appeared.[13] In it, Leonard Kornberg (1955) recounts his experiences in teaching 15 disturbed boys at Hawthorn-Cedar Knolls, a residential school near New York City. His teaching approach was based primarily on psychoanalytic thought and drew heavily on the interpersonal therapeutic process—"dialogue" and responding to "I" and "otherness." As he puts it, "The essential classroom event is the transaction of meaning among more than two persons, as contrasted with the two-person contact of a therapy situation" (Kornberg, 1955, p. 132). This emphasis on interpersonal relationship and psychiatric-dynamic ideas is predominant in the literature of the 1950s.

By the mid 1950s it was recognized that systematic procedures were needed to identify disturbed children in the public schools. Eli Bower and others began research in California that culminated in publication of the screening instrument devised by Bower and Lambert (1962) and other writings of Bower (1960, 1969).

---

[13] The books that appeared before 1955 are not primarily descriptions of classroom teaching, although Redl and Wattenberg discuss mental health in teaching and others (e.g., Bettelheim, 1950; Hymes, 1949; Pearson, 1954; Prescott, 1954; Redl & Wineman, 1951, 1952; Slavson, 1954) examine the relationship between psychoanalysis, psychotherapy, other forms of treatment, and mental health efforts and education. Also Axline (1947) and Moustakas (1953) describe play therapy with children. Until the early 1960s probably the most explicit teaching methods for children with behavior disorders were found in the classic books by Strauss and Lehtinen (1947) and Strauss and Kephart (1955).

Concern for teaching disturbed children had grown by the late 1950s to the extent that an initial study of teacher preparation was reported by Mackie, Kvaraceus, and Williams (1957). The last years of the decade were auspicious ones for the field because numerous individuals were attaining new vantage points on the education of disturbed children: Pearl H. Berkowitz and Esther P. Rothman were collaborating in New York City; William C. Morse and Nicholas J. Long were working at the University of Michigan's Fresh Air Camp for disturbed children; Frank M. Hewett was beginning his studies with severely disturbed children at the University of California at Los Angeles; Nicholas Hobbs and William C. Rhodes began conceptualizing new strategies at George Peabody College in Nashville, Tennessee; William M. Cruickshank and Norris G. Haring were conducting research projects in the public schools of Maryland and Virginia; and Richard J. Whelan was developing a directive, structured approach to teaching disturbed children at the Menninger Clinic in Topeka, Kansas. The activities of these and other individuals resulted in a wave of publications and research activities which burst upon the field in the 1960s and 1970s.

1960 to the Present

A steady stream of events after 1960 led to the current diversity of theory and practice in the education of disturbed children. While much of the theoretical groundwork was laid prior to 1960, it was only after that point that specific classroom practices were articulated. Special classes for disturbed children in the public schools had proliferated by this time to such a degree that planning guidelines were published (Hollister & Goldston, 1962) and a nationwide survey of special classes was conducted (Morse, Cutler, & Fink, 1964). Professionals banded together in 1964 to form a new division of the Council for Exceptional Children called the Council for Children with Behavioral Disorders. Various curriculum designs for behavior disordered children were outlined (Kauffman, 1974a; Rhodes, 1963), and curricula to teach specific social-interpersonal skills were developed (Fagen, Long, & Stevens, 1975; Goldstein, 1974; Ojemann, 1961). A series of three annual conferences on the education of emotionally disturbed children was held at Syracuse University, bringing together educators and psychologists of divergent viewpoints (Knoblock, 1965, 1966; Knoblock & Johnson, 1967). Preparation of personnel to work with disturbed children received federal support in 1963 with the enactment of Public Law 88–164 (amending PL 85–926 of 1958). The National Society for Autistic Children was founded in 1965 and The Association for the Severely Handicapped was organized in 1974, reflecting increased interest in the field. It would be impossible to review all of the important events and trends of the years since 1960, but several of the more critical developments will be summarized.

Psychoanalytic View

In 1960, Berkowitz and Rothman published their now classic book, *The Disturbed Child: Recognition and Psychoeducational Therapy in the Classroom*. This book describes various classifications of disturbed children, but the last four chapters explain the teacher's role and classroom procedures. The underlying theory of the book is psychoanalytic, and the approach suggested is quite permissive. In a later book Berkowitz and Rothman (1967a) pull together descriptions by several individuals of a variety of programs for disturbed children in New York City. Together they further delineate their concept of clinical teaching (Rothman & Berkowitz, 1967a), propose a paradigm for a clinical school (Rothman & Berkowitz, 1967c), and describe methods of teaching reading to emotionally disturbed children (Rothman & Berkowitz, 1967b). In other works of the late 60s, Berkowitz reports the status of public schools in treatment centers (Berkowitz, 1967), and Rothman relates her work at the Livingston School for disturbed, delinquent girls (Rothman, 1967). In other publications of the 1970s, Berkowitz (1974) describes her continued work in institutional schools in New York City and Rothman (1970, 1974) writes more about her involvement with the Livingston School.

Psychoeducational Approach

Just as the later publications of Berkowitz and Rothman reflect a movement from the strictly psychoanalytic perspective and toward a more pragmatic stance, the work of Morse and others at the University of Michigan in the 1960s shows a tendency toward emphases on practical considerations and ego development. Morse and Long, in collaboration with Ruth G. Newman, published the first edition of a landmark volume in 1965, *Conflict in the Classroom* (Long, Morse, & Newman, 1965). This book brings together the ideas of Redl and Morse regarding the *life space interview* but includes several disparate viewpoints, ranging from the psychoanalytic (e.g., Freud, 1965) to the behavioral (Haring & Whelan, 1965). The life space interview (LSI) grew out of Redl's work at Pioneer House in Detroit in the 1940s and 1950s. At or shortly after the time of a behavioral crisis, the teacher (or other child worker) could conduct an LSI in order to strengthen the child's ego and to help the child to understand and interpret correctly the problems he/she had just encountered (Long & Newman, 1965; Morse, 1953, 1965a; Morse & Wineman, 1965; Redl, 1959a). It is also in the writings of the 1960s that Morse explains his idea of the *crisis teacher*—a teacher skilled in LSI techniques and remedial teaching who would be prepared to take over the management and teaching of a difficult child for a short period of time (during a behavioral crisis), and to obviate the need for full time special class placement (Morse, 1965b, 1971a, b). More recently, Fagen, Long, and Stevens (1975) present a psychoeducational self control curriculum and Fagen (1979) describes psychoeducational methods for adolescents.

Humanism

As Martin (1972) notes, individualism and humanism are forces shaping special education's future. Concern has been expressed for the particular educational needs of black and other minority group children, especially those from inner city areas and poverty backgrounds (Dennison, 1969; Dokecki, Strain, Bernal, Brown, & Robinson, 1975; Johnson, 1969, 1971; Rothman, 1970, 1974). For emotionally disturbed children it has been suggested that radical departures from past educational practices are needed. *Countertheorists* who depart markedly from tradition and are not accepted typically as fellow professionals by established authorities in their fields, have as an aggregate become a strong force since the mid 1960s. Many of the individuals who are a part of this group consider themselves to be *humanists* and subscribers of the freedom and openness called for by Carl Rogers (1969) and others (Kohl, 1970; Kozol, 1972; Leonard, 1968; Neill, 1960).

> Counter theory is what countertheorists say and do. Usually it begins with the school or the child and works back to the theory from there. It means a bent toward the humanistic ideas of writers like Abraham Maslow [1962, 1968]. It is a tendency toward freer education, more in the hands of the student and less determined from above than in most models. Often it means a spirit of rebelliousness and innovation. And it is not so much a body of theory as it is a praxic. (Burke, 1972, p. 577)

In special education for disturbed children, pleas for freedom, openness, and humanism are made by Dennison (1969), Grossman (1972), Knoblock (1970, 1973; 1979), Knoblock and Goldstein (1971), Schultz, Heuchert, and Stampf (1973), and Trippe (1970).

Ecological Approach

The 1960s also saw the rise of the *ecological* approach to disturbed children. Based primarily on the writing of Hobbs (1965, 1966, 1968, 1974) and Rhodes (1965, 1967, 1970), this approach calls for intervention not only with the disturbed child but also with his home, school, and community.[14] The most important project associated with the ecological approach is Project Re-ED. After having worked extensively in the mental health field in this country and having observed the European *educateur* programs,[15] Hobbs, along with Rhodes, Matthew J. Trippe, Wilbert W. Lewis, Lloyd M. Dunn, and others began Re-ED programs in Tennessee and North Carolina in the early 1960s. Re-ED schools focused on health rather than illness, teaching rather than treatment, learning rather than fundamental personality change, the present and future rather than the past, and on the total social system of the child rather than the child's intra-psychic processes exclusively (Hobbs, 1965). In the initial Re-ED schools, children were served in a residential setting during the week but returned home on weekends. A central aspect of Project Re-ED was the selection and training of the *teacher-counselors*, who carried out the moment-to-moment and day-to-day work with children, and the liaison teachers, who maintained communication and coordination with the child's home and regular school class (Hobbs, 1966, 1974). Work with the Re-ED model continues (Lee, 1971; Weinstein, 1969), and initial evaluations appear to support the efficacy of the approach. Furthermore, the initial work of Hobbs and Rhodes appears to have given impetus to the research and writing of others (e.g., Graubard, 1976, Graubard, Rosenburg, & Miller, 1971; Rosenburg & Graubard, 1975; Swap, 1974, 1978).

Behavioral Approach

In the late 1950s and early 1960s some special educators began making explicit use of basic behavior principles and behavior modification techniques (cf. Forness &

---

[14] Hobbs, Rhodes, and others draw upon the theoretical formulations and field work of ecological psychologists such as Roger C. Barker and Herbert F. Wright (Barker & Wright, 1949, 1954; Barker, 1968; see also Gump, 1975).

[15] See Linton (1969, 1970) as well as Hobbs (1974) for description of the *educateur* programs.

MacMillan, 1970; Kazdin, 1978). The behavior modification frame of reference was derived primarily from the basic research and writing of B.F. Skinner (Skinner, 1953). However, its initial application to the education of disturbed children was the work of many individuals, a number of whom were influenced by the work of Heinz Werner, Alfred Strauss, Laura Lehtinen, Newell Kephart, and others who devised methods of teaching brain-injured children at the Wayne County training School in the 1940s.

William M. Cruickshank and his colleagues conducted an experimental public school program for brain-injured and hyperactive children (many of whom had emotional difficulties) in Montgomery County, Maryland in the late 1950s. The report of this project (Cruickshank et al., 1961) describes a highly structured program similar in many ways to that outlined earlier by Strauss and Lehtinen (1947). The emphasis in the report is on control of extraneous stimuli and the use of a consistent routine and consistent consequences for behavior. Shortly after the Montgomery County Project, Norris G. Haring and E. Lakin Phillips extended the concept of structure to work with emotionally disturbed children in the public schools of Arlington, Virginia (Haring & Phillips, 1962; Phillips & Haring, 1959; Phillips, 1967). In their books, their major hypothesis is that disturbed children lack order, predictability, and consistency in their environment and that these children need the stability and consistent demands found in Cruickshank's program. They particularly emphasize the use of consistent consequences for behavior (a basic behavior modification principle). A structured approach as defined by Haring and Phillips consists of three primary elements: clear directions, firm expectations that the child would perform as directed, and consistent follow through in applying consequences for behavior. Later in the 60s, Haring collaborated with Richard J. Whelan at the University of Kansas Medical Center in order to refine and extend the concept of structure (Haring & Whelan, 1965; Whelan & Haring, 1966), which was extended even further in the late 1960s and into the 1970s by Haring and Phillips to include the behavior modification technology of direct daily measurement of behavioral rates (Haring, 1968, 1974a; Haring & Phillips, 1972). Whelan, Haring's collaborator at Kansas University, had previously developed a structured approach to teaching at the Southard School of the Menninger Clinic in Topeka, Kansas (Whelan, 1963, 1966). Whelan has expanded and refined the concept of structure and the use of behavior principles with disturbed children (Whelan, 1974; Whelan & Gallagher, 1972).

Other individuals were also pioneering the behavioral approach to disturbed children. Herbert C. Quay and his associates contributed immeasurably to the classification of disordered behavior (Quay, 1975, 1979). The report of Zimmerman and Zimmerman (1962) was a prelude to an outpouring of behavior modification research with disturbed children in the latter part of the decade. Their simple anecdotal reports of how they resolved two behavior problems—temper tantrums and refusal to write spelling words—by systematic use of consequences was to be followed by a spate of technically sophisticated reports in the behavior modification literature, little of which can be cited here. It is sufficient to mention that many behavioral psychologists, including many who were interested in special education and emotionally disturbed children, made tremendous strides in therapeutic endeavors in the 1960s and 1970s (Goodall, 1972).

One behavioral psychologist interested in special education was Frank Hewett. Two of his areas of activity are particularly worthy of note. First, in the middle 1960s, he designed an *engineered* classroom that employed a token (point) system as well as special curricula and centers of activity. His Santa Monica Project, as an early trial of his program was called, has become a frequently cited and widely emulated behavioral approach (Hewett, 1967, 1968). As part of his research and training activities, Hewett also proposed a hierarchy of educational tasks for disturbed children (Hewett, 1964a) and a hierarchy of competencies for their teachers (Hewett, 1966). He has continued to write of his research and training using behavioral methods (Hewett, 1970, 1971, 1974). The second area in which his efforts deserve notice is the teaching of severely and profoundly disturbed children. Through the systematic use of operant conditioning (reinforcement) techniques he was able to teach speech and reading skills to an autistic boy (Hewett, 1964b, 1965).

Finally, in the 1960s and 1970s, there was a dramatic increase in interest and effort in the education of the severely and profoundly handicapped, including disturbed children.[16] The formation of The Association for the Severely Handicapped and the National Society for Autistic Children has already been noted. Probably the intervention techniques that gained widest acceptance in this era and proved themselves to be most effective with psychotic children were behavior modification methods. Although the professionals making contributions in this area are too numerous to name, the work of O. Ivar Lovaas must be mentioned. First at the University of Washington and later at the University of California at Los Angeles, Lovaas and his colleagues researched the teaching of language and daily living skills to autistic and schizophrenic children (Lovaas, 1966, 1967; Lovaas & Koegel, 1973; Lovaas, Koegel, Simmons, & Long, 1973; Lovaas, Young, & Newsom, 1978; Devany, Rincover, & Lovaas, 1981). His work, along with that of others who employed operant conditioning techniques, demonstrates that the severely and profoundly disturbed child can learn when appropriate conditions are arranged and that one need not wait for this learning to occur spontaneously.

Projects and Legislation

Two major special projects with long range implications for disturbed children were conducted in the 1970s. In order to delineate clearly and to synthesize the diverse ideologies and practices in the field, William C. Rhodes and others at the University of Michigan began the Conceptual Project in Emotional Disturbance in the early 1970s. Recognizing the fragmentation and conflict in the field, but also the commonalities and the mood of ecumenicalism among various factions, Rhodes set about to clarify the conceptual models and their associated methods of intervention (Rhodes & Head, 1974; Rhodes & Tracy, 1972a, b). His work has become a standard reference in the field. The Project on Classification of Exceptional Children was directed by Nicholas Hobbs in the early 1970s. This project was

---

[16] Part of the reason for this increase in interest and effort was due to litigation in which the parents of exceptional children were plaintiffs. Court decisions that *all* children, including the severely and profoundly handicapped, have a right to public education provided the impetus for local schools to make provisions for such children and for the Office of Special Education (U.S. Department of Education) to support training programs for teachers of such children.

conducted (at the request of Elliot L. Richardson when he was secretary of Health, Education and Welfare) in order to examine the consequences of labeling exceptional children of all categories, including the behaviorally disordered. The results of the project (Hobbs, 1975a, 1975b) reflect the stigmatizing and damaging effects of an inadequate classification and labeling process, an issue of intense concern in the first half of the 1970s.

In 1975, PL 94-142 was signed into law and went into effect in September, 1978. It is a complex and prescriptive piece of legislation, the details of which are not discussed in this book (see Bateman & Herr, 1981; Martin, 1979, for discussion). The law's central feature is the requirement that *every* handicapped child, including those categorized as seriously emotionally disturbed, be given a free, appropriate education. The intention of the law certainly cannot be faulted, and some of its effects without doubt will be salutary. Troubled children who are identified as emotionally disturbed cannot now legally be excluded from school or denied an appropriate education because they are handicapped. However, the law represents an unfulfilled promise. At the beginning of the 1980s, only about 1/4 of the federal government's conservative estimate of the number of disturbed children were being provided special education. The prospect is not good for all such children being served within the near future. Limited economic resources, shortage of trained personnel, non-normative classification systems, technical requirements of the law, and lack of pressure for services from parents of nonpsychotic disturbed children are factors working against dramatic increases in the number of disturbed children that will receive special education (Kauffman, 1980; Magliocca & Stephens, 1980).

IN RETROSPECT

The view presented in this chapter reflects the vision of one individual at one point in time and calls to mind the insightful comments of Eisenberg (1969).

> Historiography is a constant dialogue between past and present; it takes new form from the grounds of the shifting present. The historian 25 years hence will almost certainly view our recent past from perspectives quite different from our own, having at his command new viewpoints and more distance from the controversies in which we are still engaged. We can only hope he will be kind to those of us then still alive, and show due respect for our venerability if not for our perspicacity.   (p. 389)

SUMMARY

Children with behavior disorders have been recognized throughout history. Before 1800, most such children were considered possessed, wicked, or idiotic. In the nineteenth century efforts to educate disturbed children began, first in lunatic asylums and institutions for idiots and later in houses of refuge, detention centers, or public school classes for truants, troublemakers, or backward children. The mental hygiene and child study movements of the early twentieth century highlighted the problems of behavior disorders in children and led to efforts to deal with disturbed children more effectively in homes and schools. In the 1940s several syndromes of severely disturbed behavior were clearly described. Several psychoanalytically oriented educational programs began in the late 1940s and the 1950s. The 1960s and early 1970s were periods of rapid growth in educational interventions for disturbed children. Diverse theories ranging from psychoanalytic to behavioral led to divergent educational practices. Besides the forces of psychoanalysis and behaviorism, the field was influenced by growth of ecological and humanistic psychology. Recently there has been renewed concern for the severely and profoundly disturbed child and the negative effects of labeling and classifying.

Several of the important events in the history of the field are summarized in Table 2-1.

TABLE 2-1 Chronology of Some Important Events Relating to Children with Behavior Disorders, 1799-1980

1799 — Itard publishes his report of the wild boy of Aveyron

1825 — House of Refuge, first institution for juvenile delinquents in the United States, founded in New York; similar institutions founded in Boston (1826) and Philadelphia (1828)

1841 — Dorothea Dix begins crusade for better care of the insane

1847 — State Reform School for Boys established in Westborough, Massachusetts, the first state institution for juvenile delinquents

1850 — Massachusetts incorporates school for idiotic and feebleminded youth at urging of Samuel Gridley Howe; Edward Seguin moves to the United States

1866 — Edward Seguin publishes *Idiocy and Its Treatment by the Physiological Method* in America

1871 — *Ungraded* class for truant, disobedient, and insubordinate children opens in New Haven, Connecticut

1898 — New York City Board of Education assumes responsibility for two schools for truant children

1899 — First U.S. juvenile court established in Chicago

1908 — Clifford Beers publishes *A Mind that Found Itself*

1909 — National Committee for Mental Hygiene founded; Ellen Key publishes *The Century of the Child*; William Healy founds the Juvenile Psychopathic Institute in Chicago

1911 — Arnold Gesell founds the Clinic for Child Development at Yale University

1912 — Congress creates the U.S. Children's Bureau

1919 — Ohio passes law for state wide education of the handicapped

1922 — Council for Exceptional Children founded

1924 — American Orthopsychiatric Association founded

1931 — First psychiatric hospital for children in the United States is founded in Rhode Island

1935 — Leo Kanner publishes *Child Psychiatry;* Loretta Bender and others begin school for psychotic children at Bellevue Psychiatric Hospital in New York City

1943 — Leo Kanner describes *early infantile autism*

1944 — Bruno Bettelheim opens the Orthogenic School at the University of Chicago

1946 — New York City Board of Education designates *600* schools for disturbed and maladjusted pupils; Fritz Redl and David Wineman open Pioneer House in Detroit

1947 — Alfred Strauss and Laura Lehtinen publish *Psychopathology and Education of the Brain-Injured Child* based on work at Wayne County Training School in Northville, Michigan

Table 2—1 (continued)

1950 — Bruno Bettelheim publishes *Love is Not Enough*

1953 — Carl Fenichel founds the League School in Brooklyn, first private day school for severely emotionally disturbed children

1955 — Leonard Kornberg publishes *A Class for Disturbed Children*, first book describing classroom teaching of disturbed children

1960 — Pearl Berkowitz & Esther Rothman publish *The Disturbed Child* describing permissive, psychoanalytic educational approach

1961 — William Cruickshank et al. publish *A Teaching Method for Brain-Injured and Hyperactive Children*, reporting results of a structured educational program in Montgomery County, Maryland; Nicholas Hobbs and associates begin Project Re-ED in Tennessee and North Carolina

1962 — Norris Haring and Lakin Phillips publish *Educating Emotionally Disturbed Children*, reporting results of a structured program in Arlington, Virginia; Eli Bower and Nadine Lambert publish *An In-School Process for Screening Emotionally Handicapped Children* based on research in California

1963 — PL 88-164 provides federal money for support of personnel preparation in the area of emotionally disturbed

1964 — William Morse, Richard Cutler, and Albert Fink publish *Public School Classes for the Emotionally Handicapped: A Research Analysis*; Council for Children with Behavioral Disorders established as a division of Council for Exceptional Children

1965 — Nicholas Long, William Morse, and Ruth Newman publish *Conflict in the Classroom;* National Society for Autistic Children founded; First Annual Conference on the Education of Emotionally Disturbed Children held at Syracuse University

1968 — Frank Hewett publishes *The Emotionally Disturbed Child in the Classroom,* reporting the use of an *engineered* classroom in Santa Monica, California

1970 — William Rhodes begins Conceptual Project in Emotional Disturbance, summarizing theory, research, and intervention in the field

1974 — Association for the Severely Handicapped founded

1975 — Nicholas Hobbs publishes *Issues in the Classification of Children* and *The Futures of Children* reporting the work of the Project on the Classification of Exceptional Children

1978 — PL 94-142 (enacted in 1975) requires free, appropriate education for *all* handicapped children, including the seriously emotionally disturbed

1980 — Statistics show that about .5% of school age children are receiving special education services as seriously emotionally disturbed, only about 1/4 of a very conservative estimate of prevalence

chapter 3

Screening, Classification, and Assessment

The most severely disordered behavior of children is easy to detect, even when the children are very young. There is no difficulty in arriving at a consensus of rational people that such behavior deserves a deviance label and calls for intervention. But the majority of disordered behavior is not so readily identified; indeed, *disordered* fades into *normal* amid a haze of conjecture and, in specific cases, divided opinion of well schooled experts. Consequently, it is often considered desirable to reduce the size of the population being considered during the identification process, that is, to devise an effective and efficient means of screening out from further consideration those children who are almost certainly not disturbed and screening in for further study those who probably are.

Identification of children as disturbed is not very informative—the label for the general category does not give any indication of what kind of behavior to expect from a particular child, except that some of the child's behavior will be aberrant. There are hundreds of ways that children can show aberrant behavior. For the sake of clearer communication, and because classification is basic to scientific investigation, those who study disturbed children have tried to devise ways of classifying disordered behavior (see Menninger, 1963, for many examples of psychiatric classification). Behaviors with common attributes are clustered together under various labels. For example, the problem behaviors exhibited by Henry (see p. 5) might be considered representative of a *conduct disorder*. This label denotes a specific type of behavioral difficulty and leads to the prediction that the child will exhibit hyperaggressive or "acting out" behaviors rather than shyness, passivity, and withdrawal.

Once a child is identified as disturbed it is important to make an evaluation of the child's behavior and situation so that an appropriate intervention can be planned. Determining precisely the nature and extent of the problem, finding its possible causes and exacerbating factors, designing methods of changing it, and monitoring the outcome constitute the process of *assessment*. The term diagnosis has been largely replaced by assessment in the behavioral literature because diagnosis connotes the classification of disease. In the vast majority of cases, there is no evidence that disordered behavior is a disease in any usual sense of the term.

This chapter addresses general issues in screening, classification, and assessment that are pertinent to discussion in each of the following chapters. Greater attention is given to the process of assessment than to screening and classification because at this point in the development of behavioral science, assessment is more helpful to understand the origins and management of disorders. Assessment in the general case is discussed in this chapter; assessment techniques specific to particular types of disorders are taken up in subsequent chapters.

SCREENING

Effective screening means becoming a good "suspectition" (Bower, 1969). It means being able to pick out cases that are not immediately obvious to anyone and being able to identify incipient problems—those just beginning—with a high degree of accuracy. The reason for screening children for behavior disorders, or any other handicap for that matter, is based on the assumption that early identification and early treatment will be more effective, efficient, and humane than to let problems fester until they arouse the concern of even hardened observers. Furthermore, PL 94–142 requires efforts to identify *all* handicapped children (including all those who are seriously emotionally disturbed). Yet very few school systems or communities carry out systematic and effective screening for disturbed children. It is easy to see why; many more children would be referred as a result of systematic screening than could be served by special education (Hobbs, 1975b; Morse, Cutler, & Fink, 1964). And identification of children as handicapped when they cannot be provided with special education has potentially disastrous negative effects on children and their parents (Keogh & Becker, 1973; Wallace & Kauffman, 1978).

Effective screening techniques are available. For example, teachers' ratings are quite reliable, effective, and efficient, especially when several teachers' judgments are obtained over a period of time (Bower, 1969; Bower & Lambert, 1962; Maes, 1966; Nelson, 1971; Schaefer, in press). However, most school systems have financial resources to find trained personnel for only a small fraction of the children who would be identified by mass screening. And there is seldom any question about which children are the *prime* candidates for the limited services that are available.

Screening for behavior disorders among infants and preschool youngsters is particularly problematic. Certainly, there are severely disturbed children (usually considered *autistic*) who are perceived by their parents as being "different" from birth or from a very early age. Adequate pediatric care, however, will result in identification of most of these and other cases where extremely troublesome behavior is part of pervasive developmental disorders. But trying to select the infants and preschoolers who need special education and related services because of relatively *mild* behavior disorders is quite another matter. No one has figured out how to do that reliably as yet, primarily for three reasons. First, a child's behavioral style or temperament in infancy interacts with parenting behavior in order to determine later behavior patterns. For example, "difficult" behavior x at age 10 months is not predictive of inappropriate behavior y at age 6 years. Behavior management techniques used by parents and teachers from 10 months to 6 years need to be taken into account (Chess & Thomas, 1977; Thomas, Chess, & Birch, 1968). Second, parents vary markedly in their tolerance for behavioral differences in children. Since a problem *is* a problem primarily by *parental* definition in the preschool years, it is difficult to decide on a standard set of behaviors that are deviant. Exceptions, as noted before, are obvious developmental lags. Third, the school itself is a potential source of behavior problems—its structure, demands for performance of new skills, and emphasis on uniformity may set the stage for disorders that simply do not appear until the child enters school.

Hobbs (1975b) suggests issues that should be considered in selecting or devising any screening program for handicapped children.

1. Who should do the screening: regular classroom teachers, special educators, psychologists, or parents?
2. What is known about the reliability and validity of screening instruments? Are they appropriate for specific developmental levels and fair to various cultural or ethnic groups?

3. Does screening identify cases that are not obvious? Is there anything actually gained beyond providing services to children already known to be
disturbed?

4. Are "false positives" and "false negatives" obtained during screening, and
what happens as a result? Are children often misidentified as disturbed or
are truly disturbed children overlooked? When they are, how prompt and
effective is the corrective action?

5. When children are identified as needing further study or special services as a
result of screening, do they actually get what they need?

6. Is screening more cost-effective than periodic, comprehensive assessment of
children already receiving services?

These are critical questions for evaluating screening programs. But for the foresee-
able future they are moot questions in most schools and communities. Economic
realities and the limits of social policy severly limit possible responses of most
schools and communities to the results of effective screening.

CLASSIFICATION

Classification, basic to any science, is determined by reliably observed phenomena. The classification of a given phenomenon usually has a clear relationship to
the nature, origin, or course of the phenomenon in question. Psychiatry, mimicking
the empirical classification of diseases in physical medicine, has devised systems of
classification of *mental disease* (mental "illness") that have an intriguing mystique
but little substance (American Psychiatric Association, 1980; Group for the
Advancement of Psychiatry, 1966). That is, the psychiatric classification of
behavior disorders has been based on unverifiable assumptions. Classes include
"diseases" of personality structures and conjectures about disorders of hypothetical
parts of the psyche that are not open to direct measurement. Understandably,
therefore, the usual psychiatric systems of classification have been quite unreliable,
and a given classification has had little or no implication for treatment (Achenbach
& Edelbrock, 1978; Harris, 1979). Newer classification systems, especially
behavioral or dimensional systems (Quay, 1979) have tended to be more reliable
and valid because they are based (to a greater extent) on the direct observation of
specific behaviors.

Psychiatric Classification

The newest psychiatric system of classification is the third edition of the American
Psychiatric Association's *Diagnostic and Statistical Manual of Mental Disorders*,
usually referred to as DSM-III (American Psychiatric Association, 1980). In
DSM-III there is a section on disorders usually first evident in infancy, childhood,
or adolescence. The clinician diagnosing an infant, child, or adolescent is first to
consider the diagnostic categories from this section. If no appropriate diagnosis can

be found in this section, then the clinician is to consider diagnoses listed in other (adult) sections of the manual. Diagnoses in other sections most often applicable to children or adolescents are listed as:[17]

- organic mental disorders
- substance use disorders
- schizophrenic disorders
- affective disorders
- schizophreniform disorders
- anxiety disorders
- somatoform disorders
- personality disorders
- psychosexual disorders
- adjustment disorders
- psychological factors affecting physical disorder

Diagnoses from the childhood or adolescence section may be given to adults if, as children or adolescents, they manifested any of these conditions and if the condition has persisted and no adult category is appropriate (APA, 1980, p. 35).

The manual suggests that the childhood and adolescent disorders can be grouped under five major headings according to the predominant area of disturbance:

    I. Intellectual
        Mental Retardation
   II. Behavioral (overt)
        Attention Deficit Disorder
        Conduct Disorder
 III. Emotional
        Anxiety Disorders of Childhood or Adolescence
        Other Disorders of Childhood or Adolescence
  IV. Physical
        Eating Disorders
        Stereotyped Movement Disorders
        Other Disorders with Physical Manifestations
   V. Developmental
        Pervasive Developmental Disorders
        Specific Developmental Disorders
        (APA, 1980, pp. 35–36).

The actual DSM-III categories that apply primarily to infants, children, and adolescents are shown in Table 3–1.

---

[17] Brief definitions of many of the terms used in DSM-III are found in the glossary.

TABLE 3–1   Diagnostic Categories of DSM III for Disorders Usually First Evident in Infancy, Childhood, or Adolescence

---

Mental Retardation

Mild
Moderate
Severe
Profound
Unspecified

Attention Deficit Disorder

With hyperactivity
Without hyperactivity
Residual type

Conduct Disorder

Undersocialized, aggressive
Undersocialized, nonaggressive
Socialized, aggressive
Socialized, nonaggressive
Atypical

Anxiety Disorders of Childhood or Adolescence

Separation anxiety disorder
Avoidance disorder of childhood or adolescence
Overanxious disorder

Other Disorders of Infancy, Childhood, or Adolescence

Reactive attachment disorder of infancy
Schizoid disorder of childhood or adolescence
Elective mutism
Oppositional disorder
Identity disorder

Eating Disorders

Anorexia nervosa
Bulimia
Pica
Rumination disorder of infancy
Atypical eating disorder

Stereotyped Movement Disorders

Transient tic disorder
Chronic motor tic disorder
Tourette's disorder
Atypical tic disorder
Atypical stereotyped movement disorder

Other Disorders with Physical Manifestations

Stuttering
Functional enuresis

Table 3-1 (continued)

Functional encopresis
Sleepwalking disorder
Sleep terror disorder

Pervasive Developmental Disorders

Infantile autism
Childhood onset pervasive developmental disorder
Atypical

For each of the categories the manual provides information about the disorder's essential features, associated features, age at onset, sex ratio, prevalence, usual course, familial pattern, impairment, complications, predisposing factors, and criteria for diagnosis. There is no doubt that DSM-III represents a considerable improvement over earlier psychiatric classification systems (Harris, 1979). Yet its widespread acceptance and use outside the psychiatric profession seems unlikely. First, it has official status only when used by physicians. Second, as of early 1980 the American Psychological Association has not endorsed the system (Foltz, 1980). Third, the system seems to suffer from the same problems of unreliability, lack of validity, and medical/disease orientation that have severely limited the usefulness of previous psychiatric classification systems. Fourth, alternative classifications based on more reliable, empirical data are becoming known widely.

Behavioral Classification

Quay (1979) has abstracted the features of the ideal classification system. First, the categories should be *operationally defined*, that is, the behaviors that constitute a category should be defined so that they can be measured. Second, the system should be *reliable*; an individual must be classified consistently the same way at the same time by different observers so that assignment of someone to a category is consistent over a reasonable period of time. Third, the categories should be *valid*, meaning that assignment to the categories could be determined in a variety of ways (for instance, by a variety of observational systems or rating scales) and assignment to a category is highly predictive of particular behaviors. Fourth, classification should have clear *implications* for treatment and prognosis. Finally, the classification system should account for all cases (be *complete*), but consist of the fewest possible mutually exclusive categories (*parsimonious*). Behavioral or dimensional classification systems approximate 'more closely the ideal than any alternatives available presently.

Dimensional classifications are descriptions of behavioral dimensions or clusters of highly intercorrelated behaviors. This multivariate approach uses complex statistical procedures such as factor analysis to reveal which problem behaviors tend to occur together to form a syndrome or dimension. In early studies (Ackerson, 1942; Hewitt & Jenkins, 1946) behavior traits were obtained from reports in children's case histories. The behaviors were listed and then *clustered* by visual inspection of the data. More recently, however, researchers rely upon more formal statistical analyses to determine the interrelationships among behaviors. A large number of studies use factor analytic techniques and data ranging from problem checklists to information obtained from life history ratings and questionnaires. Herbert C. Quay, his colleagues, and other investigators used such studies to identify several stable and pervasive behavior patterns among children (Quay, 1975, 1979).

In a recent analysis of behavior checklists, Von Isser, Quay, and Love (1980) again found the same dimensions:

1. *Conduct disorder* involves such characteristics as overt aggression, both verbal and physical; disruptiveness; negativism; irresponsibility; and defiance of authority—all of which are at variance with the behavioral expectations of the school and other social institutions.
2. *Anxiety-withdrawal* stands in considerable contrast to conduct disorders, involving, as it does, overanxiety, social withdrawal, seclusiveness, shyness, sensitivity, and other behaviors implying a retreat from the environment rather than a hostile response to it.
3. *Immaturity* characteristically involves preoccupation, short attention span, passivity, daydreaming, sluggishness, and other behavior not in accord with developmental expectations.
4. *Socialized aggression* typically involves gang activities, cooperative stealing, truancy, and other manifestations of participation in a delinquent subculture.   (pp. 272–273)

Table 3–2 provides a more detailed listing of the characteristics that have often been associated with each of these four dimensions.

In previous studies, these dimensions or factors were sometimes given different names. *Anxiety-withdrawal* was sometimes called *personality problem*, *immaturity* was sometimes called *immaturity-inadequacy*, and *conduct disorder* was sometimes called *unsocialized aggression*. Furthermore, not every previous study found all four dimensions. But as research has accumulated over the past two decades, the dimensions have become more firmly established as reliable and valid categories of problem behavior (Quay, 1979).

The dimensions of disordered behavior described by Quay and his colleagues have been found in special education classes for emotionally disturbed children. Quay, Morse, and Cutler (1966) report that conduct disorders and immaturity were the predominant behavioral difficulties in their study of classes for emotionally disturbed children. Personality problems (anxiety-withdrawal) constituted a relatively small proportion of these children's troubles. Essentially the same finding is reported by McCarthy and Paraskevopoulos (1969). They also provide data showing that the emotionally disturbed children in their study exhibited more problems along all dimensions than did learning disabled or average children. See Figure 3–1.

Classification according to these three or four dimensions, however, is hardly sufficient for purposes of behavioral assessment. Good assessment requires more definitive description and measurement of specific behavior problems. Nevertheless, for the majority of *mildly* or *moderately* behavior disordered children these dimensions are useful in that types of problems can be discussed meaningfully. Description of *severe* disorders seems to demand a different system of categories.

TABLE 3–2 Frequently Found Characteristics Defining Four Behavioral Dimensions

Conduct Disorder

Fighting, hitting, assaultive
Temper tantrums
Disobedient, defiant
Destructiveness of own or other's property
Impertinent, "smart," impudent
Uncooperative, resistive, inconsiderate
Disruptive, interrupts, disturbs
Negative, refuses direction
Restless
Boisterous, noisy
Irritability, "blows-up" easily
Attention-seeking, "show-off"
Dominates others, bullies, threatens
Hyperactivity
Untrustworthy, dishonest, lies
Profanity, abusive language
Jealousy
Quarrelsome, argues
Irresponsible, undependable
Inattentive
Steals
Distractibility
Teases
Denies mistakes, blames others
Pouts and sulks
Selfish

Socialized-Aggression

Has "bad companions"
Steals in company with others
Loyal to delinquent friends

Belongs to a gang
Stays out late at night
Truant from school
Truant from home

Anxiety-Withdrawal

Anxious, fearful, tense
Shy, timid, bashful
Withdrawn, seclusive, friendless
Depressed, sad, disturbed
Hypersensitive, easily hurt
Self-conscious, easily embarassed
Feels inferior, worthless
Lacks self-confidence
Easily flustered
Aloof
Cries frequently
Reticent, secretive

Immaturity

Short attention span, poor concentration
Daydreaming
Clumsy, poor coordination
Preoccupied, stares into space, absent-minded
Passive, lacks initiative, easily led
Sluggish
Inattentive
Drowsy
Lack of interest, bored
Lacks perserverance, fails to finish things
Messy, sloppy

Adapted from H. C. Quay, Classification. In H. C. Quay & J. S. Werry (Eds.), *Psychopathological disorders of childhood* (2nd ed.). New York: Wiley, 1979. Pp. 17–18, 20–21.

Classification of Severe Disorders

Conduct disorder, anxiety-withdrawal, and the other dimensions described by Quay and others can vary from relatively minor deviations to very marked and serious problems. However, some children's behavior is characterized by differences that are not just the extreme case of conduct disorder, anxiety-withdrawal,

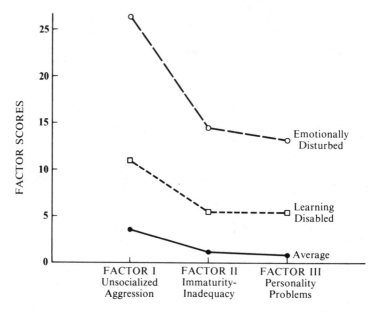

FIGURE 3-1   Mean factor scores for emotionally disturbed, learning disabled, and average children on Behavior Problem Checklist.

Note. From "Behavior Patterns of Learning Disabled, Emotionally Disturbed, and Average Children" by J. M. McCarthy and J. Paraskevopoulos, *Exceptional Children,* 1969, *36,* 71. Copyright 1969 by The Council for Exceptional Children. Reprinted by permission.

and so on. Their behavior appears to be qualitatively as well as quantitatively different from normal behavior. They are frequently described as inaccessible, unreachable, or out of touch with reality, and they often function like children considered to be mentally retarded. It is common for them to be unresponsive to other people, have bizarre language and speech patterns or no functional language at all, exhibit grossly inappropriate behaviors, lack everyday living skills, or perform self-injurious or stereotypical, ritualistic behaviors. There is not much debate about whether or not such severely disturbed children, usually referred to in the general case as *psychotic,* can be identified as a group that is distinctly different from less severely disturbed children. But there is considerable debate about how the general category of *childhood psychosis* can be subdivided in a reliable, helpful way. As Werry (1979a) points out, there have been several suggestions for classes and much disagreement about the subcategories. But the most common way to distinguish between the two major subgroups—infantile autism and childhood schizophrenia—is age of onset. If the onset of the disorder occurs earlier than 30 months, the child is considered *autistic*; if onset occurs after the age of 30 months, the child is considered *schizophrenic.* While there is much overlap in the behavioral characteristics of these two groups, it is easy to see the reason for the distinction by age of onset. One need only examine the frequency of first-observed psychotic behavior in children at different ages. Figure 3–2 shows that onset is more frequent before the age of 30 months and after the age of 12 years than between those ages.

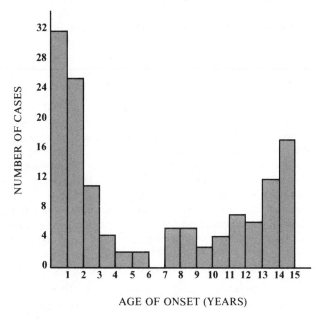

FIGURE 3-2 Distribution of cases of childhood psychosis by age of onset. Data from Kelvin (1966) and Makita (1966).

From M. Rutter, "The Development of Infantile Autism," *Psychological Medicine*, 1974, *4*, 148.

Many autistic children are described by their parents as being odd or obviously different from birth—aloof, cold, and unresponsive. It is extremely unusual, according to the data presented in Figure 3-2, for a child to begin to exhibit psychotic behavior during middle childhood. Thus, early childhood psychosis (infantile autism) and later childhood or adolescent psychosis (childhood schizophrenia or, according to DSM-III, "childhood onset pervasive developmental disorder") form two groups that can be differentiated on an objective basis.

The debate about just what is necessary and sufficient to distinguish psychotic from retarded children and to differentiate autistic from schizophrenic children is not over. Aside from an apparent consensus that children can be both retarded and psychotic and that autism is best distinguished by onset of the characteristics before the age of two and one-half years, there is little agreement about distinguishing characteristics. According to DSM-III, the diagnostic criteria for infantile autism are, in addition to onset prior to 30 months:

- pervasive lack of responsiveness to other people ("autism")
- gross deficits in language development
- peculiar speech patterns (for example, echolalia, metaphorical language, reversal of pronouns) if speech is present
- bizarre responses (for example, resistance to change, peculiar interest or attachments to objects)

- absence of delusions or hallucinations characteristic of schizophrenia (pp. 89–90)

The World Health Organization has provided the following description of autism:

> Responses to auditory and visual stimuli are abnormal and there are usually severe problems in understanding of spoken language. Speech is delayed and, if it develops, is characterized by echolalia, reversal of pronouns, immature grammatical structure and inability to use abstract terms. There is generally an impairment in the social use of both verbal and gestural language. Problems in social relationships are most severe before the age of 5 years and include an impairment in the development of eye-to-eye gaze, social attachments and cooperative play. Ritualistic behavior is usual and may include abnormal routines, resistance to change, attachment to odd objects and stereotyped patterns of play. The capacity for abstract or symbolic thought and for imaginative play is diminished. Intelligence ranges from severely subnormal to normal or above. Performance is usually better on tasks involving rote memory or visuo-spatial skills than on those requiring symbolic or linguistic skills.   (Rutter, 1972, pp. 326–327)

The case of Donald (described by Kanner, 1973a—see Chapter 2, p. 47) is an example of autism. Other such examples are described by Kanner, Rodriguez, and Ashenden (1972).[18] A mother said of her autistic son:

> Although he has talked clearly, using big words and sentences since he was 18 months old, he still had never spoken *with* us—that is, carry on a conversation or even answer simple yes and no questions. He lives completely in a world of his own. As an infant he had not smiled like other children. At 2 years, he knew the alphabet and numbers. He never used the first person in speaking.   (p. 21)

Another mother described her four year old autistic son as "retarded" and "withdrawn:"

> He is happy in his own world. He was about three years old before he knew members of the family. He has certain stereotypes,' has to touch telephone poles, will lay sticks against the pole and walk round and round. He talks better than he understands. (p. 14)

DSM-III defines childhood onset pervasive developmental disorder as gross and sustained impairment of social relationships beginning between the age of 30 months and 12 years, with the child exhibiting at least three of the following characteristics:

- sudden excessive anxiety, catastrophic reactions to everyday events, inability to be consoled when upset, or unexplained attacks of panic
- narrow or inappropriate affect and extreme lability of mood
- resistance to change in the environment or insistence on sameness
- odd movements, such as peculiar postures, hand movements, or walking movements
- abnormal speech characteristics

---

[18] Kanner's classic article (1943) contains lengthy and fascinating descriptions of autistic children. His original article is reprinted in Howells (1971).

- oversensitivity or undersensitivity to stimuli
- self-mutilation

As in autism, there is the absence of delusions or hallucinations that characterize schizophrenia in adults (DSM-III, 1980, p. 91).

Childhood schizophrenia is described by the World Health Organization as:

. . . a group of psychoses in which there is a fundamental disturbance of personality, characteristic distortion of thinking, often a sense of being controlled by alien forces, delusions which may be bizarre, disturbed perception, abnormal affect out of keeping with the real situation and autism.   (Rutter, 1972, p. 320)

The case of Wanda (Payne et al., 1979. See Chapter 1, pp. 9–10) is an example of schizophrenic behavior in childhood. During her childhood Wanda was diagnosed variously as autistic and schizophrenic, illustrating the confusion about the application of these diagnostic labels.

Although systematized delusional thinking and hallucinations in preadolescents are rare, they are sometimes a part of the severe behavior disorders of preadolescents.[19] Stutte and Dauner (1971) report the case of an 11-year-old schizophrenic boy with a highly developed pattern of bizarre thinking.

vignette

Thomas believes he is the son of a union between Christ and an unknown goddess. God stands at the top of a universe which is divided into two camps. Christ and those who strive for good in the world (including Thomas himself) are on one side, and the members of the Counter Gang, to whom Thomas eventually assigns a place in the "Community of Saints," are on the other.

The Gang, which incorporates the evil in the world and is in constant feud with the good, is an incessant threat to Thomas' body and life. As the son of Christ, he was a wild boar in a former existence. It is his task now to rid the world of the Gang which plans to prepare for him an agonizing death. Since nowadays no one is crucified, he will be crushed between two millstones until the blood squirts from his fingers.

Among other things, the boy sees black men with horns. His explanations: "world regulators"; "dear, sweet, little devils with radical power, recognized by the color of their tails;" "young female creatures" whose eyelid lines give them away as members of the Gang. (p. 416)

Summary of Classification

Progress has been made in the classification of behavior disorders, but an ideal system has not yet been devised. The latest psychiatric classification system, DSM-

---

[19] For additional descriptions of hallucinations and delusions in children and adults, see Green (1964) and Kaplan (1964).

III, an improvement over earlier versions, is not likely to be used outside the psychiatric profession. Behavioral classification, in which behavioral characteristics are clustered along a few statistically derived dimensions, seems most reliable and useful at the present time. Four major behavioral dimensions have been identified through research: conduct disorder, anxiety-withdrawal, immaturity, and socialized aggression. Severe disorders—childhood psychoses—are characterized by qualitatively as well as quantitatively deviant behavior. Childhood psychoses are usually subdivided into autism (onset before 30 months of age) and atypical psychosis or childhood schizophrenia (onset later than 30 months of age).

ASSESSMENT

Reliable classification of behavior disorders can not be accomplished without some sort of assessment procedure. Dimensional classification depends on observation and ratings of children's behavior. Competent classification using DSM-III requires careful observation of the child's behavior, and an assessment of the child's physical status, past level of functioning, and factors that may be causing stress in his or her life (APA, 1980). But the level of assessment necessary for appropriate classification is not necessarily sufficient to plan an intervention or to evaluate the outcome.

Adequate assessment for the purpose of intervention requires careful attention to a wide range of factors that may be important in the origin and modification of problem behavior. In many cases it involves evaluation of all domains of the child's functioning; during the developmental periods of life a serious lag in any one of these domains is likely to increase the risk of disordered behavior (Ciminero & Drabman, 1977; Evans & Nelson, 1977; O'Leary & Johnson, 1979). Thus a thoroughgoing assessment includes careful appraisal not just of the child's problem behavior but also of the social-interpersonal context of the behavior and the child's general physical status, language, cognitive development, academic skills, and those perceptual-motor skills that are relevant to play, independent functioning, and participation in sports activities. Such an assessment usually depends on the combined efforts of several professionals—a teacher, a psychologist, and a physician, at the minimum.

One important consideration in assessment is that children almost never refer themselves for evaluation. Children are typically brought to the attention of specialists by their parents, teachers, or other adults. The assessment is thus almost always prompted by adults' judgments of children's behavior rather than the opinions children have about themselves. Referral of children by adults has two immediate implications. First, the assessment must involve appraisal of at least one referring adult as well as the child. Appraisal of the adult(s) referring the child is necessary to validate the concern over the child's behavior and to discover how the adults' responses to the child might be contributing to the problem. Second, attempts must be made to determine the child's own view of the situation. No humane and ethical approach to disordered behavior can disregard or treat as trivial the child's opinions of his or her treatment. Some children's opinions are not accessible because of their lack of communication skills and some children's opinions must be overruled because they are clearly not in their own best interest. Still, children's rights must be protected and children's opinions must be weighed seriously when they can be determined.

Another thing to consider is that behavior problems are not always what they first appear to be. Sometimes it is difficult to find an explanation of the difficulty, not because the cause of disordered behavior is buried deep in someone's psyche but simply because it is hard to obtain all the relevant facts. Consider the case of Ray.

vignette

The Case of Ray[20]

Throughout elementary school, Ray was described by his teachers as a bright, cooperative, and sociable student. His work habits and general attitude toward school were very good. He achieved at or above grade level in all subjects and was very popular among his peers. A similar general description was given by all of Ray's teachers during the first few months of junior high school. By the middle of seventh grade, however, Ray's behavior had changed dramatically.

Ray began to be absent from school with increasing frequency. He dropped out of all the extracurricular activities in which he had formerly participated. His teachers reported that he did not often complete assignments, frequently daydreamed in class, and was generally uninvolved in class activities. His grades dropped below passing.

Ray's teachers attempted to alter his behavior by a variety of means. Verbal praise, additional privileges, and points exchangeable for tangible rewards were all given contingent upon appropriate behavior, but these did not produce the desired behavior changes. Curricular modifications were made repeatedly, but Ray remained uninvolved in classroom activities. In fact, he was absent from school more and more frequently as time went on. He was unwilling to discuss the problem with his teachers or the guidance counselor. Phone calls and letters to his parents went unanswered. Only after being warned of a potential fine for truancy did Ray's parents agree to discuss the situation with school personnel. A conference was arranged with Ray, his parents, teachers, and guidance counselor.

During the conference, Ray's parents stated that he remained at home during his absences from school. The relationship between Ray and his mother appeared to be overly solicitous (they greeted each other with a kiss and held hands during most of the discussion). Ray's father was attentive, but generally silent throughout the conference. Both parents agreed to make certain that Ray would attend school regularly.

---

[20] The case of Ray was contributed by Jim Krouse.

Over the next few weeks Ray's attendance improved only slightly, however. The case was then referred to the school mental health team which was comprised of the teachers, guidance counselor, social worker, school psychologist, and psychiatrist. Reviewing the case, the psychiatrist emphasized that Ray had unmet dependency needs and was experiencing separation anxiety. The teachers initiated activities recommended by the psychiatrist to enhance his self concept, increase his independence, and develop his sense of autonomy and control. Demonstrable results in terms of increased attendance rates were not evident after a month of such efforts.

As the final effort prior to legal action against Ray's parents, the social worker made a home visit on a day on which Ray was absent. Upon her arrival, the social worker found Ray comforting his obviously battered mother. His mother revealed that her husband, an alcoholic, had been fired from his job a few months earlier. During this period of unemployment, he frequently drank excessively and became physically abusive toward her. However, when Ray was home, his father typically was not abusive or beat Ray's mother less severely than when Ray went to school.

Ray's case illustrates the point that assessment may need to involve more than an assessment of the child's problem *per se*. A child can hardly be expected to attend and be interested in school when he knows that his attendance will likely result in the beating of his mother. There is not always a hidden cause for children's problem behavior, but sensitive and thorough assessment of the child's circumstances sometimes shows the child's behavior to be reasonable, given the circumstances of his/her life.

Methods of Assessment

A full blown assessment usually results in a report or psychological and educational evaluation that is used by school or clinic personnel. This forms the basis on which to label and place the child and is the starting point for an intervention program. Although PL 94–142 does not prescribe the assessment methods to be used in making such evaluations, the law does indicate that such evaluations constitute a related service to which all handicapped children are entitled. Obviously, such evaluations are necessary for writing the individualized education plans required by the law. Furthermore, the procedural safeguards guaranteed by the law give the parents or guardians of handicapped children access to all relevant records involved in identification, placement, and planning for their children and the right to challenge the adequacy of any evaluations made by school personnel (Bateman & Herr, 1981; Martin, 1979, 1980).

Ciminero and Drabman (1977) have noted that an adequate evaluation typically includes the following elements:

- results and interpretation of standardized tests
- results of behavioral observations or checklists

- recommendations for placement or special services
- recommendations for teaching and behavior management

The methods used to obtain relevant information and to arrive at recommendations may vary from case to case, but they typically include at least the following:

- standardized tests of intelligence and achievement
- interviews with the child, parents, and teachers
- observations or ratings of behavior

In some cases, personality tests, a physical examination, or psychophysiological measures are included. The value and limitations of each of these assessment methods will be discussed briefly. (For a more detailed discussion see Ciminero & Drabman, 1977; Evans & Nelson, 1977; O'Leary & Johnson, 1979).

Standardized Tests

There are sound reasons to administer standardized tests of intelligence and achievement as part of an assessment. Tests allow one to estimate what a given child has learned and to measure what a child has learned in comparison to age mates. It can provide a description of the child's current abilities and point to areas in need of instruction. A test of intelligence provides evidence of the child's learning in general skill areas, whereas a test of academic achievement taps more specific skills.

Although there are good reasons to use standardized intelligence and achievement tests, there are also serious pitfalls in their use. The pitfalls include bias in favor of certain cultural, ethnic, or socioeconomic groups—bias in terms of a disproportionate number of children from one of these groups who score within a certain range on a given test. The pitfalls also include a margin of error in the scores children achieve at a given testing, changes in scores over time or after instruction, and failure of the scores to predict important outcomes. The limitations of standardized testing, especially intelligence testing, have received so much attention in recent years that their future is somewhat uncertain (Bateman & Herr, 1981; Resnick, 1979). Court decisions may make moot the question of whether or not to rely on standardized tests, at least in their present form. That is, the courts could invalidate the use of many test scores, especially IQs as presently determined, to make decisions about educational planning and placement. Legal battles are being fought over these questions:

- Who constitutes a legitimate comparison (or standard) sample for a given child?
- What general and specific areas of learning are most important to measure?
- How accurately must a test measure something to be a legitimate assessment tool?
- What must a test predict, and how accurately, to be of value in planning?

If standardized intelligence and achievement tests are not declared legally irrelevant, it would be wise to use them. But it is important to avoid some of the erroneous assumptions and flagrant misuses that prompted the siege of litigation against them. An *IQ* derived from a standardized test is *not* a measure of intellectual *potential* and it is *not static or immutable*; it is merely a measure of general learning in certain areas compared to the children of the same age comprising the standardization sample. It is only a *moderately* accurate predictor of what the child is likely to learn in the future *if no special intervention is provided*. It must be remembered that the child's performance on a given test on a given day can be influenced by many factors and that even under the best of conditions the score obtained is an estimate that indicates a range in which the child's "true" score is likely to fall.

In spite of their limitations, standardized tests of intelligence can be used with appropriate caution and awareness and be helpful in assessing areas of strength, weakness, and progress for the majority of handicapped children, including those who are seriously disturbed. Alternatives to standardized testing are entirely subjective appraisal (a strategy that has limitless potential for bias and faulty prediction), simply ignoring the question of assessment (defining intelligence and academic achievement as irrelevant considerations regardless of how they are measured), or using criterion-referenced tests. Criterion-referenced tests are those which do not explicitly compare a child's performance on a set of tasks to a normative group but rather indicate whether a child has or has not achieved a specific skill. Ultimately, a criterion-referenced test is a standardized test with a single "yes-no" score or criterion rather than an aggregate score. That is, a criterion-referenced test presents many of the same problems of any other standardized test—possible bias because of the criteria that are chosen, invalidity of the criteria as measures of performance, variability of students' performance, and so on (McClung, 1979). Many of the objections to well known intelligence and achievement tests are based on criticisms of *inappropriate* use and interpretation of the scores—on unintelligent or unprofessional psychometric procedures that can ruin the value of any assessment technique.

Personality tests. *Personality* tests have come under much less fire in recent years than intelligence and achievement tests, although there is considerably less support for their reliability and validity (O'Leary & Johnson, 1979). They probably have not been attacked often in court because they are seldom used as the primary criterion for special education placement. Tests of personality are supposed to measure consistent *traits* or underlying psychological mechanisms that account for characteristic patterns of behavior. Such tests include *projective* instruments like the *Rorschach* and other ink blot tests, the *Thematic Apperception Test* (TAT), the *Family Relations Test*, and sentence completion tests or questionnaires. The value of these and similar tests in understanding children's behavior and planning effective educational and behavior change programs has not been demonstrated by empirical research (O'Leary & Johnson, 1979).

Interviews

Interviews vary widely in their structure and purpose. They can be free wheeling conversations or follow a line of questioning designed to obtain information regarding specific behaviors or developmental milestones. And they can be conducted with verbal children as well as adults.

Skillful interviewing is no simple matter. When it is obvious or even suspected by a child, or the adults who are responsible for a child that troublesome behavior is in question, it is not easy for an interviewer to keep the interviewee(s) from getting defensive. And an interview in which answers represent intentional half truths, misleading information, or avoidance of issues is not going to be of much value in assessment. Consider the difficulty in obtaining helpful information from Ray and his parents in the case of Ray described in this chapter. Furthermore, one must maintain a healthy skepticism about the accuracy of interview responses that require memory of long-past events. It's also important to weigh carefully the subjective opinions of interviewees, especially when their responses are highly emotionally charged or seriously discrepant from other subjective reports or objective evidence.

Interviews should help the person conducting an assessment to get an impression of how the child and significant others interact and feel about each other. Also, they should help to decide what additional types of assessment are needed. But interviews can accomplish these ends only to the extent that the interviewer has great interpersonal skills, has the experience and sensitivity to make sound clinical judgments, and is able during the interview to focus on obtaining information about relevant behaviors and events that happen around them—that is, about the child's desirable and undesirable behaviors, the contexts in which they tend to occur, and the typical reactions they receive.

Kanfer and Grimm (1977) have outlined ways in which an interviewer can organize questioning to obtain information that is helpful in defining the problem and making tentative plans for intervention. The interview should help to clarify which of the following characteristics are problems:

I. *Behavioral deficits*, such as lack of information about how to behave; lack of specific social skills; lack of skills required for self-monitoring and self-control; lack of access to or responsiveness to important reinforcers, or lack of daily living skills

II. *Behavioral excesses*, such as debilitating anxiety or preoccupation with self

III. *Inappropriate environmental control*, such as deviant sexual responses or insensitivity to violence; unavailability of opportunity to practice desirable behaviors; or inefficient organization of activities

IV. *Inappropriate responses to self*, such as misperception of one's abilities; unrealistic evaluations or predictions; or inaccuracy in describing one's internal states

V. *Inappropriate contingencies*, such as lack of reinforcement for appropriate behavior; reinforcement for inadequate or undesirable behavior; excessive reward for desirable responses; or random reinforcement (or reward that is not dependent on any particular kind of behavior).

As Kanfer and Grimm (1977) note, descriptions of behaviors, competencies, environmental conditions, and consequences obtained in interviews may be helpful, but they are often inaccurate and cannot be relied upon uncritically. There is no adequate substitute for direct observation of behavior. Furthermore, discrepancies between the reports given to interviewers and information obtained from direct observation are important to note, for they can sometimes be crucial in the decision about how to design an intervention. For example, if teachers report that they frequently praise appropriate and ignore inappropriate behavior but direct observation shows that appropriate behavior is usually ignored and inappropriate behavior is frequently criticized, then the teachers' misperceptions will likely have to be taken into account in an intervention plan.

Observations and Ratings

Traditional personality assessment places relatively little emphasis on observation of the child's behavior in everyday settings, but emphasizes instead the child's responses to projective tests and observations of the child's free play in the clinic. It is not surprising that such assessment methods lack reliability and frequently yield suggestions for teaching and behavior management that seem obtuse or irrelevant. Without the constraints imposed by a psychodynamic conceptual model that supposes the real problem to be hidden within the child's unconscious motivation, common sense suggests that direct observation of the problem behaviors when and where they occur might lead to useful ideas about how to change them. The commonsense notion of direct behavioral observation in the child's natural environment is supported by behavior principles that define environmental events that occur just before and just after a behavior as important controlling factors. And, indeed, direct behavioral observation has become a nearly indispensable part of the adequate assessment of any child referred for evaluation because he or she exhibits seriously inappropriate behavior.

An extensive technology of direct observation and recording of behavior has been developed (Dancer, Braukmann, Schumaker, Kirigin, Willner, & Wolf, 1978; Sulzer-Azaroff & Mayer, 1977). Not all problems of reliability and validity of direct observational data have been entirely eliminated. Nevertheless, reliability sufficient to serve most purposes can be readily attained by the majority of observers; and the beneficial outcome of countless assessments using direct observation attest to its validity. An appropriate behavioral observation system allows one to answer questions such as these:

- In what settings (home, school, math class, or playground) is the problem behavior or behavioral deficit exhibited?
- With what frequency, duration, or amplitude does the behavior appear in various settings?
- What happens immediately before the behavior occurs that seems to set the occasion for it, and what happens immediately afterward that may serve to strengthen or weaken the response?
- What other inappropriate responses are observed?
- What appropriate behaviors could be taught or strengthened to lessen the problem?

For a variety of reasons, it may be impossible for someone assessing a child to do extensive observation and recording of the child's behavior in everyday settings. Under such circumstances the adults who have spent an appreciable amount of time with the child (parents, peers, siblings, or teachers) might be asked to rate the child's behavior on a scale consisting of numerous behavioral descriptions. Some behavioral rating scales (Quay, 1977; Schaefer, in press; Von Isser, Quay, & Love, 1980) yield data that are useful in describing the typical behaviors of the child. Behavioral dimensions derived from rating scales were described earlier in this chapter.

Physical and Psychophysiological Measures

It is well known that physical disorders and diseases can affect the way both adults and children behave. Thus, if there is any reason to suspect that a child referred for assessment of disordered behavior has a physical ailment, a thorough physical check-up should be suggested.

Sometimes the search for causes of behavior disorders includes the neurology and physiology of the child, and uses neuropsychological or neurophysiological measures such as various electroencephalographic techniques, electrical conductance of the skin, and heart rate. Feuerstein, Ward, and LeBaron (1979) point out that there may be potential for use of these techniques in the future. However, they conclude that "to date, it appears that these time-consuming, relatively costly assessments are no more useful than what is generally completed in a standard psychological/behavioral evaluation" (Feuerstein, et al., 1979, p. 274).

Assessment Strategies and Clinical Judgment

An emphasis on objective, reliable methods of assessment might give the impression that there is seldom a need for subjective appraisal or sensitive clinical judgment. Although reliable, empirical methods are important and advances in the technology of assessment will undoubtedly lead to increased objectivity and precision, it seems unlikely that clinical judgment can ever be replaced completely in the assessment process (Ciminero & Drabman, 1977). Interpersonal relationships—the stuff of behavior disorders—can be described as objective responses of people to each other. But there are nuances in relationships that are difficult or impossible to assess quantitatively, and sensitivity to the subtleties of relationships can enhance technical virtuosity in assessing interpersonal problems.

Assessment of Person Variables

In the social learning theory of Bandura (1977, 1978) and Mischel (1973, 1976), *person variables* include emotional states and thoughts that are linked with behavior and environmental events. Behavioral assessment until recently has tended to ignore these person variables, but there is growing interest in evaluating what children say to themselves about their behavior (Evans & Nelson, 1977; O'Leary & Johnson, 1979). That is, there is interest in: (a) how children instruct themselves during problem solving or in exercising self control; (b) what or who children believe is responsible for their behavior (that is, children's causal attributions); and (c) how changing what children say to and about themselves can induce other behavioral changes (Henker, Whalen, & Hinshaw, 1980; Kneedler, 1980; Meichenbaum, 1979, 1980; O'Leary, 1980). The assessment of convert self-verbalizations is still at a primitive stage of development compared to direct observation techniques for overt behaviors. Presently, it appears that assessment of person variables is a promising area for research, but it is clear that no magical results will be obtained simply by considering what children think and feel about themselves and their behavior. A realistic hope is that consideration of verbal mediators or self-statements will, in some cases, add a useful dimension to other, better established techniques of behavioral assessment.

Assessment and Social Validation

Those who are responsible for the assessment of children must be concerned not just about the scientific or technical quality of their work but about the social validity of the outcomes of their efforts as well. Social validity means that the clients (those parents, teachers, and children) who are ostensibly being helped, as well as those who intervene, are convinced (a) that a significant problem is being addressed, (b) that the intervention procedures are acceptable, and (c) that the outcome of intervention is satisfactory. Social validation is the process of evaluating the clinical importance and personal/social meaningfulness of intervention efforts in addition to any statistically significant outcomes or resultant research implications. As Kazdin (1977) points out, social validation involves social comparison and subjective evaluation. That is, it involves comparison to a peer group who do not exhibit the disorder for which the client was referred and the subjective judgments of specially trained and/or nonprofessional persons about the client's behavior. To the extent that a child's behavior is markedly different from that of a valid comparison group before intervention but indistinguishable from that comparison group's behavior after intervention, social validity is established by social comparison. And, to the extent that the perceptions of clients and trained observers are that the quality of the child's behavior is unacceptable before intervention but markedly improved or desirable after intervention, social validity is indicated by subjective evaluation.

SUMMARY

Screening is the efficient and effective selection for further study of those children who probably are disturbed. Systematic screening for emotional disturbance is carried out by few schools and communities because far more children would be referred than could be served. Screening very young children for mild or moderate behavior disorders presents particular problems.

Psychiatric classifications of childrens' behavior disorders have not been helpful to nonphysicians. Behavioral classifications based on statistical analyses of behavioral ratings have resulted in the description of relevant behavioral dimensions. Quay and his associates have identified four behavioral dimensions: conduct disorder, anxiety-withdrawal, immaturity, and socialized aggression. Today, severe behavior disorders (psychoses) of children are classified most frequently according to age at onset: autism indicates onset before 30 months of age and schizophrenia or atypical psychosis signifies onset after 30 months. Both autism and schizophrenia involve behavior that is qualitively different from that of normal or moderately disturbed children, including gross and sustained impairment in ability to establish and maintain relationships with other people.

Assessment includes defining the problem, noting possible causes or contributing factors, designing an intervention, and evaluating outcomes. Methods of assessment include standardized tests, personality tests, interviews, direct observation of behavior, behavioral ratings, physical examination, and psychophysiological measures. Subjective clinical judgment will always be required, even with advances in the technology of objective behavioral assessment. Assessment of covert, person variables (for example, self-verbalizations) is being given increasing attention, as is the social validation of assessment and intervention techniques.

part two

Origins of Behavior Disorders

chapter 4 _____

Family Factors

The nuclear family, consisting of father, mother, and children, has been considered traditionally a central factor in early personality development in all societies (Clausen, 1966). While the nuclear family deserves close scrutiny as a model context for child development, it is obvious that a substantial proportion of children are now reared in other social contexts, particularly in single-parent families. Regardless of whether the family is intact or broken, a child's kin are the first people to whom he or she must become oriented, and the nexus of kinship is the entry into a larger social context and culture. Given the primacy of family relations in children's social development, it is understandable that the origins of behavior disorders have been sought in the structure, composition, and interactions of family units. The notion that the composition and structure of the family can provide a simple basis for prediction of behavioral pathology has proved to be a tantalizing will-o'-the-wisp. Family size, birth order, presence of grandparents or other relatives in the home, broken families, father absence, maternal employment, and the presence of stepparents, for example, have not been shown to be in *themselves* sufficient to produce behavioral pathology (Biller & Davids, 1973; Clausen, 1966; Herzog & Sudia, 1973; Rutter, 1979; Yarrow, 1964). Research also shows that when considered separately, parental control techniques, marital relationships, maternal or paternal dominance, parental personality, or role assignment within the family are not predictive of mental health or behavioral pathology (Becker, 1964; Bell, 1971; Clausen, 1964; Martin, 1975). Such family variables appear to be predictive of the child's behavior development only in complex interactions with each other and with other factors, such as socioeconomic status, ethnic origin, and the child's age, sex, and temperamental characteristics. Nevertheless, it appears that broken homes, father absence, parental separation, divorce, chaotic or hostile family relationships and socioeconomic level increase children's vulnerability to behavior disorders (Hetherington & Martin, 1979; Martin, 1975; Rutter, 1979). When several factors that increase vulnerability occur together—for example, poverty, parental hostility, and illness requiring hospitalization—their effects are not merely additive but multiplicative. That is, the occurrence of two such factors together more than doubles the probability that a child will develop a behavior disorder. When a third factor is added, the chance of disorder is several times higher.

Rutter's (1979) review of recent research on maternal deprivation and related family factors in behavior disorders points out some of the complexities in family influences. For example, one might be tempted to conclude that separation of the child from one or both parents always works serious mischief with the child's psychological and behavioral development. That conclusion is not tenable because a variety of other circumstances must be taken into account. In an intact family, parental discord may exert a more pernicious influence than parental separation. A good relationship with one parent may sustain a child even though parental discord is pervasive or separation occurs, and the interaction of the child's constitutional or temperamental characteristics with parental behavior may be more important than parental separation or disharmony. In addition, factors outside the home (school, for instance) may lessen or heighten the negative influence of family factors. Some children do not succumb to extreme disruption or disintegration of their families.

The precise reason why some children are invulnerable to negative family influences is not known. Future research may reveal those family factors that are related causally to disordered behavior and what factors protect children from stress. Such research will likely be guided by a conceptual model of how families may influence children's behavior.

CONCEPTUAL MODELS OF FAMILY INFLUENCE

As Hetherington and Martin (1979) point out, there are a number of alternative theories of child development, each suggesting how the interaction of parents and children contribute to personality development and behavior disorders. Some of these theories are supported by more scientific evidence than others. Those theories having the clearest support from replicable empirical data and having the clearest implications for intervention are discussed here.

The Learning Model

A learning model of family influence is derived from research of basic learning processes, primarily the research and theory of B. F. Skinner, Albert Bandura, Walter Mischel, and their colleagues and students. From the social learning theory perspective, both normal and deviant behavior are induced and sustained by several ubiquitous learning processes, primarily the processes of reinforcement (reward), punishment, and observational learning (for example, modeling and imitation). Behavior that is rewarded will persist, whether or not that behavior is maladaptive or the parents' *intent* is to reward it. Consequently, parents may inadvertently reward their children's temper tantrums by allowing them to have their own way. Parents may reinforce their children's aggression with attention by scolding them when they hit other children, but by ignoring them otherwise. Parents may unwittingly induce school failure by providing negative or inadequate models of interest in academic matters and by failing to provide their children with reinforcement for good academic performance.

In short, the learning model rests on the assumption that children learn patterns of behavior. Therefore, inappropriate behavior represents inappropriate learning (Bijou & Baer, 1961; Patterson, 1971). In the give and take of family interactions, both normal and disturbed, the behavior of children and their parents exerts reciprocal influence—parents are taught by their children and vice versa. The behavioral intervention hypothesis is that if family interactions can be restructured so that more adaptive patterns of behavior are rewarded, the child (and parents) will learn to behave more appropriately.

One of B. F. Skinner's students, C. B. Ferster, articulates a theory of autism (1961). His hypothesis is that autistic children exhibit their characteristically bizarre behaviors and show marked deficiencies in behavior primarily because their parents provide inadvertent reinforcement for increasingly inappropriate behavior while providing little or no rewards for appropriate responses. As Lovaas and Koegel (1973) point out, there is little research evidence to support Ferster's hypothesis. There is a great deal of scientific research evidence to indicate that reinforcement techniques derived from modern learning theory can be used to *change* disturbed children's behavior, including the behavior of severely and profoundly disturbed children. However, as Ross (1974) and others note, there is a fallacy in the argument: *post hoc, ergo propter hoc* (after the fact, therefore before the fact). The methods used to change maladaptive behavior do not necessarily reveal the causal factors that gave rise to that behavior. It is not safe to assume that disturbed behavior is caused by inappropriate reinforcement contingencies simply because appropriate contingencies of reinforcement have been shown to be effective in resolving the problem. Penicillin effectively cures strep throat, but it is not safe to assume that the infection was due to a lack of penicillin. As Ainsworth (1973) comments, ". . . merely because environmental manipulation may modify behavior in desirable directions, this does not prove that natural processes of development follow the same cause-effect line implied by the therapeutic practice" (p. 10).

The learning model has provided little direct evidence regarding the ways in which families *produce* behavior disorders in children, but it has yielded a veritable flood of data showing how families can gain control over disordered behavior by using the principles of social learning.

The Interactional-Transactional Model

It has become increasingly apparent to child development specialists that parents' influence on their children's behavior does not overshadow in importance the influence of children's behavior on their parents. With increasing frequency researchers are suggesting that perhaps undesirable family interactions or parental behaviors are as much a reaction of family members to a deviant child as they are a cause of the disturbed child's behavior (for example, Bell, 1968; Bell & Harper, 1977; Martin, 1975; Patterson, 1975; Sameroff & Chandler, 1975). As Martin (1975) states:

> At the moment of birth, parent and child begin an interactive drama that will evolve its own unique character and destiny. Affection, joy, antagonism, openness, withdrawal, demands, and acquiescence will be interchanged according to each dyad's own pattern— a pattern that is likely to vary considerably according to circumstances and over time. (p. 463)

This interactional perspective does not compete with the learning model but elaborates upon it. Interactions and transactions between individuals are the central theme in interpreting developmental data. And the data may indeed include reinforcement, punishment, imitation, and other teaching techniques consistent with learning theory. It is the emphasis on reciprocity of influence from the earliest parent-child interactions and the pervasiveness of reciprocal influence in all subsequent interactions that distinguishes the interactional-transactional model.

An example of the type of research on which the interactional-transactional model is based is provided by Clarke-Stewart (1973). She carefully recorded the interactions between 36 mothers and their firstborn children (9 to 18 months of age) over a nine-month period. Repeated observations were made in the homes of these mothers, both in structured and in spontaneous situations. Analysis of the observational data indicated that mothers who were highly responsive to their infants and provided a lot of stimulation in the form of talking and playing had more intelligent babies, that is, maternal responsiveness and stimulation appeared to increase the child's cognitive growth. In the area of social development, however, the child's behavior appeared to have a controlling relationship to the mother's, for the child's looking at, smiling at, and vocalizing to the mother seemed to increase the mother's responsiveness to demands and distress signals. Clarke-Stewart's findings, then, suggest a reciprocal pattern of influence in which the mother's responsiveness and stimulation facilitate the child's cognitive development and the child's positive social-emotional signals to his mother increase maternal responsiveness and sensitivity.

Sameroff and Chandler (1975) postulate that the outcome of child care is positive to the extent that the child elicits or is provided with nurturance, but that a child is a "high risk" for later difficulties to the extent that he elicits negative responses from the environment. Even in the case of child abuse, where it has in the past been assumed that the variables of over-riding importance are the psychological characteristics of the parents, Sameroff and Chandler (1975) interpret the problem in interactional-transactional terms. The abused child's temperament may contribute to his parents' tendencies to abuse him: "Children with difficult temperaments or physical disorders may increase their own chances of being abused, whereas siblings of a less bothersome nature are likely to receive only minimal abuse" (p. 237).

The role of the child in contributing to his or her own abuse has been reviewed also by Parke and Collmer (1975). They found that there are socio-cultural factors that appear to increase the chance of child abuse: The parents' own history of being abused as children, social isolation from the community, too many children, poverty and undereducation, and a cultural environment that condones violence and harsh physical discipline. Still, certain characteristics of children seem to invite abuse. That is, a child appears to become a likely target for abuse to the extent that he/she is unattractive, is difficult to care for because of illness or prematurity, is irritable, or is unresponsive to loving attention or discipline. Older children as well as infants who are abused are characterized by unattractiveness and by behavior that typically calls forth negative responses from adults: For example, a high activity level, irritability, and defiance of discipline.

Research findings by George and Main (1979) and Mulhern and Passman (1979) are consistent with the hypotheses of Parke and Collmer (1975) and Sameroff and Chandler (1975). George and Main studied abused toddlers in a daycare center and found that they exhibited a set of negative behaviors that distinguished them from non-abused youngsters. The abused children physically assaulted their peers, harassed and seldom made friendly advances toward their adult caregivers, and often avoided friendly overtures. These responses of abused children, according to George and Main, were similar to those of children who are rejected by their mothers.

One hypothesis about parent-child interaction in child abuse is that parents are "taught" to become increasingly punitive by their children's responses to punishment. For example, if the child exhibits behavior that is aversive to the parent (for example, whining), the parent may punish the child (by slapping). If the punishment is successful, and the child stops the aversive behavior, then the parent is negatively reinforced by the consequence. The next time the child whines, the parent is more likely to try slapping again in order to get relief. If at first the child does not stop whining, the parent may slap harder or more often to try to quiet the child. Thus the parent's punishment becomes increasingly harsh as a means of dealing with the child's increasingly aversive behavior. Mulhern and Passman (1979) present data from a laboratory study showing that mothers escalate their punishments in attempts to "teach" their sons, lending support to the hypothesis that children's responses to parental punishment are involved in child abuse.

The case of child abuse has been discussed here in some detail because, until rather recently, little attention was given to the interactive effects of children and parents on each other. Formerly, child abuse was seen as a problem of parental behavior, and intervention was directed at changing parents' responses to their children. The interactional-transactional model includes consideration of how abused children influence their parents. It suggests that intervention should deal directly with the abused child's undesirable behavior as well as with the parents' behavior (George & Main, 1979).

An interactional–transactional model is not confined to any one area of child behavior. The application of this model is being made to nearly every conceivable topic in child development. For example, Keller and Bell (1979) recently investigated how children's behavior (for example, looking at an adult and answering promptly when questioned) influenced adults' methods of trying to induce the children to perform acts of altruism. Clearly, the notions that (a) children have effects on adults that are equal to adults' effects on children and that (b) family interactions can be understood only when the reciprocal influences of parents and children on each other are taken into account, both represent a significant advance in theories of child development and psychopathology.

INTERACTION IN FAMILIES OF DISTURBED CHILDREN

Numerous attempts have been made in recent years to identify in experimental studies the specific patterns of interaction that distinguish the families of emotionally disturbed children. Many of the studies of family interactions have involved direct observation of family members in a laboratory situation. Typically, the family has been given a problem to solve or a topic for discussion, and then the ensuing interactions have been recorded for later analysis (Love & Kaswan, 1974; Mishler & Waxler, 1968). The following discussion will look at differences between disturbed and normal family patterns, the results of behavioral analyses of patterns, and an in-depth view of two common family interactions: Attention to crying and parental discipline.

Differences in Disturbed and Normal Family Patterns

In many studies the researchers have looked for differences between normal and disturbed children's families in terms of conflict, affective expression, dominance, and clarity of communication. It would seem reasonable to accept the assertion that disturbed and normal families differ rather markedly and specifically in the manner in which their members interact. Nevertheless, research so far has not yielded data that will allow one to state conclusively how interactions are different in normal and disturbed families. Part of the failure of researchers to show consistent differences in disturbed and normal families can be attributed to the sheer complexity of family relations and the multitude of variables (for example, socioeconomic status, sex, age, family composition, and size) that influence them. In addition, researchers often fail to design studies that include adequate sampling methods and experimental controls. A recent review of the literature on family interactions reveals that many studies failed a reasonable test of scientific rigor and, consequently, have yielded very equivocal findings (Jacob, 1975). In those studies that have been designed adequately, the results have often been inconclusive, contradictory of previous findings of other well designed studies, or unable to show significant differences between disturbed and normal families. As Jacob (1975) summarizes, "it would appear that family interaction studies, although based on a potentially sound methodological strategy, have not yet isolated family patterns that reliably differentiate disturbed from normal groups" (p. 56; see also Goldstein & Rodnick, 1975).

An additional reason for the failure of family interaction research to show reliable differences is perhaps due to the problem of measurement. Not only have measurement techniques varied greatly from study to study, making comparisons very difficult or impossible (Jacob, 1975), but also the variables measured may not have been the crucial ones (see also Hetherington & Martin, 1979). Subjective self-reports and measurement of verbal interactions during discussion of a hypothetical question in a laboratory setting, for example, may be less crucial for detecting differences between normal and disturbed families than measuring, through naturalistic observation, the discipline techniques used by the parents in the home.

One recent trend in parent-child research should be noted here. Until a few years ago, nearly all the research involving family influences on infants and young children focused on mother-child interaction. It is now widely recognized that father-child interactions are important in children's development, and research involving the father's role is increasing dramatically (Earls, 1976; Lamb, 1977).

Behavioral Analyses of Family Interaction

The work of G. R. Patterson and his colleagues (e.g., Patterson, 1973; Patterson & Fleischman, 1979; Patterson & Reid, 1970; Patterson, Reid, Jones, & Conger, 1975) involves direct observation and measurement of the behavior of parents and children in the home. Their careful behavioral analyses of the interaction in families who have aggressive and nonaggressive children show that for the families studied, there was an identifiable pattern of family interaction associated with aggressive child behavior. That is, the interaction in families with aggressive children was characterized by exchange of negative, hostile behaviors, whereas the interaction in families with nonaggressive children tended to be mutually positive and gratifying for parents and children. In the families with aggressive children, not only did the children behave in ways that were highly irritating and aversive to their parents, but their parents relied primarily on aversive methods (hitting, shouting, threatening, and so forth) to control their children. Thus, children's aggression in the family seemed both to produce counteraggression and to be produced by punitive parenting techniques. Patterson's data clearly show a pattern of negative interaction and coercion in the families of aggressive children, but he did not find that punitive parents caused aggressive behavior to develop in their children to any greater extent than aggressive children caused their parents to become punitive. The interactive-transactional effects of aggressive children and their parents on each other are obvious, but Patterson et al. (1975) demonstrated that many parents can be trained to control their own responses to their children in order to modify their children's aggression.

Other behavioral researchers (Lobitz & Johnson, 1975; Wahler, Winkle, Peterson, & Morrison, 1965) found that specific parent-child interactions that maintain undesirable child behavior can be identified and changed. Once the specific problem behaviors of parents and their children are identified and the relationships among parent and child behavior are analyzed, therapeutic intervention consists of rearranging the consequences provided by one individual (usually the parent) for the other (usually the child). For example, a typical aggressive interaction in one family begins with a reasonable parental command, followed by the child's noncompliance, followed by the parent's nagging, and the child's increased opposition. In this case the parent may be taught, among other things, to give the command only once, to provide praise for compliance, and enforce time-out (brief social isolation) for noncompliance.

In summary, *in situ* behavior analyses have led to the identification of maladaptive interaction patterns in families of disturbed children but have also shed more light on the design of therapeutic intervention than on the origins of disordered behavior.

Influence of Specific Child-Rearing Practices

The discussion to this point may lead one to adopt an overly negative or pessimistic view of the possibility of identifying family factors in the development of disordered behavior. Research of certain child-rearing practices has indeed provided a clear indication of how some behavior disorders may be given impetus or be exacerbated. As stated previously, it is not safe to assume that the etiology of behavior has been established on the basis of data showing how behavior can be changed. One can demonstrate how an extant behavioral repertoire can be modified and, therefore, show how the *course* of behavioral development can be altered (Lobitz & Johnson, 1975). The child-rearing techniques used by parents may, then, contribute to the development of disordered behavior in combination or interaction with the child's present responses.

The influence of some specific child-rearing practices on children's behavior has been rather clearly indicated by research (see Ainsworth, 1973; Becker, 1964; Martin, 1975; Risley & Baer, 1973). Attention will be given here to two topics: Adults' attention to crying and techniques of parental discipline. Excessive crying is a frequent concern of parents of infants and normal young children, of parents of older children with incipient behavior disorders, and of parents of seriously disturbed children. Crying, too, is often a prominent part of the temper tantrums exhibited by many normal and disturbed children. Typically, adults are thrown into a quandary by such crying, wondering whether or not they should attend to the child's crying or ignore it. Techniques of parental discipline for inappropriate conduct are, naturally, a primary and urgent concern of the parents of difficult-to-manage children, many of whom are considered to be disturbed.

Attention to Crying

In several experimental studies, the crying of normal infants and young children has been responsive to the social consequences provided by parents or other adults (Etzel & Gewirtz, 1967; Hart, Allen, Buell, Harris, & Wolf, 1964; Williams, 1959). In research studies, crying and temper tantrums of disturbed children have been observed to change with the adults' social response (Risley & Wolf, 1967; Wolf, Risley, & Mees, 1964). When the adults paid solicitous attention to the child's crying or gave in to the child's demands, crying increased in frequency. When the child's crying was ignored or punished, crying decreased in frequency, especially if noncrying behavior was reinforced. Basing their ideas on a succinct review of the research, Risley and Baer (1973) suggested several conclusions:

1. Crying may be operant (i.e., behavior affected by its *consequences*) or respondent (i.e., behavior *elicited* by antecedent events, such as pain).
2. Reinforcement of respondent crying may prevent the child's adaptation to the eliciting stimulus (e.g., pain).
3. Terminating an episode of crying by paying attention to the child or giving in to demands increases the likelihood of future crying episodes; but ignoring the child's crying, isolating him or her from social contact, or using appropriate punishment procedures decreases the probability that the child will cry more often in the future.

Two studies of crying reviewed by Risley and Baer deserve special attention because of their implications for child-rearing practices in infancy and early childhood. Etzel and Gewirtz (1967) found that they could change the amount of crying done by two infants (6 and 21 months old) by varying adults' attention to crying and noncrying behavior. The healthy infants were awaiting adoption on the well-baby ward of a hospital. They cried more frequently than normal infants—frequently and demandingly enough that Etzel and Gewirtz dubbed them *Infants Tyrannotearus* to convey the nature of their tyrannical demands for attention (for example, being picked up, held, and rocked) from the hospital staff. If crying was extinguished (not paid attention to) on the ward throughout the day, the babies did not cry. The experimenters also found that they could decrease crying during experimental sessions by ignoring crying and by attending to and reinforcing noncrying with a variety of stimuli (smiling, talking, ringing bells, showing hand puppets, and so on), even though the ward staff attended solicitiously to crying during the rest of the day.

The classic case study by Williams (1959) showed the dramatic effects parental behavior had on excessive crying and tantrums. The subject of his report was a 21-month-old boy who had been seriously ill during much of the first 18 months of his life. The child continued to demand the special attention and care he had received during his months of illness, although he was growing considerably healthier and was gaining weight and vigor. He extorted special care from his parents and his aunt by tyrant-like tantrum behavior when his wishes were thwarted. His parents and his aunt alternated turns at putting him to bed at night and for his afternoon nap. Putting him to bed was not a pleasant chore, for he would insist that the adult stay with him until he fell asleep. The adult, therefore, was confronted with a task requiring one-half to two hours each bedtime. If the parent or aunt tried to read during this bedtime vigil, he would cry until the adult put the reading material down. It was decided that an extinction procedure would be used for this tyranni-cal behavior. The child would be put to bed in a pleasant and relaxed manner and the adult would then leave the room, close the door, and not return, regardless of how the child might rage and scream. The assumption was that without the rein-forcing effect of the parents' or aunt's acquiescent return to the child's room, the behavior would diminish. The assumption proved to be correct. As shown in Figure 4-1, the child screamed for 45 minutes the first time the extinction procedure was carried out, but he did not cry at all the second time. The third time he was put to bed and ignored, he cried for about 10 minutes, but the length of his tantrums then fell gradually to zero. By the tenth occasion he no longer fussed at all when the parent put him to bed and left the room. About a week later, the child again cried and fussed when the aunt put him to bed. The aunt provided reinforcement by re-turning to his room and staying with him until he fell asleep—the battle was resumed. The second extinction (shown by the broken lines) followed the course of the first: Crying ceased after a few days of being put to bed without reinforcement for tantrums. No additional bedtime tantrums were observed during the next two years.

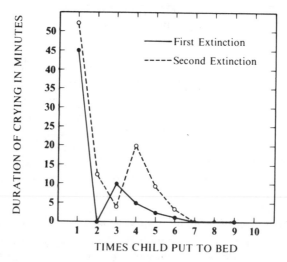

FIGURE 4-1   Length of crying in two extinction series as a function of successive occa-sions of being put to bed.

Note. From "The Elimination of Tantrum Behavior by Extinction Procedures" by C. D. Williams, *Journal of Abnormal and Social Psychology,* 1959, *59,* 269. Copyright 1959 by the American Psychological Association. Reprinted by permission.

It would then seem warranted to conclude that there are clear and simple implications for parents: Never pay attention to your child when he or she is crying, but do pay frequent attention when the child is not crying. However, the implications are not quite that simple. First, it is obvious that if the child is hurt or frightened seriously, failure to attend to the child in order to care for and comfort would not only be cruel but could also endanger the child's responsiveness to adults as social reinforcers (that is, it is desirable for children to associate caring adults with escape from aversive situations).[21] Second, in Bell and Ainsworth's study (1972), mothers' responsiveness to their infants' crying early in the first year of life was associated with noncrying modes of communication during later infancy, while maternal *un*responsiveness to crying during the first year was associated with *increased* frequency of crying later on (see also Ainsworth, 1973).[22] Ainsworth's (1973) review of research suggests that sensitivity of the mother to the infant's needs, including prompt attention to crying, is most likely to lead to the development of a noncrying, happy, compliant child, at least if she also cares sensitively for him/her when the child is not crying (Parsley & Rabinowitz, 1975). In his review of research, Rutter (1979) notes that prompt maternal attention to crying—what might be called *sensitive responsiveness*—has produced mixed results. It is not completely clear what sensitive responsiveness means, but it may involve parental ability to discriminate between differences in children's cries and to appropriately respond. It may mean that the parent who is sensitively responsive may be able to interpret the child's cries, to know which ones signify pain or discomfort and which ones signify boredom or anger, and to take appropriate action.

In summary, one need not worry about "spoiling" a child by sensitive or gentle treatment. This includes the times the child cries as an infant and can include crying responses to fright or pain as an older child. On the other hand, tyrannical crying and tantrums need not be tolerated at any age, and can be extinguished by withdrawing attention for crying and providing copious attention for noncrying behaviors.

Parental Discipline

How parents manage their children's crying is a small part of the broader topic of parental discipline. The conclusions reached in the case of crying can be extended to suggest general guidelines regarding parental control of other undesirable child behaviors.

1. Be sensitive, warm, and caring in relationships with children.
2. Consistently ignore misbehavior, unless it is threatening to life or health.
3. Offer frequent attention and rewards for appropriate behavior.

---

[21] For further discussion of this point and speculation regarding deficiencies in autistic children's association of adults with escape from aversive stimuli, see Lovaas, Schaeffer, & Simmons (1965). Becker's (1964) discussion of love-oriented versus power-assertive parental discipline and the reviews of Ainsworth (1973) and Martin (1975) on infant-mother attachment are also relevant.

[22] Bell and Ainsworth's analysis of their data has been questioned by Gewirtz and Boyd (1977a). See Ainsworth and Bell (1977) and Gewirtz and Boyd (1977b) for further discussion. Note that Gewirtz and Boyd's criticism is *not* intended to refute the plausibility of Bell and Ainsworth's hypothesis.

These three rules may be fundamental to good parental discipline, but they represent an oversimplification of the research findings regarding the effects of parental control techniques.

Becker (1964) suggests two major dimensions along which parental discipline techniques can vary: Restrictiveness versus permissiveness, and warmth versus hostility. His review of research led him to the conclusion that love-oriented (warm) methods of discipline and permissiveness (that is, a high degree of tolerance in areas such as neatness, orderliness, toilet training, sex play, modesty, manners, noise, obedience, and so forth) foster desirable social growth, whereas power-assertive (hostile) methods of discipline and restrictiveness (strict rule enforcement) inhibit social development. However, the two dimensions of warmth-hostility and restrictiveness-permissiveness *interact* to affect the child's social development. In his opinion, parents whose discipline is *warm and restrictive* are likely to have submissive, dependent, polite, neat children who are minimally aggressive, friendly, and creative. On the other hand, parents who use *warm and permissive* discipline are likely to have socially outgoing, active, creative, independent children who are able to assume adult roles and show minimal self-aggression. *Hostile and restrictive* parents will tend to have socially withdrawn, "neurotic" children who are shy and quarrelsome with their peers, show maximal self-aggression, and have difficulty assuming adult roles. Parents who are *hostile and permissive* in their discipline will tend to have highly aggressive, noncompliant, delinquent children. Furthermore, *consistency* in discipline—sameness over time, agreement between parents, predictability of consequences, and congruity between instructions, rewards, and models—is a crucial factor in the outcome. In general, he believes, consistency will smooth out difficulties and inconsistency will aggravate problems. Even though consistent, love-oriented, permissive discipline seems to facilitate socialization and inconsistent, hostile, restrictive disciplinary measures are typically debilitating, Becker (1964) concludes that "There are probably many routes to becoming a 'good parent' which vary with the personality of both the parents and children and with pressures in the environment with which one must learn to cope" (p. 202).

A more recent review of parental discipline techniques (Martin, 1975) leads to the same conclusions reached by Becker (1964) insofar as children's aggression is concerned: Parents who are generally lax, uncaring, and rejecting in their attitudes toward their children—but also are harsh, hostile, and inconsistent in discipline—tend to have hostile, aggressive children. However, Becker's conclusion that parental restrictiveness produces withdrawn-neurotic behavior is not supported by Martin's review. Martin's analysis does reaffirm the pernicious effects of parental rejection and nonacceptance and the desirable outcome of sensitivity to children's needs, reinforcement for appropriate behavior, and love-oriented methods of dealing with misbehavior.

The contention that discipline techniques are not simple or predictable in their effects without taking into consideration the behavioral characteristics of both parent and child is given direct support by the longitudinal study of Thomas, Chess, and Birch (1968); see also Chess and Thomas (1977) and Thomas and Chess (1975). The thesis advanced by Thomas and Chess is that every child is born with a "temperament"—a behavioral style or characteristic way of responding to situations—that determines behavioral development only in interaction with environmental variables, including parental behavior and schooling. Some children are "difficult," showing a temperament that includes negative mood, intense reactions, irregularity in biological functions, slowness to adapt to new stimuli or environmental changes. Others are "easy," in that they are characterized by just the opposite behavioral style. Depending on how they are managed by their parents and other adults, for example, teachers, easy and difficult children (as well as those with other temperaments) may develop behavior disorders or develop desirable behavior patterns. The following provides an example of the different outcomes of parental management of difficult children.

vignette

The differences in the developmental courses of difficult children which result from differences in parent-child interactions are illustrated by the contrasting behavioral courses of two of the study children. Both youngsters, one a girl and the other a boy, showed similar characteristics of behavioral functioning in the early years of life, with irregular sleep patterns, constipation and painful evacuations at times, slow acceptance of new foods, prolonged adjustment periods to new routines, and frequent and loud periods of crying. Adaptation to nursery school in the fourth year was also a problem for both children. Parental attitudes and practices, however, differed greatly. The girl's father was usually angry with her. In speaking of her, he gave the impression of disliking the youngster and was punitive and spent little or no recreational time with her. The mother was more concerned for the child, more understanding, and more permissive, but quite inconsistent. There was only one area in which there was firm but quiet parental consistency, namely, with regard to safety rules. The boy's parents, on the other hand, were unusually tolerant and consistent. The child's lengthy adjustment periods were accepted calmly; his strident altercations with his younger siblings were dealt with good-humoredly. The parents waited out his negative moods without getting angry. They tended to be very permissive, but set safety limits and consistently pointed out the needs and rights of his peers at play.

By the age of $5\frac{1}{2}$ years, these two children, whose initial characteristics had been so similar, showed marked differences in behavior. The boy's initial difficulties in nursery school had disappeared, he was a constructive member of his class, had a group of friends with whom he exchanged visits, and functioned smoothly in most areas of daily living. The girl, on the other hand, had developed a number of symptoms of increasing severity. These included explosive anger, negativism, fear of the dark, encopresis, thumb sucking, insatiable demands for toys and sweets, poor peer relationships, and protective lying. It is of interest that there was no symptomatology or negativism in one area where parental practice had been firmly consistent, i.e., safety rules.

The boy, though his early handling had been difficult for his parents, was never considered by them to have a behavioral disturbance. They understood that the youngster's troublesome behavior was the expression of his own characteristics. With this constructive parental approach, these troublesome items of behavior did not become transformed into symptoms of a behavior disorder. The girl, in contrast, suffered the consequences of parental functioning which was excessively stressful for a child with her temperamental attributes and developed a neurotic behavior disorder. . . . (Thomas et al., 1968, pp. 82–83)

Summary. It is very clear that specific child-rearing practices that influence the course of the child's development can be identified, but that the particular effects of any one of these practices will depend on the psychological characteristics and the current behavioral repertoire of the child in combination with the parents' control techniques.

FAMILY FACTORS IN SPECIFIC BEHAVIORAL CHARACTERISTICS

Childhood Psychosis

Using the term *childhood psychosis* to denote all severe and profound behavior disorders (subsuming under it the categories *autistic, schizophrenic, symbiotic, atypical,* and so forth), there is little sound evidence, if any, indicating that parents *make* children psychotic. The same negative statement could be made regarding parents as the cause of the more specific syndromes subsumed under the general category *psychotic* (Ross, 1974; Werry, 1979a). The families of many severely and profoundly disturbed children seem to be indistinguishable from the families of normal children (Byassee & Murrell, 1975; DeMyer, Pontius, Norton, Barton, Allen, & Steele, 1972; Fenichel, 1974). For example, Lennox, Callias, and Rutter (1977) found no differences on tests of thought disorders between parents of autistic children and parents of normal children. Cantwell, Baker, and Rutter (1977) found that mothers of autistic children and mothers of children with developmental receptive aphasia spoke in very similar language to their children.

In the cases where there is obviously behavioral pathology in the family, the problem may be as much (perhaps more) a result of the disruptive influence of the disturbed child on the parents and siblings as it is a matter of pathogenic parental influence on the child. The trauma experienced by parents when they have a seriously handicapped child is great, and all of the blame for the ensuing problems in the family cannot be laid at the parents' door (Roos, 1975). As stated previously, however, once maladaptive behavior has become established in the child, parental or sibling responses to it may serve to maintain, attenuate, or otherwise modify it.

Juvenile Delinquency and Conduct Disorder

Delinquent, or law-violating, behavior obviously is learned from the child's social environment. The social environment includes not only the child's family but the peer group and peer culture, which are particularly important in the case of delinquency. In fact, it has been suggested that the lower class culture is a generating milieu for gang delinquency (Miller, 1958; see also Short, 1966). It must be recognized, too, that juvenile delinquency takes many forms (socialized gang delinquency, isolated delinquency, crimes against property, aggression against people, and so forth), and differs statistically according to age, sex, and socioeconomic level of the youth involved; therefore one would hardly expect to find uniform family backgrounds for all delinquents. Indeed, "a complete contrast in family relationships does not differentiate delinquents from nondelinquents" (Cavan & Ferdinand, 1975, p. 193). Nonetheless, certain types of families and parental discipline techniques are found more frequently to apply to delinquent than to nondelinquent youths. The findings of several classic studies of delinquents' families (Gluek & Gluek, 1950, 1962; Healy & Bronner, 1926; McCord, McCord, & Zola, 1959) have been confirmed repeatedly over the years: The risk of delinquency is increased within broken, disorganized homes in which the parents themselves have an arrest record and are lax in discipline (permissive, indifferent, or neglecting) but are also hostile, rejecting, capricious, and cruel in punishing their children (Becker, 1964; Cavan & Ferdinand, 1975; Hetherington & Martin, 1979; Robins, West, & Herjanic, 1975; Short, 1966). While a host of factors interact to produce delinquent behavior and the negative effects of some factors (e.g., an absent or a hostile, rejecting father) can be at least partially offset by others (e.g., a warm and loving mother), the pathological influence of extreme family hostility, conflict, and disorganization can hardly be questioned.

Most studies of delinquency have involved boys rather than girls or have not separately analyzed the data for females. Offord, Abrams, Allen, and Proushinsky (1979) studied Canadian families with delinquent daughters and found that delinquent girls tended to come from broken homes, have mothers who were considered mentally ill, have fathers with records of criminal behavior, and have parents with a history of being on welfare. The factor most clearly distinguishing delinquent from nondelinquent girls was the frequency of broken homes. These findings do not indicate that parental separation *causes* female delinquency, but that parental discord and separation are part of the family characteristics correlated with law violation by girls.

Until very recently, there was little or no reason to question the assertion that "the family correlates of early antisocial aggression and most forms of delinquency appear to be similar" (Hetherington & Martin, 1979, p. 257). That is, research reviewed by Becker (1964), Martin (1975), and Hetherington and Martin (1979) pointed to similar family factors related to law violations and the aggressive, acting-out (but not necessarily delinquent) behavior known as *conduct disorder* (see Chapter 3). However, Moore, Chamberlain, and Mukai (1979) recently presented data indicating that "aggressive behavior and adolescent criminal behavior represent different developmental tracks that are not necessarily related" (p. 346). They found that while stealing was highly predictive of later contact with the juvenile court, aggression in the home was not. Some aggressive children are thieves; others are not.

The study of Moore et al. (1979) was of a small sample, and the findings must be considered tentative. Even if the findings are reliable, however, the family factors in delinquency and those in conduct disorder are not necessarily different.

Table 3–2, for example, shows that stealing is one behavior associated with conduct disorder, but additional research may show that stealers are a distinct subgroup of children with conduct disorders, most of whom are destined to become delinquent. Future research of family characteristics associated with specific child behaviors might show that different family characteristics are involved in the case of stealers than in the case of nonstealers.

Anxiety-Withdrawal

Anxiety-withdrawal, which is discussed in detail in Chapter 9, includes such characteristics as excessive shyness, lack of assertiveness, depression, and excessive fears (see Table 3–2). Hetherington and Martin (1979) reviewed research showing that anxious, withdrawn children tend to come from homes where at least one (more often both) parent is "neurotic" and where there is marital conflict. It is certainly plausible that anxious, withdrawn parents teach their children to behave as they do. And it is clear that in many cases of withdrawal or fearfulness, one or both parents are overly restrictive, demanding, or overprotective of their children. However, the extent to which family interaction, as opposed to biological factors or influences from outside the family, accounts for anxiety and withdrawal is not known precisely.

School Failure

The family's contribution to school failure plays a secondary role in most cases, for it is axiomatic that the school is responsible for the child's learning. However, parents undoubtedly contribute toward or detract from their child's success at school in several ways: their expressed attitudes toward school, academic learning, and teachers; their competence or lack of success in school; and their disinterest in or reinforcement of appropriate school-related behaviors, such as attending regularly, completing homework, reading, and studying. Gesten, Scher, and Cowen (1978), for example, found that "homes characterized by lack of educational stimulation appear to produce children who are prone to learning problems" (p. 254).

Family composition and structure may, perhaps, have some effect on academic achievement. The father's absence apparently has little or no effect on school success (Herzog & Sudia, 1973), but it is plausible that highly educated parents and academically successful older siblings will, in most cases, tend to facilitate achievement.

Thomas et al. (1968) found in their subjects that the interaction of the child's temperament and the parents' behavior management techniques could add to or subtract from the child's adaptation to school (see also Thomas, 1971). When parental standards and family interactions were markedly different from the standards and characteristic social situations the child faced at school, sometimes a problem resulted. Because teachers, peers, or both rejected or ridiculed the child for behaving in ways that were acceptable at home, the child sometimes then developed a behavior disorder. "Easy" children for the parents then became "difficult" at school.

vignette _____

For example, the parents of 4-year-old Hal . . . worried because he let the other children take his toys, did not defend himself but, instead, came home crying. This behavior represented qualities in their son of which his parents did not approve and never had approved. The basic issue, however, was that the other children as a group ganged up on Hal because of his inappropriately formal manners and his habit of asking with meticulous politeness to share their toys; they saw him as a strange creature. Hal's formalistic manners actually were the direct reflection of the standards and approaches imposed by his parents, who were not aware that his politeness would cause him to become the target of teasing. They considered the other children badly brought up but, even so, they wanted their son to be manly and capable of standing up for his rights.

Another child, Isobel . . . , who presented with a learning difficulty in second grade, was of concern to her parents because they honored education highly and knew the youngster to be above average in intelligence. On the surface it appeared that the child had not adapted, despite her intellectual ability, to their academic standards. However, Isobel's learning difficulty stemmed from her unwillingness to take instruction, and this, in turn, derived from the parental focus on uniqueness, the right of each person to be individual. They encouraged self-expression in the child, and simultaneously she developed a disregard for rules in play with peer groups and in learning situations in school. When engaged in dramatic play, Isobel was outstanding in her creative imagination and no problems arose. When in the classroom, however, she did not consider the group directions to be her concern and expected individual instruction. The net result was failure to build an educational base because the environment simply had no provision for the child who refused to avail herself of group instruction and required, no matter how pleasantly, the teacher's entire attention. (Thomas et al., 1968, p. 88)

In contrast to the foregoing cases, parents of "difficult" children contributed, through proper management in terms of the child's temperament, to making them "easy" (or at least easier than otherwise) at school. Jimmy, a difficult child whose parents managed him well by good-natured but firm and consistent routine, is an example.

vignette _____

Homework had been done haphazardly in the earlier grades. The parents then established a firm and unvarying rule of no television during the week and gave him a specific time, place, and set of conditions for doing his homework. The initial tantrums when these rules were applied gradually gave way to compliance, and the youngster gave his full attention to mastering the work. There was still periodic distress when new subject material was introduced, and Jimmy would become absolutely certain that he would never learn it. During these periods the child would slam his way in and out of rooms and assure his family that he was the dumbest boy in the class. The parents laughed through such sessions, knowing that these would soon be displaced, as they were but a minor aspect in the child's eventual good adaptation. (Thomas et al., 1968, p. 84)

Psychophysiological Disorders

Psychophysiological disorders are physical disorders assumed to be caused by psychological factors, often by parent-child relationships. Reliable evidence pointing to parent-child relations as a *causal* factor in physical disorders is at best meager. Although parent-child conflict may indeed be associated with physical illnesses and disorders of many types, it is seldom the case that the causes of such physical problems can be clearly and properly attributed to nonbiological factors (see Werry, 1979c).

FAMILY CONTROL OF DISORDERED BEHAVIOR

The discussion thus far has uncovered no proof that family factors *cause* disordered behavior in children. Beyond the ethereal speculations of some psychoanalysts, the strongest evidence for a causal relationship is derived from data showing that family members can indeed change the course of a child's behavior, and a retrospective analysis of this nature cannot be said to hold much weight of evidence. The absence of strong evidence for a family-based etiology should not be a reason for despair. Effective intervention and efficient means of correcting behavior disorders do not always depend on discovery of the cause of the problem. Furthermore, the range of problems that have been dealt with successfully through family intervention and the variety of techniques for changing troublesome behaviors that have been employed by family members are great (Atkeson & Forehand, 1979; Berkowitz & Graziano, 1972; Johnson & Katz, 1973; O'Dell, 1974; O'Leary & Wilson, 1975). Not only have parents been taught to manage a wide array of problem behaviors in their nonpsychotic children, but parents have been trained to serve as therapists for their own severely and profoundly disturbed offspring (Kozloff, 1973; Schopler & Reichler, 1971). In some cases, siblings of behaviorally handicapped children have been used as therapeutic change agents (Colletti & Harris, 1977; Doleys & Slapion, 1975). Also, it has been shown in at least one case that parents who could not modify the disruptive behavior of their child were taught by the child (after training in the use of behavior modification techniques) to pay attention to appropriate behavior, not to inappropriate acts, thereby reducing disruptiveness (Fedoravicius, 1973).

The literature clearly indicates the benefits to be derived from proceeding with intervention in the absence of firm conclusions regarding etiology. Nonetheless, the search for causal factors arising from the family and other sources should not be abandoned. Primary prevention does require at least identification of the conditions under which behavior disorders are likely to appear, if not the specification of etiological agents. A new approach to assessing the conditions which increase the chances that a child will develop disordered behavior is the study of children "at risk."

FAMILIES AND THE CONCEPT OF RISK

One strategy for unravelling the seemingly impossible tangle of family factors that *may* give rise to behavioral pathology in children would be to experiment with families. That is, researchers could purposely manipulate family variables in order to induce behavior disorders in children, taking care to control extraneous variables that could cloud the outcome. If researchers could produce behavior disorders at will, then the *etiological* variables could be identified. At present, intervention research is able to identify only *therapeutic* variables that can be manipulated in order to ameliorate behavior disorders.

Even if researchers could conduct the required experiments with families (a task far more difficult than it at first appears), it would not be an acceptable approach for obvious moral and ethical reasons. An alternative approach to the study of etiology is intensive longitudinal study of individuals for whom the *risk* of developing a behavior disorder is high. In the case of schizophrenia, such longitudinal study of children at risk—children whose chances of becoming schizophrenic at some time in their lives are assumed to be greater than normal—has recently been initiated (Garmezy, 1974 a, b, c; Neale & Weintraub, 1975). Mosher and Gunderson (1974) suggest that risk research is a natural outgrowth of previous investigations that have shown both genetic and environmental factors to be important in the etiology of schizophrenia.

Researchers seeking the origins of schizophrenia have traditionally concentrated their attention upon the systematic experimental analysis of schizophrenic patients' behavior. But although this approach has yielded any number of putative etiological clues, attempts to evaluate the significance of differences found between normal and schizophrenic subjects have been stymied by a major and seemingly insuperable methodological problem—the impossibility of determining whether abnormalities observed in already manifest, diagnosed schizophrenics reflect a cause or a consequence of illness. To circumvent this problem, a cadre of enterprising researchers have turned to a promising and relatively new research strategy: The study of individuals deemed particularly vulnerable to schizophrenia prior to the manifestation of illness. By following vulnerable individuals from their earliest years through the period of risk, these investigators hope to identify preexisting biochemical, physiological, psychological, or life-history characteristics which consistently differentiate those who ultimately develop schizophrenia from those who do not. (p. 13)

Much of the work currently in progress is concerned with development of schizophrenia in adulthood. However, as Garmezy (1974) and Robins (1974) point out, adult psychopathology and childhood behavior disorders, especially those of the acting-out aggressive type, may represent a continuum of social incompetence. One must, therefore, be concerned with the factors that increase *children's* risk of developing problem behavior. Identifying the factors that produce high risk for children is not an easy task. Poverty, malnutrition, neglect, abuse, parents who are deviant, failure at school—all are known to increase the child's chances for abnormal development. Presently there is more error than accuracy in predicting maldevelopment on the basis of any one of the factors known to contribute to it. Furthermore, even though it may be possible to identify factors that increase risk of school failure from information on a child's birth certificate—for example, birth order, race, mother's education, legitimacy, month when prenatal care began—it is not correct to assume that these risk factors *cause* later school or behavioral problems (Ramey, Stedman, Borders-Patterson, & Mengel, 1978).

SUMMARY AND IMPLICATIONS
FOR SPECIAL EDUCATION

Attempts to pinpoint the origins of behavior disorders in family relationships have met with little success. Family relationships are best viewed as *contributing* factors in behavioral development. Although there are studies in which family members intervened in children's behavior disorders and changed the course of their development, convincing evidence is lacking that families cause children to behave abnormally in the first place. Methodological weaknesses in studies of family interaction probably account for some of this lack of evidence. In cases where parental behavior is most plausibly tied to the origins of deviant behavior in children, such as the case of parental discipline, a strong case can be made for the assertion that the effects of specific types of discipline depend on interaction with the temperamental characteristics of the child. The child's behavior influences that of the parent, as well as vice versa, and child-rearing patterns therefore must be interpreted as an interactional and transactional process. Recently initiated longitudinal studies offer some hope for identifying the factors, including factors related to family life, that increase children's risk for developing behavior disorders.

Given what is known today regarding the family's role in children's behavior disorders, it would be extremely inappropriate for special educators to adopt an attitude of blame toward parents of troubled children. The special education teacher must realize that the parents of a disturbed child have experienced a great deal of disappointment and frustration and that they too would like to see the child's behavior improve.[23] In the light of numerous studies showing that parents can intervene successfully in their children's behavior disorders, the special educator would be well advised to try to enlist the aid of the child's parents. The family is obviously a crucial part of the child's psychological ecology. Although the teacher may be successful in working directly with parents, it is often highly desirable to obtain the help of a school psychologist, social worker, liaison teacher, or other professional whose role includes parent counseling.

---

[23] For first-hand accounts by parents whose children are severely disturbed, see Chapin (1972), Park (1972), Turnbull and Turnbull, (1978), and Wechsler (1972).

chapter 5 _____

Biological Factors

In light of the conclusions of the previous chapter, a biological view of behavior disorders has particular appeal. Psychological models of behavior cannot account for all behavioral variations in children. On the other hand, advances in medicine, genetics, and physiology make plausible the suggestion of a biological basis for all behavior disorders. It is undeniable that the central nervous system is involved in all behavior, and that all behavior involves neurochemical activity. Furthermore, genetic factors alone are potentially sufficient to explain all variation in human behavior (Eiduson, Eiduson, & Geller, 1962). It may seem reasonable to believe that disordered behavior always implies a genetic accident, disease, brain injury, brain dysfunction, or biochemical imbalance.

Attractive as this answer may appear on the surface, the assumption that disordered behavior is simply a result of biological misfortune is misleading. It must be recognized that much of the so-called evidence linking biological factors to behavior disorders is presumptive. A case in point is the presumption of minimal brain dysfunction or minimal brain damage (MBD) in children who are hyperactive and distractible. As will be discussed further, many hyperactive children have been diagnosed as having MBD on the basis of their behavior alone—on the basis of purely presumptive evidence that their brains actually are damaged or dysfunctioning. Furthermore, as Lovaas (1979) points out, even if a biological cause of troublesome behavior can be confirmed, the cause will not likely lead to a prescription for treatment of the behavior disorder.

At this point, several facts need to be clarified. First, in *nearly all* cases of mental illness (including psychosis) no reliable *direct* evidence of biological disease or disorder can be found. It must therefore be *presumed* that there is a physical basis for the disorder if one wishes to implicate biological factors (Szasz, 1960; Werry, 1979 a, b). Second, it is certain that environmental influences interact with and modify the behavioral manifestations of biological processes. Even in the field of genetics where the determinants of behavior operate in apparent isolation from environmental forces, it is now clear that the environment plays an important role in shaping inherited traits (McClearn, 1964; Scarr-Salapatek, 1975); consequently, one cannot point to behavior disorders as purely biological in nature. Third, although biological factors clearly are involved in behavior disorders, their status as *causal* agents can in many cases be questioned.

One must conclude that the effects of biological factors on behavioral development apparently are considerable, but that these effects frequently are neither demonstrable nor simple. While biological factors can influence behavior, environmental conditions can modify an individual's biological status. At this juncture in the behavioral sciences, it may be more useful to examine the biological factors that increase the risk of behavioral maldevelopment than to attempt to find direct and simple biological causes for behavior disorders. With these points in mind, we turn to a consideration of (a) biological factors that *can* cause disordered behavior, (b) disorders that are often thought to have a biological base, and (c) psychophysiological disorders (physical illnesses or disorders thought to have a psychological origin).

BIOLOGICAL MISFORTUNES—IMPLICATIONS

Genetic Anomalies

Children inherit more than physical characteristics from their parents. For example, there is considerable research indicating that in the Caucasian populations in the United States and Europe, genetic factors account for a large proportion (perhaps 50 percent to 75 percent) of the differences in intelligence (Gourlay, 1979; Scarr-Salapatek, 1975). Although mental retardation may result from non-hereditary factors (for example, impoverished experience, malnutrition, accident, disease), the risk for retardation in the offspring of retarded parents is considerably higher than the risk for the children of nonretarded persons. Furthermore, some mental retardation syndromes, such as the chromosomal anomaly known as Downs' syndrome (mongolism), are direct expressions of reproductive misfortunes (Reed, 1975).

There is little or no evidence that the specific behavioral characteristics of mildly and moderately disturbed children are genetically transmitted. However, some type of genetic misfortune obviously contributes to psychotic disorders that can occur in children (Freedman, 1971; Gunderson, Autry, & Mosher, 1974; Hanson, Gottesman, & Mechl, 1977; Heston, 1970; Kety, 1976; Reed, 1975). Genetic factors clearly play a role in children's psychoses that begin near the age of puberty or thereafter, but there is little evidence supporting genetic causes of psychoses beginning before 5 years of age (Hanson & Gottesman, 1976).

The exact genetic mechanisms responsible for a predisposition to schizophrenia are still unknown, but the research clearly shows an increase in risk for schizophrenia and schizophrenic-like behavior (often called *schizoid* or *schizophrenic spectrum* behavior) in the relatives of schizophrenics. The closer the genetic relationship between the child and a schizophrenic relative, the higher the risk that the child will develop the condition. The heightened risk cannot be attributed solely to the social environment or interpersonal factors.

In the past two decades there has been considerable interest in a genetic variation among males, the *karyotype XYY syndrome*. The normal complement of sex chromosomes in males is XY, the Y supposedly contributing the "maleness." The extra Y chromosome in some males (approximately .2 percent of the male population) is imagined to produce hyperaggressive characteristics. The reason to suspect that XYY males are more aggressive is that in samples of men institutionalized for criminal behavior of various sorts, the XYY chromosome pattern occurs more frequently than in the general population. Furthermore, Nielson, Christensen, Friedrich, Zeuthen, and Ostergaard (1973) saw in their study more truancy, vagabondage, impulsiveness, and difficulties at school in the childhoods of XYY males who had a history of psychiatric hospitalization (or other problems) than in a comparison group of criminal men with "more or less similar behavioral characteristics."

As Achenbach (1974) and Bandura (1973) point out, much of the research on the XYY question must be viewed with great caution because of problems in research design and sampling methods. In the Nielsen et al. (1973) study, for example, the meaning of the findings is quite unclear because the criteria for selecting subjects were so vague. There appears to be no sound research to support the hypothesis that the XYY variation produces hyperaggressive males. Furthermore, Kellerman (1977a) showed that the hyperaggressive behavior of a 7 year old boy who had the XYY chromosomal variation could be controlled with typical behavior modification procedures. The boy's parents, when taught to provide consistent consequences, controlled his temper tantrums, destructive and defiant behavior, hitting of other children, and other unacceptable behaviors. The boy became well behaved enough so that his evening dose of methylphenidate (Ritalin) could be eliminated, and his parents were able to leave him with a babysitter while they went on a weekend vacation. Thus, even if chromosomal anomaly does contribute to hyperaggression in XYY males, that behavior can be changed using behavioral techniques that involve making the child's environment predictable, consistent, and conducive to appropriate conduct.

The XXY male, who has an extra female chromosome, has certain physical and mental characteristics that are well known. Small testicles, sterility, tallness, thinness, and long arms and legs, often accompanied by low intelligence and unstable personality, are characteristics of males with the XXY or Klinefelter's syndrome (Money, 1970).

A variety of genetic anomalies result in moderate or severe mental retardation (Crandall, 1977; Reed, 1975). Two examples are described here because they involve behavior disorders in addition to mental retardation.

The case of phenylketonuria (PKU—a genetically transmitted metabolic disorder) is perhaps the most noteworthy case in which a biochemical irregularity has been identified and can be treated in order to prevent mental retardation and accompanying behavior problems.

> PKU is a disorder of amino acid metabolism in which the enzyme phenylalanine hydroxylase is missing. This enzyme has a crucial role in the utilization of phenylalanine, a very common component of the diet. In its absence, phenylalanine cannot be converted to tyrosine but instead accumulates in the tissues and is partly transformed into phenylpyruvic acid and other metabolites. In some way, as yet unknown but perhaps related to myelin formation, the accumulation of these abnormal metabolites prevents normal development of the brain, and mental retardation is the usual result. Other symptoms are irritability, athetoid movements, hyperactivity, and blond coloration. About one-third of the children have convulsive seizures. (Reed, 1975, p. 83)

If PKU is detected soon after birth and phenylalanine is eliminated from the diet until the child's brain is no longer damaged by abnormal metabolities (until middle childhood), mental retardation can be prevented. If the child goes untreated, he or she may not only be retarded but also exhibit schizoid behavior, hyperactivity, uncontrollable temper tantrums, seizures, and athetoid movements (clumsy movements usually associated with cerebral palsy). Dietary restriction of phenylalanine after the child has become retarded will not reverse the mental retardation but may help to alleviate the behavior problems (Reed, 1975).

Some severely disturbed children exhibit *self-injurious behavior*. In most cases of self-injurious behavior (SIB) there is no known biological cause, although biological variables are receiving increasing attention in research (deCatanzaro, 1978).

There is, however, a genetic anomaly in which SIB is a distinctive part of the syndrome. The Lesch-Nyhan syndrome is a severe neurological disorder caused by the lack of the enzyme hypoxanthine-guanine phosphoribosyl transferace (Nyhan, 1976; Reed, 1975). Without this enzyme the urine cannot be properly metabolized and there is a great excess of uric acid in the urine. The syndrome is very rare and is sex-linked, occurring once in about 50,000 male births.

Lesch-Nyhan disease results in early death, the victims seldom living beyond their teens. The first neurological symptoms appear at about 6 months of age, when it is noticed that the infant cannot sit unsupported or crawl. Choreoathetoid (slow jerking) movements and scissoring of the legs develop, and the child appears to be severely retarded. At about 3 years of age compulsive self-mutilation appears. The SIB may involve biting the lips or fingers, head banging, and hitting and biting other persons and objects. No effective treatment is known, but constant physical restraint and extracting the teeth are commonly recommended in order to reduce self-mutilation. Behavior modification techniques can be helpful (Nyhan, 1976), and new drug treatments for this disorder are being researched (Castells, Chakrabarti, Winsberg, Hurwic, Perel, & Nyhan, 1979). Genetic counselling is clearly indicated, as carriers and affected fetuses can be identified.

Difficult Temperament

From birth, all children exhibit a temperament—a behavioral style. It is initially determined, apparently, by several factors that operate prior to birth, including genetic makeup, the physical status of the mother during pregnancy, and perinatal trauma. The point is that infants begin life with an inborn tendency to behave in certain ways. The newborn has a way of behaving that is determined predominantly by biological factors, and how a baby behaves at birth and in the first weeks and months thereafter will influence how others respond. Temperament can be changed by the environment in which the child develops, but a difficult temperament may increase the child's risk for behavior disorder. It would be inappropriate to view temperament as anything other than an initial behavioral style that may interact with environmental influences to cause a behavior disorder. As Thomas et al. (1968) state:

> Temperament is not immutable. Like any other characteristic of the organism, its features can undergo a developmental course that will be significantly affected by environmental circumstances. In this respect it is not different from height, weight, intellectual competence, or any other characteristic of the individual. The initially identified pattern of the young child may be relatively unchanged by environmental influences, or it may be reinforced and heightened, diminished, or otherwise modified during the developmental course. (pp. 4–5)
>
> Neither in theory nor in fact would we expect a one-to-one relation to exist between a specific pattern of temperament and the emergence of a behavior problem; temperament, in and of itself, does not produce a behavior disorder. (p. 9)

Based on their longitudinal study of 136 children in New York City, Thomas et al. (1968) describe nine categories of temperamental characteristics (see also Thomas, 1971):

1. *activity level*—How much the child moves about during activities such as feeding, bathing, sleeping, and playing

2. *rhythmicity*—the regularity or predictability with which the child eats, sleeps, eliminates, and so on

3. *approach or withdrawal*—how the child responds initially to new events such as people, places, toys, and foods

4. *adaptability*—how quickly the child becomes accustomed to or modifies an initial reaction to new situations or stimuli

5. *intensity of reaction*—the amount of energy expended in reacting (positively or negatively) to situations or stimuli

6. *threshold of responsiveness*—the amount or intensity of stimulation required to elicit a response from the child

7. *quality of mood*—the amount of pleasant, joyful, and friendly behavior compared with unpleasant, crying, and unfriendly behavior exhibited by the child

8. *distractibility*—the frequency with which extraneous or irrelevant stimuli interfere with the ongoing behavior of the child in a given situation

9. *attention span and persistence*—the length of time a child will spend on a given activity and the tendency to maintain an activity in the face of obstacles to performance

Chess, Thomas, and their colleagues found that children with any temperament might develop behavior disorders, depending on the child-rearing practices of their parents and other adults. Children with difficult temperaments were most likely to develop troublesome behavior. In their subjects, a difficult temperament was characterized by irregularity in biological functioning, mostly negative (withdrawing) responses to new stimuli, slow adaptation to changes in the environment, frequent display of negative mood, and a predominance of intense reactions. A difficult temperament may elicit negative responses from a child's caretakers and increase the probability that he or she will exhibit inappropriate or undesirable behavior in future years (see also Chess & Thomas, 1977).

Brain Damage or Dysfunction

The brain can be traumatized in several different ways before, during, or after birth. Physical insult during an accident or during the birth process may destroy brain tissue. Prolonged high fever, infectious disease, toxic chemicals (such as drugs or poisons taken by the child) also may damage the brain. Probably the most frequently suspected or known cause of brain damage in children, however, is anoxia (also known as *hypoxia*), a seriously reduced supply of oxygen. Anoxia often occurs during birth but may also occur during accidents or as a result of disease or respiratory disorders later in life.

No one can argue against the fact that children's brains can be, and often are, damaged. One can argue, however, that the behavioral manifestations of brain injury cannot be predicted, except within broad limits (Rutter, Graham, & Yule,

1970; Werry, 1979b). Sameroff and Chandler (1975) found little in their review of the literature to support the contention that children who suffered perinatal trauma (including anoxia) but show no obvious brain damage are greater risks for later deviance than children who have not suffered perinatal trauma (see also Koupernik et al., 1975). In fact, the abnormal behavior of children with anoxia or other birth complications appeared to decline with age unless the children were from homes in which child-rearing practices exacerbated behavioral difficulties. Thomas et al. (1968) found in their longitudinal study that one pattern of behavioral dysfunction could not be considered to fit all cases of brain damage. A further finding of Thomas et al. was that in cases in which a child's central nervous system was damaged, parental management and other features of the social environment determined whether or not behavior disorder was manifested (Thomas & Chess, 1975).

Brain damage can run the gamut from massive destruction, resulting in a vegetative state or death, to imperceptible trauma having no discernible effects on behavior or intellectual functioning. Along the continuum of insult from mild to severe are degrees of damage which, depending also on the age of the individual and the locus of the damage, may result in specific leaning disabilities: epilepsy, cerebral palsy, mental retardation, or a variety of other disorders. The diagnosis of brain damage is often difficult. It is an error to assume that suspected damage to the brain can actually be confirmed. As Werry (1979b) has stated, "under the circumstances, the diagnosis of brain damage or dysfunction in the majority of children with behavior disorders is no more than an enlightened guess. Furthermore, even where the diagnosis of brain damage can be firmly established, there is as yet usually no way of proving that it is causally related to the behavior observed" (p. 98).

The brain may function improperly due to accidental physical damage or other causes, such as congenital malformation or biochemical irregularity. Naturally, brain dysfunction *can and often does* produce aberrant behavior. However, it cannot be concluded that disordered behavior necessarily results from brain dysfunction. Many children and adults exhibit disordered behavior in the absence of any other evidence of neurological malfunctioning.

The assumption that behavior disorder implies brain dysfunction has led to much confusion and debate, especially in the case of what has been referred to as "minimal" brain dysfunction (MBD). The term *minimal brain dysfunction* was coined to apply to children who have learning difficulties and exhibit other maladaptive behavior—usually hyperactivity, and sometimes distractibility, perceptual problems, motor awkwardness, or other "soft" neurological signs. Brain dysfunction in these cases is said to be "minimal" because, although it is assumed to exist, it cannot clearly be detected by reliable tests. "Soft" neurological signs are not diagnostic of MBD and not all MBD children show them. The signs include behaviors that are seen in a relatively high proportion of normal children—clumsiness in gross or fine motor movements, abnormal eye movements, frequent tics and grimaces, disturbed body position sense, left-right confusion, awkward gait, poor visual-motor performance, reading disabilities, and so on (Kornetsky, 1975). Thus, the term MBD is ill-defined and represents a presumed etiology.

Even with recent advances in neurology, the assessment of brain dysfunction leaves much room for error and speculation (Werry, 1979b). For example, the electroencephalogram (EEG) is a method of recording the electrical activity of the brain. Its usefulness in diagnosing brain dysfunctions and behavior disorders is often grossly exaggerated (Feuerstein et al., 1979; Freeman, 1967). Koupernik et al. (1975) comment:

> It can sometimes tell us something about disorder of the brain; it cannot tell us about the person's abilities and disabilities . . . . It cannot, except in rare instances, tell us whether a person has a brain lesion or epilepsy but it may tell us what sort of epilepsy he has. (p. 118)

In short, anything less than gross pathology or dysfunction of the central nervous system ordinarily leaves in doubt the etiology of behavior disorder. The lack of knowledge regarding brain dysfunction as a factor in behavior disorders applies to cases of severe and profound disturbances, and to a lesser degree, to mild disorders as well.

Nutritional Errors

The work of Cravioto and his colleagues (Cravioto & DeLicardie, 1975) clearly indicates the devastating effects of severe malnutrition in children, especially young children (see also Garn, 1966). Malnutrition reduces the child's responsiveness to stimulation and produces apathy. The eventual result of serious malnutrition (especially severe protein deficiency) is retardation in brain growth, irreversible brain damage, mental retardation, or some combination of these effects. Apathy, social withdrawal, and school failure are expected long-term outcomes if children are nourished improperly (see Ashem & Jones, 1978; Cravioto, Gaona, & Birch, 1967). Knapczyk (1979) points out that hypoglycemia, vitamin or mineral deficiencies, and allergies can influence behavior and that teachers should be aware of these potential problems.

In recent years, the idea has been advanced that disordered behavior is, in some cases, a direct result of the ingestion of certain foods (for example, wheat flour or fresh fruits) or food additives (for example, colorings or preservatives). Finegold (1975) suggests, for example, that children's hyperactivity often is caused by food additives. One theory is that some dietary substances are toxins (chemicals that cause direct damage to the body). Another idea is that some foods produce an allergic reaction that causes behavior disorders (foods that trigger an immunological reaction). So far, the evidence regarding dietary control of behavior problems is inconclusive (Taylor, 1979). Although some studies have shown a relationship between problem behavior and food coloring (Rose, 1978; Swanson & Kinsbourne, 1980; Weiss, Williams, Margen, Abrams, Caan, Citron, Cox, McKibben, Ogar, & Schulz, 1980) or certain classes of foods (for example, O'Banion, Armstrong, Cummings, & Strange, 1978), others have failed to find any causal connection (Bird, Russo, & Cataldo, 1977; Harley, Matthews, & Eichman, 1978). Recent research strongly suggests that food chemicals do produce a highly reliable, negative behavioral response in *some* children (Rose, 1978; Swanson & Kinsbourne, 1980; Weiss et al., 1980). Research also suggests that food dyes can affect nerve functioning at a molecular level, that is, produce changes in the release of neurotransmitters (Augustine & Levitan, 1980).

Physical Illness and Disability

Obviously, a child who is physically ill is more prone to irritability, withdrawal, or other behavior problems. The result of some diseases (for example, encephalitis) can be permanent damage to the brain. In most cases in which the child's behavior is disordered during a physical illness, the behavior problem is transitory; and residual effect is likely to be a function of solicitous attention by her caretakers during the illness.

Changes in children's behavior may accompany certain physical disorders (Bakwin & Bakwin, 1972), such as rapid or protracted salt depletion, hyperthyroidism, or hypoglycemia (low blood sugar). When appropriate medical treatment or dietary change is provided, the behavior problems ordinarily are resolved.

Children's physical status influences their perceptions and behavior. To the extent that a child is hungry, tired, or uncomfortable, he or she will be more prone to exhibit behavior that adults and other children find irritating and inappropriate.

Physical disability associated with chronic health impairment, crippling, or disfigurement can have a profound effect on a child's psychological functioning, especially during adolescence and early adulthood (Verhaaren & Connor, 1981). In some cases, physical disabilities appear to trigger depression or suicide (Bryan & Herjanic, 1980).

Body Type Conducive to Psychopathology

Folklore has typed the fat person as pleasure seeking and jolly, the thin person as nervous, suspicious, and sickly. Common sense seems to dictate the conclusion that a person's self-perception and behavior will be affected by his/her body type and stature. Observation does indeed tend to bear out the fact that children who are ahead of the norm in physical growth tend also to be ahead in intellectual and behavioral development (Garn, 1966). But marked deviation from the age norm for height and weight can be a deleterious factor in the child's emotional development. There is some evidence to indicate that psychotic children are frequently below the norm in height, weight, and skeletal maturity, though there is no reason to believe that their retardation in growth *causes* psychosis (Dutton, 1964).

A theory of psychopathology that hypothesizes a relationship between body type and behavior has been proposed by Sheldon (Sheldon, 1967; Sheldon, Hartl, & McDermott, 1949). In his writings, Sheldon describes three somatotypes (body builds), each associated with a distinct temperament or behavioral style, each prone to certain types of psychiatric disorders. Although Sheldon's theory provides a way of organizing observations of body types, temperaments, and behavior disorders, there is little or no empirical data showing anything beyond a correlational or associative relationship between body build and psychopathology. Body type cannot be considered to cause behavior disorder, but persons having a certain somatotype are, perhaps, predisposed to exhibit certain behavioral characteristics more often than others. Glueck and Glueck (1950), for example, found that juvenile delinquents most often had a strong, muscular build (Sheldon's "mesomorphic" body type) and there are some data linking a thin, fragile body (Sheldon's "ectomorphic" body type) to schizophrenia (Heston, 1970; Verghese, Large, & Chiu, 1978).

BEHAVIOR DISORDERS WITH SUSPECTED BIOLOGICAL BASES

Hyperactivity and Distractibility

The problems of hyperactivity and distractibility are discussed in detail in Chapter 7. It is sufficient to point out here that "organicity," or, brain damage or brain dysfunction, has historically been the suspected cause of hyperactivity and distractibility in children (Hallahan & Cruickshank, 1973; Hallahan & Kauffman, 1976). Current opinion and theory include suspicion that a variety of biophysical factors are involved, including brain damage or brain dysfunction, heredity, food additives, and other biochemical irregularities. Some proponents of a biological view argue that the prompt therapeutic response of some hyperactive and distractible children to stimulant drugs, massive doses of vitamins ("megavitamin" or "orthomolecular" therapy), or dietary elimination of food additives indicates a biological etiology. However, as mentioned previously, such "evidence" must be evaluated cautiously, and at this time one cannot conclude on the basis of sound data that hyperactivity and distractibility are typically caused by biological factors (Kauffman & Hallahan, 1979; Werry, 1979b).

Childhood Psychosis

In general, there is more evidence for a biological etiology of childhood psychosis than of milder behavior disorders. The same can be said for severe mental retardation and other handicapping conditions—extreme deviation from the norm is more likely to have an identifiable biological cause than less marked or nominal deviation. However, this fact should not lead one to believe that the etiology is known in most cases of childhood psychosis or severe mental retardation. It is unfortunately true that the causes in the vast majority of instances remain a mystery. One is only safe in stating that in a very few cases the cause is obviously brain damage (Bollea, 1969), and that in many cases biological factors are strongly suspected (Werry, 1979a; White, 1974). Several biological elements that are felt to be factors in cases of psychosis are:

1. genetic predisposition
2. developmental lag
3. biochemical irregularity
4. neuropathology

Genetic Predisposition

It has been confirmed that genetic factors contribute to the etiology of schizophrenia. As stated earlier, the closer the genetic relationship of an individual to a schizophrenic, the more likely it is that the individual will become schizophrenic or show schizoid tendencies (Kety, 1976). Figure 5-1 shows the correspondence of the degree of genetic relationship to the incidence of schizophrenia and schizoid behavior. The diagonal line on the graph represents the theoretical (expected) proportion of relatives who would be schizophrenic if schizophrenia were transmitted simply by a dominant gene. Obviously, the transmission of schizophrenia and related behavioral characteristics is not a simple dominant genetic effect; a genetic component is involved, but its mechanism is not presently known and is, likely, very complex. Additionally, other inherited characteristics (body type, intelligence) and the social environment undoubtedly modify the genetic factors that are operative in schizophrenia.

Most of the genetic studies of schizophrenia have involved adults. However, as mentioned previously, schizophrenia may occur in children and there is little or no reason to suspect that bizarre behavior, distorted thinking and perception, and abnormal affect represent a different genetic factor in children than in adults, except, perhaps when the onset of the disorder occurs before the age of 5 years (Fish, 1977; Hanson & Gottesman, 1976; Rutter, 1972).

One indication that infantile autism is a different disorder than schizophrenia is that the incidence of psychosis in the relatives of autistic children is not as high as

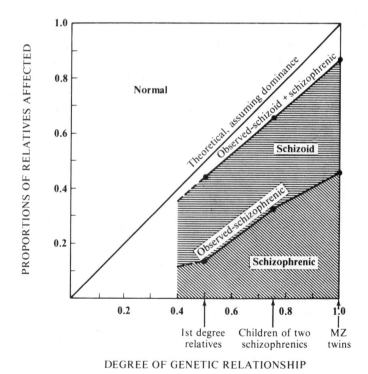

FIGURE 5-1   Observed and expected proportion of schizoids and schizophrenics.

Note. From "The Genetics of Schizophrenic and Schizoid Disease" by L. L. Heston, *Science,* 1970, *167,* 16 January 1970, 253. Copyright 1970 by American Association for the Advancement of Science. Reprinted by permission.

it is in the relatives of children with schizophrenia (Eisenberg & Kanner, 1956; Rutter, 1972; Rutter & Bartak, 1971). It is comparatively unusual for an autistic child to have a close relative who is psychotic (except in the case of identical twins, who have the same genetic makeup). Folstein and Rutter (1977) have found in studies of twins that there appears to be a definite genetic contribution to some cases of autism. However, they caution that environmental factors are implicated as well, even if there is a genetic contribution, and that the specific nature of the heritability factor is unknown.

In summary, it is clear that genetic factors play a role in childhood psychosis and, perhaps, autism. In the case of childhood schizophrenia, Rutter (1972) concludes that "it is equally necessary to note that the mode of inheritance and what is inherited remain unknown. Is it a predisposition in terms of personality traits which is inherited or is it a direct vulnerability to a disease which is handed on genetically? We do not know" (p. 322). A similar conclusion is warranted for nearly all types of severe and profound behavior disorders.

Developmental Lag

Lauretta Bender, for several decades one of the foremost authorities in the field of children's behavior disorders, believes that genetic factors determine a child's vulnerability to childhood psychosis but that the disorder is triggered by a biological crisis, such as perinatal anoxia, severe illness, or accident (Bender, 1956, 1969). According to Bender, the psychotic child is unable to discard the primitive patterns of behavior established during the embryonic stage of development. The child's behavior represents a biological defect that includes failure to develop neurologically beyond the level of an infant in some respects.

Evidence of "pandevelopmental retardation" in childhood psychosis—disruption of maturation in physical growth, gross motor and visual-motor performance, cognitive development, muscle tone, and perhaps other areas of development—is reviewed by Fish (1977). Fish suspects that such pervasive developmental deviations are linked to genetic factors, although environmental conditions can contribute significantly to the outcome. According to Fish, psychotic children and children who will later become psychotic (preschizophrenics) are characterized by integrative disorders of the central nervous system, including periods of disruption in the normal timing, sequence, and organization of development. The neurological defect is not a single, fixed defect but a "disorder of the timing and integration of neurologic maturation" (p. 1303) which can vary in its manifestations and severity. DeMyer (1975) also presents evidence of a developmental lag in the intellectual, language, and perceptual-motor performance of psychotic children. Lovaas, Koegel, and Schreibman (1979) review studies showing that autistic children are developmentally delayed in selective responding to stimuli in the environment.

In summary, evidence to date suggests that psychotic children are in many ways not affected by a mysterious behavioral difference that sets them apart from normal children. Rather, much of the behavior of psychotic children closely resembles the behavior of normal but younger children. It may be that childhood psychosis is most accurately conceptualized as a peculiar, marked, and pervasive developmental delay.

Biochemical Irregularity

It has long been considered that psychotic individuals may be lacking some essential biological substance which is necessary for normal central nervous system function and/or that they may be producing a toxic biochemical which suppresses or destroys the ability of their central nervous systems to function normally. Consequently, the body fluids and neural tissues of psychotic persons have been studied and compared to those of normal persons. Psychotic and retarded individuals have also been administered a wide variety of chemicals in attempts to improve their behavior (Campbell & Small, 1978; Sprague & Ullmann, 1981; Sroufe, 1975).

The results of efforts to find and treat biochemical irregularities related to psychosis and retardation for the most part have been disappointing. It is true that in some cases the troublesome behavior of psychotic and retarded children improves with medication, but cure or even uniform improvement has not been achieved. Missing or toxic biological substances have not been reliably linked to behavioral deficiencies except in a few specific and relatively rare cases (Ritvo, 1977; Werry, 1979a, b; White, 1974).

Neuropathology

Some of the factors already mentioned, such as Bender's and Fish's hypotheses of a maturational lag in childhood schizophrenia, imply some sort of pathological process in the central nervous system. In addition, Goldfarb (1961) speculates that psychoses of childhood may result from either brain damage or psychosocial factors.

Rimland (1964) believes that infantile autism is a neurological defect, probably due to damage to the brain caused by an *excess* of oxygen in infancy. The damage, he speculates, involves a particular part of the brain—the reticular formation in the brainstem that governs the integration of current perceptions with memory and emotion. As a consequence of this damage, the autistic child suffers from a basic cognitive deficiency—inability to relate current to past experience and inability to integrate or attach meaning to sensations. Because there is so little continuity from one experience to the next, the child lives in a world that is always new and frightening. The child cannot establish relationships with people. Hence, the autist develops a pathological insistence on sameness and exhibits stereotyped ritualistic behavior. In spite of brain damage, the constant experience of newness can be attenuated by incessant repetition. Anything that will lessen novelty and increase familiarity will make the child's too-novel world more manageable. In Rimland's opinion, once the autist establishes familiarity with an object or event by repetition, the child reacts negatively to changes in that part of his/her environment. Sameness keeps the child from losing a tenuous contact with reality.

DesLauriers and Carlson (1969) advance a neuropathological theory slightly different from Rimland's. Like Rimland, they propose that the autistic child cannot relate new stimuli to remembered experience. In addition, they believe that the child is developmentally arrested by an "internal stimulus barrier" involving two arousal mechanisms in the brain. Arousal System I, supposedly located in the reticular formation, is thought to be the source of energy for activation of behavior. Arousal System II, supposedly located in the limbic-midbrain, is thought to mediate incentive and reward (i.e., positive reinforcement). In the normal individual these two arousal systems operate reciprocally when learning takes place: Arousal System I first dominates Arousal System II and provides energy (drive) for activating behavior. But once the behavior occurs Arousal System II becomes dominant over and suppresses Arousal System I so that reinforcement and its associated affect will occur. In the autistic, the reciprocation and equilibrium between the arousal systems is destroyed so that the child is driven by System I to behave but is not affected by the consequences (rewards) of his/her behavior because System II is suppressed. Thus they believe that their theory, unlike Rimland's, better accounts for the autistic child's lack of affective attachment as well as ritualistic and self-stimulatory behavior.

> The imbalance is in the direction of sustained ascendancy of System I over System II; i.e., sustained suppression or inhibition of System II by System I. The result of this purported imbalance is a severe disturbance of affect; severe limitation of learning, or ability to establish meaningful associations; and goal-less, aimless, repetitive, and stereotyped behavior, without any apparent adaptive value aside from pure stimulus input. (DesLauriers & Carlson, 1969, p. 64)

The inborn organic deficiency of autistic children can be overcome, DesLauriers and Carlson believe, either by many, many repetitions of learning trials and reinforcement or by presenting a training trial under conditions of very high affective arousal (see DesLauriers, 1978).

Although it seems nearly certain that some kind of neuropathology is involved in most or all cases of childhood psychosis, there is little certainty about the exact nature of the organic problem (Werry, 1979a, b). It is apparent that wherever or however the central nervous systems of such children are damaged or malfunctioning, the results are developmental problems involving language, perception, and attention (cf. Churchill, 1972, 1978; DeMyer, 1975; Hermelin & Frith, 1971; Hingtgen & Bryson, 1972; Ornitz, 1974).

In summary, a strong case can be made for neurological disorder as an underlying cause or contributing factor in childhood psychosis. However, the exact nature of the disorder is unknown. The assumption that brain damage is involved does not imply that medical treatment will be effective, nor does it imply that environmental factors do not contribute to the disorder.

PSYCHOPHYSIOLOGICAL DISORDERS

Physical illnesses or disorders that are believed to be caused by an individual's psychological state are called *psychosomatic* or *psychophysiological* disorders. Investigations of psychophysiological disorders in children have focused on the idea that certain physical illnesses do indeed result from psychopathology. Since the roots of psychological disturbances are usually assumed to grow from the child's early experiences, especially relationships with parents, there has been a focus on parental psychopathology and parental mishandling of developmental tasks (for example, toilet training or separating from mother). As Werry (1979c) observes, psychoanalytic theory has dominated child psychiatry. This circumstance, unfortunately, has led to the acceptance of correlational data as evidence that psychopathology *causes* physical disorders. Experimental data are needed (few such data are available at this time) to show whether or not specific psychological disorders, or psychological stresses in general, cause physical symptoms. It could be, of course, that (a) physical symptoms and psychological disorders are merely coexistent and not causally related at all, (b) physical illness causes psychological stress, or that (c) both physical illness and psychological stress are caused by a third factor or combination of factors.

Psychophysiological disorders involve disruption of normal biological processes: breathing, eating, eliminating, moving, and the like. The following discussion will take an individual look at each of these problems.

Breathing Disorders

Some children have chronic respiratory difficulties that are sufficiently serious to require special medical attention. By far the most common disorder in this category is asthma—"paroxysms of difficulty in breathing, particularly in expiration, resulting from an episodic narrowing of the bronchioles or penultimate fine airways in the lung" (Werry, 1979c, p. 137). Asthma-producing parental behaviors have not been identified, although Purcell, Brady, Chai, Muser, Molk, Gordon, and Means (1969) have shown in their studies that some asthmatic children improved when they were separated from their families. The children who showed improvement were those whose asthma attacks were triggered frequently by emotional reactions. Thus, it may be speculated that for some asthmatic children, inappropriate learning involving emotional responses to family interactions contributes to their attacks. More recent research tends to confirm a relationship between asthma attacks and dependence on the mother as well as anxiety (on the part of the mother or the child) about separation (Purcell, 1973; Williams, 1975).

Eating Disorders

Children may be problem eaters because they eat too much (and consequently become obese), because they eat too little (sometimes so little that their self-imposed starvation—technically known as *anorexia nervosa*[24]—threatens their lives), or because they eat inedible or dangerous material (a behavior known as *pica*). Parents and siblings do, of course, provide models which children may imitate, but the examples set by parents, brothers, and sisters are not sufficient to account for the origin of all children's pathological eating patterns. While it is not clear that reinforcement by the family for inappropriate food-related behavior is the instigating factor in the development of psychophysiological disorders involving eating, research has shown that the principles of learning can be employed by the family and other individuals in order to resolve behavior problems associated with food,

---

[24] Anorexia nervosa is seen primarily in adolescent girls and is frequently accompanied by menstrual disorders, usually amenorrhea (see Halmi, 1974, for further description). Many anorexic children deny that they are emaciated, and it is not unusual for them to express the opinion that they are too fat. Psychoanalytic interpretations usually suggest fear of sexual maturity, association of eating with pregnancy, desire to maintain childlike dependence, fear of cannibalistic impulses, and so on (Lipton et al., 1966; Senn & Solnit, 1968).

including anorexia nervosa (Agras, Barlow, Chapin, Abel, & Leitenberg, 1974; Kellerman, 1977b).

Gastric Disorders and Colitis

Chronic vomiting, peptic ulcers, colitis, and related disorders like the psycho-physiological problems already discussed, have not been demonstrated to result from parental behavior or other family variables. It is known that gastric function can be dramatically affected by emotional experiences, but psychological variables alone do not account for such things as ulcers and irritable colons (Werry, 1979c). It should be noted that gastro-intestinal disorders are subject to change through environmental manipulation (Daniels, 1973; Spergel, 1975).

Elimination Disorders

Incontinence of feces (*encopresis*) and urine (*enuresis*) are the two most frequently mentioned psychophysiological disorders associated with elimination. Chronic constipation (in some extreme cases known as *psychogenic megacolon*, which may result in an enlarged and blocked colon) and chronic diarrhea (which in the extreme can be life-threatening, especially in infancy) are also included in this category. Psychoanalysts have typically had a heyday with cases of the sort involving elimination, interpreting the problem as a rather direct manifestation of underlying personality conflicts arising during the anal stage of development. Toilet training is, obviously, a function parents perform; and it is reasonable to believe that parental mishandling of toilet training is partially responsible for some cases of elimination disorders, especially those cases that do not have an identifiable medical etiology (such as a defective bowel or urinary system). Even here, however, one must make *causal* inferences with caution. One of the strongest indications that deficiencies in parental teaching may be a factor in the etiology of some children's elimination problems is the literature showing that behavior principles (learning theory) can be employed with great success to teach initial toileting behaviors (Madsen, 1965) and therapeutic management by parents of their children's eliminative disturbances (Ayllon, Simon, & Wildman, 1975; Bach & Moylan, 1975; Blechman, 1979).

Movement Disorders

Neither psychoanalytic theory nor behavior principles has led to any firm conclusions regarding the etiology of tics (sudden, repetitive, involuntary movements of certain muscles), stereotyped movements usually referred to as self-stimulation (thumbsucking, hair twirling, hand flapping, headbanging, rocking), or self-injurious behavior (Werry, 1979c). Nevertheless, a behavior modification approach to such problems of stereotyped and self-injurious movement has indicated that they can be ameliorated by the judicious use of reinforcement and punishment (see Johnson & Katz, 1973; Kozloff, 1973; O'Leary & Wilson, 1975).

Skin Disorders

There is no believable evidence that parental behavior or other family interaction variables cause children to have eczema or other skin disorders (Lipton, Steinschneider, & Richmond, 1966). It is noteworthy that Allen and Harris (1966) were able to teach a girl's mother to use behavior modification techniques to decrease excessive scratching, a common problem associated with skin disorders.

Summary. In general, one must conclude that there is little or no sound evidence showing that psychological factors *cause* physiological disorders of any type in children (Hetherington & Martin, 1979; Lipton, et al., 1966; Ross, 1974; Werry, 1979c). In fact, Werry (1979c) concludes that there is little or no evidence that *any* disorders (except perhaps, anorexia nervosa) are truly psychophysiological (that is, physical disorders caused by psychological factors). It is known that physiology plays a part in all behavior (in some behaviors a more prominent part than in others), and that children may be born with a predisposition for certain physiological disorders. It is also known that parental management can change the course of children's psychophysiological disorders once they have been manifested.

SUMMARY AND IMPLICATIONS
FOR SPECIAL EDUCATION

Several biological misfortunes may contribute to the origins of behavior disorders. These biological factors include genetic anomalies, difficult temperament, brain damage or dysfunction, nutritional errors, physical illness and disability, and body types conducive to psychopathology. Certain behavior disorders, especially hyperactivity, distractibility, and childhood psychosis are suspected of having biological bases. In the case of childhood psychosis, genetic predisposition, developmental lag, biochemical irregularity, and neuropathology are thought to be possible contributing factors.

Psychophysiological disorders are, by definition, physical illnesses or disorders that have a *presumed* psychogenic origin. However, no sound evidence exists to indicate that physical illnesses or disorders involving breathing, eating, eliminating, and so on are directly caused by psychological factors, except perhaps, in the case of anorexia nervosa. Behavioral disorders may accompany physical illnesses or disorders, and stress or parental mismanagement may contribute to worsening of physical illness or behavior problems. Appropriate parental management may contribute to the amelioration of behavioral difficulties associated with physical symptoms.

Although there is suggestive evidence, there is no conclusive evidence for a biological etiology of the vast majority of cases of behavior disorders in children. It is quite clear that when biological factors are operative in the causation of behavioral disorders, they do not operate in isolation from or independently of environmental (psychological) forces. The most tenable view at this time is that biological and environmental factors interact with one another in the causation of behavior disorders, and that either biological or environmental variables may be manipulated in order to exacerbate or attenuate many behavioral difficulties. It seems reasonable to postulate a continuum of biological casualty ranging from mild, undetectable organismic faults to profound accidents of nature and a correlated continuum of behavior disorders ranging from mild to profound to which these biological accidents contribute.

As mentioned previously, it is highly inappropriate for special educators to adopt an attitude of blame toward the parents of behavior disordered children. Educators also must not conclude hastily that all behavior disorders have a biological origin and therefore decide erroneously that all such disorders are best handled by medical intervention. Not only is there a tenuous tie between behavior disorders and biological causative factors, but even if a biological cause can be identified in a given instance there may be no direct implications for change in educational methodology. To be sure, special educators should work with other professionals in order to obtain the best possible medical care for the children in their charge. But it must be remembered that

> where the brain lesion or disorder is a nonprogressive one, there is often no advantage in treatment to identifying the cause or the anatomical or physiological disorder. All the child's various abilities and disabilities must be evaluated and then treatment given for his visual, auditory, language, motor, learning, emotional, and social deficits; his pre-, peri-, or postnatal insult is in the past and is untreatable.   (Koupernik et al., 1975, p. 114)

Special educators cannot provide medical intervention and must not allow speculation regarding biological etiologies to excuse them from the task of teaching appropriate behavior to disturbed children.

chapter 6

School Factors

The role of the school in the development of childrens' behavior disorders deserves particularly careful scrutiny by educators. The school environment is the one variable over which teachers have the greatest amount of control. Certainly it is true that outside factors influence children's in-school behavior, and some children present behavior problems at the time of their entry into the educational system. These already behavior disordered children obviate searching for the school's contribution to the emergence of their initial problems, but it is still necessary to examine how the school may worsen or ameliorate existing behavior disorders. Many children do not develop behavior disorders until after they enter school, and for these children one must consider the possibility that the school experience is a primary factor in the origin of their difficulty.

Besides the family, the school is probably the most important socializing influence on the child. For children, success or failure at school is tantamount to success or failure as a person, since school is the occupation of children (and a preoccupation of many). Success at school is of fundamental importance for healthy development and post-school opportunity; therefore the intelligence and academic achievement of disturbed children will be examined in considerable detail.

INTELLIGENCE

As mentioned in Chapter 3, intelligence tests are most reasonably viewed as tests of general learning in areas that are important to academic success. The following discussion should be interpreted with the understanding that IQ refers only to performance on an intelligence test. IQs are moderately good predictors of how children will perform academically and how they will adapt to the demands of everyday life. Furthermore, IQ tests are the best *single* means we now have to measure what we call *intelligence*. Therefore, it is worth considering the IQs of disturbed children even though *intelligence is not reflected only by one's performance on a test*.

Mildly and Moderately Disturbed

Generally, it has been assumed that disturbed children fall within the normal range of intelligence. If the IQ falls below 70, the child is typically, though not always, considered to be mentally retarded. This is true even though behavior problems may be the primary concern. The rationale for considering children with IQs in the retarded range to be something other than MR (that is, ED or LD) is that emotional or perceptual disorders have prevented them from performing up to their "true" capacity.

The average IQ for mildly and moderately disturbed children (those not considered psychotic) is apparently in the low normal range, with dispersion of scores from the educable mentally retarded level to the gifted level. However, Morse, Cutler, and Fink (1964) in their survey of 298 public school classes for the emotionally handicapped, found the distribution of IQ to be negatively skewed. More children were found at the higher levels of intelligence than would be expected in the normal population. The average IQ of the sample of Morse et al. was in the bright normal range with a sizeable proportion of the children scoring in the superior range or above. Still, about 10 percent of the sample scored below 70 IQ. These findings of Morse and his colleagues are at variance with the findings of other investigators who found a positive skew in the distribution of disturbed children's IQ scores. There was a greater frequency at the lower levels of intelligence than expected in the normal population.

In a study of disturbed children excluded from the Los Angeles schools, Lyons and Powers (1963) found that most of the children had IQs in the 70 to 90 range. Stone and Rowley (1964) found that for 116 children referred to a child psychiatry service, the mean IQ was 96.5 (the range of scores was from 62 to 135). Graubard (1964) reported that for the 21 children in his study who had been institutionalized for two to eight years (and all of whom had been adjudicated by the juvenile courts as delinquent or neglected), the average IQ was 92.3 (range = 71 to 108). A study by Motto and Wilkins (1968) provided data that the average IQ for 48 children in a state mental hospital was 94 (range = 72 to 136, with more scores below normal than above).[25] Bower's extensive survey of children in California revealed that the average IQ score was significantly lower for children identified as emotionally handicapped than for the normal children in the same school classes (92.9 compared to 103.2). Bortner and Birch (1969) studied the intellectual performance of 116 brain damaged and 131 emotionally disturbed children enrolled in special schools. These disturbed children were characterized by subnormal intellectual functioning, having a mean IQ of 88. Hallahan, Gajar, and the author conducted a survey of the IQ scores of 376 public school children classified as ED, LD, or EMR. The mean IQ for the 120 ED children was 91 (range = 62 to 137). Finally, the longitudinal work of Rubin and Balow (1978) provides data supporting the notion that the tested intelligence of behavior disordered children is significantly lower than that of normal children. For their sample of nearly 1,400 subjects, the average IQs of children never identified by teachers as behavior problems were 109 and 107 on the Stanford-Binet and Wechsler tests, respectively, but the average scores of children consistently identified as behavior problems (by three or more teachers) were 96 and 92 on these same tests. The average IQ of children inconsistently identified as behavior problems was 102.

Clearly, there has been enough research of the intelligence of disturbed children compared to normal or other groups of exceptional children to draw at least tentative conclusions. Today, the bulk of the current literature reports findings that while the majority of mildly and moderately disturbed children fall only slightly below average in IQ, there are a disproportionate number of disturbed children (in comparison to the normal distribution) representing the dull normal and mildly retarded range of intelligence and relatively few disturbed children in the upper

---

[25] Data regarding samples of children in institutions and special schools are being discussed under the heading of "mildly and moderately disturbed" rather than under the heading "severely and profoundly disturbed" at several places in this chapter in apparent contradiction of some definitions. This reflects not only the limitations of definitions but also lack of specificity in the descriptions of samples in the studies reviewed and extremely hetrogeneous institutional populations. In general, *severely and profoundly* is being used in this chapter to refer to psychotic (e.g., schizophrenic, autistic) children, many of whom are institutionalized, and *mildly and moderately* is being used to designate all other behavior disordered children (e.g., delinquents and neglected, conduct disordered children), some of whom are institutionalized.

ranges of IQ. Coupled with the IQ data obtained from disturbed children, the consistent finding that a lowered IQ is a correlate of school disorder of all types (MR and LD as well as ED) suggests a distribution like the one portrayed in Figure 6–1. The hypothetical curve for the mildly and moderately disturbed (not psychotic) shows a mean of about 90 to 95 IQ with more children falling at the lower IQ levels and fewer at the higher levels than in the normal population. If this hypothetical distribution of intelligence is correct, then one could predict a greater frequency of academic failure and socialization difficulties in mildly and moderately disturbed children on the basis of IQ alone.

Severely and Profoundly Disturbed

It has long been suspected that even though severely and profoundly disturbed children function at a retarded level in most areas of development, they are not *really* retarded. Kanner's (1943) description of early infantile autism strengthens the belief that such children are potentially normal in intelligence. DeMyer (1975) observes that in the case of autistic children:

> The reasons for this belief were the presence of splinter skills, "intelligent" faces, few reports of motor dysfunction, and "refusal" to perform when age-appropriate items from intelligence tests were presented to them. One widely held theory advanced to explain these "facts" was that most if not all autistic . . . children had anatomically normal brains and that relatively high splinter skills were a "true" reflection of their potential intelligence. If the right treatment key could be found, then the seriously delayed verbal intelligence would advance in an accelerated fashion to catch up with the splinter skills and with the norms of the child's chronological age.   (pp. 109–110)

Within the past several years, data have been accumulated to indicate that the IQs of most autistic and other psychotic children can be reliably and validly determined and that the majority of such children score in the moderately to mildly retarded range of intelligence (Bartak & Rutter, 1973; DeMyer, 1975; DeMyer et al., 1974; Lovaas, Koegel, Simmons, & Long, 1973; Rutter & Bartak, 1973). Some psychotic children have IQs in the severely to profoundly retarded range, and a small number achieve normal or above IQs. For example, DeMyer (1975) found the mean IQs for several autistic groups ranging from 29.7 to 61.0 (overall mean for the groups = 44.8); Bartak and Rutter (1973) found average IQs for their autistic groups ranging from 48 to 66. It seems reasonable to hypothesize on the basis of available data that intelligence is distributed among severely and profoundly disturbed children as indicated in Figure 6–1. The average IQ is likely around 50 with the vast majority of scores falling between 25 or 30 and 70 or 75. Although DeMyer (1975) found verbal IQ to be considerably less than performance IQ for autistic children, she saw no significant differences between the verbal scores of autistic and non-psychotic, subnormal comparison children.

It is clear that although severe behavior disorders occur across the entire spectrum of intelligence, they occur most frequently in individuals who are of less than average IQ. Compared to other categories of severely disturbed individuals, autistic children tend to test lowest in intelligence. Severely disturbed children tend to have general intellectual deficiencies, and they often have particular problems dealing

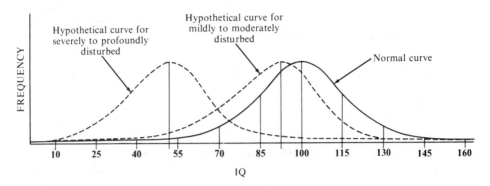

FIGURE 6-1 Hypothetical frequency distributions of IQ for mildly to moderately, and severely to profoundly disturbed compared to a normal frequency distribution.

with tasks that require language or higher cognitive skills. However, the developmental retardation of these children is associated with poorer prognosis (Eggers, 1978), since even with the best behavioral and intervention presently available (Werry, 1979a) it tends to persist over time.

Implications of Low IQ

There is convincing evidence that disturbed children tend to be lower in IQ than normal children and that the more severely disturbed the child, the lower the IQ is likely to be (DeMyer et al., 1974; Lovaas et al., 1973). It would be indefensible to argue that children are disturbed *because* their intelligence is low. The correlation between IQ and level of disturbance does not imply a causal relationship. Moreover, it is well known that IQ can indeed be biased against certain cultural groups or handicapped children. Still, the IQs of disturbed children appear to be the best single predictor of what one can expect in terms of educational achievement and later adjustment. DeMyer (1975) and Rutter and Bartak (1973) report that, in their subjects, IQ at initial evaluation was a good predictor of academic and social skill achievement in autistic children. The predictive power of IQ for less severely disturbed children's academic achievement and future social adjustment is well known (Garmezy, 1974; Robins, 1966, 1974, 1979; Rutter, 1972; White & Charry, 1966). Thus, intelligence may be a causal factor in behavior disorders, and it is connected intimately with school achievement and adaptive behavior.

ACHIEVEMENT

Academic achievement is usually assessed by standardized achievement tests. There is danger in placing too much confidence in such tests, for they are not very accurate measures of academic aptitude, nor are they very precise measures of the academic attainment of the individual handicapped child. Nevertheless, scores on achievement tests do allow comparisons between the performance of normal and disturbed groups, and such comparisons are valuable in assessing and predicting the school success of disturbed children.

Mildly and Moderately Disturbed

One of the earliest studies of the academic achievement of disturbed children (Tamkin, 1960) found no greater academic retardation in a sample of 34 recently institutionalized children than one would expect to find in a normal sample. Tamkin's data from the *Wide Range Achievement Test* show that 32% of his sample were educationally retarded, 27% were achieving at grade level, and 41% were academically advanced beyond their grade level. Arithmetic achievement was found to be significantly lower than reading achievement.

Tamkin's study has been criticized repeatedly, primarily because he used chronological age rather than mental age as the basis for determining achievement expectation. Graubard (1964) notes also that none of the children in Tamkin's sample were considered delinquent or seriously conduct disordered, raising the question of a biased or inadequate sample. The criticism regarding Tamkin's use of chronological age rather than mental age has been raised by those who have found both lower IQ and lower academic achievement in disturbed children (Stone & Rowley, 1964; Graubard, 1964; Motto & Wilkins, 1968). Thus, unless Tamkin's sample was truly unrepresentative of disturbed children, that is, normal or above normal in IQ, his use of mental age would have resulted in findings even more discrepant from those of subsequent studies. That is, to the extent that Tamkin's children were below normal in IQ, their achievement would have been greater relative to mental age than to chronological age, and his sample would have been evaluated as even more academically advanced.

Most of the studies completed subsequent to Tamkin's have shown the majority of disturbed children to be academically retarded. Stone and Rowley (1964) tested 116 children referred for psychiatric services and found that based on chronological age and scores on the *Wide Range Achievement Test*, 59% were academically disabled, 21% were achieving at grade level, and 20% were academically advanced. Judgments of expected achievement based on mental age showed 52% disabled, 19% at grade level, and 29% advanced. Reading achievement was significantly higher than arithmetic achievement. In Stone and Rowley's sample, 48% of the children were in the grades expected for their chronological age, 9% were placed above the expected grade, and 43% (including six children placed in special education classes) were in grades below their expected level. In the Morse et al. (1964) survey of 298 special classes for disturbed children, teachers perceived most of their pupils as being academically retarded, but no test data regarding academic achievement were obtained. When Graubard (1964) based expected achievement on mental age and compared performance of 21 institutionalized disturbed children on the Metropolitan and Stanford Achievement tests, the children were found to be severely disabled in reading and arithmetic. He found no significant difference between reading and arithmetic achievement. In a subsequent study, Graubard (1971) compared reading achievement of 108 disturbed children in special schools to their scores on a behavior problem checklist (Quay & Peterson, 1967). Although the overall results did not indicate any greater reading retardation for the group of disturbed children than one would expect to find in a group of nondisturbed children, he found that the higher the child's score on the conduct disorder dimension of the behavior problem checklist, the greater the child's retardation in reading. The review of Silberberg and Silberberg (1971) indicates that academic failure can be expected in a very high proportion of delinquent (conduct disordered) children.

Congruent with most of the previous findings, Motto and Wilkins (1968) observed uniform academic retardation in arithmetic and reading for 42 of the 48 children in their sample from a state mental hospital population. The children were academically deficient regardless of whether expected achievement level was based on chronological or mental age. Bower (1969) reported several large-scale studies of disturbed children's achievement in arithmetic and reading as compared to the achievement of their normal peers in grades four, five and six. The disturbed children scored significantly below the other children in classes at each grade level. The achievement deficiencies of the disturbed children were greater in arithmetic than in reading, and their deficiencies became more marked with each succeeding grade level. The author and his colleagues, D.P. Hallahan and A. Gajar, recently surveyed the academic achievement of 99 children classified as emotionally disturbed in a public school system in Virginia. Using mental age as the basis for computing expected achievement, the disturbed children were found to be educationally retarded an average of .7 years in reading, 1.6 years in spelling, and 1.7 years in arithmetic (as measured by the *Wide Range Achievement Test*). Finally, Rubin and Balow (1978) found that children identified consistently by teachers as behavior problems scored significantly lower than children identified inconsistently or never identified on tests of achievement in reading, spelling, arithmetic, and language. Furthermore, the consistently identified children were significantly more often retained in grade than were the other children.

There have been few studies of academic failure in disturbed children in school subjects other than reading and arithmetic. Kitano (1959) and Glavin and DeGirolamo (1970), however, found that disturbed children have specific problems in spelling.

Together, the results of research now lead to the conclusion that most mildly and moderately disturbed children are academically deficient even when it is taken into account that their mental ages are typically slightly below those of their chronological age mates. It is not clear whether deficiencies in arithmetic achievement are most likely to be the same as or greater than the deficiencies in reading achievement. Conduct disordered children appear to be more prone to academic failure than withdrawn or personality-problem children.

Severely and Profoundly Disturbed

Compared to their age mates, few severely and profoundly disturbed children are found to be academically competent. Many such children will be functioning at the level where training is most important in self-help skills (i.e., toileting, dressing, feeding, bathing, grooming, etc.), language, and play skills (DeMyer, 1975; Devany, Rincover, & Lovaas, 1981; Lovaas et al., 1973; Rutter & Bartak, 1973). The highly intelligent, academically competent, schizophrenic child is a rarity; most autistic and schizophrenic children will be severely deficient in academic attainment and will require prolonged, directive instruction in a carefully controlled teaching environment if they are to attain functional academic skills (Koegel & Rincover, 1974; Rincover & Koegel, 1977; Rutter & Bartak, 1973)

Implications of Academic Underachievement

Low achievement and behavior disorders (as well as all other school disorders, such as mental retardation and learning disability) go hand in hand. It is not clear, however, whether disordered behavior causes underachievement or vice versa. In some cases the weight of evidence may be more on one side of the issue than the other, but in the majority of instances, the primary causal relationship is quite unclear. As will be discussed further in this chapter, there is reason to believe that underachievement and disordered behavior affect each other reciprocally. Disordered behavior apparently makes academic achievement less likely, and underachievement produces social consequences that are likely to foster inappropriate behavior. In any case, the deleterious consequences of educational failure insofar as future opportunity is concerned are so clear that one must view the augury for disturbed children with alarm.

> Educational attainment and opportunity are linked in many ways. Abundant evidence supports the view that education affects income, occupational choice, social and economic mobility, political participation, social deviance, etc. Indeed, educational attainment is related to opportunity in so many ways that the two terms seem inextricably intertwined in the mind of the layman and in the findings of the social scientist. (Levin, Guthrie, Kleindorfer, & Stout, 1971, p. 14)

BEHAVIOR PREDICTIVE OF ACADEMIC SUCCESS OR FAILURE

Intelligence tests originated early in the twentieth century for the purpose of predicting the academic success or failure of school children. Although IQ is not inerrant, especially in the individual case, it is a fairly accurate predictor of academic success or failure on an actuarial (statistical) basis. In recent years, however, educational researchers have become increasingly interested in delineating the overt classroom behaviors (other than performance on tests) that are associated with academic accomplishment. That is, there has been a search for behavioral characteristics that will improve the prediction of achievement beyond the accuracy attainable with intelligence tests alone. One of the reasons for this interest in behaviors related to achievement is the hope that if such behavioral characteristics can be identified, then it may be possible to improve academic performance by teaching the behaviors associated with it. For example, if attentiveness is found to be positively correlated with achievement, then it might be possible to increase achievement by teaching children to pay "more" or "better" attention. Conversely, if achievement is negatively correlated with certain "dependency" behaviors, then one might be successful in increasing achievement by reducing in frequency the child's dependent characteristics. Implicit here is the assumption that the identified behavioral characteristics have more than a *correlational* relationship to achievement—there is the implicit assumption of a *causal* link by which certain overt behaviors at least partially *determine* achievement.

The causal relationship between overt classroom behavior and academic success or failure is not entirely clear. Although it has most frequently been the strategy of teachers and educational researchers to modify overt behavior in the hope of improving performance on academic tasks, it has recently been suggested that direct modification of academic performance will effectively eliminate certain classroom behavior problems (Ayllon & Roberts, 1974; Kirby & Shields, 1972; see also Hallahan & Kauffman, 1975). It may be that while under some circumstances one may effectively change overt nonacademic behavior by reinforcing academic performance, under other circumstances modification of nonacademic responses is necessary in order to improve academic achievement. Even though more research data are required in order to draw firm conclusions regarding causal relationships, it is now rather clear what types of classroom behavior are correlated with academic success and what types of behavior are inimical to achievement.

Swift and Spivack (Spivack & Swift, 1966; Swift & Spivack, 1968, 1969a, b, 1973) have conducted numerous studies in which teachers rated children's overt classroom behavior. After the teachers' ratings were analyzed along behavioral dimensions, the dimensions or "factors" were correlated with academic achievement. Slightly different rating scales have been used at different grade levels, but essentially the same results have been obtained from kindergarten through high school. In the elementary school, Swift and Spivack (1969b) found poor achievers unable to maintain successful and positive interaction with the learning environment. Instead, the children:

1. engaged in behavior that required teacher intervention and control.
2. were overdependent on the teacher.
3. had difficulty concentrating and paying attention.
4. entered the classroom with fewer ideas and materials than achieving children.
5. became upset under the pressure of academic achievement more often than achieving children.
6. often did "sloppy" work or responded impulsively.
7. frequently became involved in teasing, annoying, or interfering with the work of other children.

At the secondary level, 13 behavioral factors related to achievement were identified. Junior high and senior high school students who were high achievers were found to score high on factors 1 through 5, while low achievers were found to score high on factors 6 through 13. As described by Swift and Spivack (1973; Spivack & Swift, 1977) the factors include the list following.

Factor 1: Reasoning ability. Behaviors in this category include being effective in applying a new principle to an unfamiliar problem; being quick to grasp a new concept presented in class; being effective in making inferences and working out answers when given the facts; and being able to sift out the essential from the unessential in what is read or heard.

Factor 2: Originality. The student exhibiting original behaviors brings up other points of view in class so that they may be discussed; brings things to class that relate to a current topic, comes up with original or unique thoughts which are unusual but relevant; and prepares homework or project assignments in an interesting and original fashion.

Factor 3: Verbal interaction. In this category, the student is assessed as to whether or not questions are asked in order to get more information, raises questions or volunteers information, and participates actively in classroom discussions.

Factor 4: Rapport with teacher. A student considered to have rapport with the teacher engages the teacher in conversation before or after class; is liked by teacher as a person; and is responsive or friendly in a relationship with the teacher in class (versus being cool or detached).

Factor 5: Anxious producer. An anxious producer does more work than he is assigned (carries assignments beyond the minimal requirements); seems overly concerned that he has the correct directions (will check it after class, ask that it be repeated); and is prone to feel he must master all of the details before he is satisfied.

Factor 6: General anxiety. A student exhibiting anxiety is outwardly nervous about taking tests; is openly nervous during class (physically tense, quivering voice, fearful); and flusters, blocks, or becomes ill at ease in verbal expression.

Factor 7: Quiet-withdrawn. The quiet-withdrawn student is very quiet and uncommunicative and responds to questions with monosyllables or gestures; is oblivious to what is going on in class (not "with it") and seems to be in his own private world; is inconspicuous in class; and lacks social interaction with peers in class.

Factor 8: Poor work habits. A student's poor work habits are exhibited by coming in late to class; having poorly organized work; coming to class having lost, forgotten, or misplaced books, pencil, or other class materials; and failing to turn in assignments on time.

Factor 9: Lack of intellectual independence. A student demonstrating . . . lack [of intellectual independence] is likely to quit or give up when something is difficult or demands more than usual effort; relies on the teacher for directions and to be told how to proceed in class; is prone to want the teacher to do all the work for him or make things easy for him; and is swayed by the opinions of his peers in class.

Factor 10: Dogmatic-inflexible. The inflexible student is dogmatic or opinionated in the way he thinks; is prone to want quick black or white answers to questions; and is not receptive to others' opinions (does not listen, interrupts).

Factor 11: Verbal negativism. Behaviors characteristic of this factor are being critical (in a negative way) of peers' opinions, questions, or work in class; speaking disrespectfully to the teacher in class; and criticizing, belittling, or making derogatory remarks concerning the importance of the subject matter of the course.

Factor 12: Disturbance-restlessness. The student fitting in this category acts physically restless in class or is unable to sit still; annoys or interferes with the work of peers in class; has to be reprimanded or controlled by the teacher; and is a compulsive talker.

Factor 13: Expressed inability. The student who expresses inability to cope with achievement demands tells the teacher he is not capable of doing the work expected (underestimates his ability); complains that the work is too hard; and expresses the feeling that too much work has been assigned.   (pp. 393–394)*

---

* Reprinted from "Academic Success and Classroom Behavior in Secondary Schools" by M. S. Swift and G. Spivack by permission of The Council for Exceptional Children, copyright 1973 by The Council for Exceptional Children.

Other researchers (Cobb, 1972; Mckinney, Mason, Perkerson, & Clifford, 1975; Pusser & McCandless, 1974; Samuels & Turnure, 1974) report congruent findings: the child who is inattentive, not task oriented, overdependent, and low in verbal and social-interpersonal skills is most likely to be an academic failure. In severely disturbed (autistic) children, Koegel and Covert (1972) provide experimental evidence that self-stimulation is a type of behavior incompatible with learning. In short, it appears that children who are academic failures are most likely to be children who are easily distracted from academic tasks and have difficulty attending to relevant stimuli. Many underachievers are also social misfits or isolates. The antisocial child is typically a school failure (Robins, 1966, 1974).

Another concomitant of underachievement is impulsivity—the tendency to make quick, erroneous judgments rather than taking the time necessary to reflect on the choices and the task long enough to make a correct response. The reflective versus impulsive child is described by Kagan (1965), and the implications of impulsivity for special education are discussed by Epstein, Hallahan, and Kauffman (1975). If an impulsive "cognitive style" does contribute to school failure, then it will be quite important to find effective means of teaching a more reflective approach to school tasks. Evidence showing that two characteristics—impulsivity and problems in selective attention to relevant stimuli—are closely related (Hallahan, Kauffman, & Ball, 1973), in addition to the literature on training children to be more reflective, suggests that perhaps one needs to teach underachieving children a *strategy* for approaching academic problems rather than just correct responses to specific tasks (Finch & Spirito, 1980; Lloyd, 1980; McKinney & Haskins, 1980).

SCHOOL FAILURE AND LATER ADJUSTMENT

Low IQ and academic failure often foretell difficulty for children. A higher proportion of children with low IQ and achievement will experience adjustment difficulties as adults than will children high in IQ and achievement. Furthermore, a high proportion of antisocial and schizophrenic adults are known to have exhibited low academic achievement as children (Bower, Shellhammer, & Daily, 1960; Robins, 1966; Watt, Stolorow, Lubensky, & McClelland, 1970).

It must be understood, however, that below normal IQ and academic achievement alone do not spell disaster for the child's later adjustment. *Most* mildly retarded children whose IQs are below normal and whose achievement may lag even behind their mental ages do not turn into social misfits, criminals, or institutional residents in adult life. They are considered to be problems only during their school years (Kolstoe, 1975). The same can likely be said of *most* children with learning disabilities, whose academic retardation marks them as school failures. Even among mildly and moderately disturbed children the prognosis is not poor *just* because the child has a low IQ or fails academically.

"Follow-back" studies in which the childhoods of adult psychotics or sociopaths are researched by interviews and examination of the records of schools, clinics, and courts show the adult prognosis for children who exhibited certain characteristics (Bower et al., 1960; Robins, 1966; Watt et al., 1970; see also Garmezy, 1974; Robins, 1974, 1979). In general, these studies revealed that school failure is a part of the pattern identified as "premorbid" (i.e., the pattern predictive of later mental illness, especially in boys). Premorbid girls may be more prone to withdrawal, immaturity, and introversion, whereas premorbid boys may be more likely to show underachievement, negativism, and antisocial behavior (Watt et al., 1970). Aside from maladaptive behavior of some sort, however, low intelligence and achievement are not as highly predictive of disordered behavior in adulthood. School failure, then, cannot be considered by itself to *cause* adult social failure.

When low IQ and academic incompetence are accompanied by serious and persistent "conduct disorder"—antisocial behavior characterized by hostile aggression—the risk for later adjustment is most grave (Robins, 1966, 1979). Even here one must be cautious in drawing causal inferences, but if there is a casual connection between achievement and antisocial behavior, then there are implications for education.

> It is well-known . . . that children with antisocial behavior are usually seriously retarded in academic performance. We do not know at this point whether academic failure usually preceded or followed the onset of the antisocial behavior. If experiencing academic failure contributes to the occurrence of antisocial behavior disorders, then it is clear that preventive efforts should include efforts to forestall failure through programs such as those currently endeavoring to improve the IQs and academic success of disadvantaged children either by educating their parents to stimulate them as infants or through a variety of educationally oriented daycare and preschool programs. No one has yet measured the effect of these programs on behavior disorders.   (Robins, 1974, p. 455)

Summary. Low IQ and school failure alone are not as highly predictive of adult psychopathology as when they are combined with serious conduct problems. The outlook for the child is particularly grim when he or she is at once relatively unintelligent, underachieving, and highly aggressive. If conduct disorders are fostered by school failure, then programs designed to prevent school failure may contribute to the prevention of antisocial behavior.

Intelligence, Achievement, and Antisocial Behavior

Given that antisocial behavior (for example, hostile aggression, theft, incorrigibility, running away from home, truancy, vandalism, sexual misconduct), low intelligence, and low achievement are interrelated in a complex way, it may be important to clarify their apparent interrelationship. Figure 6-2 shows a hypothetical relationship among the three characteristics. The various shaded areas in the diagram should be interpreted as representing the *approximate* proportions in which it is hypothesized that various combinations of the three characteristics occur. As indicated by the diagram, relatively few children exhibiting antisocial behavior are above average in IQ and achievement (Area *A*); most are below average in IQ and achievement (Area *D*) and a few are below average in only IQ (Area *B*) or only achievement (Area *C*). Whereas the majority of underachieving children are low in IQ (areas *D* and *G*), they are usually not antisocial (Area *G* is much larger than Area *D*). Some children are low in IQ but not in achievement (areas *B* and *E*) or vice versa (areas *C* and *F*), but relatively few of these children

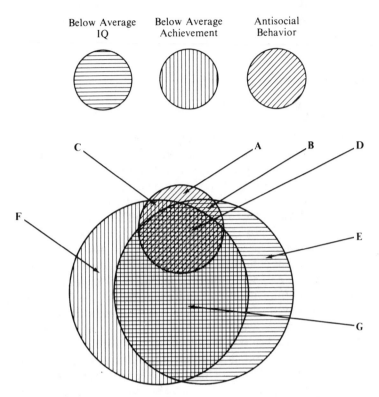

FIGURE 6-2 Hypothetical relationships among below average IQ, below average achievement, and antisocial behavior.

Note. A = antisocial behavior, average or above IQ and achievement
B = antisocial behavior, below average IQ
C = antisocial behavior, below average achievement
D = antisocial behavior, below average IQ and achievement
E = below average IQ
F = below average achievement
G = below average IQ and achievement

are antisocial (Area *E* is much larger than Area *B*, and Area *F* is much larger than Area *C*).

Keep in mind that additional factors enter the picture to determine the adult outcome for children with a given combination of characteristics. The severity of the child's antisocial behavior, the parents' behavior, and perhaps social class will influence whether or not behavioral difficulties will persist into adulthood. To the extent that children exhibit many antisocial behaviors at high frequency, have parents who are themselves antisocial or abusive, and come from a lower social class (which may be determined by their parents' behavior), they have a greater chance of being hospitalized as mentally ill or incarcerated as a criminal when they become adults (Robins, 1979). Also, one must remember that many children who are low in intelligence, low in achievement, antisocial, or some combination of these do not exhibit serious behavior disorders as adults. *Any prediction of adult behavior based on childhood behavioral characteristics is subject to a great amount of error.*

THE SCHOOL'S CONTRIBUTIONS TO BEHAVIOR DISORDERS

We have seen that below average intellectual functioning and below expected academic achievement are characteristics of children with behavior disorder. Combined with serious conduct disorder, low intelligence and achievement are a poor augury for normal adult psychological status. Although school failure is not known to cause behavior disorders, it is a frequent concomitant of maladaptive behavior and a possible contributor to maladjustment. On the other hand, it may be argued that maladaptive behavior makes academic success unlikely and contributes to school failure. One could logically take the position that the school can contribute both to the children's social difficulties and to their academic incompetence.

It seems highly likely that the demands of school and the child's social and academic repertoire affect each other reciprocally. As Glidewell and his associates observe (Glidewell, 1969; Glidewell, Kantor, Smith, & Stringer, 1966), there is a circular reaction between the child and the social structure of the classroom. Children who are healthy, intelligent, upper-middle class, high achieving, high in self-esteem, and adroit in interpersonal skills enter the classroom at a distinct advantage. Such children are likely to make approach responses to others, who are likely to respond positively; and these advantaged children will be sensitive to the responses of others toward them and be able to use their intelligence to further enhance their power and status. Intelligence and achievement beget social acceptability, self-esteem, accurate social perception, and status, all of which in turn induce positive social responses from others and facilitate achievement.

Turning to the other extreme, consider the child who enters the classroom with less vigorous health, with limited intellect, inadequate interpersonal skills, and from the lower classes. He is likely to have a low level of self-esteem and relatively high anxiety. The data indicate that he is likely to initiate interaction with his peers and the teacher with awkwardness, and that he is likely to induce responses which are, at best, a restrained embarrassment, or at worst, hostile ridicule. He is likely to feel humiliated to some degree, and he is likely to respond with some degree of either aggression or withdrawal, or both in alternation. If he responds with aggression, he is likely to promote counteraggression. If he responds with withdrawal, he is likely to promote some sort of passive rejection or counterwithdrawal. It has even been noted (Lippitt and Gold, 1959) that the low-status boys—often aggressive and troublesome—evoke more criticism from the teacher than do their high-status classmates while the low-status girls—often overdependent and passive—receive more support from the teacher. Although the teacher's reaction is understandable, it increases hostility and dependency, respectively. The response of the others—peers or teacher—to this child's interaction attempts are not likely to increase his self-esteem or his interpersonal skills. He is likely to distort his perception of the responses by denial or projection in order to protect whatever limited self-esteem he can marshall in the face of his rejection by others. His utilization of his intelligence is likely to be reduced. Again, a self-sustaining circular process is established. Rejection breeds defensiveness, perceptual distortions, further aggression or withdrawal, and reduction of self-esteem. Further aggression or withdrawal and further counteraggression or passive rejection complete the circle, and symptoms of emotional conflict and disturbance appear.   (Glidewell et al., 1966, p. 248)*

Thus, how the school affects the child's emotional or behavioral development will depend to some extent, at least, on the child's characteristics when entering the education system. The same type of interaction between the child's temperament and the child-rearing techniques of parents appears to occur between the child's temperament or behavioral style and the social and academic demands of the school. The child who is slow to approach others, has irregular work habits, is slow to adapt to new situations, and is predominately negative in mood is most likely to have difficulty in school, though any temperamental characteristic is susceptible to amelioration with proper handling (Glidewell, 1969; Thomas et al., 1968).

The school, like the family and physical status, does not operate unilaterally as a determinant of children's behavioral development. Nevertheless, it is possible to identify classroom conditions and teacher reactions to pupil behavior that make behavioral difficulties more likely to grow. The following discussion will look at five specific (though not mutually exclusive) ways in which the school can contribute to the development of disordered behavior and academic failure. Briefly, these ways are:

1. insensitivity to children's individuality
2. inappropriate expectations
3. inconsistent management
4. instruction in nonfunctional and nonrelevant skills
5. nefarious contingencies of reinforcement

Insensitivity to Children's Individuality

Special educators of all persuasions—psychoanalytic, psychoeducational, humanistic, ecological, and behavioral—recognize the necessity of meeting the *individual* needs of pupils. Some (e.g., Rubin & Balow, 1971) speculate, in fact, that the large proportion of school children identified as having learning and behavior disorders is a reflection of the refusal of the educational system to accommodate individual differences. By making the same academic and behavioral requirements of each child, the school forces many normal children who are only slightly different from most into the role of academic failures or social deviants. Through its inflexibility and stultifying insistence on sameness, the school creates conditions that inhibit or punish the healthy expression of individuality. In an atmosphere of regimentation and repression of individual expression, many children will respond with resentment, hostility, or passive resistance to the "system."

Thus, by squelching individuality and demanding uniformity, the school may contribute to the learning and behavior problems of the very children whose optimum development it is supposed to facilitate. For the child unfortunate enough

* From L. W. Hoffman & M. L. Hoffman (Eds.) *Review of Child Development Research*, Vol. 2, 248. © 1966 Russell Sage Foundation. Reprinted by permission.

to be more than slightly different from the norm in learning or behavior, the message in some classrooms is clear: "To be myself is to be bad, inadequate, or unacceptable." Under such conditions, it is likely that the children's self-perception becomes negative, their perceptions of social situations become distorted, and their intellectual efficiency and motivation decline. The outcome may be that the child becomes caught in a self-perpetuating cycle of conflict and negative influence as described by Long (1974) and Glidewell et al. (1966).

Insensitivity to individuals is not, of course, something that emanates from "the school" as an abstraction: School administrators, classroom teachers, and other pupils are the persons who are sensitive or insensitive to expressions of individuality. School administrators can create a tolerant or a repressive mood in schools—not only in the way they deal with children but also in the way they deal with adults. Teachers are primarily responsible for the classroom emotional climate and for how restrictive or permissive, individualized or regimented the child's school day will be. Children's peers may demand strict conformity regarding dress, speech, or deportment for social acceptance, especially in the higher grades. On the other hand, peers may be an easygoing, open group in which a boy or girl can find acceptance even though he or she is quite different from the group.

Empirical evidence is not abundant that behavior disorders are caused by insensitivity to children's individuality on the part of school administrators, teachers, and peers. Evidence that such insensitivity may be a feature of the school experience of many disturbed children can be readily found. Glidewell et al. (1966) review research in which it was shown that the social structure of the classroom is profoundly affected by teacher behavior. If the teacher delegates power to children and shows acceptance of all children in the class, there tends to be more pupil-to-pupil interaction, less interpersonal conflict and anxiety, and more autonomous work, independent thought, and moral responsibility. Highly rigid, authoritarian teachers who show acceptance of only the children who please them most might be expected, then, to be associated with greater numbers of learning and behavior problems.

The work of Thomas et al. (1968) clearly shows that the growth of behavior disorders is quickened by failure on the part of adults to treat children in accordance with their temperamental individuality. One of the "difficult" children described by Thomas et al. (1968), Richard, was a very persistent child. His case illustrates how the rigidity of the school and the insensitivity of teachers and other children can play a part in creating behavior problems. In the first grade, Richard had temper tantrums (up to 5 per day) and the school was threatening to force the parents to withdraw him unless both they and Richard undertook psychiatric treatment.

vignette

Initially, the tantrums were precipitated whenever Richard objected to stopping what he was doing and moving on to a new activity. As time passed, the number of incidents that would evoke a tantrum increased, especially since the other children had begun to laugh at his crying. Concurrently, he had begun, with much persistence, to ask his teacher that he be taught formal reading. This was not possible inasmuch as the school's educational philosophy emphasized reading readiness procedures in the first grade, and the postponement of instruction in formal reading itself to the second or third grade. (p. 154)

Richard's behavior was much improved when the parents placed him in a different school where he was allowed to spend longer than other children on a given activity (e.g., reading or writing) before shifting to another task and provided more instruction in reading, writing, and arithmetic. During the remainder of the first grade through the third grade, his tantrums did not reoccur because his teachers approved of his persistence in working on his assignments. In the fourth grade, however, his tantrums began again. One of the incidents in his fourth year at school is a particularly clear example of insensitivity on the part of teacher and peers.

Then a poster contest for public school children was announced. The teacher had obtained a specified number of poster papers, selected the children from the class who were to be permitted to enter the contest, and gave them paper. Richard did not get any and, quite innocently, assumed that it would be all right to get his own poster paper. He proceeded to do so and then brought in his finished poster. The teacher interpreted this as insubordination, scolded him for being disobedient, and tore up his poster. The other children laughed, and Richard erupted by flinging his notebook, which hit the teacher on the nose. The teacher reported this to the principal, which made the episode automatically an assault charge with mandatory dismissal of the child. (p. 167)

The foregoing discussion is not intended to be an indictment of all rules, regulations, or demands for conformity in the classroom or school. Certainly, there are rules that must be maintained for the safety and well-being of all. No social institution can exist without some requirements of conformity, and the appeal for tolerance of "individual expression" cannot reasonably be interpreted to mean *anything* should be accepted. Nevertheless, insensitivity to children as individuals and needless repression of their uniqueness clearly can contribute to behavior disorders. Children like "to have a piece of the action," and when they are allowed to participate in self-determination of their lives in the classroom, the results are often improved behavior and academic performance (Lovitt, 1977).

Inappropriate Expectations

Ever since Rosenthal and Jacobson published *Pygmalion in the Classroom* (1968), there has been concern among educators and critics of education that teachers' expectations of children may become "self-fulfilling prophecies." Dunn's now classic article, "Special Education for the Mildly Retarded—Is Much of It Justifiable" (1968), which is a rallying point for those opposed to the use of categorical labels in special education, adds to the concern that children may fail because they are expected to. The assumption has been that a label, such as *retarded*, carries with it an expectation of lower performance. The teacher's lowered expectation for children labeled as *exceptional* (for example, *emotionally disturbed*) will be communicated in subtle ways to them and they will indeed fulfill this expectation. However, it may be too that children's expectations for *themselves* influence their performance (cf. Rappaport & Rappaport, 1975).

While no one has brought forward reliable empirical data indicating that teachers' expectations *in themselves* influence children's behavior, it is plausible that teachers do behave differently toward children depending on their expectations for them. That is, it is not difficult to imagine that if teachers have low expectations for a particular child, then they may treat that child in a different way than they treat another child for whom they have high expectations. The differences in the ways teachers treat the two children may involve types and difficulty of assignments and instructions, frequency of contact, social praise and criticism, responses to questions, evaluation of performance, and other features of teacher behavior. Some of these differences in teacher behavior may be quite subtle and yet be very powerful in their effects on children.

Meichenbaum, Bowers, and Ross (1969) conducted research in which they found evidence that the "teacher expectancy effect" may indeed be associated with changes in teacher behavior. Children for whom teachers were given the expectation that they would be "potential intellectual bloomers" improved significantly more in appropriate classroom behavior and objective measures of academic performance than control students for whom the expectation was not induced. Measurement of the teachers' behavior showed that they behaved differently toward children for whom the higher expectations were created—the teacher significantly increased positive interactions or significantly decreased negative interactions with the "high expectancy" pupils. Meichenbaum et al. (1969) conclude from their data: "It appears one means of modifying behavior of both teachers and pupils is to modify the teacher's perception or label of the students' academic potential" (p. 315).

If the hypothesis regarding the relationship between teacher expectation and teacher behavior is in fact correct, then it will be important to know whether or not labels implying that a child's behavior is deviant carry with them a set of lowered expectations (see Herson, 1974). Studies by Foster, Ysseldyke, and Reese (1975) and Ysseldyke and Foster (1978) provide some evidence that *emotionally disturbed* is a label that may bias teachers toward an expectation of lower than normal academic performance and poorer than normal social adjustment. Foster et al. (1975) found that undergraduate and graduate special education students rated a normal child (shown on video tape in a variety of situations, including testing and free play) lower in behavior and performance if they were told the child was emotionally disturbed than if they were told the child was normal. Ysseldyke and Foster (1978) found the same biasing effect for the label "learning disabled" as for "emotionally disturbed." Admittedly, there is danger in generalizing from the results of these studies, but if it is true that the label *emotionally disturbed* and similar labels do negatively influence teachers' expectations then one might hypothesize the following:

A child is presented to the teacher bearing a deviancy label, and the teacher in turn approaches the child with a mental set based on preconceived expectancies. If the child shows signs of normalcy, these may, to some extent, alter the teacher's preconceived expectancies. This research suggests though that these normal behaviors can be misinterpreted as typical of negatively categorized children. Logic dictates that an experimenter bias affect may then come into play, with the teacher behaving toward the child in ways consistent with the bias. If the child responds to the bias, he may in turn reinforce the teacher's expectancies. (Foster et al., 1975, p. 473)

DeStefano, Gesten, and Cowen (1977) compared primary grade teachers' and school mental health workers' judgments about hypothetical children with specific behavioral characteristics. The teachers viewed children with behavior problems as more difficult and less enjoyable to work with and as having a poorer prognosis. That is, teachers had a more negative impression of working with behavior problem children and saw such children's futures in more negative or pessimistic terms than did mental health workers.

The research and speculation on the effects of teacher bias should not lead one to the conclusion that simply expecting normal behavior will help disturbed children to improve. After all, it is quite clear that most disturbed children *are* lower in tested intelligence, academic achievement, and social adjustment than normal children. Many disturbed children are *very* far below their normal age mates in numerous areas of development, and to expect normal performance from them would be to deny reality. Kirk (1972) forwards the notion that a discrepancy between the child's ability and adults' expectations for his or her performance contributes directly to the development of disordered behavior. For many disturbed children, according to Kirk's thinking, one might surmise that too high rather than too low expectations on the part of the teacher contribute to the problem.

Kirk bases his concept of discrepancy between potential and expectation on his own clinical observations and on extrapolations from experimental research with animals and children. He notes that experimental psychologists have found aggression, regression, and resignation to be frequent outcomes of frustration. That is, in experimental situations where they are extremely frustrated, animals and children may either become aggressive in trying to reach their goal, regress to an immature level of behavior, or simply give up. If the school requires that children perform in ways that they cannot, the children are placed in a highly frustrating situation. Becoming angry and upset, exhibiting silly, irrational, or immature behavior, or simply becoming a truant may be the response of a child who is being frustrated by unreasonable expectations.

If too low expectations are self-fulfilling prophecies and too high expectations are overly frustrating, then one might reasonably ask what expectations can be held for children without running the risk of contributing to the development of disordered behavior. Expectations for *improvement* are always in order. The implication here is that the teacher knows the child's current level of academic performance or adaptive social behavior and can specify a reasonable level of improvement along a measurable dimension. If *reasonable* is defined by the child and teacher together, then the expectation will be neither too low nor too high.

Inconsistent Management

One of the major hypotheses underlying the structured approach to educating disturbed children (Haring & Phillips, 1962; Phillips, 1967) is that a lack of structure or order in the daily lives of such children contributes to their difficulties. When children cannot predict the responses of adults to their behavior they become anxious, confused, and unable to choose appropriate behavioral alternatives. If at one time they are allowed to engage in a certain misbehavior without penalty and at another time they are punished, then the unpredictability of the consequences for their behavior encourages them to act inappropriately. If they cannot depend on favorable consequences following their good behavior, then there is little incentive for them to perform well.

The major support for the contention that inconsistent behavioral management fosters disordered behavior is found in the child development literature (Becker, 1964; Hetherington & Martin, 1979). If one can extrapolate from the findings that inconsistent parental discipline adversely affects children's behavioral development, then it seems highly likely that inconsistent behavior management techniques in the school also will be negative in their effect. Certainly one may surmise at the very least that capricious, inconsistent discipline in the classroom will contribute nothing toward the child's learning of appropriate conduct. If inconsistent management is not clearly at the root of behavior disorders, it does at the least obviously contribute to the perpetuation of behavioral difficulties.

Instruction in Nonfunctional and Nonrelevant Skills

One way for the school to increase the probability that students will misbehave or be truant is to offer instruction for which pupils have no real or imagined use. Not only will such "education" fail to engage the attention of pupils, it will also increase the likelihood of their social maladaptation by wasting their time and substituting worthless information for knowledge that would allow them to pursue rewarding activities.

The question of the *relevance* of education to the child's life has plagued teachers for a long time. The question is more than whether or not the instruction being offered is known by the teacher or other adults to be important for the child's future. In order for the question to be resolved, the *child* must be convinced that the learning he or she is asked to do is now or will be important. It is up to the teacher to convince the child that the instruction is in some way worthwhile. Otherwise the classroom will be merely a place for the child to avoid or disrupt. For some children with a history of school disorder, this convincing will require the provision of "artificial" reasons to learn, such as extrinsic rewards for behavior and performance.

Nefarious Contingencies of Reinforcement

From the viewpoint of behavioral psychology, the school can contribute to the development of behavior disorders in two very obvious ways: by providing reinforcement of inappropriate behavior and by failing to provide reinforcement for desirable behavior. There is a great deal of evidence that appropriate contingencies of reinforcement can be devised in order to remediate disordered behavior. It is reasonable to suspect on the basis of that evidence that inappropriate reinforcement contingencies account for a large proportion of the behavior disorders seen in children in school. (Scientific confirmation of the truth of that suspicion would depend on arranging contingencies of reinforcement to produce disordered behavior in normal children, an experiment not likely to be carried out.)

Many types of reinforcement can be offered in the classroom, ranging from the teacher's praise to tangible reinforcers such as candy, trinkets, or money. Perhaps the reinforcer most endemic to the classroom is the teacher's attention. Time after time, experimental studies have shown that when teacher attention is provided during appropriate child behavior but withheld during undesirable behavior, improvement results (Nelson, 1981; Sherman & Bushell, 1975). For example, Zimmerman and Zimmerman (1962) withheld teacher attention when an institutionalized emotionally disturbed child was throwing temper tantrums but provided attention when he was behaving well. In this way they extinguished his tantrums in a short time.

Hall, Panyon, Rabon, and Broden (1968) conducted an experiment in an inner-city sixth grade classroom (in which the pupils exhibited high rates of disruptive and other nonstudy behavior) that provides a particularly clear illustration of the effects of teacher attention on appropriate behavior. They measured not only the time pupils spent in study behavior during a half-hour period each day but also the attention of the teacher to pupils who were engaged in study behavior during the period. As shown in Figure 6–3, the children spent only about 45% of their time studying, and the teacher seldom attended to studying children during the baseline phase of the study (sessions 1 through 17). During the Reinforcement$_1$ phase, the teacher was told to attend more frequently to studying children, as he did according to the graph for teacher attention to study. During this phase, they received more teacher attention for studying, and the pupils improved markedly in their study behavior. When, for the sake of experimentation, the teacher returned to his baseline mode of operation (i.e., paying little attention to pupils who were studying, as shown in the Reversal phase), study behavior dropped sharply. High rates of studying were then reinstated by returning to the procedure of having the teacher attend to studying children (as shown in the Reinforcement$_2$ phase). Post checks up to five months later showed that the teacher was continuing to attend to studying children and the children were continuing to maintain a high percentage of study behavior.

Copeland, Brown, and Hall (1974) found that having the school principal pay attention to appropriate pupil behavior was an effective means of improving the problem behaviors shown by pupils in an inner-city elementary school. Chronically truant children began attending school more often when the principal came into the classroom and gave them a few words of praise on the days they came to school. Low-achieving students improved their academic performance when they were sent to the principal's office for praise contingent on their achieving specified criteria. Having the principal recognize the improving students and the highest performing students in two classrooms resulted in an increase in achievement of the pupils. By spending only a few minutes each day giving attention to desirable behavior of children, the principal was able to effectively improve children's academic and behavioral characteristics.

In a study with 12 seventh grade boys who exhibited behavior problems, Mar-

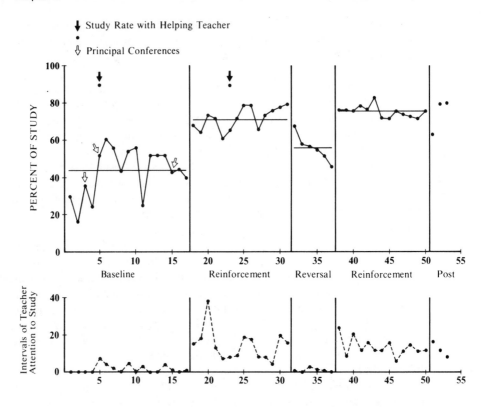

FIGURE 6–3 A record of class study behavior and teacher attention for study behavior during reading period in a sixth grade classroom: Baseline—before experimental procedures; Reinforcement₁—increased teacher attention for study; Reversal—removal of teacher attention for study; Reinforcement₂—return to increased teacher attention for study; Post—follow-up checks up to 20 weeks after termination of experimental procedures.

Note. From "Instructing Beginning Teachers in Reinforcement Procedures Which Improve Classroom Control" by R.V. Hall, M. Panyan, D. Rabon, and M. Broden. *Journal of Applied Behavior Analysis*, 1968, *1*, 317. Copyright 1968 by Society for the Experimental Analysis of Behavior. Reprinted by permission.

lowe, Madsen, Bowen, Reardon, and Logue (1978) found that teacher praise for following classroom rules, especially when combined with token reinforcement (points exchangeable for snacks on Fridays), was effective in reducing rowdiness and off-task behaviors. Increasing positive teacher attention to the desirable behaviors of these boys was more effective by far than a nondirective counseling approach.

In the interactional or transactional model of behavioral influence is found the notion that children and adults exert *reciprocal* influence on each other. It is reasonable to believe that teachers' and problem students' mutual praise and criticism become important factors in the maintenance of behavior, and that mutual hostility could be defused beginning with either teacher *or* pupil. Polirstok and

Greer (1977) trained an eighth grade girl who was frequently verbally abusive (and who received primarily disapproving, critical comments from her teachers) to increase her approving, complimentary comments to her teachers. In response to what they described as her "remarkable socialization" and new-found "maturity," her teachers reversed their tendency to interact with her in a predominantly negative way. Thus it is illustrated that nefarious contingencies of reinforcement are not a one-sided factor in classroom disharmony but an influence on both teacher and student conduct. In the typical educational setting, however, it is to be expected that the teacher will have the responsibility for making the first move toward providing positive consequences for desirable behavior.

Summary. There is a tremendous weight of empirical evidence showing that children's classroom behavior can be altered by manipulating the contingencies of reinforcement, even when the reinforcement is so natural a part of the classroom as teacher attention. It takes no great backlog of classroom observation nor any great acumen to see the potential implications of this evidence for discussion of the school's contributions to the development of behavior disorders. Children whose behavior is a problem often receive a bonanza of attention for misbehavior while receiving little or no attention for appropriate conduct. Even though the attention they receive for misbehavior is often criticism or punishment, it is still attention and is quite likely reinforcing for whatever they are doing. The effect of attention for misbehavior and nonattention for good deportment is likely to be perpetuation of the miscreant's deeds, regardless of the *intentions* of the teacher or other adult.

SUMMARY AND IMPLICATIONS
FOR SPECIAL EDUCATION

There are convincing data to indicate that, as a group, disturbed children score lower than normal children on intelligence tests and that they are academic underachievers compared to children of the same mental age. The behavior exhibited by disturbed children is inimical to academic learning. It is not clear that low academic achievement and low intelligence cause emotional disturbances; nor is it clear that disordered behavior causes low intelligence and achievement. Disordered behavior and underachievement may influence each other reciprocally. Academic failure and low intelligence, when combined with serious antisocial conduct disorders, portend social adjustment problems in adulthood. The school may contribute to the development of behavior disorders in children in several ways:

1. School administrators, teachers, and other pupils may be insensitive to the child's individuality.
2. Teachers may hold inappropriate expectations for children.
3. Teachers may be inconsistent in managing children's behavior.
4. Instruction may be offered in nonfunctional (i.e., irrelevant) skills.
5. Inappropriate contingencies of reinforcement may be arranged by school personnel.

The teacher of the disturbed must be prepared to work with children who are usually intellectually and academically deficient as well as deviant in their social behavior, although some disturbed children are superior intellectually and academically. Teaching the disturbed demands not only the ability to instruct children with an extremely wide range of intellectual and academic levels but also the ability to teach social and other nonacademic behaviors (for example, good work habits, attention strategies, independence) that make scholastic success possible. The most crucial tasks of the teacher as a preventative agent are to foster academic success and lessen the child's antisocial conduct. Academic failure and antisocial behavior predict limited future opportunities and probable future maladjustment.

Although we have discussed how disorders are affected by the family (Chapter 4), by biology (Chapter 5), and by the school, the answer to the question "Why did this child become emotionally disturbed?" is, in most cases, "No one knows." However, one can identify conditions in the child's family, biology, and school experiences that contribute positively or negatively to the ongoing development of the child. Pinpointing exactly the etiology of a behavior disorder is not usually necessary in order to provide effective intervention. Even in the few cases where the cause is unmistakable, it is usually true that nothing can be done to remove the causal factor (e.g., an abused child cannot relive earlier years, and brain damage cannot be repaired).

The most valuable perspective for the teacher is to examine the present environment of the child in order to detect those factors that contribute to disordered behavior and those that encourage healthy behavioral development. It is the teacher's primary task to modulate the school environment in ways that will contribute to desirable behavioral and academic growth.

part three

Four Facets of Disordered Behavior

chapter 7 _____

Hyperactivity, Distractibility, and Impulsivity

In Chapter 1 it was stated that disturbed children induce negative feelings and behaviors in others. Among the many ways disturbed children have of bothering or irritating others are hyperactivity, distractibility, and impulsivity—moving about too much, failing to pay proper attention, and acting without thinking. Extremely hyperactive, distractible, and impulsive children may upset their parents because they are difficult to live with at home. In school, too, such children are typically unpopular. Incessant movement, impulsiveness, noisiness, irritability, destructiveness, unpredictability, flightiness, and other similar characteristics of exceptional children are not endearing to anyone—parents, siblings, teachers, and schoolmates included.

Hyperactivity, distractibility, and impulsivity are particularly unpleasant child characteristics for parents and teachers because they entail serious problems in behavior management.

> It is not unusual for the parent to relate numerous incidents from early childhood which depict a child as an exceedingly rambunctious "pest," always into places where he should not be. This very same child, when confronted with the demands of the school situation, can quickly become a nightmare for even the best of teachers who have not had the background necessary to cope with distractible and hyperactive children. It takes only one of these children to create chaos. (Hallahan & Kauffman, 1976, p. 150).

The developmental aspects of hyperactivity, distractibility, and impulsivity are important to recognize. A high level of seemingly undirected activity, short attention span, and impulsive behavior are frequently observed in normal young children. As normal children grow older, they gradually become better able to direct their activity into socially constructive channels, to attend for longer periods and with greater efficiency, and to consider alternatives before responding. Thus, it is only when motoric activity, attentional skills, and impulse control are markedly discrepant from that expected for children of a particular age that the child's behavior is considered to require intervention. Besides age, sex of the child may be an important developmental factor in these characteristics. Boys are far more frequently referred for problems of hyperactivity, distractibility, and impulsivity than are girls. Sociocultural differences also appear to be related to these problems, since hyperactive, distractible, and impulsive children appear to be seen more often in lower-income or "culturally disadvantaged" groups.

The characteristics of hyperactivity, distractibility, and impulsivity were brought to the attention of special educators in the 1940s by Heinz Werner, a developmental psychologist, and Alfred A. Strauss, a neuropsychiatrist.[26] Both Werner and Strauss emigrated to the United States after Hitler's rise to power in Germany. At the Wayne County Training School in Northville, Michigan, and the Cove schools in Racine, Wisconsin, these men, their colleagues, and their students pioneered in the assessment and education of retarded children who were presumed, because of their behavioral characteristics, to be brain damaged. Their work with mentally retarded children led eventually to concepts forming a foundation for the field of "learning disabilities" (Hallahan & Kauffman, 1976). Werner and Strauss described in considerable detail the characteristics of "brain-

---

[26] For further discussion of the history of hyperactivity see Ross and Ross (1976).

injured" children, many of whom today might be labeled *emotionally disturbed, learning disabled,* or *mentally retarded.* Included among the behavior disorders they describe in these children are hyperactivity, distractibility, and impulsivity. Their descriptions of "brain-damaged" children are of historical and contemporary importance for the following reasons:

1. They tie together conceptually a cluster of related characteristics, specifically perceptual problems, problems of attention, and excessive motility, which today's research has not yet unraveled.

2. They imply that hyperactivity, distractibility, and impulsivity are *caused* by brain pathology, an idea that still has many proponents.

3. They describe characteristics that are now known to apply to several categories of exceptional children, most notably the learning disabled, emotionally disturbed, and educable mentally retarded.

Strauss, along with Laura Lehtinen, described the classroom behavior of children with these problems in the classic volume *Psychopathology and Education of the Brain-Injured Child* (Strauss & Lehtinen, 1947). Strauss and Lehtinen note that many of the children with whom they worked would be considered hyper-aggressive or antisocial due to their extreme disinhibition as well as overmotility and disordered attention. They describe these children as victims of brain pathology that prevents normal and effective deployment of attention.

The brain-damaged organism, as we know, is abnormally responsive to the stimuli of the environment, reacting unselectively, passively, and without conscious intent. When such a hypervigilant organism—one whose reactibility is beyond his own control —is placed in a situation of constant and widespread stimulation, he can only meet the situation with persistent undirected response. The brain-injured child is therefore the focus of the teacher's permanent reminders to "tend to his own work." He pivots in his seat to watch the activity of the children sitting near him. His attention is caught and held by any child who leaves his place. Any noise may cause him to attend; any motion seemingly insignificant may attract him. The teacher will repeatedly find him gazing at pictures and decorations while the lesson is neglected on his desk.

He presents a picture of a child who is extremely mobile in attention and activity, unduly attracted by the doings of others or by the presence of normally inconspicuous background stimuli, inconstant and variable in interests, lacking persistence and sustained effort.

While the distractibility of most brain-injured children is observable in their psychomotor behavior, there are a few children in whom this symptom is not obvious. Such a child is equally handicapped in a learning situation. He is the one who sits quietly at his desk, apparently absorbed in work; at the end of the period his lesson is uncompleted; he is adjudged lazy or a daydreamer. Close observation reveals that a brain-injured child of this type is constantly at the mercy of stimulus details provided by the pictures and page numbers in his book, by flaws and marks on the paper, or by any features of the material which are, for the normal person, additional or irrelevant; he wanders away from his intended goal under the influence of the shifting and uncontrolled associations of his own thoughts. This child is described as inattentive, and certainly with respect to the purposes of the teacher or other members of the class he is. From the child's point of view, however, his seeming inattentiveness is the expression of an abnormally attentive condition. The countless irrelevant stimuli which the normal child disregards the brain-injured child is unable to withstand.   (pp. 129–130)*

For more than three decades, then, it has been known that some exceptional children exhibit a cluster of interrelated behaviors:

1. excessive motor activity of an inappropriate nature, often referred to as *hyperactivity* or *hyperkinesis*
2. inability to selectively attend to the appropriate or relevant stimuli in a given situation, or overselectivity of attention to irrelevant stimuli, often referred to as *distractibility*
3. disinhibition or a tendency to respond to stimuli quickly and without considering alternatives, often referred to as *impulsivity*

Over the years these characteristics (sometimes considered to be a part of the "Strauss syndrome," after A. A. Strauss) have been noted to occur frequently in ED, LD, and MR populations (Campbell, 1974). The description and research of these characteristics have been particularly important for special educators because they consist of behaviors that appear to preclude good social adaptation and school achievement.

A hyperactive child may be impulsive or distractible. That is, many children described by clinicians as hyperactive are also described as impulsive and distractible. Yet there is relatively little empirical research indicating the extent to which hyperactivity, distractibility, and impulsivity are intercorrelated. The important point to consider here is that hyperactivity, distractibility, and impulsivity are behavioral characteristics that according to clinical judgments can, and very often do, occur together.

HYPERACTIVITY

Definition and Measurement

One of the ironies about hyperactivity in children is that although frequently talked and written about, it is still very imprecisely defined (Ross & Ross, 1976). Part of the problem in defining *hyperactivity* is the difficulty in measuring it. Measurement of children's motoric activity can be accomplished at this time in one of two ways: direct observation, or the use of mechanical devices attached to the child's body. Direct observation requires many hours of work and is susceptible to errror and unreliability (Evans & Nelson, 1977; O'Leary & Johnson, 1979). Mechanical devices are expensive, and susceptible to failure (Schulman, Stevens, & Kupst, 1977). Both direct observation and mechanical devices carry with them the danger of the child's reaction to measurement (that is, the possibility that children will behave differently while their behavior is being recorded than while they are not being observed or recorded). The problem of reaction might in time be overcome

---

* From *Psychopathology and Education of the Brain-Injured Child* by A. A. Strauss and L. L. Lehtinen-Rogan, 1947, p. 129 130. Copyright 1947 by Grune & Stratton. Reprinted by permission.

because the child adapts to the presence of an observer or becomes accustomed to having the mechanical gadget attached to his/her body. Even so, one can not blindly assume that the measures obtained are truly representative of children's behavior when they are *not* being observed.

Hyperactivity is sometimes measured with behavior rating scales. The best known of these scales are the Teacher Questionnaire (TQ) and the Parent Questionnaire (PQ) developed by C. Keith Conners (1969, 1973). The TQ and PQ were devised for the purpose of measuring children's responses to drugs, but they have also been used frequently to choose samples of hyperactive children for research studies and to measure the responses of hyperactive children to other than medical interventions. As Conners and Werry (1979) point out, such scales can yield reliable and useful data even though they are not direct counts of the child's responses; rating scales "are, in essence, algebraic summations, over variable periods of time and numbers of social situations, of many discrete observations by parents, teachers, or other caretakers in which an unconscious data reduction process operates to produce a global score or frequency estimate" (p. 341).

Granting that direct and reliable measurement of a child's actual behavior can be had, however, there remains the problem of judging whether or not it represents activity that is *hyper*. Although there are comparative data for various populations on Conners' TQ and PQ, there are no real norms and very few data of any kind to which the child's *amount of activity* can be compared. Ultimately, judgment that the child is hyperactive or hyperkinetic is made on a subjective basis—the parent, teacher, doctor, or psychologist believes that the child is too active for his or her age and circumstance (Koupernik et al., 1975, p. 120). Very often, the observer's judgment is affected by more than just the child's excessive movement. Stewart (1970) expresses the majority view succinctly.

> Fidgeting in itself is hardly an unusual or alarming behavior in children, but it is a matter for concern when it is accompanied by a cluster of other symptoms that characterize what is known as the *hyperactive-child syndrome*. Typically a child with this syndrome is continually in motion, cannot concentrate for more than a moment, acts and speaks on impulse, is impatient and easily upset. At home he is constantly in trouble because of his restlessness, noisiness, and disobedience. In school he is readily distracted, rarely finishes his work, tends to clown and talk out of turn in class and becomes labeled a discipline problem.   (p. 94)

In one of Stewart's studies (Stewart, Pitts, Braig, & Dieruf, 1966), the mothers of 37 "hyperactive" and a similar number of nonhyperactive control group children were interviewed. Figure 7–1 shows the percentage of problems reported for each group. Although one third of the control children were reported by their mothers to be *over*active, it is quite clear that the "*hyper*active" children were characterized by a multiplicity of problems to a much greater extent than the control children.

In actuality then, hyperactivity is not defined by high activity alone. Moreover, if some children with the "hyperactivity syndrome" lose their overactivity but retain other related characteristics as they grow older, yet are still said to show the syndrome (as reported, for example, by Weiss, Minde, Werry, Douglas, & Nemeth, 1971), one is hard pressed to define what is meant by the term *hyperactivity* (Koupernik et al., 1975). Keogh (1971) points out that "Despite clinical observations of the increased quantity and speed of motoric action, there is only

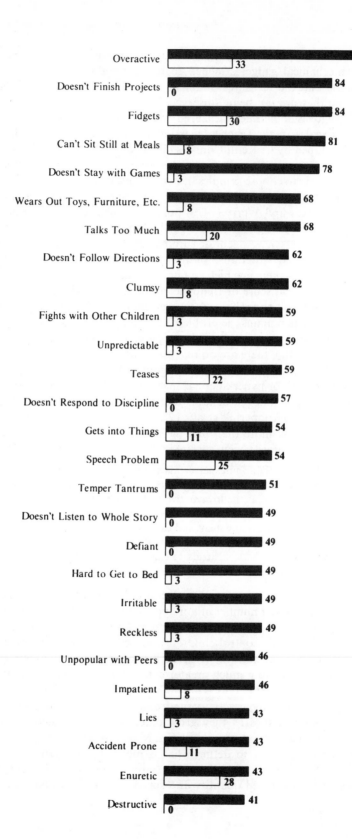

FIGURE 7–1 Symptoms of hyperactivity in hyperactive (solid bar) and nonhyperactive (open bar) children.

limited evidence to document quantitative differences in activity levels of hyperactive and normal children" (p. 101). The more recent review by Ross and Ross (1976) leads to essentially the same conclusion. Some children have very high activity levels but are socially well adapted and high achieving. These highly active children are not likely to be considered hyperactive but are apt to be labeled energetic, enthusiastic, hard working, or brilliant. The socially inappropriate character of the hyperactive child's behavior and the presence of other undesirable behavioral characteristics in addition to overactivity seem to be implicit in the definition of *hyperactivity*.

Among the characteristics associated with hyperactivity are below average performance on intelligence tests and learning difficulties (Loney, 1974; Minde, Lewin, Weiss, Lavigueur, Douglas, & Sykes, 1971; Palkes & Stewart, 1972). Ross and Ross (1976) comment that research suggests "a downward spiral in the academic facets of the hyperactive child's school performance" (p. 46). Hyperactivity probably interferes with school achievement, and lack of achievement, feelings of failure, and low motivation set the stage for high rates of socially inappropriate behavior. Thus the child is caught in a self-perpetuating negative interaction between hyperactive behavior and school failure.

Hyperactive children affront and disappoint adults by their seemingly ceaseless and irritating movement. But it is not only adults who find hyperactivity an undesirable characteristic. Typically, hyperactive children do not get along well with their peers. They are aware that they have socialization problems, and so are their parents and other children (Campbell & Paulauskas, 1979).

Hyperactivity does not seem to just disappear with maturation. Unless effective methods of intervention are found, the young child who is hyperactive today stands a good chance of being hyperactive and/or having serious social and academic problems several years hence (Campbell, Schleifer, & Weiss, 1978). Furthermore, hyperactivity and its negative concomitant characteristics (for example, poor cognitive, academic, and social skills) appear to persist into adolescence and adulthood (Hoy, Weiss, Minde, & Cohen, 1978; Ross & Ross, 1976).

Etiology

As mentioned previously, there has been for many years a presumed link between hyperactivity and brain damage or brain dysfunction. Careful examination of the research literature on the topic, however, can only lead to the conclusion that "Hyperactivity and cerebral dysfunction are neither synonymous nor mutually exclusive" (Keogh, 1971, p. 102). Some hyperactive children show definite "hard" clinical signs of brain damage, but many do not; and some children showing "hard" neurological signs are not hyperactive (Hertzig, Bortner, & Birch, 1969). Not only is the definition of hyperactivity vague, but also the pathogenic mechanism responsible for its appearance is obscure. The link between hyperactivity and brain damage—indeed the link between brain damage and any specific behavior disorder—is so weak that the educational usefulness of the concept of brain damage is questionable. The term *minimal brain dysfunction* has no substantial referents, and it is of no value to educators or psychologists (Kauffman & Hallahan, 1979).

Koupernik et al. (1975) point out that high activity levels are common in children under a variety of circumstances including:

1. normal two- and three-year old children
2. older children with mental ages of two or three years
3. very intelligent children who are highly exploratory
4. children being nagged by parents or teachers
5. anxious or depressed children
6. environmentally deprived children
7. some autistic children
8. some epileptic children

The observations of Koupernik and his colleagues highlight the multifactored nature of high activity levels and indicate that the characteristics known as *hyperactivity* probably have multiple origins. There are a great many events that may cause brain damage (for example, oxygen deprivation, physical insult, lead poisoning), and many of the circumstances surrounding *possible* brain trauma are unfavorable for the child's development. Such circumstances include poor prenatal nutrition and care of the mother, poverty, maternal smoking and drinking, chaotic or abusive home environment.

Brain damage or brain dysfunction has been the most common hypothesis about the cause of hyperactivity, but several others have been suggested as well. Some of these hypotheses point to biological factors other than brain damage; others point to psychological causes that are nonbiological, environmental factors.

One of the alternative biological explanations is that hyperactivity is inherited. Research to date offers no reliable evidence that hyperactivity is genetically transmitted, although it is plausible that genetic factors *may* give some children a predisposition to learn hyperactive behavior or *may* be one of several biological factors that, in combination with other physiological characteristics or environmental stress, lead to hyperactivity (McMahon, 1980; Ross & Ross, 1976). Another hypothesis involves food additives or food allergies (see Chapter 5). If one is willing to trust nonexperimental case studies and testimonies, there is reason to believe that food additives are *often* at fault in hyperactivity. If, on the other hand, one wants to rely on replicable data from carefully controlled experiments that make it possible to eliminate alternative explanations, then there is some scant evidence that food additives can in *some* cases be a cause of hyperactivity (Harley et al., 1978; Rose, 1978; Ross & Ross; 1976, Swanson & Kinsbourne, 1980; Taylor, 1979; Weiss et al., 1980). In short, evidence does not clearly link any particular biological factor to hyperactivity, although biological causes may well be involved in many cases.

Hypothesized psychological causes of hyperactivity range from psychoanalytic explanations to those involving social learning theory. One idea is that hyperactive children are understimulated, and their hyperactive behavior is an attempt to optimize their sensory stimulation (Zentall, 1975, 1979). There is some indication, including some psychophysiological data, that this hypothesis *may* be correct for *some* children (Hastings & Barkley, 1978). For the majority of hyperactive children, other psychological causes are more plausible and are supported by more data. The literature contains numerous studies of modeling and imitation illustrating how hyperactive behavior could be acquired by children through observation of frenetically active parents or siblings. The literature is also replete with examples of how children's inappropriate behavior can be manipulated by social attention, suggesting that hyperactivity may be taught inadvertently by parents and teachers (see Ayllon & Rosenbaum, 1977; Kazdin, 1980; Ross & Ross, 1976; Sulzer-Azaroff & Mayer, 1977). Nevertheless, it has *not* been demonstrated that hyperactivity is simply a matter of undesirable social learning.

To summarize, no one really knows at this time *why* children become hyperactive. More is known about how to control hyperactivity once it is evidenced than is known about its origins. It is likely a result of multiple causes.

Methods of Controlling Hyperactivity

Because hyperactivity often involves a cluster of related characteristics, including distractibility and impulsivity, many control techniques are designed to manage more than a high level of motoric activity. These techniques include medication, dietary restriction, behavior modification, structured environment, self-instruction, modeling, and biofeedback. The discussion here will focus primarily on the techniques' usefulness in controlling excessive motoric activity, some of which may represent impulsive responding to irrelevant or distracting stimuli.

Medication

Perhaps the most widespread notion about how hyperactivity can be controlled is that drugs can be used to "slow children down." It is not uncommon to hear lay persons as well as professionals in education, psychology, and medicine suggest that a child should be medicated if he or she is seriously and chronically disturbing to others. Many physicians obviously are open to the suggestion that prescription of drugs in such cases is warranted if they are not themselves advocates of the use of medication, for it is estimated that hundreds of thousands of children are being treated with drugs (Stroufe, 1975). In most cases, hyperactive children are placed on *stimulant* drugs such as methylphenidate (Ritalin) or dextroamphetamine (Dexedrine).

There are those who question the use of medication with hyperactive children, at least on the scale that it has been used in recent years. In fact, argument on both sides of the issue of drugs has become quite heated.

> The volatile nature of the debate over the use of drugs makes it imperative that knowledgeable teachers be aware of the issues. At this point, there is no single piece of advice on this matter that will give them a clear-cut idea of where to stand on the issue. It *is* important that teachers be aware of the *potential* power and danger of drugs and that they leave final decisions on these matters to qualified physicians.   (Hallahan & Kauffman, 1976, p. 176)

One of the strongest advocates of medicating hyperactive children is Wender (1971), who suggests that perhaps all children with suspected "minimal brain dysfunction" (which he defines quite broadly) should be given medication on at least a trial basis. Wender believes that *not* medicating children with suspected brain dysfunction may constitute medical malpractice and that it may be appropriate to continue drug treatment through the adolescent years if the child continues to have problems. Considerably more cautious views have been expressed by others. In 1971, a government sponsored panel of experts submitted a *Report of the Conference on the Use of Stimulant Drugs in the Treatment of Behaviorally Disturbed Young School Children* (see Hallahan & Kauffman, 1976, pp. 174-175). The panel reached several conclusions, including: physicians should carefully monitor dosage and side effects; drugs prescribed for young children do not necessarily lead to later drug abuse; common sense precautions should be taken, including adult administration and keeping the drugs in a safe place at home; school personnel should not coerce parents into requesting drugs for their children; pharmaceutical companies should engage only in ethical advertising through medical channels; more research is needed.

Reviews of research on the use of medication with behavior disordered children have indicated the need for more definitive data regarding the effects and side effects of drugs (Ross & Ross, 1976). Kornetsky (1975) and Sroufe (1975) urge caution in prescribing drugs, especially when alternative methods of managing disturbing behavior are available.

Sroufe (1975) is a particularly outspoken and incisive critic of careless drug treatment. His thorough and thoughtful review includes the following major points:

1. Studies of drug effects have been almost exclusively short-term assays. Practically nothing is known about the long-term effects of drugs on children's behavior.

2. Even the short-term physical side effects of drugs (e.g., loss of appetite, insomnia) have been inadequately researched. There are no research data on the possible long-term physical side effects (e.g., effects on linear growth or weight gain).

3. Little or nothing is known about the effects of drugs on conceptual abilities.

4. How particular types of children will respond to specific medications cannot be predicted with much accuracy or confidence.

5. Placebo effects (i.e., effects attributable to the fact that the child is receiving a "pill" of some kind, whether it contains the active drug ingredient or not) have not been adequately researched. The expectation set for the child when he is given the drug and the environment in which the child lives during drug treatment may have a profound effect on the outcome.

6. Behavior modification or educational intervention may often obviate the need for drugs or considerably reduce disruptive behavior. At present there is little evidence that medication is superior to behavior modification or tutoring or that drugs enhance the effects of other methods of behavioral control. Drug effects must be considered within the context of reinforcement and other environmental manipulations.

7. More research is needed to assess the possible relationship between medication prescribed for the control of young children's behavior and later drug

abuse or the availability of drugs to individuals for whom they are not intended.

8. Drug treatment may offer so facile a "solution" to behavioral difficulties that improvement of the child's home or school environment is overlooked. Drugs may be used as an excuse for avoiding professional commitment to the needs of children.

The issues involving the use of drugs to control hyperactivity are not simple, nor are they resolvable without data which must be obtained over a period of several years. Only future research by the medical profession and allied disciplines can answer questions of the value of medications and the dangers inherent in their use (see also Conners & Werry, 1979; Gadow, 1979; Sprague & Ullmann, 1981). As Ross and Ross (1976) point out, drug treatment need not be the *exclusive* intervention in hyperactivity; in some cases dietary restrictions (and others discussed below) are used as well.

Dietary Restriction

As mentioned in the discussion of etiology of hyperactivity, some individuals have guessed that certain food substances are the cause of the problem. For example, Finegold (1975, 1976) has expressed the belief that artificial colors and flavors in processed foods and some natural chemicals in certain foods cause many children to be hyperactive. Since he believes that even minute amounts of these chemicals can trigger the physiological mechanism that makes the child hyperactive, effective treatment entails careful elimination of these substances in the diet. Finegold's "K-P" diet requires elimination of a wide variety of foods, including all foods containing artificial colors or flavors and all foods containing natural salicylates (e.g., apples, berries, tomatoes, pork). Furthermore, the child is not allowed to use things like mouthwashes or toothpastes that contain artificial colors or flavors or to take medications that are flavored or coated.

Evaluating the validity of the Finegold hypothesis is not as easy as it might first appear. One must be extremely strict in imposing the diet. At the very least, the parents must keep exact records of *everything* they feed the child and must shop and follow recipes very carefully. Some researchers have gone so far as to supply all the family's food themselves just to make sure the diet is followed religiously. One must be on guard against the child's cheating, because one stick of gum or one small bite of candy taken from another child can bring a return of the hyperactive symptoms for days. One must weigh the possibility that the parents' perceptions and the child's behavior may be more affected by the rigors of the diet itself than by the chemicals involved. Finally, in controlled experiments comparing the child's behavior when the supposed chemical villains are present and when they are not (that is, the child eats the same foods each day but on some days the chemical instigators of hyperactivity are added to the foods and on some days they are not), one must be careful that placebo and active ingredient foods cannot be told apart— they must be the same in color, texture, odor, and taste.

Well controlled studies indicate that *some* children's hyperactivity is at least partly a function of food substances. It appears that younger children may be affected by food chemicals more than older children. But the claims made by Finegold (1975, 1976) may be extravagant. The research data now available only support a considerably more cautious view of how many children are adversely affected by foods, how many children's behavior would be improved by following the diet, and how much improvement could be obtained by dietary control alone (Harley et al., 1978; Rose, 1978; Swanson & Kinsbourne, 1980; Taylor, 1979; Weiss et al., 1980).

Behavior Modification

It would be dishonest to tout behavior modification as a "cure-all" or "foolproof" method of controlling hyperactivity or any other behavior problem. However, research has demonstrated that hyperactive children's noisy, destructive, disruptive, and inattentive behavior can be changed for the better by controlling the contingencies of reinforcement (see Ayllon & Rosenbaum, 1977; Hallahan & Kauffman, 1975, 1976; Sherman & Bushell, 1975; and Sroufe, 1975 for reviews of this literature). Nevertheless, one cannot assume that a behavior modification schema will automatically bring improvement. The successful use of behavior modification requires the astute application of the principles of learning to rearrangement of events in the child's environment (for example, changing *when* the child receives attention from teacher or parents). Unless the individual attempting to use behavior modification techniques is knowledgeable about behavior principles and also finely attuned to the child's individual characteristics and preferences, the child's behavior is not likely to change—at least not in the desired direction. Like medication, behavior modification can be abused and misused: it is, even when skillfully used, a powerful method that can have an unanticipated or undesirable outcome.

Modifying the hyperactive child's behavior ordinarily has meant arranging rewarding consequences to follow desirable behavior; either no consequences or punishing consequences follow undesirable behavior. This rearrangement of environmental events can be accomplished in many different ways and may involve so simple a change as shifting the teacher's attention from inappropriate to appropriate behavior (see Figure 6–3, and the accompanying description) or more complicated techniques such as token reinforcement. Both individual and group contingencies of reinforcement have been used successfully with hyperactive children (Rosenbaum, O'Leary, & Jacob, 1975).

Patterson (1965b) conducted one of the earliest studies in which behavior modification techniques were applied to the problems presented by a hyperactive child. He used a "workbox" device to reinforce nonhyperactive behavior. The device was a small box containing a digital counter and a light that could be remotely controlled. Patterson explained to the child (Earl, a 9-year-old second grader) and his classmates that whenever Earl was sitting still and paying attention for a few minutes, the counter would turn to indicate points and the light would flash. (Earl's inappropriate behavior included very frequent talking, pushing, hitting, pinching, looking about the room or out the window, walking around the room, moving his desk, tapping or handling objects). Each "point" accumulated on the counter earned one penny or one small piece of candy, and the earned rewards were divided evenly among Earl and his classmates. With immediate and frequent reward for his appropriate behavior and motivation for his classmates to help him behave well, Earl's behavior quickly improved.

The case of Henry (see Chapter 1) described by Kubany, et al. (1971) provides another example of the use of behavior modification with a hyperactive child.

vignette

Henry was a bright (IQ 120) 6-year-old described as not only hyper-active but also loud, demanding, oppositional, and disruptive.
He piled his desk with debris and refused to sit with the other children. His teacher found that scolding and reprimanding him only made his behavior worse. As shown in Figure 7–2, his behavior was a severe problem during baseline sessions (when the teacher ignored most of his misbehavior). The behavior modification procedure devised for Henry was as follows: For each two minutes (15 minutes after the first day) that Henry was in his seat and quiet, a candy or trinket was dropped into a "sharing jar," and Henry was allowed to distribute goodies to his classmates at the end of the day. The accumulation of "good behavior time" was shown on a large 15-minute timer hung at the front of the room and labeled *Henry's Clock*, which the teacher controlled by turning it off whenever Henry misbehaved and turning it on again after he had been well behaved for 15 seconds. Figure 7–2 shows that this procedure was

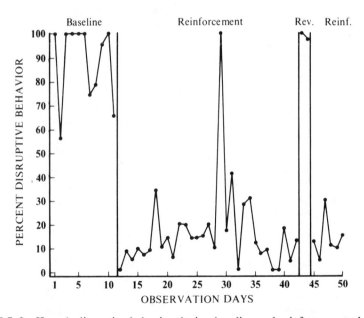

FIGURE 7-2 Henry's disruptive behavior during baseline and reinforcement phases.

Note. From "The Good Behavior Clock: A Reinforcement Time Out Procedure for Reducing Disruptive Classroom Behavior" by E. S. Kubany, L. E. Weiss, and B. B. Sloggett, *Journal of Behavior Therapy and Experimental Psychiatry*, 1971, *2*, 175. Copyright 1971 by Pergamon. Reprinted by permission.

effective in improving Henry's behavior. A "reversal" (a return to baseline conditions) and reinstatement of the behavior modification technique demonstrated clearly the causal link between the technique and the change in Henry's behavior.

Briefly stated, behavior modification techniques have been used frequently and effectively to control hyperactive behavior in the classroom as well as at home. Hyperactive behavior, like other behaviors of unknown origin, is usually susceptible to environmental influence and can be brought under control effectively and humanely by a system of rewards for appropriate responses coupled with a withholding of rewards or punishment for undesirable activity.

Drugs Versus Behavior Modification

One recent controversy in the literature has been whether drugs or behavior modification is the preferred treatment for hyperactivity. Frequently, proponents of behavior modification have argued that such techniques are an effective alternative to medication, but they have not always presented research data to back up their claim. However, some researchers have made direct experimental comparisons of the two interventions. One such comparison study was reported by Ayllon, Layman, and Kandel (1975). Ayllon et al. first recorded the hyperactive behavior and academic performance (reading and math) of three children being treated with drugs. When taken off the drugs, the children's hyperactive behavior immediately increased, although their academic performance (percent of tasks correct) did not deteriorate. Following a brief period of days a token reinforcement program was initiated. Children could earn points (tokens) by making correct academic responses, and their tokens could later be exchanged for backup reinforcers (candy, school supplies, free time, picnics). Although the children were not medicated, their hyperactivity decreased and their academic performance increased dramatically when the reinforcement program was instituted. Figure 7–3 shows the data for one of the three children (Dudley) during each phase of the study. Figure 7–4 shows the percent of time the three children were hyperactive and the percent of correct academic responses during the medication and reinforcement phases of the study. The data clearly show that hyperactivity was controlled as well with behavior modification as with drugs and that behavior modification produced better academic performance than did drugs for these children.

Kauffman and Hallahan (1979) reviewed studies in which drug treatment and behavior modification were compared, and concluded that drugs are sometimes helpful in controlling behavior. However, drug effects are always interactive with environmental effects—how a child responds to medication depends not only on the drug dosage but also on the kind of classroom or home environment the child is placed in (cf. Jacob, O'Leary, & Rosenblad, 1978; Whalen, Collins, Henker, Alkus, Adams, & Stapp, 1978). With or without drugs, behavior modification is typically effective, having some distinct advantages over medication: (a) it tends to be more specific in its effects than drugs; (b) it encourages a focus on teaching appropriate behavior in addition to concern for eliminating maladaptive responses; (c) it demands improvement of the child's environment rather than allowing

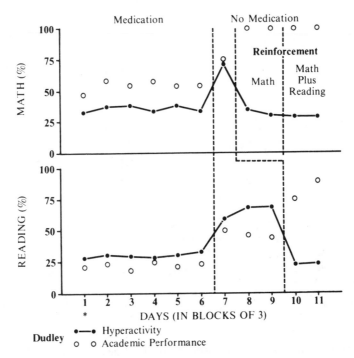

FIGURE 7–3   Dudley. The percentage of intervals in which his hyperactivity took place and (in percent) his correct math and reading performance.

Note. The first and second segments respectively show the effects of medication, and its subsequent withdrawal, on hyperactivity and academic performance. A multiple-baseline analysis of the effects of reinforcement across math and reading and concurrent hyperactivity is shown starting on the third top segment. The last segment shows the effects of reinforcement on math plus reading and its concurrent effect on hyperactivity. (The asterisk indicates one data point averaged over two rather than three days.)

Note. From "A Behavioral-Educational Alternative to Drug Control of Hyperactive Children" by T. Ayllon, D. Layman, and H. J. Kandel, *Journal of Applied Behavior Analysis*, 1975, *8*, 143. Copyright 1975 by Society for Experimental Analysis of Behavior. Reprinted by permission.

exclusive attention to the child's misbehavior; and (d) it may be used to increase the child's tendency to attribute behavioral change to his/her own action rather than to the chemical effects of pills (that is, it may tend to foster personal responsibility rather than explanations having to do with external agents).

Structured Environment: Consistency and Teacher Direction

The structured approach to teaching brain-injured, hyperactive, and disturbed children described by Cruickshank et al. (1961), Haring and Phillips (1962), and Haring and Whelan (1965) is designed to control hyperactivity. A minimum of distracting stimuli are present in the classroom. Clear expectations are created regarding children's movement about the classroom, and the classroom routine is very predictable. Consistent consequences, actually an elementary form of behavior modification, are thus applied to hyperactive and nonhyperactive behavior. The teacher is to be highly directive, making nearly all decisions for children

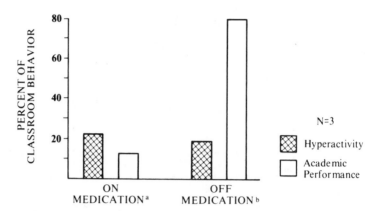

FIGURE 7-4   Average percent of hyperactivity and academic performance in math and reading for three children.

a The first two bars summarize findings from the 17-day baseline under drug therapy.

b The last two bars show results for the final 6-day period without drug therapy but with a reinforcement program for both math and reading performance.

Note. From "A Behavioral-Educational Alternative to Drug Control of Hyperactive Children," by T. Ayllon, D. Layman, and H. J. Kandel, *Journal of Applied Behavior Analysis*, 1975, *8*, 143. Copyright 1975 by Society for Experimental Analysis of Behavior. Reprinted by permission.

until such time as they can wisely manage themselves. As will be discussed further, the structured classroom of Chuickshank, Haring and their co-workers is designed to control distractibility as well as hyperactivity. The research of Haring and Phillips (1962), Haring and Whelan (1965), Hewett (1968) and others indicated that a highly structured classroom has a salutary effect on disturbed children's behavior.

Self-Instruction

In recent years, there has been a surge of interest in teaching children with learning and behavioral handicaps to use self-instructional strategies to control their inappropriate responses (Meichenbaum, 1977, 1979, 1980). Much of the research using self-instruction and other self-regulating strategies has dealt with impulsive responses; consequently, that research will be reviewed more fully under the discussion of impulsivity. However, it is noted here that some of these studies have dealt with children labeled hyperactive and that self-instruction, self-monitoring, and self-reinforcement have sometimes been used with success (for example, Bornstein & Quevillon, 1976; Varni & Henker, 1979).

Modeling

As Cullinan, Kauffman, and LaFleur (1975) point out, behavioral examples are as ubiquitously present in the child's environment as are contingencies of reinforcement. It is known that children often learn by imitating the examples or models provided by their peers or adults. One way in which modeling may be used to change hyperactive behavior is described by Csapo (1972). She found that hitting, kicking, poking, and other aggressive, hyperactive behaviors could be reduced in elementary school children by having the hyperactive children's normal peers demonstrate correct deportment and give reinforcers in order to initiate imitation. Other researchers have found modeling of desirable behavior to be an effective means to induce more attentive and less impulsive behavior in hyperactive children, as will be discussed in following sections of this chapter (see Cullinan et al., 1975; Epstein et al., 1975; Goodwin & Mahoney, 1975).

Biofeedback

Biofeedback is a way of teaching individuals to control their overt behavior or internal biological processes by "feeding back" to them information regarding their own physiological status. For example, a person may be taught control of blood pressure or brain waves by training him/her to monitor these internal activities continuously with the help of an oscilloscope or similar device. Braud, Lupin, and Braud (1975) reported a case in which a 6-year-old hyperactive boy was taught to reduce his muscular activity and tension by training him to monitor his own muscle tension. His training was carried out in a laboratory situation, but some generalization of improvement in his behavior was observed at home and at school. Schulman, Stevens, Suran, Kupst, and Naughton (1978) decreased the activity level of a highly active 11-year-old boy using a combination of biofeedback (from a portable activity-measuring device worn at the child's waist) and behavior modification techniques. The study was conducted in a typical day hospital classroom. They also increased the activity level of a lethargic (hypoactive) 10-year-old boy using the same methods in an experimental classroom. Further research and development of biofeedback techniques might in the future provide practicable methods for controlling hyperactive behavior in everyday settings (see also Lubar & Shouse, 1977; Ross & Ross, 1976; Strider & Strider, 1979).

Other Methods

In addition to the methods of control described so far, others have been tried— various forms of psychotherapy, for example. In fact, it seems that almost every strategy that has been used with any kind of troublesome behavior has been tried with hyperactivity (cf. Ross & Ross, 1976). Perhaps that in itself is a commentary on the seriousness with which adults approach the problem, the frequency of hyperactivity in exceptional children, and our lack of knowledge about the origins of such behavior.

DISTRACTIBILITY

Definition and Measurement

Distractibility is a characteristic tied closely to the construct of attention. That is, the distractible child is assumed to have difficulty "attending" to appropriate stimuli or in "deploying attention" to relevant stimuli in an efficient way. Although the concept of attention is central to psychological theories having to do with learning and academic achievement (Hallahan & Kauffman, 1976; Ross, 1976), attention itself has been difficult to define and measure. Behavioral psychologists have often measured attention by observing children directly, noting whether or not they are visually oriented toward the task materials or other appropriate stimuli (e.g., the teacher). Measuring attention by recording whether or not the child is looking at the relevant stimuli obviously has some drawbacks, the most obvious of which is that a child can be looking at a particular object but at the same time be thinking about something completely different. Some psychologists and educators have measured attention by testing children with specially designed materials and noting whether or not they respond appropriately to the stimuli they are told to attend to. The most obvious weaknesses of this assessment strategy are that the child may be able to respond appropriately in some cases without attending (that is, get some items correct just by chance) and that performance on such a laboratory task may have little or no relationship to attending to appropriate stimuli in a classroom situation. Sroufe, Sonies, West, and Wright (1973) measured attention by recording heart rate deceleration, a method presenting obvious technical problems for teachers who may wish to use it.

In spite of the problems in defining and measuring attention, research has yielded important information regarding distractibility in children. It is clear from the literature that disturbed children (and learning disabled and retarded children as well) have difficulty in giving sustained attention to the relevant aspects of academic tasks and social stimuli (see Campbell, 1974; Hallahan, 1975a, b; Hallahan & Kauffman, 1975, 1976).

Short Attention Span and Frequent Attention Shifts

It has been noted frequently that disturbed children tend to be distractible. Hewett (1968), for example, made the assessment of attention a primary part of his evaluation procedures for disturbed children. In his "engineered classroom," teaching children to attend to work provided by the teacher is the first step in his hierarchy of educational tasks. Bryan (1974) presents data indicating that learning disabled children, who share many characteristics of children labeled *disturbed*, spend less time engaged in attending to school tasks than do normal children. In many behavior modification studies with disturbed children, direct observation in the classroom or home reveals a high rate of inattentive behavior. Sroufe, Steucher, and Stutzer (1973) found heart rate changes suggesting that autistic children's attention fluctuates markedly during episodes of self-stimulation.

An operant conditioning analysis of "attention span" suggests that how long a child will attend to a particular task depends, to some degree at least, on the consequences provided for attention. If the child is given reinforcement for attending to a task, then attention span can be increased (Martin & Powers, 1967). Nevertheless, it seems clear that when disturbed children are observed directly in naturalistic situations, they are likely to be found to attend to tasks for shorter intervals of time and to shift their attention more often than normal children who are observed in similar environments. Indirect evidence for this assertion is found not only in anecdotal reports of the behavior of disturbed children, but also in studies where disturbed children rated higher than normal or learning disabled children on characteristics such as preoccupation, daydreaming, and short attention span (see Table 3-2, p. 67 and Figure 3-1, p. 68).

Underselective Attention in the
Mildly and Moderately Handicapped

Normal children become increasingly able to attend selectively to relevant visual and auditory stimuli and "screen out" or ignore irrelevant stimuli as they get older (Hagen & Kail, 1975; Hallahan, Kauffman, & Ball, 1974). The measurement of selective attention in most developmental studies has involved presenting tasks to children on which they are told to pay attention only to particular "relevant" stimuli and to ignore other "irrelevant" stimuli. After a series of experimetal trials in which they are required to respond to the relevant stimuli, they are asked questions regarding the irrelevant stimuli. To the extent that they perform well on the relevant or "central" part of the task but poorly on the irrelevant or "incidental" aspect, they are considered to have attended "selectively." For example, they may be shown a series of cards, each containing a picture of an animal and a picture of a familiar household object (the task devised by J. W. Hagen). They are told to pay attention only to the animals. They are shown one card at a time for two seconds and then the card is turned face down. After several cards are placed in a row in front of them, they are shown a cue card matching one that is face down in front of them and required to find the match. (In effect, the children are asked to perform a memory task and told to base their memory on the animals.) After a series of matching trials the children are asked to remember which household objects were paired with the animals on the cards. (In effect, they are then asked to remember something they were not told to pay attention to and which was, therefore, irrelevant.) Their performance on the serial recall involving the animals is considered their *central* recall score, and their performance on the task of pairing up objects with animals is considered their *incidental* recall score. Children who are good selective attenders do better on central versus incidental recall. An auditory measure of selective attention may involve a similar measurement paradigm but may substitute pairs of words spoken by the experimenter for pairs of pictures (see Hallahan et al., 1974).

Studies with learning disabled, mentally retarded, and cerebral palsied subjects have revealed that such exceptional children tend to be deficient in selective attention (Hagen & Huntsman, 1971; Hallahan, Kauffman, & Ball, 1973; Hallahan, Stainback, Ball, & Kauffman, 1973; Tarver, Hallahan, Kauffman, & Ball, 1976; see also Hallahan, 1975a, b). Given the findings by Hallahan, Stainback et al. that selective attention was positively correlated with mental age and negatively related to institutionalization, plus what is known of the behavioral similarities among ED, LD, and EMR children, it is a reasonable guess that disturbed children tend to be deficient in selective attention. There is good reason to suspect that many mildly and moderately disturbed children are distractible in that they have difficulty in selecting out relevant stimuli for attention while ignoring irrelevant stimuli.

Overselective Attention in the
Severely and Profoundly Disturbed

There is some reason to believe that many severely and profoundly disturbed children have more serious problems in selective attention than mildly and moderately disturbed children. The severely disturbed child may be *too highly selective* (*over*selective) in deploying attention, focusing only on a limited aspect of stimuli or on irrelevant stimuli (Lovaas, Koegel, & Schreibman, 1979). Many psychotic children respond to a narrow range of cues, perhaps to a single feature or dimension of a stimulus—they attend to such a limited or specific stimulus compared to normal children that they are retarded in their ability to learn discriminations among stimuli. Children with *under*selective attention, on the other hand, respond to many irrelevant stimuli or "extra" stimulus dimensions as well as to relevant ones—they do this to a greater extent than do normal children and consequently are inefficient learners.

The measurement of stimulus overselectivity has typically involved teaching children to discriminate among complex, (multidimensional) stimuli. For example, the child may be taught to press a bar in response to one auditory stimulus, and not to press the bar to another different sound (Reynolds, Newsom, & Lovaas, 1974). Both of the stimuli (the one signaling the child to press the bar and the one signaling *not* to press) are complex in that they are a mixture of individual sounds (perhaps a pure tone and a clicking noise) that later can be presented separately. After the child has learned to respond differentially to the two complex stimuli, the components of the stimuli are presented separately in order to see if the child learned to attend to the components *together* or learned to attend to only *one aspect* of the complex stimuli. Most normal children will continue to respond correctly when the stimulus components are presented separately, indicating that they pay attention to all relevant stimuli or elements. Conversely, most autistic children do *not* continue to respond correctly when only one stimulus component is presented—they seem to have learned the discrimination on the basis of overselective attention to only one aspect of the complex stimulus. In the visual realm, much the same measurement strategy has been used. Pairs of pictures (for example, horse-girl, bicycle-tree) have been presented during initial discrimination training with each member of the pairs being presented separately on later trials (Koegel & Wilhelm, 1973). Complex social stimuli (variously dressed boy and girl dolls) have also been used (Schreibman & Lovaas, 1973).

The difference between underselective and overselective attention is important to the selection of a teaching strategy. A child who is underselective in attending to stimuli will be an inefficient learner because he/she "takes in" too much, wasting effort on the processing of irrelevant information. The child may therefore need to be taught a strategy for focusing attention more finely and ignoring nonessential information. A child who is overselective in attending to stimuli will be an inefficient learner because he/she "takes in" too little, and focuses on so narrow a range of information that the child is unable to learn a generalization. Such a child may need to be taught a strategy to disperse attention to more aspects of stimuli and to focus on the "critical features" that allow the learning of generalizations.

The implications of overselective attention for the behavioral development of autistic children may be seen when it is remembered that much learning requires the individual to respond to stimuli presented *together*. Koegel and Wilhelm (1973) speculate that the inability to respond to multiple cues (complex or paired stimuli) may account for autistic children's failure to (a) acquire secondary reinforcers through association of neutral stimuli with primary reinforcers, (b) to acquire appropriate affect through classical conditioning, and (c) to learn through the use of prompts. Schreibman (1975) found that autistic children are indeed unable to use the prompts that normal and less severely handicapped children find helpful in learning discriminations among stimuli. Additionally, autistic children may have great difficulty learning to recognize people and situations because of their over-selective responding.

> For example, an autistic child might learn to recognize his father by the presence of his glasses, or similar superficial and potentially unreliable features. Given that condition, perhaps this accounts for why many autistic children become very upset or their behavior is distinctly altered, if even a small element of their environment is changed. For example, a father's removal of his glasses may send his child into a severe tantrum, or he may respond as if he suddenly does not recognize him. Such inconsistencies in their behavior, major behavioral disruptions with minor changes in their environment, are frequently referred to in the clinical literature on autism.   (Rimland, 1964) [Koegel & Wilhelm, 1973, p. 452]

Etiology

As with the previous discussion on the etiology of hyperactivity, little can be said definitely about the causes of distractibility—they are simply not known. However, it is worth noting that attention deficiencies may represent a developmental lag rather than a pathological process (cf. discussion Chapter 5, p. 116). Hallahan, Stainback, et al. (1973) found evidence linking the development of selective attention to mental age and hinted that underselective attention may represent a developmental lag. The data of Hallahan and his colleagues suggest that children who are underselective in comparison to their chronological age mates have the same attention characteristics as younger, normal children (Tarver et al., 1976). Lovaas, Koegel, and Schreibman (1979) speculate that overselective attention in autistic children may be more relevant to developmental level than to clinical diagnosis. Koegel and Wilhelm (1973) observed that selective responding to stimuli is characteristic of normal young children; therefore, they suggest, "By contrast . . . the autistic children do not show any mysterious deviance, but rather appear to evidence an extreme form of a process which occurs regularly in normal organisms" (p. 451).

The hypothesis that attentional deficiencies represent a developmental lag suggests that the sequence in which various attention skills are acquired is the same for all children, including handicapped children. If it is the case that attention-deficient children follow the same developmental sequence as normal children but merely progress from stage to stage at a slower rate, then perhaps their remedial instruction should follow the same course, the same sequence of skill acquisition, taken by the learning of normal children. Research has not yet indicated how underselective and overselective attention are related. It is possible that overselectivity and underselectivity are independent developmental processes. But it could be the case that they represent sequential developmental processes. Normal children may at first be overselective, then underselective, and finally efficient in their attentional strategies.

The hypothesis of a developmental lag also seems to point toward neurological dysfunction as the basis for deficiencies in attention, though by no means will the currently available data support a firm conclusion. Lewis (1975) reviews research linking measures of attention to central nervous system function in infants and young children. Still, whether the attention deficiencies seen in disturbed children are induced by environmental factors, reflect a neurological problem, or both, is unknown.

Methods of Controlling Distractibility

Structured Environment and Controlled Stimulation

Perhaps the best known educational methods for distractible children are those devised by Strauss and Lehtinen (1947) and refined by Cruickshank et al. (1961; see also Cruickshank, 1975). These methods are predicated on the assumption that the children in question (whether labeled *mentally retarded, brain damaged, hyperactive,* or *emotionally disturbed*) cannot learn to attend properly in an environment with the usual amount of stimuli.

> The distractible child exists, and, for whatever reason, he is fundamentally attracted to stimuli—visual, auditory, tactile, and probably others. We postulate that, if this is so, the response of the adult should be to reduce stimuli for as long a period of time as may be required for the child to learn appropriate attending behavior and to establish integrated perceptual-motor responses.   (Cruickshank, 1975, pp. 253–254)

In order to minimize distracting stimuli in the classroom, Cruickshank recommends

1. sound treating the walls and ceilings
2. carpeting the floors
3. covering the windows with translucent material or using frosted glass
4. covering bookshelves and cupboards so that their contents are not open to view
5. keeping bulletin boards undecorated except for special occasions or special brief periods during the day
6. providing small three-sided cubicles where children can work without the distractions present in a large open space
7. clear directions
8. predictable routine
9. firm expectations
10. consistent consequences provided by the teacher

Cruickshank believes that such environmental structure and attenuation of environmental stimuli will facilitate learning in distractible children. A heavy barrage of criticism has been directed at his ideas. Irresponsible critics equate Cruickshank's methods with barbarous treatment or mindless insensitivity to children. Intelligent detractors point to the lack of research evidence supporting the practice of minimizing environmental stimuli (e.g., Sroufe, 1975). Hallahan and Kauffman (1975, 1976) note that there has been no research in which the *total* program advocated by Cruickshank has been replicated and that many of the children with whom cubicles or other individual aspects of Cruickshank's techniques have been used may not have been highly distractible. Moreover, the attempts to replicate certain features of Cruickshank's approach have varied widely in quality (see also Cruickshank, 1975) and have been very short in duration. At this time, however, the literature appears to support only two tentative conclusions regarding reduced environmental stimuli: Attending to task may be increased, but higher cognitive tasks and academic achievement will probably be unaffected by attenuating normal classroom distractions.

The concept of optimal stimulation suggests that children will not respond favorably to excessive stimulation or to extreme sensory deprivation (see Ross & Ross, 1976). That is, there is an optimal level of sensory stimulation that produces normal behavior. Cruickshank's hypothesis is that the ordinary classroom environment contains too much stimulation for the distractible child. However, an alternative hypothesis is that distractible children need *more* stimulation than is found in the normal classroom if they are to perform normally (Zentall, 1975, 1979). Very little evidence is available indicating that heightening or lessening classroom stimulation *per se* is an effective approach to management of distractible children. It seems obvious that research is needed to indicate precisely *which* stimuli should be attenuated or eliminated and *which* stimuli should be made more salient when specific behavioral objectives have been chosen.

Modified Instructional Materials

In addition to the methods already discussed, Cruickshank and his co-workers changed the stimulus characteristics of instructional materials as a way of helping the distractible child pay attention to the right thing. Irrelevant or potentially distracting stimuli (for example, colorful illustrations on the same page as the reading materials) were eliminated from materials, and academic tasks (arithmetic problems or reading paragraphs) were often presented one at a time on separate pages. Relevant aspects or stimulus dimensions of a task (for example, operation signs in arithmetic) were often made more salient by adding color cues to highlight critical features. Research in child development lends support to the efficacy of such modifications to teaching materials. Stevenson (1972) concludes that learning can be made easier for children, particularly young children (and, by implication, chronologically older children with developmental lags) by eliminating irrelevant stimuli that they have difficulty ignoring. Stevenson also concludes that research supports the notion that heightening the differences among stimuli by having them differ in more than one aspect (perhaps color *and* form) will help children learn more efficiently. These assumptions concerning the helpfulness of modification of teaching materials apply, of course, only to cases in which the child is an inefficient learner with standard or unmodified materials. It is apparent that children with either overselective or underselective attention may benefit when instructional materials are "cleaner," and freer of irrelevant stimuli. However, the overselective attender may be hindered even by relevant information that is of help to the underselective child. For example, a mathematical operation sign might profitably be printed in color for the sake of an underselective attender, but for an overselective attender the color dimension of the stimulus might prevent learning to discriminate the form of the sign (see Schreibman, 1975, for a more complete discussion of this problem).

Modified Instructional Strategies

In the normal classroom, children are seldom told clearly and precisely how to respond to educational tasks. In the structured classrooms of Haring and Phillips (1962) and Cruickshank et al. (1961) the teacher not only made most of the decisions regarding when a child should engage in a certain activity, but also gave explicit instructions. Clear instructions regarding the relevant aspects of the task they are being asked to perform has been shown by research to improve children's attention and performance (Lovitt & Smith, 1972; Maccoby, 1967; Pick, Christy, & Frankel, 1972).

Teaching children to use verbal labels for stimuli and to rehearse the instructions they have been given or the stimuli they have been shown also appears to have merit as an instructional strategy (Hallahan & Kauffman, 1975, 1976). For example, a child may be told to verbalize each arithmetic problem or its operation sign as he or she is working the problem, to say each letter of a word aloud as it is written, or to rehearse a reading passage (Lovitt, 1977). It is important to note the limits of a method of managing distractibility. Robin, Armel, and O'Leary (1975) have noted that verbal self-instruction can be a cumbersome procedure and is, at least for some children, no better than direct instruction by the teacher. Too, verbal labeling and rehearsal imposed by the teacher may benefit younger or developmentally delayed children who are underselective in attention and have no strategy for deploying their attention. Older, nondelayed children may actually be hindered by such an instructional approach.

> It seems that at younger ages the child is more dependent upon immediate stimuli in his environment, and has not developed strategies for coping with specific task demands. The older child becomes more dependent upon his own information processing strategies; he can ignore stimuli that are irrelevant unless they conflict with his strategies. Verbal labels which are imposed externally are irrelevant, and even distracting, for the individual who does not utilize them in task performance. (Hagen, Meacham, & Mesibov, 1970, p. 57)

Thus the child's developmental level and specific attentional abilities and disabilities must be taken into account in selecting instructional strategies. Many children with underselective attention can be helped by verbal cues or prompts from the teacher. Children whose attention is overselective, though, may need a different approach in which prompts are not used or are an intrinsic part of the stimuli themselves. The prompts themselves, rather than the intended discriminative stimuli, may, for overselective children, become the basis for learning a discrimination among stimuli (Rincover, 1978; Schreibman, 1975).

Cognitive-behavior modification includes a variety of techniques such as self-monitoring, self-instruction, and self-reinforcement. As mentioned previously, these techniques have been used with hyperactive and impulsive children. The same general set of strategies has been employed for teaching distractible children to attend to academic tasks and to improve their academic performance (Hallahan, Lloyd, Kosiewicz, Kauffman, & Graves, 1979; Rieth, Polsgrove, McLeskey, Payne,

& Anderson, 1978). Lloyd (1980) has reviewed the cognitive-behavior modification research as it applies to academic tasks. He notes that many cognitive training studies have involved teaching the child a general strategy that requires asking one-self "What is my problem? What is my plan? Am I following my plan? Did I do it correctly?" If cognitive strategy training is to be successful in improving academic achievement, then it will probably have to be tailored more carefully to specific academic tasks. Cognitive training has appeal because it seems to be the kind of intervention that would have generalized effects, but research to date does not clearly indicate that it produces generalization to a greater extent than other inter-ventions. Also, Meichenbaum (1980) and O'Leary (1980) caution that, although cognitive-behavior modification (sometimes called cognitive training or strategy training) holds promise, it can not be implemented effectively without intelligent planning by the teacher. It is neither magic nor a formula for certain success.

Behavior Modification

Again and again it has been demonstrated that children will attend more to school work if favorable consequences follow their attending behavior. The report by Hall and his colleagues (1968) is typical of the results obtained when the teacher's attention is made contingent on the attending behavior of distractible pupils. In instances where children are extremely distractible and candidates for special edu-cation, stronger reinforcers than teacher attention to appropriate behavior are re-quired. In the case of Earl presented by Patterson (1965) and the case of Henry described by Kubany et al. (1971), the children's hyperactivity was decreased and their attention to tasks was increased by making extrinsic rewards (candy and trinkets) contingent on attending behavior (cf. the discussion of hyperactivity in this chapter). Many different types of rewards or reinforcers may be provided for appropriate behavior with good results, depending on the child's developmental level and individual preferences. The point is that behavior modification research has provided ample experimental evidence that children will learn to attend more to their school work when meaningful rewards are given to them for paying at-tention (see Hallahan & Kauffman, 1975, for a review of this research).

One of the best known educational programs for disturbed children in which behavior modification is used is Hewett's (1968) "engineered classroom." Hewett's Santa Monica Project included research showing that disturbed children's attention to school tasks was improved by the use of reinforcement. The details of most aspects of Hewett's program are beyond the scope of this discussion, but two features of his approach are directly relevant. First, an integral part of the operation of the engineered classroom was a system for awarding points or check marks (which children could later exchange for "backup" reinforcers such as candy and toys) to each pupil for desirable behavior. Second, the most fundamental educa-tion goal was to get the child who is inattentive to pay attention to the teacher and to academic tasks. In this system, once children learn to pay attention, they can work towards higher level goals. The way the token reinforcement or check mark system works is described below by Hewett.

The engineered classroom day revolves around the child's receiving check marks for various accomplishments. Each morning as he enters the door the child picks up a Work

Record card from the Work Record holder nearby. . . . As the child goes through the day he is given check marks reflecting his accomplishments and classroom functioning. Cards filled with check marks can later be exchanged for tangible rewards such as candy and trinkets. . . . Usually, a possible ten check marks are given by either the teacher or aide following each 15-minute work period in the classroom. During the time devoted to giving check marks (usually 5 minutes) all work done within the preceding work period is corrected and the new assignment for the next 15 minutes is given. This allows three 15-minute work periods and three-5 minute checkmark-giving periods during each class hour.

Two check marks are given if the child started his work, three if he "followed through" on an assignment, and a possible five bonus check marks are administered for "being a student." In the engineered classroom "being a student" refers . . . to how well the child respected limits of time, space, and activity and the working rights of others. . . . For some extremely inattentive children, the bonus check marks may be given "Because you put your name on the paper and paid attention to your work," even though no actual work was accomplished.   (pp. 247–249)

An important question regarding the modification of attending behavior is whether or not—once the child is ostensibly "paying attention," looking at the teacher or work—there is an improvement in academic performance. One might also ask whether reinforcing academic performance would increase both performance and attention, as suggested by Ayllon and Roberts (1974). The answer to both questions depends on the child's level of attention, ability to use attentional strategies, and ability to perform the academic tasks (Hallahan & Kauffman, 1975, 1976). The child whose attention is at a very low level initially will probably be helped by being reinforced merely for paying attention, for increased attending makes responding correctly more likely to occur. On the other hand, the child who already pays attention most of the time will not benefit much from reinforcement for attending. The child who does not know *how* to pay attention, does not know *what* to look for or *how* to search for information, must be given direct instruction in attentional strategies. Otherwise, reinforcement for looking at the teacher or task will merely reinforce looking, not performing. Reinforcing correct responses to academic tasks will probably increase attention only when the tasks are within the child's capacity and the percent of time the child attends to tasks is below average (below about 75%) to begin with; offering reinforcement for a performance the child cannot give is of no avail, and it is not reasonable to expect the child to attend to work all of the time.

IMPULSIVITY

Definition and Measurement

Impulsivity is a characteristic often associated with aggression and deficient moral development, two topics to be explored more carefully in following chapters. However, impulsiveness is also related to hyperactivity and problems in attention. The focus of the discussion here will be on impulsivity as a cognitive tempo that hinders school performance.

Disturbed children frequently are described in anecdotal reports and case studies as being impulsive or "impulse ridden." The descriptions emphasize that such children seem to be "at the mercy of their impulses," unable to keep from responding quickly and without thinking to academic tasks and to social situations. Typically, these children's impulses are wrong, and they get them into trouble. Were they to respond as quickly but yet correctly or appropriately, they would likely be considered highly intelligent. Impulsiveness is often judged subjectively by teachers or parents. As is true for hyperactivity, behavior rating scales are sometimes employed (see Kendall & Finch, 1978).

The primary tool for measuring impulsivity and its inverse, reflectivity (the tendency to take one's time and consider alternatives before responding), has been the *Matching Familiar Figures Test (MFFT)* constructed by Jerome Kagan and his colleagues (Kagan, 1965; Kagan, Rosman, Day, Albert, & Phillips, 1964). The MFFT requires children to choose from among several alternatives a line drawing of a familiar figure (for example, an airplane) that matches a standard. Each of the alternatives is slightly different from the standard, except the one that matches the standard exactly. The child is required to match a series of figures, and the latency of response (that is, the length of time taken to make the first choice) and errors are recorded for each trial. The impulsive child tends to respond very quickly and to make many errors; the reflective child tends to have long latencies and make few errors. Impulsivity as measured by the MFFT has been found to be correlated with other measures of impulsivity and with other characteristics of exceptional children, such as hyperactivity and distractibility. Brown and Quay (1977) found that behavior disordered children show a developmental lag in impulse control, as shown by their performance on the MFFT. Children with an impulsive cognitive tempo are known also to do poorer academic work than reflective children (see Epstein et al., 1975; Finch & Spirito, 1980).

The MFFT has proven to be a valuable instrument for measuring impulsivity. Nevertheless, children's performance on the MFFT may be quite different in some respects from their performance on analogous academic tasks. Bower (1975) tested behavior disordered and learning disabled children using MFFT-type items and analogously constructed match-to-sample arithmetic and reading items (see Figs. 7–5, 7–6, and 7–7). He found that children took much longer to respond and made far fewer errors on the tasks involving academics than on the tasks involving line drawings of objects. That is, children appeared to be much more reflective in cognitive tempo on the academic tasks than they were on the MFFT-type tasks. However, further analysis of Bower's data showed that children's performance on the MFFT was significantly correlated with their performance on the arithmetic and reading tasks. That is, children's latencies and errors tended to be high or low on all three measures. Thus, children tended to be slower and more accurate in an *absolute* sense when confronted with academic tasks than when asked to perform on the MFFT, but their *relative* impulsivity or reflectivity did not change—children who were quick and inaccurate tended to be so on each measure, and quickness of response was associated with errors.

Etiology

Speculation about the origins of impulsivity has followed the same lines as guesses about the etiology of hyperactivity and distractibility—inborn predisposition,

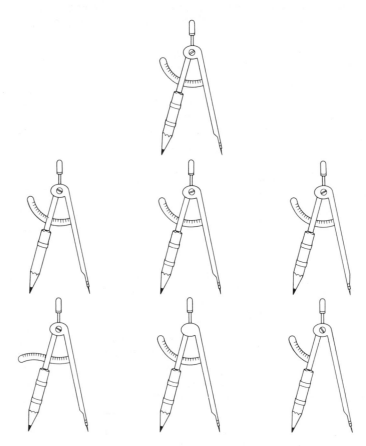

FIGURE 7–5   MFFT-type item.

Note.   Adapted from "Impulsivity and Academic Performance in Learning and Behavior Disordered Children" by K. B. Bower (Doctoral dissertation, University of Virginia, 1975). *Dissertation Abstracts International,* 367A. (University Microfilms No. 76-1071). Adapted by permission.

anxiety, cultural factors, neurological dysfunction, genetic factors, learned behavior, and so forth. The answer to the question of etiology is the same for impulsivity as for other behavior disorders: No one actually knows, and there are probably multiple causal factors involved in most cases.

One line of thought regarding the origin of impulsivity that is relevant here, though empirical data to support it are lacking, is the psychoanalytic viewpoint. Psychoanalytic theory posits a mental apparatus made up of three parts—the id, the ego, and the superego. The id is comprised of primitive instincts and provides the unconscious drive or impulse for the gratification of basic biological needs. Without the control imposed by the superego (the conscience, a largely unconscious mechanism acquired primarily from parental standards and restrictions) and the ego (the conscious, volitional aspect of the mind), the id dominates the personality. An individual whose personality is dominated by the id or "primary process" thinking is impulsive, does not stop to reflect on his/her behavior or bother to check his/her drive, and is frequently said to have a "deficient ego." It is the hypothesis of

$$
\begin{array}{r}
221 \\
-12 \\
\hline
209
\end{array}
$$

$$
\begin{array}{r}
221 \\
-21 \\
\hline
209
\end{array}
\qquad
\begin{array}{r}
211 \\
-12 \\
\hline
209
\end{array}
$$

$$
\begin{array}{r}
221 \\
-12 \\
\hline
901
\end{array}
\qquad
\begin{array}{r}
221 \\
+12 \\
\hline
209
\end{array}
$$

$$
\begin{array}{r}
221 \\
-12 \\
\hline
209
\end{array}
\qquad
\begin{array}{r}
221 \\
-12 \\
\hline
219
\end{array}
$$

FIGURE 7-6   Arithmetic item analogous to the MFFT.

Note.   Adapted from "Impulsivity and Academic Performance in Learning and Behavior Disordered Children" by K. B. Bower (Doctoral dissertation, University of Virginia, 1975). *Dissertation Abstracts International*, 367A. (University Microfilms No. 76-1071). Adapted by permission.

Redl and Wineman (1951, 1952) and others who describe disturbed children from a psychoanalytic perspective, that children are impulsive because of maldevelopment of the ego and superego. Pathological development of children's control mechanisms is assumed to arise from faulty child-rearing or traumatic life events. While the concepts of id, ego, and superego have little empirical foundation, they are used as explanatory constructs by psychoanalytically oriented psychologists and educators. Furthermore, the concept of the ego provides the basis for use of the *life space interview* as a technique for controlling impulsivity.

Methods of Controlling Impulsivity

A variety of procedures have been used to increase impulsive children's latencies, decrease their errors, and improve their performance on the MFFT. Merely re-

If you find the ring don't keep it.

If you fix the ring don't keep it.	If you find her ring don't keep it.
When you find the ring don't keep it.	If you find the ring just keep it.
If you find the ring don't drop it.	If you find the ring don't keep it.

FIGURE 7-7   Reading item analogous to the MFFT.

Note.   Adapted from "Impulsivity a Academic Performance in Learning and Behavior Disordered Children" by K. B. Bower (Doctoral dissertation, University of Virginia, 1975). *Dissertation Abstracts International*, 367A.) University Microfilms No. 76-1071). Adapted by permission.

quiring children to delay responding will, of course, increase their latencies. Forced delay, however, has not been shown to decrease errors. To decrease errors, it has been necessary in most cases to give children a strategy for scanning the alternatives and comparing them to the standard before choosing. Especially crucial for special education workers are findings suggesting that modeling, instructions, and extra motivation combined may be effective in modifying impulsivity (see Epstein et al., 1975; Finch & Spirito, 1980; Hallahan & Kauffman, 1975). Having the teacher or a peer demonstrate a reflective tempo, calling attention to exactly how one uses a scanning strategy, and providing favorable consequences for improved performance are techniques that can be used successfully in classroom settings. Other teaching methods include self-instruction, response cost, time-out, self-control curriculum, and life space interview.

Self-Control Training: Self-Instruction

Teaching children to use their own language to regulate behavior has been a successful approach with some impulsive children (Goodwin & Mahoney, 1975; Mahoney, 1974). Meichenbaum and Goodman (1969, 1971) and Palkes et al. (1968, 1971), for example, found that having children instruct themselves to be more reflective reduced impulsive errors on experimental tasks. To instruct impulsive children to slow down and to be careful in responding may not be enough to help them, but it may be helpful if these same children can be induced to tell *themselves* to stop and think before they give a response. Practical applications of a form of self-instruction to academic tasks are provided in literature by Lovitt and Curtiss (1968) and Parsons (1972), who found that requiring children who made many careless or impulsive errors in arithmetic computation to verbalize each problem or operation sign before writing their answers improved accuracy.

Typically, self-instructional training of impulsive children involves a series of steps in which verbal control of behavior is first modeled by an adult, then imitated by the child, and finally used independently by the child. On a given task, the adult first performs the task while verbalizing thoughts about the task requirements, relevant stimuli, strategies, task performance, and coping and self-reinforcement statements. For example, suppose the training task were to find matching arithmetic problems (like the task shown in Figure 7-6). The teacher might model self-instruction by saying aloud something like the following:

> Ok, now, what do I have to do? I have to find a problem down here that is just *exactly* the same as this one up here. This is going to be tough, but I just need to relax and get through it. Let's see, now. This problem is 221 minus 12 equals 209. I need to remember to make sure every part of the one I find down here is just the same. I'd better take it one part at a time just to make sure I get it right, because *every* part has to be the same. I know what I'll do, I'll just take it slow, one step at a time, and I'll cross off each one down here if I find something that's different. Because once I find something wrong, I don't have to check that one again because I know it can't be the one. Now, it's got to have 221 at the top. Let's see. This one has 221. But this one has 211 at the top, *not* 211, so it can't be right. So I'll mark it off. This one has 221, and this one, and this one, and this one, so they're ok. Now, it's got to be minus 12. This is minus 21, so it gets marked off. Minus 12 here is ok. Plus 12 can't be it. Minus 12 here is ok and here is ok. Boy, I'm really being careful, and I'm going to get it right. Ok. Now I've got to find 209 for the answer. Let's

see, 901 is wrong, 209 is right. Looks like I got it now. But I'd better check this other one too. No, 219 is wrong, so it must be this one here. I'm gonna double check just to make sure. Up here 221, down here 221. Up here minus 12, down here minus 12. Up here 209, down here 209. Got it. Wow, did I do a great job on *that!*

Next, the child might run through similar problems, imitating the teacher's verbalizations. The teacher might coach the child about appropriate verbalizations. Then trials might be given in which first the teacher, then the child, whispers the self-instructions. Finally, the teacher might model the appropriate task behavior with covert verbalization (but pointing and comparing), after which the child does the same. In most training programs, the teacher also models making occasional errors and dealing with them constructively. For example, the following might be said during the course of using the item in Figure 7–6:

Now I've got to find minus 12. Let's see, minus 12—cross it off. Oops! That is *minus* 12. I'm looking for ones that are *not* minus 12. I almost made a mistake. But I caught it, and I can just erase that line. I'm still ok, because I'm thinking and being careful. Let's see, plus 12 is *not* minus 12, so I'll cross *it* off. *Now* I'm getting it.

Cognitive training like this, adapted to the particulars of the task and the child's characteristics, has great intuitive appeal, and research indicates that the techniques hold promise when used skillfully (Meichenbaum, 1980; O'Leary, 1980). However, it is also clear that cognitive training and other self-control procedures are not a panacea for the problems presented by impulsive children. Future research will undoubtedly lead to refinements in teaching self-control and reveal also the circumstances under which self-instruction and other cognitive training methods are *not* the treatment of choice (cf. O'Leary & Dubey, 1979; Polsgrove, 1979; Rosenbaum & Drabman, 1979).

Response Cost, Time-Out, and Other
Behavior Modification Techniques

Actually, instructions, forced delay, modeling, and self-instruction are techniques that could fit under the rubric of "cognitive behavior modification." In addition to these methods, the technique of response cost—withdrawing rewards contingent on errors—has proven useful in some cases where careless errors are frequent. Finch and his associates frequently have used response cost in combination with cognitive training to reduce impulsivity (Finch & Spirito, 1980; Kendall & Finch, 1978). Lovitt (1977) and others who work with children who have learning and behavior difficulties found, for example, that some children improve their accuracy dramatically when each error "costs" them a fraction of their recess or some other desirable activity. In some cases it is helpful to require that for each error the child perform an additional task correctly (for example, for each spelling error, the child must write the word correctly five times). Azrin and Powers (1975) found that impulsive, disruptive behavior decreased when students lost recess time for being disruptive. Disruptions decreased even more, however, when pupils were required to practice the correct way of behaving (for example, raising their hands and requesting permission to leave their desks) for several minutes contingent on each episode of disruptive behavior. Time-out is a method frequently employed to reduce impulsive actions, usually extremely disruptive behavior or aggression against others. The time-out procedure typically involves removing the child from the situation in which impulsive and inappropriate behavior occurred and placing him/her, for a short while, in a relatively isolated and nonrewarding, nonstimulating environment. Time-out will be discussed further in Chapter 8, but it is noted here as a technique that is sometimes useful in controlling a child's impulsive behavior. Naturally, positive reinforcement for reflective or nonimpulsive behavior will often help the child to improve. Behavior modification procedures designed to alter hyperactivity and distractibility will probably decrease impulsivity as well.

Self-Control Training:
Psychoeducational Curriculum and Methods

Fagen, Long, and Stevens (1975) present a sequence of instructional units designed to teach children to be, among other things, less impulsive and more reflective. The units of instruction include activities calculated to help the child learn to focus attention, avoid distractions, develop memory skills, plan sequences of behavior, anticipate consequences, appreciate feelings, tolerate frustration, inhibit or delay responding, and relax.

> Taken together, the . . . skills represent an integration of cognitive and affective factors which mediate possibilities for regulating action. The presence of these skills enables a learner to make personally and socially acceptable choices regarding task requirements—choices which preclude the feelings of inadequacy which so often accompany task performance or nonperformance. Through mastery of these self-control skills, the learner incorporates the necessary self-pride and respect for open-minded reflection on available alternatives.   (Fagen et al., 1975, p. 44)

Important parts of the rationale for the self-control curriculum were borrowed from the "psychoeducational" approach to working with disturbed children. This approach emphasizes the importance of feelings, self-understanding, introspection, and insight in changing behavior. However, the curriculum described by Fagen et al. (1975) and Fagen and Long (1979; see also Fagen, 1979) goes well beyond the methods described in early writings about the psychoeducational approach and includes some techniques associated with cognitive-behavior modification. Fagen and Long (1979) present research data supporting their self-control curriculum; but unlike the cognitive-behavior modification research, which emphasizes careful analyses involving single subjects, their research involves comparison of averages for groups of children. The self-control curriculum is discussed further in Chapter 8.

Life Space Interview

The life space interview (LSI) was devised by Fritz Redl (1959a) and his colleagues (see also Redl & Wineman, 1951, 1952) as a means of building ego strength in impulsive, aggressive children. The LSI is a way of talking therapeutically with children about their behavior. Most often a LSI will be held immediately after a behavioral "crisis," since crises provide opportunities to explore with the child what happened, why it happened, and what can be done to prevent future difficulties. The assumption underlying the LSI technique is that by discussing children's behavior with them in the proper way, they will gain insight into their problems and work out solutions to their dilemmas. Insight, it is believed, will provide the basis for volitional or "ego" control.

The LSI has great appeal to most individuals who are opposed on philosophical grounds to the use of explicit behavior modification techniques. It also appeals to those whose perspective is predominately psychiatric. Although much descriptive literature can be found regarding the rationale and use of the LSI with disturbed children, experimental research of its effects on children's behavior has not been forthcoming. Proponents of the LSI must, unfortunately, base their conviction of its value on testimonial or anecdotal evidence from case reports.

SUMMARY

Hyperactivity, distractibility, and impulsivity have been known for several decades to be common behavioral characteristics of exceptional children who today are labeled *emotionally disturbed*, *learning disabled*, or *mentally retarded*. These characteristics are highly interrelated and are also closely aligned with failure at school and social maladaptation. There have been problems in defining and measuring all three characteristics, but usable methods for measuring each characteristic have been devised. The methods used to control one of the three characteristics will likely have value in controlling the other two characteristics as well. Control techniques that have been suggested include medication, dietary restriction, consistent consequences for behavior, modeling, self-instruction, controlled environmental stimuli, biofeedback, and life space interview. Other methods and combinations of techniques have been proposed, including a self-control curriculum. At this time, explicit teaching techniques falling under the general rubric of behavior modification (clear instructions, modeling, reinforcement) have clearer support in empirical research and are more useful for special educators than other approaches.

chapter 8 _____

Aggression

Aggression is not new to American children, their families, or their schools. Even cursory examination of *Children and Youth in America* (Bremner, 1970, 1971) and other similar sources will quickly reveal that coercion, violence, and brutality have been practiced by and toward children from the beginning of this country. Recognition of the historical presence of violence does not in any way, however, reduce the crisis proportions of aggression in the present-day lives of American children. Both violent adult crime and violent juvenile delinquency have increased dramatically during the past few decades. Through the media of television and motion pictures, children are being exposed to brutal acts of aggression at a rate unprecedented in the history of civilization. Assaultive behavior, disruptiveness, and property destruction by children and adolescents in schools have grown commonplace (Lefkowitz, Eron, Walder, & Huesmann, 1977).

The regular classroom teacher must be prepared to deal with aggression, for in most classes there is at least one child who is highly disruptive, destructive, or assaultive toward other children or the teacher. The teacher of disturbed children must be ready to handle an especially large dose of aggression. As will be recalled from previous chapters, conduct disorders—disruptiveness, assaultiveness, destructiveness, tantrums, defiance of authority, profanity, and kindred modes of behavior—are the variety of exasperating deportment that most frequently obtain a deviance label and result in the child's referral for special education services. The prospective special education teacher who expects most disturbed children to be withdrawn or who believes that conduct disordered children will quickly learn to reciprocate a kindly social demeanor will be soundly thumped (physically and psychologically) and, most likely, sent packing. Without effective means for controlling aggression, the teacher of behavior disordered children must develop a superhuman tolerance for interpersonal nastiness.

Two points need clarification here. First, it must be recognized that perfectly normal, emotionally healthy children perform aggressive behaviors, including temper tantrums, verbal assaults, hitting, teasing, and other acts which are part of the aggressive child's repertoire. Aggressive children perform such onerous deeds at a much higher rate and at a much later age than normal children. The socially aggressive child may, in a given interval of time, match the noxious behaviors of the normal child two-to-one or more. Whereas the normal child exhibits social aggression at a decreasing rate as he or she grows older, the socially aggressive child appears to be severely delayed in social development, behaving much like a normal 3-year-old (Patterson, Reid, Jones, & Conger, 1975). Second, aggressive behavior is frequently observed to be a component of other facets of disordered behavior. Aggression is closely linked to hyperactivity, distractibility, and impulsivity. Many aggressive behaviors are involved in delinquency and carry an implication of faulty moral judgment or immoral conduct. Under some circumstances, aggression may be interpreted to represent immaturity or developmental lag. Finally, socially withdrawn children may tolerate provocation only for a limited time, after which they strike out at their provocateurs.

The developmental significance of aggressive, antisocial behavior was touched upon in Chapter 7. It bears restating that hyperaggressive behavior in childhood is a discouraging indicator of adult adjustment, as well as a severe hindrance to childhood social development. Research shows that boys are generally more aggressive than girls. However, some of the observed sex differences might be a result of the fact that girls are observed more often than boys in situations or environments that are not conducive to aggressive acts (Barrett, 1978). Sex differences aside, the importance of teaching children alternatives to aggressive behavior can hardly be overemphasized.

DEFINITION AND MEASUREMENT

The problems of defining *aggression* recall the problems of defining *emotionally disturbed child*. Intuitively, one gets the notion "I know it when I see (or hear or feel) it," but reliance on intuition evades the issue. In order to have a fruitful discussion, one must clarify the instances of behavior that will be included and those that will be excluded from consideration, and this is not so easy a matter as it first appears. As Bandura (1973) points out, whether or not a certain behavior is considered to be aggressive may depend upon the following range of considerations:

1. Characteristics of the behavior itself (e.g., physical assaults, humiliation, property destruction) regardless of the effects on the recipient
2. Intensity of the behavior with high intensity responses (e.g., talking very loudly to a person) being labeled *aggressive* and low intensity responses (e.g., talking with low volume) being labeled *nonaggressive*
3. Expressions of pain, injury, or escape behavior by the recipient of the action
4. Apparent intentions of the performer of the deed
5. Characteristics of the observer (i.e., sex, socioeconomic status, ethnic background, child's own history of nonaggressive or aggressive behavior, and so forth)
6. Characteristics of the aggressor (the same items could be listed here as for characteristics of the observer)

Labeling an act *aggressive*, then, depends for some people on criteria inherent in the behavior itself, while for other people the criteria for labeling aggression are subjective and apart from the act per se.

Semantic quibbles aside, a useful definition of *aggression* must make clear what classes of behavior will be included and what types of activity will not. The definition offered by Bandura (1973) in his social learning analysis fits the tenor and purpose of this book:

> For purposes of the present discussion, *aggression* is defined as behavior that results in personal injury and in destruction of property. The injury may be psychological (in the form of devaluation or degradation) as well as physical. Although this formulation delimits the phenomenon in a meaningful way, it should be made clear that aversive effects cannot serve as the sole defining characteristics of aggression. Individuals who hurt others while performing a socially sanctioned function (for example, dentists repairing teeth or surgeons making painful incisions) would not be considered as acting in an aggressive manner. Nor would bulldozer operators destroying condemned buildings to make way for new construction be charged with committing aggressive acts.

Conversely, some forms of conduct would be judged aggressive even though no personal injury or property damage occurred. A person who attempted to hurt another individual by firing a gun at him or by striking him with a lethal object, but who happened to miss the unsuspecting victim, would be judged as behaving violently. As the preceding examples show, additional criteria for distinguishing between accidental and intended injury must be used both to exclude numerous pain-producing responses from the category of aggression and to include others that do not injure anyone because they are poorly executed.   (p. 5)

Typically, the measurement of aggression has involved behavior rating scales or direct observation and counting of specified acts. Projective tests (like the *Thematic Apperception Test* and personality tests provide only effete measurements of aggression (see Levine, 1966; O'Leary & Johnson, 1979). While behavior rating scales have had some utility insofar as screening populations of children for behavior disorders, factoring behavioral dimensions, and measuring the outcome of intervention techniques, they lack the precision and usefulness of direct observation and the counting of objectively defined aggressive responses. As we shall see later in this chapter, the greatest success in application of control techniques has been achieved by using strategies which involve precise measurement of discrete aggressive behaviors. The work of Gerald R. Patterson and his associates (Patterson, 1973; Patterson & Cobb, 1971; Patterson, Cobb, & Ray, 1972; Patterson, Littman, & Bricker, 1967; Patterson et al., 1975), illustrates the value of direct behavioral observation and measurement. Their data allowed them not only to assess the outcome of their therapeutic endeavors in quantitative terms but also to describe quite clearly the typical rates of behavior that can be expected from aggressive and normal children. According to the data provided by Patterson et al. (1975), a noncompliant behavior about every 10 minutes, as well as a hit and a tease about each half hour, can be expected from an aggressive child. On the other hand, a normal child might be expected to noncomply once in 20 minutes, to tease once in about 50 minutes, and to hit once in a couple of hours.

"Passive Aggression"

It is common in psychiatric literature, including the literature on children's behavior disorders, to encounter references to "passive aggression." Some mental health professionals feel that certain disturbed children find direct, overt expression of aggressive impulses to be too frightening or unproductive, and so these children express their aggression as "passivity." The concept of passive aggression evolved from psychoanalytic theory, which posits that everyone has an inherent aggressive instinct or drive which must be expressed in one form or another. As we shall see later in this chapter, the assumption of such an inherent aggressive drive is not supported by empirical data. Furthermore, *passive aggressive* is a self-contradictory term, for one cannot be aggressive (that is, cause injury or destruction) and passive (that is, be submissive or unresisting to external influence) at the same time. *Passive aggression* in the psychiatric literature has ordinarily been used to refer to such characteristics as stubbornness, procrastination, or obstructionism. The truly passive child—one who is very easily influenced to behave in a given way—may be immature, inadequate, or withdrawn, but is not aggressive. Deliberate obstructionism and failure to comply with requests or commands are indeed aggressive responses; but they are not passive because they are calculated attempts to frustrate or injure another. Thus, negativism, obstructionism, noncompliance, and so on require responses that are the opposite of submissiveness or passivity.

Situation Specificity Versus Consistency in Aggression

A continuing controversy among psychologists is whether people exhibit different behavior in different situations (situation-specific behavior) or whether individuals exhibit behavior that is consistent across situations (behavior affected by personality traits). Of course, everyone would agree that to *some* degree behavior is responsive to environmental circumstances. The controversy has to do with the *relative* amount of situational control or generalized trait that might be observed. As it applies to aggression, the controversy is characterized by the question: "Do aggressive children consistently exhibit aggressive behavior regardless of circumstances, or do they exhibit aggressive behavior only under a few specific circumstances?" Olweus (1979) concluded from a review of research that the evidence supports the notion that the level of male aggressive behavior is relatively consistent across settings and over time. Harris (1979) conducted one of the few observational studies designed expressly to address the question of situation specificity. Her findings are interesting in that they suggest a *curvilinear* relationship between the level of aggressiveness and the degree to which aggressive behavior is consistent across situations. She found that both extremely aggressive children and prosocial children were consistent across different settings (classroom and playground). However, children who were more aggressive than most of their peers, but not extremely so—"garden variety" aggressive children—were significantly more aggressive on the playground than in the classroom.

Sophisticated research is needed to answer definitely the question of situation specificity. Meanwhile, it is clear that for many children, situational factors in the school environment play an important role in determining how much aggressive behavior will be exhibited.

Assertiveness and Aggression

Psychodynamic theorists interpret normal assertiveness as an adaptive or appropriate expression of aggressive drive or aggressive instinct. Some behavioral psychologists have defined *aggressive behavior* as a subset of assertive behaviors. Patterson et al. (1967), for example, identified two characteristics of assertive behaviors: "A demand for an immediate reaction, and the implied threat of highly aversive behavior contingent upon noncompliance" (p. 4). Patterson's hypothesis is that the assertive behaviors of young children are rewarded by the compliance of parents and peers, and that reinforcement of assertiveness is a necessary (but not sufficient) condition for the development of "high-amplitude" aggressive behavior. If a child asks for candy (and thereby is assertive), the parent may reinforce the child's assertiveness by complying with the child's request. Subsequently, the child may again ask for candy, and if the parent declines to comply, the child may become more demanding (more highly assertive). If the parent finally complies, the child may learn quickly to increase assertiveness (perhaps to the level of yelling, hitting, and tantruming) to the point at which the behavior becomes intolerably aversive. The child has then learned to behave aggressively—to be overly assertive and obtain rewards by *coercion* (by behaving in a way that is aversive to others and allowing others to escape from or avoid the aversive behavior only by compliance with his/her wishes).

There is no direct evidence linking normal assertiveness to an aggressive instinct, and there is not much empirical evidence to support the notion that aggression represents assertive responses gone to seed. Patterson's hypothesis seems plausible, but it has not been resoundingly confirmed by behavioral research. When and how assertiveness becomes aggression, and the nature of the differences between assertion and aggression, are still matters for speculation.

Recent interest in the problems of unassertive individuals and popularization of "assertiveness training" have increased the confusion regarding the differences between assertion and aggression (De Giovanni & Epstein, 1978). Hollandsworth (1977) suggests that aggression be differentiated from assertion by its threatening, punitive, coercive qualities. Thus, expressing one's feelings, needs, preferences, or opinions verbally or nonverbally might be considered assertive responses. Only when assertive responses become aversive and threatening would they be considered aggressive. Hollandsworth's suggestion has intuitive appeal, but it does not resolve the problems of reliable definition and measurement. Merely stating that aggression involves threats and coercion does not make it easy to tell assertive acts from aggressive acts. For example, when does a young boy's pulling on his mother's sleeve and saying, "But I *want* that candy *now*" turn from assertiveness to aversiveness and threat? The definition of aggression will become clarified by further description and examples of specific acts. The following discussion will be divided into two sections: Aggression against others and self-injurious behavior.

AGGRESSION AGAINST OTHERS

Types of Noxious Behaviors

Several examples of aggression against others have been provided in the preceding chapters. Children's aggression may take the form of tantrums, verbal abuse, opposition (doing the exact opposite of what they are requested to do), physical assault, or even murder. Table 8–1 lists 14 noxious behaviors commonly exhibited by aggressive and normal children. Patterson and his fellow researchers have identified these behaviors and their typical rates of occurrence through many hours of naturalistic observation in the homes of families with socially aggressive and normal children. Note the marked differences between rates of aggressive behaviors in disturbed and normal children. While this list is certainly not exhaustive, it does represent the most common means by which children inflict suffering on others. Observation by Patterson and his co-workers in schools (Patterson, Cobb, & Ray, 1972) indicates that behaviors of a similar nature may be expected of aggressive children in the classroom. For example, the case of "Maude the Malevolent" illustrates the type of behavior exhibited by socially aggressive children at home and at school.

TABLE 8-1 Noxious Behaviors, Their Descriptions, and the Average Time Elapsing between Their Occurrences in Aggressive and Nonaggressive Children

Noxious Behavior	Description	Average No. of Mins. between Occurrences[a]	
		Aggressive Children	Nonaggressive Children
Disapproval	Disapproving of another's behavior by words or gestures	7	12
Negativism	Stating something neutral in content but saying it in a negative tone of voice	9	41
Noncompliance	Not doing what is requested	11	20
Yell	Shouting, yelling or talking loudly; if carried on for sufficient time it becomes extremely unpleasant	18	54
Tease	Teasing that produces displeasure, disapproval, or disruption of current activity of the person being teased	20	51
High Rate Activity	Activity that is aversive to others if carried on for a long period of time, e.g. running in the house or jumping up and down	23	71
Negative Physical Act	Attacking or attempting to attack another with enough intensity to potentially inflict pain (e.g., biting, kicking, slapping, hitting, spanking, throwing, grabbing)	24	108
Whine	Saying something in a slurring, nasal, high-pitched, or falsetto voice	28	26
Destructive	Destroying, damaging, or trying to damage or destroy any object	33	156
Humiliation	Making fun of, shaming, or embarrassing another intentionally	50	100
Cry	Any type of crying	52	455
Negative Command	Commanding another to do something and demanding immediate compliance, plus threatening aversive consequences (explicit or implicitly) if compliance is not immediate; also directing sarcasm or humiliation at another	120	500
Dependent	Requesting help with a task the child is capable of doing himself; e.g., a 16-year-old boy asking his mother to comb his hair	149	370

TABLE 8-1 (continued)

Noxious Behavior	Description	Average No. of Mins. between Occurrences[a]	
		Aggressive Children	*Nonaggressive Children*
Ignore	The child appears to recognize that another has directed behavior toward him but does not respond in an active fashion	185	244

[a] Minutes between occurrences are expressed as approximations of reported average rates per minute (e.g., for aggressive children's "whine," reported rate per minute equals 0.0360, or approximately once every 28 minutes.

Note. Adapted from *A Social Learning Approach to Family Intervention*, Vol 1: Families with Aggressive Children by G.R. Patterson, J.B. Reid, R.R. Jones, and R.E. Conger (Eugene, Oregon: Castilia, 1975), p. 5. Copyright 1975 by Castilia Publishing Company. Reprinted by permission.

vignette

Maude was only 10 when referred to ORI [Oregon Research Institute] at the behest of the school. In addition to frequent stealing episodes, and even more frequent lies, she was almost totally without friends. Her "entrance" into a game being played on the playground could be marked by her shouted commands and freely dispensed kicks and blows to those who noncomplied. What was most infuriating to peers and teachers alike was her ability to look an accusing adult in the eye and say, "No, I didn't take the money," even though faced by three eye witnesses (including the teacher). If defeated in such an encounter, she generally planned revenge such as writing notes to the teacher in the most florid prose imaginable. The notes were directed to those teachers most likely to be upset by the language. While only four feet tall, she could reduce most adults half again her size to smoldering impotence.

Her parents fared no better. Her presence in the home consisted of running battles with both of her older sisters. What she did not accomplish by verbal invectives could be won by stealthy attacks upon their belongings (e.g., a favorite picture smashed, an article of jewelry "lost," or money "mislaid"). Attempts to control her behavior were met with denials, lies, debates, giggles, and sobs. Occasionally, one or both parents would severely spank her, but both were convinced that it did little good. She was so difficult to manage that the parents had long ago given up any pretense of asking her to do chores.

The mother seemed very angry with Maude and reported later that she spent long hours ruminating about her daughter's myriad misbehaviors. She was convinced she could not be changed and had often considered institutionalization. She reported that Maude knew just what to say or how to act in order to get under her skin.

The parents listed the following as problems of greatest concern
to them:
1. Steals
2. Lies
3. Swears at home and school
4. Fights with peers
5. Not liked by other children
6. Teases siblings
7. Does not mind (Patterson et al., 1975, p. 31)

Lest the impression be given that conduct like Maude's and the attendant consternation of adults are found primarily in the behavior modification literature, it should be noted that psychoanalytic and humanistic descriptions of disturbed children—indeed, the literature representing every philosophical viewpoint—also contain frequent and graphic illustrations of children's aggression and the revulsion it produces in its victims. Unlike the behavior modification literature, which abounds with frequency data that have been obtained systematically over a period of time and plotted on a graph, the writing of nonbehaviorists is characterized by case reports highlighting a few dramatic and specific instances of aggression and summary statements regarding children's aggressive tendencies (cf. Berkowitz & Rothman, 1967; Bettelheim, 1950, 1970; Dennison, 1969; Grossman, 1965; Redl & Wineman, 1951, 1952).

Causes of Aggression

Why children begin to hurt and threaten others and why they persist in aggressing are questions that need answers. How social aggression can be prevented and how it can be controlled once it occurs are also concerns of great importance if schools and families are to be humane social institutions. Attempts to analyze the factors that instigate and maintain aggression and the control techniques that have been found most effective must be considered.

There is nothing approximating unanimity of view among social scientists and educators regarding the causes of aggression in children. For the sake of clarity and simplicity, only four major viewpoints will be discussed briefly: Biological, psychodynamic, frustration-aggression, and social learning. Variations on these four themes are subsumed under the major headings.

Biological Aspects

Hypotheses regarding the biological bases of aggression usually follow one of three lines of argument: (a) aggression is a genetically organized, instinctual behavior, shaped through evolutionary processes and controlled primarily by certain eliciting stimuli; (b) aggression is basically a response to hormonal and other biochemical action; or (c) aggression reflects electrical activity in the central nervous system.

The evidence that most aggressive behavior in humans can be explained by evolutionary or genetic factors is very weak. Bandura (1973) and others (e.g., Montagu, 1968) review data that call into question the idea that humans are innately aggressive. Although species (presumably even Homo sapiens) can be selectively bred in order to produce more aggressive strains (indicating genetic factors perhaps can influence aggressive tendencies), the evidence is overwhelming that experiential factors are far more influential than genes or instincts in determining specific aggressive acts.

There is reason to believe that hormonal changes and drugs can induce aggressive tendencies (Achenbach, 1974; Bandura, 1973). However, the evidence is far from sufficient to justify assertions that biochemicals account for aggression in humans, or even in infrahuman species. The social experience of individuals appears to be a far more potent force in accounting for aggressive behavior.

Perhaps the most popular and appealing hypothesis regarding biological instigators of aggression is that brain mechanisms determine behavior in which case, of course, biochemical and genetic factors play a role. This hypothesis gains support from observation that damage to, or electrical or chemical stimulation of, certain parts of the brain (for example, the hypothalamus or the limbic system) can facilitate or inhibit aggressive behavior. For example, the monumental work of Jose Delgado (Delgado, 1969; see also Restak, 1975) and the research of others has shown how aggression in animals and humans can be turned on or off by delivering electrical impulses to the brain. The suggestion that aggression is *simply* a function of discharges in the brain, however, is extremely naive. Delgado's work with artificially triggered aggression in animals showed that the social environment as well as neural stimulation is a determiner of aggression. The conclusions to be drawn from neurobiological research are not only that behavior is multiply determined, but also that the extent to which biological, psychological, and sociological forces instigate and maintain aggression will vary according to the species, the specific aggressive behavior, and the social conditions involved (Bandura, 1973). Delgado (1969) states:

> While neurophysiological activity may be influenced or perhaps even set by genetic factors and past experience, the brain is the direct interpreter of environmental inputs and the determinant of behavioral responses. To understand the causes and [to] plan remedies for . . . aggression in animals and man require knowledge of both sociology and neurophysiology. Electricity cannot determine the target for hostility or direct the sequences of aggressive behavior, which are both related to past history of the stimulated subject and to his immediate adaptation to changing circumstances.   (p. 132)

In summary, all behavior, including aggression, involves neurobiological processes. These biological forces, however, do not alone determine behavior (cf. Kety, 1979). The social environment of the individual is a powerful regulator of neurobiological processes and behavior.

Psychodynamic Theory

Freud and other early proponents of psychoanalytic theory believed that aggression is a basic instinctual force that causes one to perform aggressive behaviors.[27] According to Freud, aggressive behavior arises from either the "death in-

---

[27] There is, of course, a biological basis for "instincts," and psychodynamic theory embraces biological determinants of behavior. However, psychodynamic theorists explain instincts differently than ethologists; there is no necessity in ethology to construct hypothetical mental mechanisms similar to those proposed by Freud.

stinct" (Thanatos) or the "libido" (the pleasure-seeking or love-object-seeking psychic energy) or some confluence of these forces. The id—the unconscious store of psychic energy and primitive impulses—is in Freud's theory the mental apparatus containing aggression. Aggression, according to Freud's theory, is something separate from aggressive behavior: It is an entity creating a *need* for aggressive behavior. Accordingly, aggression can be expressed behaviorally as positive (socially acceptable or constructive aggression) or negative (socially unacceptable or destructive aggression), depending on the demands of the environment and, especially, on the control mechanisms of the mind (the ego and the superego). Other psychodynamic theorists, including Adler, vary Freud's theme but the basic idea of an independent motivating force called *aggression*, an unconscious impellent that guides the behavior of its unwitting victims and champions, is fundamental to the psychodynamic perspective, (see Feshbach, 1970, for a review). Examples of the assumption that aggression *causes* rather than *is* behavior are found sprinkled generously throughout the psychodynamically oriented literature. Redl and Wineman (1951), for example, write: "We have ample materials on the various disguises which particles of aggression and hate have to assume in order to sneak close to the scene of action or find open expression in fantasy or thought" (p. 25). Of aggressive children they state, "Then, under the impact of trauma or fright, the full blast of their aggression rides herd over them" (p. 29), and of a passive child who became aggressive, they say, "Behind the seemingly empty and childlike stare of his detached eyes lay an ocean of unbridled aggression, destruction, and counter hatred, which was the response to years of earlier cruelty and neglect, but which had been frozen into apathetic immobility at the time" (p. 28). Berkowitz and Rothman (1960) provide the following summary:

> Aggression is an innate instinctual impulse which may give rise to a need for aggressive behavior. Aggression which can be successfully sublimated may become socially useful, while overt aggression which is destructive in nature is an acting-out of the child's need to inflict pain and punishment upon himself or upon others. Aggressive behavior which is uncontrolled is an easily observed, obvious indicator of maladjustment.   (p. 89)

Psychodynamic theories of aggression appear to have lost many adherents in recent years, primarily because the hypotheses generated by such theories are not empirically testable. Moreover, psychodynamic theory is of very limited value in designing effective intervention techniques; other, competing ideas regarding the instigators of aggression *are* supported by abundant empirical data.

Frustration-Aggression Hypothesis

Research by learning theorists in the 1930s (Dollard, Doob, Miller, Mowrer, & Sears, 1939) led to the statement of an hypothesis that enjoyed wide acclaim for many years. The hypothesis is that frustration (defined as the blocking or thwarting of any ongoing goal-directed activity) always results in *aggression* (defined as behavior designed to injure the person at whom it is directed) and that aggression always arises from frustration. A likely contributing factor to the popularity of the frustration-aggression hypothesis is the fact that Dollard et al. connect their ideas with psychodynamic notions. Rather than ascribing aggression to innate instincts, however, they argue that frustration induces an aggressive *drive* that motivates aggressive behavior. Once frustration is encountered, the aggressive drive is automatically induced and *must* be given expression before the drive can be reduced. Thus, the frustration-aggression proposition was applauded by many individuals whose orientation was psychodynamic, as exemplified by the comments of Redl and Wineman (1951):

> The various studies in "Frustration and Aggression" have documented Freud's old suspicions along that line and have shown statistically that the mere frustration of basic needs or important goals in a child's life may be enough to produce unmanageable quantities of aggression and destructiveness or other disturbance even in children who otherwise wouldn't have had to hate so much. (pp. 25-26)

While it is true that the frustration-aggression hypothesis was constructed on the basis of empirical data showing that frustration *can* produce aggression, the theory has been laid to rest by additional research (see Achenbach, 1974; Bandura, 1973; Berkowitz, 1973). In brief, this research has shown that aggression is *not* an inevitable outcome of frustration and that several other factors besides frustration can contribute to the development and maintenance of aggression. Furthermore, the concept of an aggressive *drive* is extra baggage that is not needed in order to explain the instigation and perpetuation of aggressive behavior.

Social Learning Analysis

Bandura (1973) offers a comprehensive and incisive analysis of aggression based on social learning theory. A social learning analysis includes assessment of three major controlling influences on behavior: the stimuli that precede the behaviors in question (antecedent stimuli that control responses), feedback or reinforcement and punishment effects (consequences), and cognitive processes (what people perceive, think, and feel). Statements about the instigation and maintenance of aggression based on social learning theory tend to be much more complex than those generated by psychodynamic theory or drive theory (the frustration-aggression hypothesis). As shown in Figure 8-1, (a) instinct (psychodynamic) theory postulates an aggressive instinct that finds direct expression in aggressive behavior; (b) drive theory posits an aggressive drive that is set off by frustration and motivates aggressive behavior; (c) social learning theory asserts that aversive experiences (which may include frustration or unpleasant stimuli of any kind) produce a state of emotional arousal and that the anticipated consequences of a given behavior (which may have been gained through direct experience, observational learning, or cognitive processes) generate motivation. The outcome of arousal and motivation may vary greatly from individual to individual depending upon a variety of factors, such as reinforcement history, physiological status, and the social situation. Therefore, the same aversive experience may cause some persons to exhibit dependent behavior, others to strive to achieve, some to withdraw resignedly from the situation, still others to aggress, and so on.

The convolutions of social learning theory and the details of the research undergirding a social learning analysis of aggression are too intricate to be reviewed here. However, Bandura's review of the empirical research (Bandura, 1969, 1973; Bandura & Walters, 1959, 1963) provides several important generalizations:

1. Children learn many aggressive responses by observing models or examples. The models from which children learn aggression may be family

INSTINCT THEORY

DRIVE THEORY

SOCIAL LEARNING THEORY

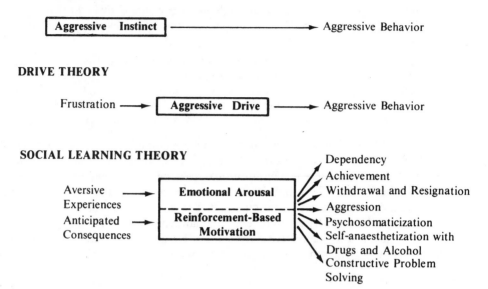

FIGURE 8-1   Diagrammatic representation of motivational determinants of aggression in instinct, reactive drive, and social learning theories.

Note. From *Aggression: A Social Learning Analysis* by A. Bandura (Englewood Cliffs, New Jersey: Prentice-Hall, 1973), p. 54. Copyright 1973 by Prentice-Hall. Reprinted by permission.

members, members of the child's subculture (friends, acquaintances, peers and adults in the child's community), or individuals portrayed in the mass media (including real and fictional, human and nonhuman individuals).

2. Aggressive models are more likely to be imitated by children when the models are of high social status and when the child sees that the models receive reinforcement (positive consequences or rewards) or fail to receive punishment for their aggression.

3. Children learn aggressive behavior when they are given opportunities to practice aggressive responses and experience either no aversive consequences or success in obtaining rewards by harming or overcoming their victims.

4. Aggression is more likely to occur when children are aversively stimulated, perhaps by physical assault, verbal threats, taunts, or insults; thwarting of goal-directed behavior; or decreases in or termination of positive reinforcement. They have learned through observation and/or practice that they can obtain rewarding consequences by engaging in aggressive behavior. The probability of aggression under such circumstances is especially high when alternative means of obtaining reinforcement are not readily available or have not been learned and when aggression is sanctioned by social authorities.

5. Factors that maintain aggression include external reinforcement (tangible rewards, social and status rewards, removal of aversive stimuli, perhaps

expressions of injury or suffering by the victim), vicarious reinforcement (that is, reinforcement obtained by observing others gain rewards through aggression), and self-reinforcement (self-congratulation or rise in self-esteem following successful aggression).

6. Aggression may be perpetuated by cognitive processes that justify hostile action: for example, by comparing one's deeds advantageously to more horrific ones, appealing to "higher" principles, placing responsibility on someone else (the familiar "I didn't start it" and "he made me do it" ploys), dehumanizing the victims (perhaps with demeaning labels such as *niggers, trash, pigs, droolers*), and so on.[28]

7. Punishment may serve to heighten or maintain aggression when there are no positive alternatives to the punished response, when punishment is delayed or inconsistent, or when it provides a model of aggressive behavior. The adult who strikes a child in order to punish him/her provides an example of aggression. When counterattack against the punisher seems likely to be successful, punishment maintains aggression.

A social learning analysis of aggression generates testable predictions about the environmental conditions that foster aggressive behavior and, as we shall see later, the ways in which the environment can be arranged to control aggression. Social learning theory has led to predictions about the genesis of aggression that are confirmed by empirical research data such as the following:

1. Viewing televised aggression will increase aggressive behavior in children, especially in males and in children who have a history of aggressiveness (Eron, Huesmann, Lefkowitz, & Walder, 1972, 1974; Friedrich & Stein, 1973; Lefkowitz et al., 1977; Stein & Friedrich, 1975).

2. Delinquent subcultures, such as street gangs, will maintain aggressive behavior in their members by modeling and reinforcement of aggression (Buehler, Patterson, & Furniss, 1966; Yablonsky, 1962).

3. Families of aggressive children will be characterized by high rates of aggression on the part of all family members and by inconsistent punitive control techniques on the part of the parents (Lefkowitz et al., 1977; Patterson, 1973, 1975; Patterson et al., 1975).

4. Aggression will beget aggression. When one person presents an aversive stimulus (e.g., hit, yell, whine) the affronted individual is likely to reply by presenting a negative stimulus of his/her own, and a coercive interaction will be the result (Patterson, 1975; Patterson & Cobb, 1971; Patterson, Littman & Bricker, 1967; Patterson & Ried, 1970). The coercive interaction will continue until one individual withdraws his or her aversive stimulus, providing negative reinforcement (i.e., escape from aversive stimulation) for the victor (see also Tedeschi, Smith, & Brown, 1974).

It is not difficult to see how social learning processes might operate in the

---

[28] For in-depth discussion of cognitive factors in social learning, see Mahoney (1974).

origins of aggression. Messer and Brodzinsky (1979) found that an impulsive cognitive tempo is correlated with aggression and with lack of concern about aggressive fantasies and the consequences of aggression. Aggressive children seem to be unduly fast and inaccurate in responding to problem-solving situations and to care little about what happens as a result of aggression. Their responses are the type that may seem to invite punitive action from their parents and teachers. Mulhern and Passman (1979) found that mothers who were ostensibly teaching their sons to avoid errors on a puzzle-solving task escalated their punishment when they believed that higher levels of punishment were effective in reducing their sons' errors. That is, when higher and higher levels of punishment were "rewarded" by fewer errors on the part of their sons (actually, feedback to the mothers was programmed elecromechanically, not by their sons' performance), mothers readily became more punitive. Moreover, the more highly punitive these mothers were in the laboratory situation, the more they indicated that they used physical punishment as a disciplinary technique in the home. Together, these two studies offer further experimental evidence supporting an interactional, social learning theory of aggression. It is plausible that children who show impulsive and aggressive behavior induce punitive discipline from their parents and teachers. Punitive discipline, especially if it is erratic and inconsistent, is likely to increase the child's anxiety and impulsive, inappropriate behavior—the very characteristics parents and teachers find aversive. If the child's aversive behavior is quickly terminated in a given instance, the adult's punishment of the child may be temporarily effective. But it may be ineffective in the long run because ever-increasing intensities of punishment are required, and the aggressive act-punitive response pattern soon becomes a vicious cycle of coercion.

Summary.   Social learning theory provides the basis for an empirically based analysis of aggression. The origin and maintenance of aggressive behavior can be accounted for to a large extent by basic learning processes, such as imitation and reinforcement. Particularly important for special educators is the implication that a social learning analysis can be a guide to the effective and humane control of aggressive behavior, as we shall see in the following discussion.

Control Techniques

How one goes about controlling aggression will depend primarily on how one views the causes of aggressive behavior. Those who view humans as inherently aggressive, driven by merciless and unalterable instincts, can offer little advice except to accept and, perhaps, to try to "channel" aggression into constructive pursuits. Alternatively, those who espouse the view that social forces are primarily responsible for the emergence of aggression will recommend modulation of the social environment. In this examination of control, three approaches of particular import for educators will be highlighted.

Psychodynamic Approach

From a psychodynamic perspective, aggression is a pervasive and unalterable aspect of every child's personality, and the objective of the teacher or other agent of control must therefore be to help the child express aggression in constructive ways. There are two fundamental ways in which a teacher can help the aggressive child according to psychodynamic tenets: first, by accepting the child's behavior and feelings; and second, by providing the child with opportunities for "catharsis." Accepting the child's feelings and behavior is important in developing a therapeutic relationship with the child (a matter of supreme importance in psychodynamic theory: see Ack, 1970; Bettelheim, 1950). Providing opportunity for catharsis (literally, *cleansing*) is important, for the aggressive child must express his/her impulses if aggression is to be reduced. We will examine the ideas of acceptance and catharsis and the evidence of their efficacy more closely.

In their classic text, Berkowitz and Rothman (1960) exemplify this approach. To be sure, they do not condone a laissez faire policy in which there are *no* limits on how children should conduct themselves in the classroom, but it must be recognized that, like Bettelheim, they recommend a very permissive approach compared to the traditional school environment. They believe that in a permissive environment where children feel accepted and free to express themselves, children develop a secure and reassuring relationship with the teacher, which is the key to behavioral and academic progress.

> A basic precept for the establishment of a good working teacher-pupil relationship is the theory of acceptance. A child has to learn to accept the teacher and the school situation. The teacher, in turn, must accept the child along with the manifestations of his difficulties. This acceptance begins the moment the child enters the classroom. The initial contact with the child lays the foundation for all future relations, and may make the difference between a teaching failure and a teaching success.   (Berkowitz & Rothman, 1960, p. 117)

To encourage a feeling of acceptance, Berkowitz and Rothman (1960) recommend that formal restrictions be relaxed, that the classroom atmosphere be noncompetitive and friendly, that individuality and self-expression be permitted, and that teaching methods be geared to realistic educational goals for each individual. In order to build trust in the child, it is necessary for the teacher to make it quite clear that no matter how the child behaves, the teacher accepts and likes him or her as an individual. Furthermore, it is necessary for teachers to allow themselves to be manipulated by the child into playing certain roles for the child's benefit.

> Frequently, the teacher can become a subservient figure who can be bullied and made to serve the ego needs of the child. In assuming this role, the teacher helps the aggressive child become less anxious, guiding his aggression, thereby preventing this aggression from falling upon other children. When it seems necessary, therefore, to acquiesce to a child's unreasonable aggressive demands, the teacher must be willing to do so. In most cases, when this child, little by little, becomes aware that his demands are being met, he also becomes more willing to relinquish them, and begins to function with less hostility and unreasonableness. (Berkowitz & Rothman, 1960, p. 125)

This psychodynamic approach to managing aggression has declined in popularity during the past decade, probably for the following reasons: (a) there is hardly any evidence to support its efficacy in reducing aggression; (b) there is some reason to believe that it is destructive and that it actually has a pernicious effect; (c) alternative methods of managing aggression are supported by data showing their efficacy. Berkowitz and Rothman (1960), Bettelheim (1950), Ack (1970), and others who advocate psychodynamic treatment offer no experimental evidence whatsoever that their methods are effective in reducing aggression. That is, there are only anecdotal reports and testimonial evidence that *acceptance* of aggression or aggressive feelings and *permission to express* aggression are effective ways of managing aggressive behavior.

More important, perhaps, than the absence of such backup data are indications that the method may make matters worse. In direct contradiction to anecdotal evidence that a permissive approach works to lessen aggression, one may find other testimonial statements that it is destructive (Fenichel, 1974, pp. 64–66). Furthermore, the mass of experimental data suggests strongly that the free expression of aggression, even if "sublimated" and directed against acceptable targets, may serve only to heighten the level of aggressive behavior (Bandura, 1973; Berkowitz, 1973; Lefkowitz et al., 1977).[29]

The idea of catharsis has been popular for a long while. Theories of aggression that postulate an aggressive drive or instinct carry an implication that aggression is *something that accumulates within the person.* The only way to get rid of aggression, therefore, is to drain off this reservoir—to cleanse or purge the self by expressing aggression in one manner or another. It has often been suggested that catharsis can be achieved through *sublimation* (expressing aggression directly but in a socially sanctioned way, such as through participation in contact sports), through *displacement* (aggressing against a substitute and socially acceptable target, such as punching a bag or doll instead of a person), or through *fantasy* (imagining aggressive acts, watching movies in which aggression is portrayed, or painting pictures depicting aggression). Berkowitz and Rothman (1960, p. 162), for example, suggest that the aggressive child might be helped by repeatedly painting scenes of violence in order to express hostility.

As Berkowitz (1973) points out, the catharsis idea has become practically a cultural truism, but it is a hypothesis that is not supported by research data. In fact, both Bandura's (1973) and Berkowitz's (1973) reviews of the research on aggression indicate clearly that instead of draining off aggressive impulses, viewing and participating in aggression *increase* aggressive behavior (Friedrich & Stein, 1973; Lefkowitz et al., 1977; Stein & Friedrich, 1975). Thomas, Horton, Lippincott, and Drabman (1977) found that exposure to TV violence had the effect of decreasing children's and adults' emotional sensitivity to acts of aggression, and of blunting their sensitivity to watching other people being hurt. One can argue on the strength of humanistic philosophy that children should feel and be accepted by the teacher even when they are aggressive, but one can find *no* substantial evidence that children's emotional sensitivity to others is enhanced or that their prosocial behavior is improved when they are allowed to watch or participate in hostile, aggressive acts or fantisies. In addition to philosophical arguments, one can marshal empirical data to support the conclusion that children should *not* be allowed to watch and practice aggression for the sake of catharsis.

---

[29] Over the years both Berkowitz and Rothman have modified their views on the issue of a permissive approach. They, as well as Fenichel (see Fenichel, 1974) have come to place more emphasis on structure and behavioral control in educating disturbed, aggressive children (see Berkowitz, 1974; Rothman, 1974; Rothman & Berkowitz, 1967a).

Psychoeducational Methods

Psychoeducational is somewhat difficult to define, but it is generally thought to mean a focus on affective and cognitive factors in behavior (cf. Fagen, Long, & Stevens, 1975, pp. 51–54). One can identify persons who describe the psychoeducational approach (for example, Carl Fenichel, Nicholas J. Long, William C. Morse, Ruth G. Newman) more easily than one can describe the major features of the approach itself. Nevertheless, it seems clear from the discourse of psychoeducational proponents that (a) the psychodynamic concepts of instincts, drives, and needs are taken into account but, (b) intervention is focused on the cognitive and affective problems of children and, (c) it is assumed that by resolving the affective and cognitive problems of children (by helping children gain *insight* into their needs and motivations), their problem behavior will be changed. Psychoeducational methods appear to be identified closely with *ego psychology* and to be derived in large measure from the writings of Redl and Wineman (1951, 1952). To some extent, psychoeducational methods are also aligned with *humanistic psychology* and the writings of Maslow (1962).

The most important tools of the psychoeducational approach are talking and experiencing. The life space interview (LSI) and exercises designed to recognize and appreciate feelings are the mainstay of the teacher's armamentarium against aggression (and other problems). Redl and Wineman (1951, 1952) and Morse and Wineman (1965) describe in considerable detail the use of LSI techniques with aggressive boys.

No experimental evidence now supports the efficacy of the LSI, only the testimony of its advocates (see Chapter 7). As in the case of the permissive, psychodynamic approach, there is testimonial evidence refuting the claims of LSI proponents. Nicholas Hobbs, a distinguished psychologist who for several years was an advocate of therapeutic strategies designed to promote insight, has stated emphatically and eloquently that his personal experience does not bear out the assumption that insight produces behavioral change (see Hobbs, 1974, pp. 148–149). In addition, the experimental literature on control of aggression strongly suggests that insight, by itself, is a relatively weak (perhaps even completely ineffective) means of changing aggressive behavior (Bandura, 1973). Regarding acceptance and expression of feelings, the evidence is even more disappointing. Not only is there a lack of data showing that to accept and express one's feelings is to overcome them or to improve one's behavior, but it seems likely that acceptance and expression of anger *by themselves and without training in how to change them* may exacerbate rather than decrease internal vituperation as well as overt aggression. As Mahoney (1974) observes "The act of perceiving oneself as 'not handling it' is often an exacerbating element in subjective distress" (p. 221).

Notwithstanding the conclusion that insight, acceptance, and expression of feelings are *in themselves* quite worthless in controlling aggression, there is reason to suspect that cognitive and affective factors can be effective *components of* strategies for reducing aggressive behavior. Berkowitz (1973) and Bandura (1973) review research showing that if the child's cognitive and affective patterns can be altered, then aggression may be lessened. For example, one can call the child's attention to the hurtful consequences of aggression, label aggression as *bad*, or make the child aware through discussion that the victims of aggression have some desirable characteristics or that they share some of his/her own characteristics. Mahoney's treatise, *Cognition and Behavior Modification* (1974), suggests that how children think and feel about aggression may contribute to how they act (and vice versa: that how they act may influence how they feel). If children's perceptions of aggression and the victims of aggression can be altered, they *may* be inclined to be less aggressive, but if they can be taught problem-solving techniques for managing aggression, there is a much better chance that they will exhibit less aggressive behavior (cf. Goodwin & Mahoney, 1975; Spivack & Shure, 1974). Certainly, cognitive awareness of one's affective responses to aggression-inducing situations and cognitive analysis of the sequence of events in such situations may be of help in controlling aggressive behavior, but the mechanisms of control appear to be built through explicit training.

Fagen et al. (1975) and Fagen and Long (1979) have significantly extended the concept of the psychoeducational approach. Their self-control curriculum involves teaching children eight clusters of skills which they describe as follows:

- *Selection*—Ability to perceive incoming information accurately.
- *Storage*—Ability to retain the information received.
- *Sequencing and Ordering*—Ability to organize actions on the basis of a planned order.
- *Anticipating Consequences*—Ability to relate actions to expected outcomes.
- *Managing Frustration*—Ability to cope with external obstacles that produce stress.
- *Inhibition and Delay*—Ability to postpone or restrain action tendencies.
- *Relaxation*—Ability to reduce internal tension. (Fagen & Long, 1979, p. 70)

The methods Fagen and Long suggest for teaching these skills include many of those used in cognitive-behavioral modification studies: self-instruction, problem-solving, modeling and rehearsal, self-determination of goals and reinforcement standards, self-observation, self-evaluation, and self-reward. The psychoeducational self-control curriculum seems designed *primarily* as a skill-building, preventative approach that includes group instruction and role playing. The cognitive-behavior modification literature is characterized by *in situ* analyses of specific behaviors of individual children. It is clear, however, that the approach described by Fagen and Long allows for work on specific problem behaviors of individual children in everyday classroom situations.

Within the past few years, two noteworthy trends in approaches to management of disruptive, hyperaggressive behavior have been seen: (a) movement of proponents of the psychoeducational approach away from ethereal, psychoanalytic speculation and toward a firmer empirical foundation for theory and methodology, and (b) recognition by proponents of the behavioral approach of the importance of internal dialogue and affective states in behavioral control. The result has been a rapprochement between psychoeducational and cognitive-behavioral interventions. The reconciliation of these two points of view has its critics who prefer the theoretical and methodological purity of mid-century behaviorism or humanism. Nevertheless, many special educators view the rapprochement as a welcome step forward. The movement toward empirical data and experimental methods on the part of psychoeducational proponents, coupled with a willingness on the part of behaviorists to experiment with cognitive-affective variables may result in reliable experimental evidence to support some psychoeducational methods that heretofore have been accepted on the basis of subjective clinical experience and dogmata.

Behavioral Intervention

In the following explanation of behavioral intervention, a few fundamental strategies and principles of social learning theory will be outlined. Several examples from the literature will be provided.

Social learning approach.   A social learning approach to control of aggression includes (a) the statement of specific behavioral objectives, (b) a system for precise measurement of behavior, and (c) techniques for changing behavior. Consequently, the outcome of the behavioral intervention can be judged quantitatively as well as qualitatively against an objective goal. Behavior change techniques are employed by the persons who have the most continuous contact with the aggressive child and the greatest amount of control over his/her immediate environment (including parents, siblings, teachers, peers), rather than therapists who see the child infrequently and work in highly artificial or contrived settings. Thus, the focus is on modification of the child's current social environment rather than on historical events. Problem behavior is dealt with as it occurs in its natural setting rather than in a counselling setting where one need rely on verbal descriptions.

As Bandura (1973) notes regarding aggressive individuals, "What most people need is not the insight that they are behaving inadequately, but the means to learn more successful ways of behaving" (p. 253), and "No amount of insightful conversation will have much effect unless the reinforcement practices of influential people in the social system change" (p. 296). Therefore, the emphasis in a behavioral approach based on social learning is on techniques of arranging the social environment to foster and reward adaptive, nonaggressive behavior. The intervention procedure requires one first to define and count instances of aggressive behavior so that an objective, quantitative assessment of the problem and its resolution can be had. Then, in order to reduce the aggression, behavioral intervention involves one or more procedures such as:

1. Modeling nonaggressive responses to aggression-provoking situations. For example, demonstrating repeatedly how to behave nonaggressively under aversive conditions, using models which may be adults or peers, live or filmed, human or nonhuman.

2. Guiding the practice of nonaggressive behaviors in real life and activities such as role playing and rehearsal in hypothetical situations.

3. Reinforcement of nonaggressive behaviors by giving rewards for specific

alternatives to aggressive responses, such as playing without hitting, or adaptive behaviors that increase the child's social competence, such as academic performance.

4. Extinction of aggression by withholding rewards for aggressive responses, such as refusing to give in to (i.e., reinforce) temper tantrums.

5. Punishing aggressive behaviors by any of three methods: presenting an aversive stimulus (e.g., spanking); withdrawing positive reinforcers, such as subtracting tokens or points already earned, or withholding a favorite food or activity; giving the child time-out, which is a brief isolation from ongoing activities and a reinforcing environment.

In brief, the theory behind behavioral intervention is built on the assumption that aggression is learned behavior; therefore, nonaggressive behavior can be taught directly. In order to teach nonaggressive behavior, it is necessary to make nonaggressive modes of behavior salient and rewarding and to remove rewarding consequences for aggression. It is also recognized that social incompetence (including academic failure and lack of skills in social interaction) and aversive, inhumane social conditions (including poverty, repression, and lack of opportunity) contribute to aggression. Therefore, programs to teach skills required for successful socialization and rectification of aversive social conditions are required.

Behavior modification techniques. Behavioral interventions often appear to be extremely simple. The apparent simplicity is often deceptive, for subtle and intricate adjustments in technique are necessary to make them work. An exquisite sensitivity to human communication is necessary to master the humane and effective application of behavior principles. Furthermore, the range of techniques that may be employed in an individual case is large, and a high degree of creativity is required in order to formulate an effective and ethical plan of action (see Maloney, Fixsen, & Maloney, 1978).

The work of Patterson and his colleagues is exemplary. Through years of painstaking observation and research in homes and classrooms, they formulated procedures that schools and families can now use to control aggressive behavior. They have been successful in controlling aggressive behavior in about two out of three cases (Patterson et al., 1975). Their work has included the use of a wide array of techniques grounded in social learning theory. In many cases they have employed contingency contracts—written agreements regarding aggressive and nonaggressive behaviors and their consequences. The case of Sam, a 10-year-old boy who had stolen bikes, destroyed school property, and physically attacked other children, provides an example (Patterson et al., 1973). Note that Sam's contract (Figure 8-2) involves both the home and the school, and the consequences of both aggressive and desirable behavior are clearly specified.

Much of the literature of behavior modification with children is devoted to the topic of aggressive, disruptive, hyperactive behavior (see Ayllon & Rosenbaum, 1977; Risely & Baer, 1973; Sherman & Bushell, 1975; Thoresen, 1973). A few examples of modification of noxious behaviors are provided here.

Controlling a hyperaggressive preschooler. Kauffman and Hallahan (1973) present the problem of a 6-year-old hyperaggressive boy (Tom) who attended a preschool designed for both handicapped and normal children.

The following is a contract between Sam and his teacher, his principal, and his counselor, in order for Sam to learn ways to behave during school. Sam will earn points during the school hours so that he can do some of the things he enjoys at home. The total number of points which can be earned each day is 50. The behaviors are the following:

Talking in a normal tone of voice, e.g., not yelling.

Cooperating with his teacher, e.g., not arguing and doing what is asked on the playground and in the halls.

Minding other teachers.

Remaining in chair unless school work requires moving in the classroom, e.g., not roaming around the room.

Talking to other children at proper times, e.g., not disturbing other children when they work.

Following his teacher's directions for work, e.g., doing the work assigned.

Sam will start with a total of 50 points each day and will lose a point for each time he does not follow the above rules. Each time he loses a point, he is to be placed in Time Out for five minutes. At the end of each school day his teacher will call his mother to give her a total of points earned for that day. Sam will be allowed five minutes of TV for each point.

For the following behaviors Sam is to be sent home from school for the day:

1. Destroying property.
2. Fighting with other children to the point of hurting them.
3. Taking property belonging to someone else.
4. Swearing.
5. Refusing to go into Time Out.

When Sam is sent home his principal will call his father to tell him what Sam has done. His principal will then call his mother so she will know that Sam is being set [sic] home. When Sam arrives home, he is to do some task around the house or yard until school is out, at which time he can follow the normal routine of the household except watching TV that night.

When Sam does not follow the rules of the lunchroom he is to be sent from the lunchroom to the principal's office without finishing his meal.

His mother will keep the number of points earned each day in order to assess Sam's progress. His mother will also continue to teach Sam reading skills until such time as he is able to handle reading material in the classroom. The therapist will continue to supervise Sam's mother until the reading program is completed. (To be signed by all parties.)

Date _Feb 3, 1971_

Sam _Sam_
Mother _Mom_
Father _Dad_
Teacher _Mr. Hanson_
Principal _Mr. Rea_

FIGURE 8-2 Sam's contract.

Note. From "Direct Intervention in the Classroom: A Set of Procedures for the Aggressive Child" by G. R. Patterson, J. A. Cobb, and R. S. Ray in F. W. Clark, D. R. Evans, and L. A. Hamerlynck (Eds.), *Implementing Behavioral Programs for Schools and Clinics* (Champaign, Illinois: Research Press, 1972), pp. 166-167. Copyright 1972 by Research Press. Reprinted by permission.

vignette _____

He had a long history of brutal treatment and neglect by his parents and was living in a foster home. Because Tom was so cruel toward other children, his peers were afraid of him and tried their best to avoid playing with him. He would often hit or kick other children. Sometimes he would climb several feet high on a play apparatus and jump off onto other children or deliberately stomp on the toys they were playing with. His play was typically extremely rough, and he often broke toys by throwing, banging, stomping on them, or using them in some other way they were not intended to be used.

The teacher was at her wit's end, having tried with no discernible success to ignore Tom's misbehavior (often impossible, since he could so easily damage other people and things) or place him in time-out (the only place available for time-out was an area under a movable water-play table—of course, it didn't work). She was quite hesitant to intervene sternly in Tom's aggressive acts, for the little Hun had vented his fury against her, at one time ripping her hose with his teeth. She also tended to ignore him (probably due to exhaustion) during the brief but identifiable periods when he was reasonably well behaved. Figure 8–3 shows the frequency of Tom's rough physical behaviors (defined as hitting, kicking, biting, pushing, or otherwise hurting another person, or throwing, kicking, breaking, or otherwise abusing equipment or materials) during 30 minutes of free play each day.

Before any intervention was begun, Tom was performing one of his rough physical behaviors at an average rate of nearly 2 per minute. Since he was getting essentially no reinforcement for appropriate behavior, the first strategy employed was to reinforce behavior incompatible with aggression. Beginning on Day 6, the teacher provided positive reinforcement for appropriate behavior after variable intervals of time averaging 3 minutes. Whenever Tom had been behaving appropriately for a short time (as little as 20 seconds in the beginning) the teacher went to him, patted him, and praised his behavior. (For example, "I like the way you're playing gently with Sam.") She also let him turn over a playing card in a previously shuffled deck (a device described by Kauffman, Cullinan, Scranton, & Wallace, 1972) and earn a prize: the same number of Froot Loops as the number on the card, a penny candy for an ace, and a chance to shoot a toy revolver eight times (no caps, and aimed at no one) for a face card. The result was a noticeable drop in roughhousing, as shown for days 6 through 11. In order to test whether the reinforcement contingency was responsible for the behavioral change, reinforcement was discontinued for two days. Figure 8–3 shows that Tom started to return to his violent ways (days 12 and 13).

From Day 14 through Day 18, Tom's behavior was recorded dur-

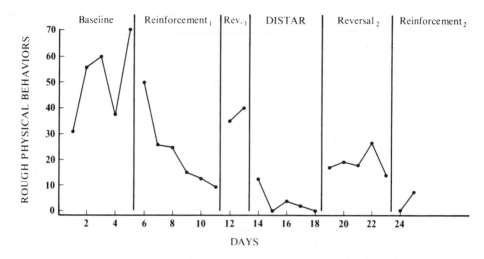

FIGURE 8–3   Frequency of rough physical behaviors per 30-minute observation session.

Note.   Reprinted with permission of publisher from: Kauffman, James M., and Hallahan, Daniel P. Control of rough physical behavior using novel contingencies and directive teaching. *Perceptual and Motor Skills*, 1973, 36, Figure 1, page 1226.

ing a DISTAR[30] session that temporarily replaced the free play activities in which his behavior had previously been observed. DISTAR is a highly structured, sequential teaching system in which each child in a small group is expected to respond according to rules established and modeled by the teacher. Children are reinforced individually with praise, pats, and/or food (for example, juice, or raisins) for appropriate behavior and/or correct responses. Misbehaving children are ignored while well-behaved children are reinforced, thus providing a model for the miscreant and vicarious reinforcement for good behavior. As Figure 8–3 shows, Tom's aggressive behavior fell to near zero during DISTAR. A return to baseline during free play (days 19 through 23) and reinstatement of the reinforcement condition (Days 24 and 25) were undertaken to show the relationship between aggressive behavior and classroom conditions. It is apparent from Figure 8–3 that both novel reinforcement for nonaggressive behavior and the combined elements (modeling, ignoring, reinforcement) of the DISTAR program were effective in reducing Tom's aggression.

Punishment.   Without question, positive reinforcement for appropriate behavior is of primary importance in strategies. Nevertheless, there are in addition behavior problems that seem to require punishment of inappropriate responses. Great care

[30] *Direct Instructional System for Teaching Arithmetic and Reading.* Chicago: Science Research Associates, 1971.

is necessary in the use of punishment, however, for ill-timed, vengeful, and capricious punishment without incentives for appropriate behavior—punishment as it is typically measured out by parents and teachers of aggressive children—will only provide a vicious model for the child. Because of its extreme aversiveness, such punishment will only provoke counteraggression and coercion.

In order to be a humane and effective aggression control technique, punishment should be:

1. used only when positive methods fail and when continuance of the behavior will result in more suffering than the punishment itself.
2. administered by persons who are warm and loving in their relationships with children when their conduct is acceptable, and who also offer ample positive reinforcement for nonaggressive responses in which the child has received instruction.
3. administered matter-of-factly, without anger, threats, or moralizing after the punishment is over.
4. administered fairly, consistently, and immediately for specific behaviors that the child knew were punishable.
5. reasonable in intensity and, whenever possible, related to the aggressive misdeed (for example, if the child breaks something, a part of the punishment may be to repair the broken item).
6. arranged, whenever possible, to involve loss of rewards (which may later be earned back by nonaggressive behavior) rather than on presentation of aversive stimuli. A loss of privileges is preferable to spanking.
7. applied early in a chain or sequence of undesirable behaviors.
8. used in conjunction with self-control techniques such as self-monitoring, self-evaluation, and rehearsal of appropriate behavior.

Three punishment techniques that have been used widely in behavior modification are *response cost, time-out,* and *overcorrection.* Response cost implies that an inappropriate response "costs" something of value, such as earned rewards or privileges—it means a fine in terms of whatever one is compelled to forfeit. Time-out means that for a specified brief period of time, the child must be isolated (perhaps in his or her room, the bathroom, or a specified area of the room—from ongoing social intercourse in which he or she can be reinforced. Overcorrection implies either (a) requiring the child to make *restitution* for damages (perhaps repairing what he/she broke *plus* additional damaged items, or giving back what he/she stole *plus* an additional amount or (b) *positive practice,* in which the child is required to practice repeatedly for a short while a more correct form of behavior, perhaps raising a hand and requesting to get out of his/her seat. (See Azrin & Powers, 1975; Foxx & Azrin, 1972; Patterson et al., 1972.)

Time-out punishment has been used effectively to help bring severe behavior problems under control. However, it is a technique that can be abused easily, and care must be taken to avoid unethical practices and violation of the rights of children and youth (Gast & Nelson, 1977; Maloney et al., 1978). First, it must be recognized that the effectiveness of time-out is dependent on the concurrent use of positive methods. The situation from which a child is "timed out" or isolated must be one in which the child has ample opportunity for reward. Second, as Gast and Nelson (1977) suggest, the time-out contingency must be carefully thought out and specific procedures must be followed to protect against unconscionable treatment of the child.

Summary. Behavior modification literature clearly supports the assertion that punishment, when carefully and appropriately administered, can be a humane and effective technique for controlling misbehavior, including aggression (cf. Baer, 1971; Bandura, 1973; Kauffman, Boland, Hopkins, & Birnbrauer, 1980; Mac-Millan, Forness, & Trumbull, 1973; Sulzer-Azaroff & Mayer, 1977). Used clumsily, vindictively, or with malice, punishment is the behavior modifier's nemesis.

Counter-control. It should be noted that aggressive children sometimes engage in counter-control of those who try to modify their behavior. That is, a component of some aggressive children's behavior is what Mahoney (1974) calls the "screw you" phenomenon—behaving exactly the opposite of the manner in which the behavior modifier urges and entices them to act. It seems as if some children take great delight in frustrating adults by being "oppositional"—often much more delight, in fact, than they take in the "rewards" and "reinforcers" being offered to them by well-meaning teachers or parents. Such children frequently endure punishment that they could easily avoid, behaving in a most "obstinate" and "self-defeating" way (but perhaps in a way *they* perceive as self-enhancing in the face of a pig-headed adult). Mahoney (1974) makes some astute observations regarding counter-controlling children.

vignette

My experiences in the group home environment and a handful of pilot investigations over the past two years have suggested a number of possibly relevant variables in counter-control phenomena. First, it appears that the presence or absence of choice may moderate oppositional patterns. This possibility was first impressed upon me by 6-year-old Aaron, our rebellious enuretic. Aaron was also a terror at bedtime—he refused to take his shower, threw temper tantrums, etc. We had painstakingly programmed reinforcement for more appropriate responses (e.g., with after-shower snacks) and consistently used the removal of privileges as negative consequences for transgressions (response cost and time-out). Nevertheless, Aaron's rebellious patterns persisted. One night, I serendipitously said, "Aaron, do you want to take your shower in the upstairs or downstairs bathroom." He stopped, smiled broadly, and said, "Downstairs!" His compliance surprised me (partly because he usually showered downstairs). An equally amazed staff member asked me what I had done to win Aaron's cooperation. We set about a naturalistic experiment. Was it the choice? We arranged a series of ministudies which varied the presence or absence of

> choice and the type of choice involved (which bathroom, color of towel, and so forth). Aaron's data were impressively consistent—when we gave him a choice, he complied enthusiastically. When we did not, he counter-controlled. Several subsequent experiences added to my hunch that choice may be an important variable in the moderation of oppositional patterns. It is interesting to note that some of the most effective treatment programs for delinquency have incorporated substantial choice options—the delinquents have some say-so in their own contingency management (Fixsen, Phillips, & Wolf, 1973). [p. 245]

Other writers also note that children's behavior often improves when they are given a say in their affairs (e.g., Lovitt, 1977). Mahoney (1974) suggests that the conspicuousness of reinforcement contingencies, modeling, and other variables probably contribute to the phenomenon of counter-control. He also notes that there has been almost no research on how best to handle this apparent form of aggression (see also Bateson, Day, McClosky, Meehl, & Michael, 1975).

Differences in Intervention Approaches

There are several critical distinctions among psychodynamic, psychoeducational, and behavioral strategies for changing aggressive behavior.[31]

Psychodynamic. As depicted in Figure 8-4, psychodynamic intervention is aimed at uncovering unconscious instincts, drives, or needs that find expression in cognitive and affective problems. The hypothesis is that creating an atmosphere of permissiveness and trust in which unconscious forces can be expressed affectively and cognitively will help the child to develop insight resulting in resolution of behavior problems. For example, if a boy has unconscious aggressive wishes involving his father and is allowed to express the need to aggress without censure by verbally assaulting his teacher (who, by *transference* has unconsciously become his symbolic father), then he may be able to gain insight into the fact that hostile wishes toward his father are acceptable and manageable and so come to control his aggression.

Psychoeducational. In contrast, psychoeducational intervention focuses on faulty cognitive and affective states rather than on their unconscious antecedents. At the same time, the existence of needs, drives, and so forth are recognized. The assumption is that by making children aware of their feelings and by discussing the nature of their aggression, they will gain insight into their maladaptive behavior and gain "ego control," (or volitional control) over their aggressive behavior. For example, if the child can be made aware that he/she has angry feelings when another child teases or "hassles", and can be helped to think through alternatives to counteraggression (for example, ignoring rather than hitting the tormentor), then

---

[31] Figure 8-4 and the accompanying descriptions represent an oversimplification of all three approaches to classroom intervention in that behavioral limits, individualized instruction at the child's level, and so on, are also recommended. The purpose here is to show clearly the contrasting emphases of the approaches.

PSYCHODYNAMIC APPROACH

PSYCHOEDUCATIONAL APPROACH

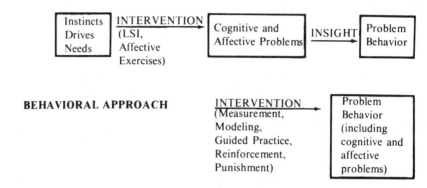

FIGURE 8-4   Diagrammatic representation of psychodynamic, psychoeducational, and behavioral approaches to intervention in problem behavior.

the child may become less aggressive. Recent developments in the psychoeducational approach involve teaching specific skills for the management of impulsive, aggressive behavior that are similar in many respects to cognitive-behavioral interventions.

Behavioral.   Behavioral intervention focuses its impact on the problem behaviors themselves, which may include cognitive and affective responses. For example, if the child hits other children, then the behavioral approach will involve intervention directed toward reducing the hitting behavior. To the extent that cognitive or affective behaviors (such as hateful thoughts or an inability to predict the consequences of teasing another child) can be identified and recorded by the child responses can be dealt with directly (perhaps with the help of the teacher, at least at first). Behavioral intervention may involve training in specific social skills that reduce aggression.

SELF-INJURIOUS BEHAVIOR

No more pitiable creatures can be found than those who attack themselves voraciously. Ordinary human decency demands that the causes and cures of self-injurious behavior be sought. Unfortunately, current knowledge regarding the origins of self-injury is not extensive, and today's available control techniques are unpalatable to those individuals who find punishment of *any* kind for *any* reason morally abhorrent.

Types of Self-Injurious Behaviors

Aggression directed against others is usually self-defeating, at least in the long run, and is therefore, in a psychological sense, self-injurious. However, this type of behavior involves actual physical trauma to the child. Many severely and profoundly disturbed children, usually labeled *psychotic*, *autistic*, or *schizophrenic*, injure themselves repeatedly and deliberately in the most brutal fashion (severely and profoundly retarded children too are often self-injurious.). Such *atavistic* (or primitive) behaviors may take a wide variety of forms, but they all have one result if left unchecked—bodily injury. If the child is not physically restrained, or if effective intervention is not instituted, then there is serious risk that the child will permanently disfigure, incapacitate, or kill himself or herself.

A complete catalog of the ways self-injury can be achieved is neither possible nor necessary. A few examples of specific self-injurious responses will suffice: Children may slap themselves or hit themselves with their fists; they may bang their heads against the wall, the floor, or pieces of furniture; they may bite or chew themselves, perhaps biting their fingers, the backs of their hands, their arms, or their shoulders; they may pull out their hair, including eyebrows, eyelashes, and pubic hair; they may scratch themselves with their fingernails or sharp objects; they may stick sharp objects such as pins and needles into their skin, joints, eyes, or ears; they may slash themselves with sharp objects such as knives or razors; they may burn themselves with cigarettes; or they may ingest poisonous substances of various kinds.

Bachman (1972) notes the range in severity of various self-injurious behaviors:

> The physical damage sustained by such behavior varies. Some individuals are "careful" and produce only minor lesions with few permanent consequences. Others, however, produce serious, permanent damage to themselves, such as blindness, loss of limb, severe bleeding, concussion, etc. These people are often physically restrained (for example, tied down to their beds) lest they produce further injury or kill themselves. As soon as their restraints are removed, the [self-injurious behavior] begins. . . . Very little other behavior is observed in these chronic self-injurers. (p. 212)

The amazing and deviant aspects of self-injurious behavior are its *rate*, *intensity*, and *persistence*. Normal children and adults sometimes perform some of the behaviors listed above. For example, it is considered normal for women to pluck out their eyebrows, for children in fits of temper to bang their heads or hit themselves, for children to play by pushing pins under the callouses on their hands, and for adults to drink alcohol. These self-directed acts of normal individuals are performed seldom enough and gently enough so that disfigurement, incapacitation, and death are highly improbable. Deviant self-injury, however, occurs so frequently and is of such intensity and duration that the child cannot develop normal social relationships and is in danger of becoming a self-made cripple or corpse.

Unless one has actually seen self-injury at work, it is difficult to grasp the human capacity for self-torture. Seeing a child battered by adults is somehow easier to believe than seeing a child who has brutalized himself or herself.

As in the case of aggression against others, self-injury is reported differently in the behavioral and the nonbehavioral literature. Nonbehaviorists provide anecdotes and general description, while behaviorists count daily the number of self-destructive acts. As we shall see later, nonbehavioral approaches have few specific and effective suggestions to offer in the case of truly atavistic children, and for this reason the literature regarding control of self-injury in children consists primarily of behavior modification studies.

Suicide

The ultimate self-injurious behavior is, of course, taking one's own life. Self-injurious behavior of the type we have been discussing thus far seldom results in immediate death. Ordinarily, these children have been considered psychotic and/or retarded for some time. Often they have been institutionalized and kept in restraints, and if they die of their self-inflicted injuries, it is a slow and agonizing death that follows a long history of atavistic behavior. There are, of course, children who make fewer but more harmful attempts at self-injury; they do not usually have a history of attempts and so have not acquired a deviance label such as *psychotic*.

Bakwin and Bakwin (1972) report historical and cross-cultural data on children's suicides. Although suicide is rarely reported in children under 10 years of age and is infrequently reported even in the early teens, it is the third most frequent cause of death (at least among Caucasian children in the United States) in young people 15 to 19 years of age (Crumley, 1979). Only car accidents, cancer, and drowning account for more deaths than suicide in the late teenage years. Hanging, strangling, poisoning, and shooting oneself are apparently the suicide techniques most often employed by individuals under 20 years of age (see Bakwin & Bakwin, 1972, for analysis by age and sex).

Adolescent suicide has increased dramatically in the past two decades. Smith (1976) notes that many adolescents who kill themselves purposely or are hospitalized due to suicide attempts have experienced school difficulties or school failure. In fact, the school performance of adolescents showing suicidal behavior is almost uniformly poor, and a large proportion of suicide and suicide attempts of teenagers occur in the spring months when school problems (e.g., grades, graduation, admission to college) are highlighted. Other factors known to be frequently associated with teenage suicide are: loss of a parent or close relative early in life; death, divorce, or separation of parents; unwanted step-parents; constant family conflict; poverty; and poor peer relationships. Crumley (1979) and Cantor (1976) found that difficulty in managing aggression was a common characteristic of suicide attempters in their studies. Crumley concluded that "intense reactions to loss, poorly controlled rage, impulsivity coupled with depression, and drug abuse seemed to be the most common pattern among . . . teenagers who attempted suicide" (p. 2,407).

Causes of Self-Injurious Behavior

Biological Aspects

The literature linking self-injury to biological factors was reviewed by deCatanzaro (1978). There is some evidence that SIB may in some cases be a result of neurological damage, inadequate pain perception or avoidance, stress and isolation, or perhaps species-protecting, suicidal behavior in individuals having defective genetic makeup. Probably the clearest connection of a specific biological factor to SIB is seen in the Lesch-Nyhan syndrome, in which an identifiable genetic anomaly produces a metabolic defect that is invariably accompanied by self-injury. At present, the Lesch-Nyhan syndrome is only a curiosity in the SIB literature—in no other case is the biological origin of the problem so clear and specific.

As deCatanzaro (1978) and Kety (1979) point out, biological factors need not, and probably do not, operate independently of nonbiological factors. There is good reason to believe that most of the time biological and psychological factors are interactive in a complex way in the causation of aberrant behavior. For example, social learning may not be involved in causing self-injury to appear, but nevertheless can be an important factor in its exacerbation and maintenance or in its control. And it is reasonable to believe that different causal factors may predominate in different types of SIB or different individual cases involving responses that are topographically similar.

The fact that biological and nonbiological factors are complex and interactive causal factors does not mean that biological contributions to SIB are impossible to identify. For example, the study of adoptive and biological relatives of individuals with certain disorders can suggest the heritability of those disorders. As discussed in Chapter 5, such studies have revealed a genetic factor in schizophrenia. The work of Kety and his associates suggests a genetic factor in suicide. Figure 8–5 is a graphic representation of the genetic contribution. The data shown are for adopted individuals only, meaning that the observed differences between groups can not be attributed to the variable of adoption and that the effects of biological relationship and psychological environment can therefore be untangled. If living with depressed people in the family were the dominant factor in suicide, then the adoptive relatives of adopted people who are depressed (C) ought to have a higher rate of suicide than the biological relatives of those who are adopted and depressed (A). Furthermore, if suicide has primarily psychogenic causes, then the adoptive relatives of depressed people who are adopted (C) ought to have a higher suicide rate than the adoptive relatives of nondepressed adoptees (D). But Figure 8–5 shows a suicide rate 13 times higher for group A than for group B, 6.5 times higher for group A than for group C, and equal rates for groups C and D. Thus a genetic link to suicidal behavior is indicated. The data shown in Figure 8–5 do not rule out psychological factors in suicide, but they do suggest a genetic contribution.

Psychodynamic Analyses

Berkowitz and Rothman (1960) aptly sum up the psychoanalytic view of self-aggression—*guilt*. According to their analysis, aggression against the self may take the form of specific SIB, accident proneness, or depression.

> A child experiences severe mental anguish when he does not wish to preoccupy himself with his difficulties, but still cannot escape from them. Self-torture is based upon self-recrimination, blaming oneself for all adverse conditions of life as they befall the individual, even to the point of assuming blame for events over which the individual clearly has no control. It is the result of a direct expression of guilt feelings from which the individual suffers. All self-aggressive tendencies, whether they be an acute or chronic depression, a specific self-destructive act, or a proclivity for accidents, are the expression of guilt which the child unconsciously experiences and for which he is unconsciously try-

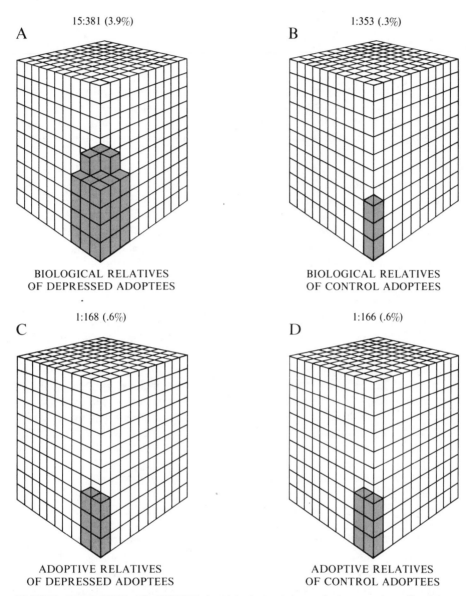

HIGHER INCIDENCE OF SUICIDE in biological relatives of adoptees who suffered from depression compared with the incidence in their adoptive relatives and in the relatives of control adoptees who had no mental illness suggests a genetic factor in suicide. Each ratio shows the number of relatives who committed suicide with respect to the total number of relatives. Data come from a study by the author [Seymour Kety], David Rosenthal of National Institute of Mental Health, Fini Schulsinger of University of Copenhagen and Paul H. Wender of University of Utah.

FIGURE 8-5

Note. From "Disorders of the Human Brain" by Seymour S. Kety, *Scientific American*, 1979, *241*(3), p. 206.

ing to atone. The guilt stems from the fear connected with the uncontrollable instinctual drives which the child feels are base and unacceptable.   (p. 83)

Bender (1948) suggests that children's aggression stems from deprivation during the early years. When children are seriously deprived of parental affection they interpret the deprivation as an expression of aggression against themselves and "counteract" this aggression from the parents with aggression of their own. Unconsciously, such children come to believe that since they are not loved they are not worthy of love, and so turn the blame and punishment for "unloveability" on themselves.

Psychoanalytic formulations of the causes of SIB are not confirmed by scientific experimentation. The experimental work of Lovaas and his colleagues (e.g., Lovaas, Freitag, Gold, & Kassorla, 1965) and studies reviewed by Bachman (1972) suggest that SIB can be accounted for in part without appeal to hypothetical unconscious mechanisms. Furthermore, literature showing successful treatment of atavisms by psychoanalytically oriented methods, even if one includes nonexperimental case reports, is almost nonexistent.

Social Learning Analysis

Social learning analyses of the etiology of SIB are still quite speculative. Most of the data supporting a learning theory view are drawn from informal observation of the typical social circumstances in which SIB occurs, or from experimental research of the ways in which SIB may be reduced. Informal observations provide no scientific basis for statements of causal relationships, and, as we have discussed previously, successful treatment of a disorder does not necessarily indicate its origin. The factors underlying the appearance and maintenance of SIB in its many forms are obviously complex and not easily ferreted out. There are, too, moral reasons for not experimentally inducing SIB in humans merely to show its origins in a scientific manner (see Frankel & Simmons, 1976).

Cognitive mechanisms appear to be a factor in SIB, for some severely disturbed children obviously engage in chronic self-derogation. Mahoney (1974) notes the pervasiveness of self-criticism in our culture and speculates on the possible pernicious effects cognitive self-flagellation may have on behavior. It is quite reasonable to believe that derogatory self-thoughts precede suicide attempts and, at least in some cases, SIB. The literature on cognitive behavior modification does *not*, however, suggest the use of psychoanalytic therapy for cases of pathological self-critical thoughts. Manipulation of the antecedents (e.g., situational cues) and consequences of self-derogation according to the principles of social learning theory may at present be the most effective approach.

Evidence from certain animal research indicates that SIB can be produced by positive reinforcement. For example, Schaeffer (1970; see also Bachman, 1972) taught monkeys to bang their heads by reinforcing them for successive approximations of SIB. Casual observation of people who perform SIB, especially children who hurt themselves, will show that in many cases SIB nets the self-injurer a great deal of attention. One behavioral hypothesis is that the reinforcement derived from attention is at the root of SIB. This hypothesis is suggested too by the fact that in some cases removal of attention for SIB (combined with reinforcement for non-SIB) or punishment for SIB has been successful in eliminating it.

Another behavioral hypothesis is that SIB is a form of self-stimulation—noninjurious, repetitive, stereotyped acts that seem to serve no other function than to provide sensory feedback (self-stimulation is discussed further in Chapter 9). Saying that SIB is a type of self-stimulation certainly sheds no light on its causes, but it does connect SIB with another type of behavior commonly seen in psychotic individuals. One reason to suspect that SIB and self-stimulation are related phenomena is that they often respond to much the same modes of behavior therapy (cf. Azrin, Gottlieb, Hughart, Wesolowski, & Rahn, 1975; deCatanzaro, 1978).

Carr, Newsom, and Binkoff (1976) suggest that sometimes self-injury may be produced and maintained by *negative* reinforcement.

vignette

They experimented with an 8-year-old mildly retarded, psychotic boy, Tim, who hit himself in the face frequently whenever demands were made for his performance of simple skills—those required by a teacher in school. Tim's SIB was high in situations where demands were made but low in (a) nondemand situations, (b) situations in which demands were inserted in a context of pleasant story-telling, and (c) following a signal that no more demands would be made in an experimental session. During sessions including only demands, Tim's SIB gradually increased. These results and anecdotal observations of the child led Carr et al. to hypothesize that SIB is, for some individuals, an *escape* response—a *response reinforced by the termination of an aversive stimulus* (in the case of Tim, demands for performance). Thus, removal of social attention (extinction or time-out) contingent on SIB may be effective in some cases, but in cases in which the social interaction connected with teaching is aversive, removal of attention and demands for performance may provide negative reinforcement for the child's self-injury.

Summary.   A social learning analysis leads to the conclusion that SIB may be a response to peculiar contingencies of reinforcement, in which (a) the self-attacker rarely receives attention or other forms of reinforcement for adaptive behavior but is rewarded with attention when he aggresses against himself, or (b) SIB is negatively reinforced by escape from social situations that are aversive to the self-injurer. Once SIB is learned, it interferes with the learning of other adaptive responses that can lessen its usefulness in obtaining attention and other rewards (see Bachman, 1972; Bandura, 1973, pp. 304–309; Frankel & Simmons, 1976; Lovaas & Koegel, 1973, pp. 244–245; Lovaas et al., 1965). A social learning analysis provides a guide to effective methods of reducing SIB by controlling the social environment, as we shall see in the section on behavioral intervention.

Control Techniques: Behavioral Intervention

Johnson and Baumeister (1978) note that treatment of SIB has included physical restraint, drugs, extraction of teeth, and psychosurgery. The most common methods employed involve some form of reinforcement and punishment contingency. Because other techniques for controlling severe atavistic behavior in children have failed miserably, only behavioral interventions will be discussed. A brief review of recent developments will be provided, as the techniques are still in the testing stage and complete descriptions would be quite lengthy.

A little over a decade ago, behavioral researchers found that some children's SIB could be reduced by using time-out. When SIB was followed immediately by a brief period of social isolation, during which time the children could not receive attention for SIB, they became less atavistic (Wolf, Risley & Mees, 1964). At about the same time it was noted that positive reinforcement for noninjurious behavior combined with time-out or ignoring SIB also had a therapeutic effect in some cases (Lovaas et al., 1965). Although these methods (time-out or ignoring combined with positive reinforcement) continue to be used successfully in some cases, there are children who seem to be quite unaffected (cf. Frankel & Simmons, 1976). Furthermore, such methods have an obvious disadvantage in severe cases of SIB— they are slow to take effect and thus are very painful for the child. Consequently, techniques with more immediate and powerful effects were sought.

Lovaas and his colleagues (Lovaas, Schaeffer, & Simmons, 1965; Lovaas & Simmons, 1969) and Tate and Baroff (1966) found that immediate punishment in the form of painful (but nonconvulsive and harmless) electric shock almost immediately stopped SIB, even in children who were savagely atavistic for years and seemed destined to spend the rest of their lives restrained. In spite of the fact that electric shock punishment has had consistent and dramatic effects on SIB, many behavior modifiers are dissatisfied with the use of shock. The principal drawbacks to its use are that (a) its effects tend to be restricted to the setting in which shock is delivered. A *generalized* cessation of SIB often does not occur because the child may stop SIB only in the room(s) where he was shocked or in the presence of the person(s) who administered the shock; (b) it is extremely distasteful and anxiety provoking to most therapists to administer painful contingent shock to children, despite the obvious therapeutic benefits (see Azrin et al., 1975; Corte, Wolf, & Locke, 1971; Risley, 1968). Consequently, researchers are looking for still other methods to control SIB.

Two other techniques involving the use of punishment contingent on SIB have been tried with success. Baumeister and Baumeister (1978) held ammonia capsules under the noses of severely retarded self-injurious children contingent on their SIB. The ammonia fumes were highly aversive and were effective in reducing self-injury. Mayhew and Harris (1979) found that squirting citric acid solution (at a concentration similar to lemon juice) into the mouth of a profoundly retarded boy contingent on his SIB was effective in reducing self-injury, especially when reinforcement was provided for social behavior incompatible with SIB.

The work of Carr et al. (1976) suggests that an effective approach for some children might involve making explicit demands for performance. While not allowing the child to escape from a teaching situation by exhibiting SIB, make the social context of the demands highly positive, perhaps through stories or other activities the child does not find aversive.

An innovative set of procedures has been tested during the past few years by Nathan Azrin and his research group. Some of these methods were first used to reduce autistic behaviors or self-stimulation in psychotic and retarded children (Azrin, Kaplan, & Foxx, 1973; Foxx & Azrin, 1973). Other aspects of the treatment have been used to control aggressive, disruptive behavior (Webster & Azrin, 1972). As used by Azrin et al. (1975), the treatment involves a combination of the following procedures:

1. *Positive reinforcement for outward-directed activities.* Abundant attention, praise, back-stroking, snacks, games, and other rewards were given for appropriate, nonself-injurious activities.

2. *Required relaxation.* Contingent on SIB, the individuals were told they were overexcited and agitated and would have to go relax on their beds for two hours. The person was gently prompted to put on a hospital gown and lie on the bed, hands at sides (where they could not be used for SIB), for two hours.

3. *Hand control.* Contingent on SIB, the individual was required to perform simple arm exercises (e.g., extended arms down at sides, then out from shoulders to the side, then over head) on command from the instructor for 20 minutes.

4. *Hand-awareness training.* The individuals were instructed to keep their hands away from their heads and to occupy their hands in ways incompatible with SIB (e.g., to clasp their hands behind their backs or to hold onto the arms of a chair). Gestures, pointing, and touching were used along with verbal instructions when needed, and positive reinforcement was given for keeping hands away from the head.

These amazingly "homespun" treatment techniques provided by Azrin and his fellow researchers were immediately and lastingly effective in reducing SIB to a very low level. The methods were used with eleven different institutionalized persons whose SIB had lasted anywhere from .5 to 31 years and whose IQs ranged from 6 (in the profoundly retarded range) to 80, suggesting that the procedures have generalized applicability. Furthermore, some components of the procedures used by Azrin et al. have been used with success by others: relaxation training (Steen & Zuriff, 1977) and forced arm exercise (deCatanzaro & Baldwin, 1978).

It must be remembered that the behavioral interventions reviewed here, including those of Azrin, are more complex than their brief descriptions indicate. The methods were individually tailored to the person's characteristics, carefully sequenced, and gradually faded out over a period of time. It would be inappropriate to attempt to apply any of the techniques mentioned here without adequate training and supervision.

SUMMARY

Aggression involves physically or psychologically harmful behavior directed against others or oneself. Biological factors may contribute to the origin, instigation, and maintenance of aggression, but by themselves, biological processes do not predict or explain aggressive behavior. Theories of aggression based on psychodynamic principles or the concepts of instincts and drives have yielded little in the way of explanations of or treatment for aggression. In fact, psychodynamic theory and theories postulating an aggressive drive led to the misconception that aggressive behavior can be lessened by the expression of pent-up aggressive impulses and feelings. Social learning theory has provided a framework to explain how aggressive behavior is learned and how it can be modified. Experimental research based on social learning theory has yielded abundant data showing that modeling, reinforcement, punishment, instructions, and other fundamental learning processes can be used to induce aggression in children as well as to eliminate it.

chapter 9

Withdrawal, Immaturity, and Inadequacy

It is not uncommon to hear the opinion that quiet, withdrawn children who seldom or never deliberately bother anyone are the "sickest" group of children with behavior problems. Psychodynamic theory, no doubt, has fostered the notion that the child who expresses anger and hostility is somehow in better mental health than the one who "keeps aggression bottled up." Obviously, this idea of "bottled-up" aggression can rest comfortably only on the assumption that aggression is an entity that accumulates behind mental restraints and had best be vented. At least three points can be made in refutation of the theory that withdrawn children have pathologically checked their aggression and can be helped toward mental health by being induced to express their wrath. First, there is scant evidence that most withdrawn children have dammed up their aggression. Aggression is sometimes misattributed to withdrawn behavior on the strength of psychodynamic conviction that *all* children *must* express aggression one way or another, even if it is expressed by passivity or withdrawal.[32] Second, the prognosis for withdrawn, "neurotic" children is much better than the prognosis for those who are hostile and antisocially aggressive (Robins, 1966). Third, "cathartic" expression of aggression is counterproductive—it does not reduce the child's tendency to aggress and may actually increase aggressive behavior (see Chapter 8).

Besides the theoretical premises of psychodynamic theory, two arguments based on nonexperimental observations of behavior are frequently made in support of the repressed-aggression hypothesis. First, it has been noted that some withdrawn children become aggressive after they have been placed in a "therapeutic" environment (Redl & Wineman, 1951, p. 28; see Chapter 8). Given what is known about how children learn aggression and recent data regarding the effects of adults' expectancies on children's behavior (Meichenbaum et al., 1969; Foster et al., 1975; see Chapter 6), it is entirely plausible that such cases of withdrawn-turned-aggressive children do not illustrate the surfacing of repressed aggression at all. That is, social learning theory predicts that if a child were exposed to extremely aggressive peer models (as was the case in the example cited by Redl & Wineman), especially in the presence of adults who condone and expect the cathartic discharge of aggressive impulses, he or she would quickly learn to behave aggressively. Second, dramatic episodes in which previously withdrawn and presumably nonaggressive individuals suddenly and inexplicably have gone on a homicidal rampage are thought to illustrate "the breaking of the dam" which holds back aggression. Although such startling cases of sudden aggression sometimes occur in individuals who have been loners—people who are socially withdrawn and inept —Bandura's (1973) research of the previous conduct of several mass murderers (e.g., Charles Whitman and Howard Unruh) revealed that these killers had practiced and become extremely proficient in various forms of aggression prior to their sprees. Apparently in these instances of unpredicted and heinous crimes, ;

---

[32] Karl Menninger (1963), a well-known proponent of dynamic psychiatry, notes the absurdity of the diagnosis "passive-aggressive personality" (p. 203). Nevertheless, he also argues that *every* symptom of mental illness, whether social withdrawal, immaturity, inadequacy, or overt aggression is somehow an expression of the death instinct, that is, inherent aggressive, destructive tendencies (see especially his Chapter IX).

accounts in the newspapers and other media tended to play down the previous aggressive behavior of the criminals in order to provide a more sensational story. There are, to be sure, instances of unpredictable aggression which are out of character with past behavior. However, it is also clear that the occurrence of aggression in previously nonaggressive individuals is rare. The best predictor of aggression is a history of aggressive acts, and there is no proof to substantiate evaluating the few cases of bizarre, unpredictable aggression in psychodynamic terms (cf. Lefkowitz et al., 1977). Unusual environmental factors offer a more plausible explanation of these quirks (see Bandura, 1973, pp. 178-182).

Although the fundamental problem of withdrawn children is not aggression, they are seriously handicapped in social development by behavioral excesses and deficiencies. The withdrawn child behaves in a manner that inhibits the growth of normal, warm, and satisfying human relationships. Closely allied with patterns of withdrawal are two other types or classes of behavior deficiencies—immaturity and inadequacy. The behaviors of immature children are characteristic of the responses of children who are much younger chronologically. Children whose behavior is inadequate have failed to learn the skills necessary to cope with the demands of their environment.

Withdrawal, immaturity, and inadequacy are frequently linked together. When the problems created by such behavioral excesses and deficiencies are not severe, they are often associated with the terms *psychoneurotic* or *neurotic* child. In their extreme forms, withdrawn, immature, and inadequate behaviors are associated with the labels *psychotic, autistic, schizophrenic,* or *retarded.* For clarity and simplicity, the following discussion will be organized under two major headings: withdrawal and immaturity-inadequacy. Remember, however, there is much overlap among these classes of behavior.

WITHDRAWAL

Withdrawal involves behavior that keeps people at a distance physically and emotionally. Withdrawn children may be deficient in behavior that brings them into social contact with others. They may be lacking in approach responses, such as looking at, talking to, playing with, and touching their peers or adults. Usually, they are also lacking in responsiveness to others' initiations of social contact. Indeed, research of social interaction in field settings and in the laboratory strongly suggests that the isolate or withdrawn child does not engage in social reciprocity—the exchange of mutual and equitable reinforcement between pairs of individuals— which is characteristic of normal social development (Combs & Slaby, 1977; Strain & Shores, 1976). The withdrawn child lacks specific social skills in making and keeping friends. The developmental significance of withdrawal and social isolation should be noted. Although children's hostile aggression carries a poor prognosis for later psychiatric status, so does extreme withdrawal and social isolation, especially in girls (Watt et al., 1970).

In addition to deficiencies in approach and responsiveness (social reciprocity), some children exhibit behavioral excesses that detract from normal social development. Some withdrawn children "retreat" into fantasy, becoming so absorbed in their imaginations that their interaction with others is restricted. The withdrawn child may engage in excessive self-stimulation which prevents attention to social cues and limits social learning. Self-stimulation may take a wide variety of forms, but it can be recognized easily as any repetitive, stereotyped act which seems to serve no other function than to provide sensory stimulation.

Withdrawal is not an all-or-nothing problem. It is normal for all children under some circumstances to exhibit withdrawn behavior to a moderate degree. The behaviors comprising withdrawal may occur with any degree of severity, ranging along a continuum from the social reticence of normal children in new situations to the profound isolation of apparently "unreachable" psychotics. Two levels of withdrawal will be discussed here: the relative social isolation (compared to normals) of children with mild and moderate behavior disorders, and the profound withdrawal associated with infantile autism and similar severe disorders.

Social Isolation

In nearly any classroom from the preschool level through classes for adults, one may observe individuals who are distinguishable by their lack of social interaction. *Nonentity, wallflower,* and other similar terms seem to fit their level of social responsiveness. Frequently, their social withdrawal is accompanied by immature or inadequate behavior which makes them the targets of ridicule or taunts. They are friendless loners who are apparently unable to avail themselves of the joy and satisfaction of social reciprocity. Unless they can somehow be induced to change their behavior, they remain isolated from close and frequent human contact and the attendant developmental advantages afforded by such social interaction.

Etiological Considerations

We have already discussed the weakness of psychoanalytic assumptions that withdrawal represents the manifestation of aggressive drive. True, some children exhibit alternating periods of aggression and social withdrawal, but it is more reasonable, in the light of research evidence undergirding social learning theory, to interpret such variations in behavior as responsiveness to changing environmental conditions than to view them as different symptomatic expressions of a single underlying and unobservable instinct. Social learning theory predicts that some children, particularly those who have not been taught appropriate social interaction skills and those who in the past have been punished for attempts at social interaction, will be typically withdrawn. These same children may, however, learn to counter-aggress against others who attack them, or to attack unsuspecting victims when the consequences of their assaults seem likely to be favorable, as discussed in Chapter 8.

It is quite likely that the mildly or moderately withdrawn child will be an anxious individual and have a low self-concept. However, the conclusion that anxiety and low self-concept *cause* withdrawal and social isolation is not justifiable on the basis of research data. It is more plausible that anxiety and low self-concept result from the child's lack of social competence. Parental over-restrictiveness or social incompetence, lack of opportunity for social learning, and early rebuffs in social interaction with peers may contribute to a child's learning to play in isolation from others and to avoid social contact. Parents who are socially obtuse are likely to have children whose social skills are not well developed (Sherman & Farina, 1974), probably because socially awkward parents provide models of undesirable behavior and are in no position to teach their children the skills that will help them become socially attractive. Aversive social experiences may indeed produce anxious children who have little self-confidence and evaluate themselves negatively. Anxiety and self-derogation may, thereafter, contribute to reticence in social situations and help to perpetuate social incompetence. Nevertheless, the child's temperamental characteristics, in combination with early socialization experiences and the nature of the current social environment, probably account for the development of social isolation. The social learning view of isolate behavior, which focuses on the factors of reinforcement, punishment, and imitation, carries direct implications for intervention and suggests ways to remediate isolation by teaching social skills (see Gelfand, 1978).

Definition and Measurement

Social isolation is sometimes defined as rejection or nonacceptance by peers. Frequently, rejection and acceptance are measured by a questionnaire or game in which children are asked whom of their peers they would *most* like to play with (or sit, work, or party with) and whom they would *least* like to interact with in some way. The results of this procedure are then analyzed to find not only the social "stars" in the group (those to whom many peers are attracted) but also the "isolates" (those not chosen as playfellows or workmates by anyone) or "rejectees" (those with whom their peers want to avoid social contact). When the results are displayed graphically as a *sociogram*, one can readily see the social structure of the group and observe the status of isolates or rejectees (see Gronlund, 1959).

More precise measurement of social interaction may be obtained by direct daily observation and recording of children's behavior (Buell, Stoddard, Harris, & Baer, 1968; O'Connor, 1969; Strain, Shores, & Kerr, 1976; Strain & Timm, 1974). *Social isolates* may thus be defined as children who have a markedly lower number of social interactions than those of their peers. When the child's social interaction is measured directly and continuously, it is possible to assess precisely and reliably what effects intervention methods designed to teach social interaction skills are having on the child's behavior. The value of direct daily measurement of behavior will become obvious in the discussion of intervention techniques. However, it should be noted that sociometric status and direct measurement of social interactions, though both important, do not necessarily reflect the same problems related to social isolation (Gottman, Gonso, & Schuler, 1976). A child could, for example, have a relatively high rate of positive social interaction and still be a relative social isolate: His or her interactions might involve relatively few peers and be characterized by a superficial or artificial quality (cf. Walker, Greenwood, Hops, & Todd, 1979). Thus, adequate measurement of social skills or social isolation requires attention to the rate of interactive behaviors, qualitative aspects of social interaction, and children's perceptions of social status.

Intervention

One approach to the problem of withdrawal is to try to improve the child's self-concept, under the assumption that this will result in the child's tendency to engage more often in social interactions.[33] Children may be encouraged to express their feelings about their behavior and social relationships in play therapy or to engage in therapeutic conversations with a warm, accepting adult. As children come to feel accepted and able to express their feelings openly, their self-concepts will become more positive. It is believed that the incidence of their positive social interactions will, therefore, increase as well. Attempts to remediate social isolation without teaching specific social skills or manipulating the child's social environment are usually ineffectual. Few data show that a child's self-concept *causes* behavior, or that a child's self-concept can be improved without first improving behavior. When children's appraisal of their own behavior is unrealistic, then bringing self-perception into line with reality is, to be sure, a worthy goal. When children are indeed withdrawn, attempting to convince them of their social adequacy without first helping them to learn the skills of social reciprocity is dishonest. However, if children can be taught to change their behavior, then a positive shift in their self-concept can be supported and facilitated based on their improved responsiveness (cf. Morena & Litrownik, 1974).

By arranging appropriate environmental conditions, it is possible to teach socially isolated children to reciprocate positively with peers and adults. This may involve providing situations conducive to social interaction: providing toys or equipment conducive to social play and bringing the isolate child into proximity with other children who have social interaction skills. Specific behavioral intervention strategies include (a) providing reinforcement for social interaction (perhaps in the form of praise, points, or tokens), (b) providing clear examples of peer models of social interaction and training in social skills, or (c) having peer confederates provide social interactions. Of course, all three of these methods may be used together. Experimental research showing the effectiveness of these procedures is readily available (Gelfand, 1978).

Wahler (1967), Strain and Timm (1974), and others show that a child's peers can be induced to modify the isolate child's social interaction (see also Strain, in press). Buell et al. (1968) showed that social interaction could be increased by reinforcing a child for using outdoor play equipment, and Quilitch and Risley (1973) found that certain types of toys facilitate social play while other toys tend to promote solitary activity. Several studies demonstrated that isolate children's social interaction with their peers could be increased markedly if adults paid attention to them when they are engaged in social or cooperative play and if they ignore them when they were alone (Allen, Hart, Buell, Harris, & Wolf, 1964; Hall & Broden, 1967; Hart, Reynolds, Baer, Brawley, & Harris, 1968). In some instances, it has been necessary to instruct the child directly in social play skills or to prompt him/her with instructions to begin social interaction. Research also reveals the value of

---

[33] Self-concept is often measured by children's responses to questionnaire items, such as "I'm pretty sure of myself," "I often wish I were someone else," "I'm never unhappy," and "Kids usually follow my ideas." (see Coopersmith, 1967)

modeling appropriate social behavior as a technique to remediate social isolation. Keller and Carlson (1974), O'Connor (1969, 1972), and Evers and Schwarz (1973), found that socially withdrawn children who watched films depicting pleasant, appropriate social interaction among other children quickly increased their level of socialization. The following descriptions of research studies illustrate each of the three major types of interventions that have proven successful.

Adult Social Reinforcement

The report of Hall and Broden (1967) illustrates the use of adult social reinforcement and the value of direct daily measurement in assessing behavioral change.

vignette

The subject of their report was a 9-year-old, brain-injured boy who during baseline sessions spent an average of only about 17% of his time in social (parallel or cooperative) play (see Figure 9-1, Section A). Hall and Broden noticed that he obtained considerable attention from the teacher during isolate play, typically in the form of invitations or encouragement to join other children in their play activities. Assuming that the teacher's attention was reinforcing the child's social isolation, Hall and Broden arranged for the teacher to ignore the child when he was engaged in isolate play but to attend to him when he was engaged in social play. By making the teacher's attention contingent on the child's social interaction, the percentage of time the child spent in social play was increased dramatically (Figure 9-1, Section B). In the beginning (sessions 9 through 11), the child so seldom played with other children that there were few opportunities to reinforce him with attention; therefore, beginning with Session 11 (Point a in Figure 9-1), he was first reinforced for approximations of social interaction (approaching or looking at other children). After the child's social play had been increased, the experiments tested the effect of the contingencies of reinforcement by reversing the conditions under which the teacher attended to the child. Figure 9-1, Section C, shows that when the teacher attended to the child only while he was playing alone, his behavior reverted to that of an isolate. Re-establishing the contingency requiring the child to engage in social play in order to receive teacher attention resulted in reinstatement of the prevous gains (Section D of the graph). Follow-up after three months showed that the child's social behavior was maintained.

Walker et al. (1979) found that there is an optimal strategy for reinforcing the social interaction of withdrawn children. When reinforcement is contingent on initiating interactions or responding to (or answering) initiations, social interactions have a stilted, artificial character. However, when reinforcement is provided for maintaining interactions, children spend more time engaged in meaningful social interaction.

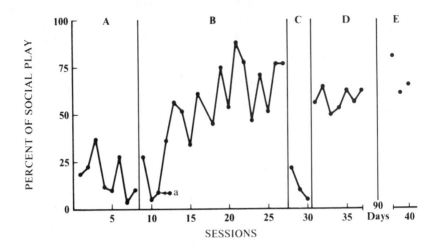

FIGURE 9-1   Record of a brain-injured, 9-year-old's rates of social play.

A = Baseline period—prior to experimental procedures

B = Reinforcement period—social reinforcement of social play by boy's teachers

C = Reversal period—reinforcement of nonsocial play

D = Return to reinforcement period—reinforcement of social play

E = Post-experiment period—three months after termination of the experiment

a = Beginning of Session 11

Note. From "Behavior Changes in Brain-Injured Children through Social Reinforcement" by R.V. Hall and M. Broden, *Journal of Experimental Child Psychology*, 1967, 5, 474. Copyright 1967 by Academic Press. Reprinted by permission.

Peer Models and Social Skills Training

The work of O'Connor (1969) illustrates the power of appropriate peer models in overcoming social isolation. After carefully selecting (on the basis of direct behavioral observation *and* teacher judgment) 26 nonisolate children and 13 isolates from nine nursery school classes, O'Connor separated the isolates into an experimental group and a control group. The children in the experimental group were shown a 23 minute sound and color film portraying children interacting in a nursery school, with narration calling attention to the social activities. The children in the control group saw a 20 minute film showing Marineland dolphins performing acrobatic tricks. Immediately after watching the films, the children returned to their classrooms and were observed as they played there. Figure 9–2 shows the results for the experimental and control groups and a comparison between isolate and nonisolate children. After having viewed the film depicting social interaction, the isolate children in the symbolic modeling condition interacted much like nonisolates, whereas the control children who watched the dolphins doing tricks did not change their behavior. Although the symbolic modeling treatment had a much more dramatic effect on some children than on others, all the children in the experimental condition increased in social interaction. The results of O'Connor's

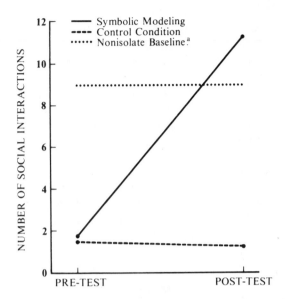

FIGURE 9-2   Mean number of social interactions displayed by subjects in the modeling and control conditions, before and after the experimental sessions.

a Dotted line represents the level of interactions manifested by 26 nonisolate children who were observed at the pre-test phase of the study.

Note. From "Modification of Social Withdrawal through Symbolic Modeling" by R.D. O'Connor, *Journal of Applied Behavior Analysis*, 1969, *2*, 19. Copyright 1969 by Society for the Experimental Analysis of Behavior, Inc. Reprinted by permission.

work are consonant with the findings of other researchers who have found that watching films in which desirable social behavior is demonstrated by others induces prosocial behavior in children (cf. Friedrich & Stein, 1973, 1975; Stein & Friedrich, 1975).

It is important to recognize that the modeling approach used by O'Connor has not always been successful (Gelfand, 1978; Gottman, 1977). As Gelfand (1978) points out, it is important to consider the appropriateness of the peer model (social status, age, sex, and general similarity to the child who is observing), the characteristics of the withdrawn children being treated, and the specific techniques used (whether the narration provided is first-person or third-person), and the extent to which the model is socially reticent initially.

Symbolic modeling or peer modeling alone is not always successful. They may be combined with social skills training that includes instructions and role playing designed to teach specific socially appropriate behaviors. For example, Gottman et al. (1976) added instruction and role playing in friend-making and communication skills to the use of film models. This approach was successful and included some of the features of cognitive-behavioral interventions that were discussed in Chapters 7 and 8. Bornstein, Bellack, and Hersen (1977) found similar social skills training effective in increasing assertiveness in children who were excessively passive, acquiescent, and unable to confront antagonists.

Use of Peer Confederates

The use of peers as agents of behavioral change in withdrawn children has been extensively investigated by Strain and his associates (Strain, 1977, in press; Strain et al., 1976, 1977). Strain's approach has often been to carefully train individual peers to initiate social interactions with a withdrawn, target child. The peer confederates are trained by the experimenter in brief sessions. The adult models the desired social initiation. Then the child confederate role plays the appropriate initiation while the adult experimenter plays the part of a withdrawn child. Table 9-1 illustrates the procedures used by Strain et al. (1977) to train two 4-year-old confederates to increase the social interactions of withdrawn children of about the same age. The work of Strain and his colleagues has amply demonstrated the feasibility of training individual young children to serve as effective intervention agents.

Ragland, Kerr, and Strain (1978) have devised similar techniques for using peers to modify the behavior of autistic children.

TABLE 9–1   Training Procedures Employed during Each of Four Confederate Instructional Sessions

Training Procedures	Desired Confederate Behavior	Consequences and Schedule of Delivery
SESSION 1		
The experimenter instructs the confederate that he is going to learn how to help the experimenter by getting other children to play with him. The experimenter indicates that asking children to play a particular game is what they will practice first. Experimenter then models appropriate behavior and asks confederate to try asking him to play (sequence has 10 repeats).	"Come play", "Let's play school", "Let's play ball", etc.	Experimenter delivers social praise to confederate on an FR 2 schedule.* Experimenter ignores every other response, then says, "Many times children will not want to play at first, but you need to keep asking them to play."
The experimenter instructs the confederate that it is also important to give children toys to play with. The experimenter models appropriate behavior and asks confederate to try giving him something to play with when he invites him to play (sequence has 20 repeats).	verbal behavior identical to that shown above plus handing a play object (ball, block, toy truck, etc.) to experimenter	Experimenter delivers social praise to confederate on an FR 2 schedule. Experimenter ignores every other response, then says, "Sometimes children won't play, even when you ask nicely and give them something to play with, but you will need to keep trying very hard to get them to play."
SESSIONS 2, 3, 4		
Repeat of Session 1	Same as Session 1	Same as Session 1

* Social praise was given for every other correct response.

Note. From Strain, P.S., Shores, R. E., & Timm, M.A. "Effects of Peer Social Initiations on the Behavior of Withdrawn Preschool Children," *Journal of Applied Behavior Analysis*, 1977, *10*, 289–298. Copyright 1977 by the Society for the Experimental Analysis of Behavior, Inc.

While Strain and others have trained individual confederates to initiate social contacts, Kandel, Ayllon, and Rosenbaum (1977) have used groups of children to intervene in the social withdrawal of their peers. Kandel et al. worked from the assumption that other children elicited anxiety and, therefore, social withdrawal. In one case they used a technique called "flooding"—presenting a feared stimulus at high intensity for a protracted period of time until it no longer elicits anxiety and withdrawal. They described their subject as follows:

vignettes

1 Paul, aged 4, diagnosed as having minimal cerebral dysfunction, chronic anxiety, and extreme episodes of hyperactivity, was the only child of a 25-yr-old mother and a 65-yr-old father. He scored in the average range of the Stanford-Binet, obtaining a 92 rating. Because of extreme emotional problems, he had been dismissed from three nursery schools during the two-week period before entering the school in this study.

When Paul was observed at the nursery school for the first time, he was screaming and crying, talking to himself, frequently clinging to the teacher, and avoiding interaction with other children. His teacher reported that he became so violently angry when confronted with other children that he could not be trusted with a group. She also stated that after his mother left him at school in the morning, he became hysterical and panicky, constantly asking about her return. Paul's mother stated that he had never interacted with children, and that the family neither associated with nor lived near any young couples with children. (Kandel et al., 1977, pp. 76–77)

Paul's behavior was recorded during free play periods in two settings: the classroom and the playground. Two specific types of behavior were recorded: self-talk and social interaction. The objective of the intervention was to increase social interaction and decrease self-talk, which was associated with isolate behavior. First, baseline data were obtained (see data plotted on left side of broken vertical line, Figure 9-3). The intervention (flooding) was as follows:

2 In the classroom, a procedure whereby Paul was flooded with children eager to interact with him was in effect during Sessions 11 through 17. The children were highly motivated to interact with Paul, since the therapist had brought a new toy truck into the classroom. Immediately, about 15 children expressed their desire to play with it, and were told they first had to play with Paul for about 2 minutes. This resulted in their asking, "Who is Paul?" "How do we play with him?" The therapist suggested that the children ask Paul about his toy cars or playfully wrestle with him (wrestling solely for the purpose of preventing Paul from escaping was prohibited by the therapist). This produced a barrage of child-

ren calling for Paul, asking him questions, and having physical contact with him (i.e. wrestling and holding his hand). Although Paul attempted to escape from these interactions during the first two sessions of treatment, it was difficult for him to find the solitude or the time to talk to himself with several children searching for him.

A flooding procedure was also initiated on the playground, beginning at Session 20 and lasting through Session 22. This was effected by telling the children they could earn some candy by interacting with Paul for about 20 minutes. At least four children started after Paul, called for him, asked him questions, and had physical contact with him. Paul attempted to escape from these interactions during the first of these playground sessions; yet such escape was not easy even with two acres of land on which to run away!

Three-week follow-up. Three weeks after the final session of treatment on the playground, during which baseline conditions were in effect (i.e. Paul was no longer flooded by children, and incentives for these children to interact with him were removed), three days of measurements were taken for interaction and self-talk in both settings.

Five-month follow-up. Five months after the final session of flooding on the playground (one week before the end of the school year), measurements were taken for a day for interaction and self-talk in both settings. Again, no incentives were given to the other children to interact with Paul. One week later Paul's family moved out of the town. (Kandel et al., 1977, p. 77)   ·

The results are shown in Figure 9-3. Although no specific interactional skills were taught, Paul began to interact with his classmates once they were induced to make overtures to him. For a second case, Kandel et al. found that the flooding technique used with Paul produced extreme anxiety, resistance to interaction, and attempts to escape. Therefore, instead of having seven children at a time try to play with the child, only two at a time were rewarded for playing with him. Using this "systematic exposure" instead of flooding, the researchers obtained results similar to those shown for Paul.

Research clearly shows that isolated children's peers can be *induced* to intervene effectively. However, a study by Furman, Rahe, and Hartup (1979) shows that the age of the peers that isolated children are *allowed* to interact with may be an important factor in the development of social skills. Furman et al. found that merely allowing a young isolate child to play with another child who was a year or two younger resulted in dramatic increases in the social interaction of the isolate with his/her age mates in the regular preschool classroom. The researchers speculate that playing with a younger child in a one-to-one situation is therapeutic for the withdrawn child because the older child is given a chance to exert *leadership* in play with a high probability of success. It is highly probable that the older, isolate child will be assertive, direct social activity, and obtain a positive response to these social initiatives when playing with a younger child.

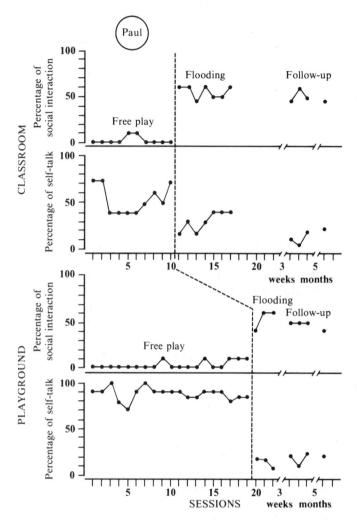

FIGURE 9-3 Paul's social interaction and self-talk in the classroom and on the playground. These two measures are based on the number of 1-minute intervals during which these behaviors occurred out of the total number of intervals per session. Free play and follow-up designate the periods of observation in the absence of flooding. The broken line shows the multiple baseline design across settings (classroom and playground).

Note. Reprinted with permission from J. J. Kandel, T. Ayllon, & M. S. Rosenbaum. "Flooding or Systematic Exposure in the Treatment of Extreme Social Withdrawal in Children," *Journal of Behavior Therapy and Experimental Psychiatry*, 1977, *8*, 77. Copyright 1977, Pergamon Press, Ltd.

Summary.   Social isolation may arise from, or at least be exacerbated and maintained by, the constraints of overrestrictive or unskilled parents, punishment for social approach responses, inadvertent reinforcement of isolate play, or lack of opportunity to learn and practice social reciprocity. The isolate child can often be induced quickly and easily to adopt more outgoing and socially responsive behavior by arranging appropriate conditions in the environment, such as opportunity to observe social interaction and to obtain reinforcement for social responses. Reinforcement by adults for social responses, peer modeling of appropriate social skills and social skills training, and use of peer confederates have been effective in bringing children out of social isolation.

Autistic Withdrawal

One of the primary features of infantile autism is the child's unrelatedness to people. Extreme withdrawal is not, however, found exclusively in children categorized as autistic. Many psychotic children and some who are severely mentally retarded effectively shut out the social world to such an extent that their withdrawal may be considered autistic, due to their profound isolation.

As has been discussed in previous chapters, there are several different views of the causes of infantile autism, none of which can be regarded as having an unshakeable foundation in empirical research data. The lack of evidence delineating the causes of autism is matched by lack of agreement regarding the specific behaviors that comprise the syndrome. Because of the lack of data and consensus regarding definition and causes, the following discussion will be focused on four characteristics of extreme withdrawal that may be exhibited by children regardless of whether or not they have been labeled *autistic*. The term *autistic withdrawal*, then, should be interpreted to mean extreme social isolation, irrespective of the child's diagnostic label. The four important types of behavioral characteristics associated with autistic withdrawal are (a) unresponsiveness to social stimuli, (b) gaze aversion, (c) language disorders (including muteness and echolalia), and (d) self-stimulation and fantasy.

Unresponsiveness to Social Stimuli

During the first year of life, normal children show increasing awareness of and responsiveness to their social environment. They recognize their mother and other familiar faces, develop a social smile in response to hearing or seeing familiar persons, lift their arms in anticipation of being picked up, engage in social games with glee (such as babbling, patty-cake, peek-a-boo, and so on), delight in close physical contact with their parents, and in many additional ways interact positively and reciprocally with other people. Children who do not display such social responsiveness early in life are often thought to be autistic, retarded, brain injured, or even deaf or blind. Many such children seem to be completely oblivious to what is going on around them, and it is no surprise that their parents and other adults begin to wonder if they can see or hear. Such lack of social contact and *failure to cuddle* or adapt their posture to that of the adult who is holding them give the impression that they lack interest in or even reject human relationships. If, as they get older, children do not respond to language (do not come when called or follow verbal directions), they become a management problem for their parents and other adults.

Autistic withdrawal often goes beyond simple *un*responsiveness to stimuli. It may become very obvious that the children can see because of their adept locomotion and manipulation of objects and their avoidance of certain visual stimuli.

It may also be obvious that they can hear, for they might respond sensitively to some auditory stimuli. One may wonder, in these cases, whether or not such children have perceptual or information processing problems. Can they make sense of what they see and hear? Or are they deliberately "screening out" certain social stimuli in order to maintain their isolation in a private world? Because some profoundly withdrawn children often respond with exactly the opposite of what is requested, we known that such children *can* "make sense" of auditory and visual social stimuli (cf. Steucher, 1972). *Negativism* is a frequent feature of some autistic children's behavior, and it requires attention to and understanding of social stimuli (Wallace, 1975). It is, of course, a highly effective way of keeping most people at bay and maintaining social isolation. Negativism combined with bizarre mannerisms and self-injurious behavior quickly produces perplexity or revulsion in most adult caretakers.

The challenge of penetrating and changing the private world of the autistically withdrawn child is not easily met, and it must be honestly recognized that autistic withdrawal remains an enigma even for the foremost researchers in the field. At this point in the histories of psychology and special education, facile explanations of the phenomenon or its cure should be recognized as exhibitions of ignorance. Nevertheless, it is now clear that permissive treatment approaches (which are based on the assumption that gratification of children's psychological needs is sufficient to improve their behavior) are nothing more than superstitions derived from psychoanalytic theory. As Des Lauriers (1962) comments:

> It is difficult to conceive that a schizophrenic could develop more adequate patterns of need satisfaction simply by gratifying his needs, any more than it is of any great profit to have a young pianist practice over and over errors and mistakes he makes in interpreting a piece of music and ever hope that he will eventually play this piece commendably. (pp. 98-99)

Those investigators who have experienced notable success in bringing profoundly withdrawn children out of their isolation (e.g., DeMyer, Des Lauriers, Ferster, Kozloff, Lovaas, Steucher, and Wing) agree that successful treatment demands the teacher's active intrusion into the child's experience and the use of a structured (as opposed to permissive) approach. Although the rationale provided to justify their use may vary markedly from one individual to another, simple games (touching, imitating, chasing, peek-a-boo) are often employed in overcoming autistic withdrawal (cf. the teaching suggestions and theoretical viewpoints of Des Lauriers & Carlson, 1969; Ferster, 1968; Lovaas, 1967; Maurer, 1969; and Steucher, 1972). For example, Lovaas (1967) suggests the use of simple games as reinforcers for other social behaviors, while Des Lauriers and Carlson (1969) comment on the use of such games as a means of overcoming the affective imbalance caused by defective arousal systems and establishing the child's identity as a person (see Chapter 5, p. 118).

Lovaas (1967) delineates two strategies for building social responsiveness in autistically withdrawn children. One method is to offer positive reinforcement (in the form of praise, hugs, food, or other positive reinforcers) for social responses, such as eye contact, imitation, or following directions. In cases where social reinforcers (e.g., praise, hugs, or other social contact) are not effective in changing the child's behavior and cannot be made effective by pairing them repeatedly with primary positive reinforcers (e.g., food), Lovaas uses a second method—pain reduction. That is, Lovaas, Shaeffer, and Simmons (1965) used negative reinforcement—escape from or avoidance of electric shock—as a means of teaching autistic children social responses. In their study, the children were placed barefoot in a room with an electrified grid on the floor. A nearby adult beckoned the child by leaning toward him and calling "Come to me." If the child approached the adult on request, he was not shocked. If he did not come within three seconds, the current was turned on and he was given a push toward the beckoning adult. The shock was terminated as soon as the child moved toward the inviting adult, whether he was pushed or moved spontaneously. As soon as he escaped or avoided the shock, the child was given profuse positive social reinforcement. With a few brief sessions of such escape-avoidance training, Lovaas and his colleagues produced dramatic and long-lasting changes in autistic children's behavior. The children quickly learned social responsiveness of various sorts, and their inappropriate behavior (self-stimulation and aggression) quickly declined. Lovaas et al. do not, as some may be tempted to believe, advocate the use of pain avoidance as a technique in cases where positive techniques will achieve the therapeutic goal, and it should be recognized that the use of painful or aversive stimuli play a comparatively minor role in Lovaas's work.

It is interesting to note some similarities and differences in the work of Lovaas et al. and that of Des Lauriers and his colleagues (Des Lauriers, 1962; Des Lauriers & Carlson, 1969). Although both advocate the paradigm of escape-avoidance coupled with positive reinforcement, the particular stimuli and rationale differ radically. While Lovaas uses reinforcement and punishment techniques based on an operant conditioning analysis of behavior, Des Lauriers employs direct and forceful intrusion into the child's life under the assumption that the child's affective arousal system is defective. The adult using the Des Lauriers method expresses emphatic displeasure and disapproval (a likely anxiety-arousing and aversive situation for the child) but changes his or her expression to obvious pleasure and approval as soon as the child adopts alternative desirable behavior. In rationale and in method, it is easy to see that Lovaas and Des Lauriers differ substantially. However, both assume that withdrawn children lack behaviors that *can* be taught directly, that such children usually learn only under increased anxiety and arousal, and that teaching methods must be predominantly positive. Des Lauriers and Lovaas do not shrink from the necessity of making demands on the child and suppressing inappropriate behavior which interferes with the learning of adaptive social responses.

Although we do not delve into the nuances of educational or therapeutic methods here, it should be clear that several divergent theories regarding the etiology and nature of the problem have led to teaching methods that share a common tenet—profoundly withdrawn children will not be helped if they are left to their own devices or merely allowed the freedom to behave as they wish in the presence of a passive, permissive, always-approving adult.[34] Although it is agreed by

---

[34] There are reports of autistic withdrawal having been overcome after several years of psychoanalytic therapy or play therapy in which the teacher was not intrusive or structured in approaching the child. These cases seem likely to represent the occasional spontaneous, "miraculous" (completely inexplicable) instances of improvement or recovery in children who have received no specific therapy or education.

the majority of workers in the field that social intrusion and social structure must be imposed upon children if they are to be helped, there is no consensus regarding *why* this is so. Whether teaching methods are successful because they overcome reinforcement deficiencies, psychoneurological defects, a developmental lag, perceptual disorders, or other conditions or combinations of factors remains unknown.

Gaze Aversion

It is normal for individuals to look at each other's faces and gaze into each other's eyes at least occasionally during social interactions. How often and for how long one person fixes a gaze on the other as well as where he/she directs the gaze may depend on a variety of factors, including social status, physical proximity, and the emotional valence of the interaction (cf. Kendon, 1967). Lack of eye contact is often interpreted as inattention or unwillingness to enter into an interpersonal relationship. Continuous eye contact extending over an unusually long time, especially if physical proximity is close, is typically perceived either as threatening assertiveness or as amorousness. Thus, the significance of gaze fixation in social interaction is readily apparent.

A very frequent component of autistic withdrawal is gaze aversion, or failure to establish eye contact with others. Autistic children are frequently described as looking "through" or "beyond" other people or as looking "out of it" because they do not focus on others' faces. Hutt and Hutt (1969) documented the avoidance of eye contact by autistic children. They took motion picture films of autistic and normal children in various social situations with peers and adults. The films showed that autistic and normal children performed many of the same motor responses, but that autistic children almost never looked directly at other people's faces, whereas normal children often did so. In the film, the autistic children seemed to rely on their peripheral vision and very quick, furtive glances at others who were not looking at them at the same time (and so could not make eye contact) in order to interpret social cues. Such gaze aversion, Hutt and Hutt (1969) believe, makes adults feel ill-at-ease and shut out and also has the function of appeasing or inhibiting the attack of other children.

Hutt and Hutt (1969) also placed normal and autistic children in a room that was bare except for environmental fixtures (door, windows, lights, light switches, and sink) and cutout drawings of various faces mounted on small stands. There were five cutouts: a blank face (no features), a smiling human face, a sad human face, a monkey face, and a dog face. The amount of time children spent looking at each face was recorded by an observer. Compared to normal children, autistic children spent little time looking at the human faces (especially the smiling one) and spent a great deal of time looking at or manipulating the environmental fixtures. Thus, autistic children seem to have an aversion for looking at the human face even when it is represented symbolically. Hutt and Hutt (1969) and Hutt and Ounsted (1966) interpret gaze aversion in biological terms. Their hypothesis is that due to a defect or dysfunction of the central nervous system, autistic children are in a chronically high state of neurophysiological and behavioral arousal. Gaze aversion may function to reduce such arousal. Therefore, they suggest that their first encounters with an adult should be low-keyed, tactile, and arousal-reducing.

Prolonged familiarization is especially necessary in social encounters. The teacher, therapist, or nurse must remain as unobtrusive as possible and should not at first attempt to make direct face-to-face encounters with the child; such encounters predictably will produce catastrophic reactions. It is better to apparently ignore the child until there is some observable unfreezing of his posture and he shows some signs of rudimentary exploration of the environment. This, of course, demands great self-discipline on the part of the teacher whose natural reaction to an unresponsive child is to try to stimulate him. (Hutt & Hutt, 1969, p. 9)

Des Lauriers and Carlson (1969) also believe that autistic children suffer from a basic neurophysiological malfunction or imbalance involving arousal. However, in direct contradiction to Hutt and Hutt, they suggest that the autistic child is under-aroused and can learn only under conditions of heightened affective arousal. Consequently, Des Lauriers and Carlson stress the importance of establishing eye contact and overcoming gaze aversion by using intrusive techniques. To teach eye contact, they report using simple games (similar to peek-a-boo, hiding, and jumping) and physical restraint of the child's head by the teacher, forcing the child to look at the adult's face (see Des Lauriers & Carlson, 1969, pp. 151–153). In contrast to Bettelheim (1967), who sees gaze aversion and other characteristics of autistic withdrawal as indications that children have turned their backs on a world that has rejected them, Des Lauriers and Carlson believe that autists want to discover their own bodies and environments, but must be painstakingly taught what normal children learn quickly and easily. The autist's hypoarousal is simply a neurophysiological barrier that must be circumvented through special instruction.

Lovaas (1969; 1977), who does not believe that an underlying neurophysiological dysfunction is the cause of gaze aversion, is another researcher who notes the crucial importance of teaching the autistic child to visually attend during language training. Without visual fixation on the teacher's face, it is unlikely that the child will learn the imitative repertoire of speech movements and sounds necessary to acquire language. Lovaas' method of teaching visual attention involves giving the verbal command "Look at me" and, in order to obtain a response, using a prompt such as holding the child's head or holding food in front of the teacher's face. Once the child looks at the teacher, he/she is immediately reinforced with food and/or praise for having attended. Lovaas (1967) also reports that looking and smiling at adults have occurred as a result of using pain reduction to establish social reinforcers and to eliminate social unresponsiveness in autistic children.

The causes and biological meaning of gaze aversion are not clear. It is obvious that gaze aversion is a disturbing social behavior of many autistically withdrawn children, and that one of the first steps in teaching such children must be the establishment of appropriate eye contact. Methods of overcoming the problem of averted gaze include games requiring looking at another person, prompts, and reinforcement for eye contact.

Muteness, Echolalia, and Other Language Disorders

Language is a primary vehicle for social interaction, and it is a common observation that most autistically withdrawn children have severe language disorders. A high proportion of children diagnosed as autistic are mute and approximately 50% have no oral language at all. Many are echolalic, parroting back whatever they hear, or reverse pronouns, for example, using *he* for *I*, or *her* for *me*. Some profoundly withdrawn children are neither mute nor echolalic but have no *functional* language, for their speech consists of random jargon or neologisms which cannot be used for meaningful communication. A few very withdrawn children (seldom considered autistic) are electively mute—they talk, but only to a select few persons (such as their mothers or other members of their immediate families) or only under extremely unusual circumstances (elective mutism will be discussed further under the section "Immaturity-Inadequacy"). Unquestionably, the language problems of autistically withdrawn children represent an extreme detriment to their social development. Some researchers have gone so far in appraising the language disorders of psychotic children as to suggest that a severe language deficiency is the necessary and sufficient cause underlying the behavior that characterizes autistic and schizophrenic children (see Churchill, 1978).

The reason (or reasons) why profoundly withdrawn children exhibit severe disorders of language is unknown. It is known that many mute and echolalic children can learn functional language skills, but there is considerable divergence of opinion regarding how such skills are best taught. Hewett (1965), Lovaas and his colleagues (Lovaas, 1977; Devany et al., 1981), and Risley and Wolf (1967) developed detailed operant conditioning procedures for teaching language to mute and echolalic children. Their methods involve first teaching the child a repertoire of motor and verbal imitations; in the case of echolalic children this is not necessary, for they already imitate excessively. Then control of imitative responding is transferred to appropriate social stimuli, such as the questions "What is this?" or "What is Bobby doing?" The language instruction is very specific, highly structured, carefully sequenced, and involves many thousands of learning trials. Each successive approximation of functional speech is reinforced by the teacher. Gradually, the child is taught longer sentences under more varied conditions until, it is hoped, the learning generalizes to everyday circumstances. The researchers who have employed these teaching methods have often come under attack, not only because some individuals believe their techniques are cold, mechanical, and cruel, but also because the children sometimes never obtain true language competence. Some children who are taught language in this manner may never move beyond robot-like repetition of the words or phrases they are taught and may never be able to generalize the rules of language to new situations. In spite of attack and criticism, it cannot be denied that that operant conditioning techniques have been used humanely by most researchers and that marked gains in the use of functional speech have been made by many autistic children in behavior modification programs (see Hewett, 1974, pp. 125–126; Lovaas, 1977; Schiefelbusch, Ruder, & Bricker, 1976).

The approach taken by Des Lauriers and Carlson (1969) to teaching language is quite different in some respects from that of other researchers who use behavior modification. Although Des Lauriers and Carlson obviously use the principles of modeling and reinforcement in their work, they use these techniques almost as an incidental part of their more "natural" or nativistic methods. That is, they do not have a definite plan or program for teaching specific language responses, but encourage vocalization and language usage as part of the games they play and the experiences they share with children. They provide a great deal of stimulation by singing and talking to the child (modeling) and become highly enthusiastic (provide social reinforcement for) over the child's use of words. According to their report, their autistic children's speech, once they acquire it, is not inappropriate, purely echolalic, out of context, or nonsensical. However, it should be recognized that Des Lauriers and Carlson do not provide the kind of precise measurement and documentation of language acquisition that is part of the operant conditioning literature.

An alternative to oral language has reportedly been used with some success with autistic children. Creedon (1973) taught simultaneous manual signing (usually used by the deaf) and spoken language in an attempt to shape the existing behavior (e.g., hand posturing) of autistic children into a usable communication system. Carr and his colleagues (Carr, Binkoff, Kiloginsky, & Eddy, 1978) taught four autistic children to use manual signs for common objects. However, Carr et al. found that even though the names of the words were said during the manual communication training, three of the four children apparently learned nothing about oral language from their training—they responded only to the visual stimuli. Carr (1979), in a review of research, concludes that simultaneous communication training (signing and talking) does not seem likely to be successful in getting mute children to talk. However, children who have good skills in verbal imitation seem to show gains in speech following simultaneous communication training. Other researchers (Konstantareas, Webster, & Oxman, 1979) have found that training in simultaneous communication has been successful not only in improving communication skills but behavior in other areas as well. Further research is needed before firm conclusions can be drawn about the value and limitations of manual signing and simultaneous communication with psychotic children.

Attempts have been made to compare operant conditioning techniques with less highly structured methods of teaching. Ney, Palvesky, and Markely (1971) compared the effectiveness of operant conditioning and play therapy in improving the social behavior and communication skills of severely disturbed boys. Rutter and Bartak (1973) conducted a comparative study of structured (emphasis on teaching specific skills) and permissive (allowing regression) education for autistic children. In general, the results of both of these studies and data from other sources (e.g., Lovaas et al., 1973) give rather clear support to the contention that a directive, structured approach based on operant conditioning principles will produce better outcomes on measures of social and language behavior than will a less structured, more permissive approach.

Excessive Self-Stimulation and Fantasy

The repetitive, stereotyped nature of self-stimulative behavior has already been briefly described. It may take an almost infinite variety of forms, ranging from staring blankly into space or at a particular object, to rocking one's entire body, flapping one's hands, rubbing one's eyes, or licking one's lips. Lists of self-stimulatory behaviors exhibited by children included in a study conducted by Koegel, Firestone, Kramme, and Dunlap (1974) are shown in Table 9–2. Self-stimulation is, apparently, a way of obtaining sensory feedback that is self-reinforcing or self-perpetuating. It is a form of behavior not likely to stop for long unless demands for other incompatible responses are made or it is actively suppressed. This appears to be true of most self-stimulation of psychotic or retarded

TABLE 9-2 Complete List of Self-stimulatory Responses for Subject *1* and Subject *2*.

Subject 1

1. eye crossing
2. finger manipulations (moving the hands with continuous flexion and extension)
3. repetitive vocalizations (excluding recognizable words)
4. feet contortions (tight sustained flexions)
5. leg contortions (tight sustained flexions)
6. rhythmic manipulation of objects (repeatedly rubbing, rotating, or tapping objects with fingers)
7. grimacing (corners of mouth drawn out and down, revealing the upper set of teeth)
8. staring or gazing (a fixed glassy-eyed look lasting more than 3 seconds)
9. hands repetitively rubbing mouth
10. hands repetitively rubbing face
11. mouthing of objects (holding nonedible objects in contact with the mouth)
12. locking hands behind head
13. hands pressing on or twisting ears

Subject 2

1. staring or gazing (a fixed glassy-eyed look lasting more than 3 seconds)
2. grimacing (corners of mouth drawn out and down, revealing the upper set of teeth)
3. hand waving vertically or horizontally with fingers outstretched in front of eyes
4. hands vigorously and repetitively rubbing eyes
5. hands vigorously and repetitively rubbing nose
6. hands vigorously and repetitively rubbing mouth
7. hands vigorously and repetitively rubbing ears
8. hands vigorously and repetitively rubbing hair
9. hands vigorously and repetitively rubbing clothes
10. hands vigorously and repetitively rubbing objects
11. hand flapping in air
12. hand wringing (hands alternately rubbing and clutching each other)
13. finger contortions (tight sustained flexions)
14. tapping fingers against part of body or an object
15. tapping whole hand against part of body or object
16. mouthing of objects (holding nonedible objects in contact with the mouth)
17. rocking (moving the trunk at the hips rhythmically back and forth or from side to side)
18. head weaving (moving head from side to side in a figure-eight pattern)
19. body contortions (sustained flexions or extensions of the torso)
20. repetitive vocalizations (excluding recognizable words)
21. teeth clicking (audibly and rapidly closing teeth together)
22. tongue rolling and clicking
23. audible saliva swishing in mouth
24. repetitive tapping feet on floor
25. repetitive tapping toes inside shoes (visible through canvas tennis shoes)
26. leg contortions (tight sustained flexions)
27. repetitive knocking knees against each other
28. repetitive knocking ankles against each other
29. tensing legs and suspending feet off the ground
30. head shaking (rapid small movements from side to side)
31. tensing whole body and shaking

Note. "Increasing Spontaneous Play by Suppressing Self-stimulation in Autistic Children" by R. L. Koegel, P. B. Firestone, K. W. Kramme, and G. Dunlap, *Journal of Applied Behavior Analysis*, 1974, 7, 523. Copyright 1974 by Society for the Experimental Analysis of Behavior, Inc. Reprinted by permission.

individuals, and it is also true for some self-stimulatory behavior (e.g., nail biting) of ordinary people. As Sroufe, Steucher, and Stutzer (1973) suggest, self-stimulation is probably seen in some form in everyone's behavior and varies only in its subtlety, social appropriateness, and rate. In autistically withdrawn children, self-stimulation is often obvious, socially inappropriate, and exhibited at such a high rate that the child engages in few other pursuits. Thus, like most behaviors, self-stimulation is considered normal or pathological depending on its social context and rate.

Causes.   The factors that cause autistically withdrawn children to become pathological self-stimulators have been the topic of conjecture, but no convincing evidence supporting any of the speculation has been uncovered. Among the many suggestions that have been made regarding the origin of self-stimulation is the hypothesis that stereotypy results from defects in the part of the central nervous system controlling arousal (cf. Des Lauriers & Carlson, 1969). Self-stimulation is quite common in sensorily deprived (for example, blind) children, and control techniques found useful with autistically withdrawn children may be applied as successfully with the sensorily deprived. Not surprisingly, then, it has been suggested that autistic self-stimulation is the result of perceptual disorders—that it is, in effect, one way for the autistic child to keep in touch with a perceptually inconstant world (see Rutter & Bartak, 1971). The more fruitful types of research examine the meaning of self-stimulatory behavior to autistic children, its relationship to other behaviors of such children, and alternative means of controlling its rate.

Meaning.   Aside from the fanciful hypotheses of psychoanalysts, there has been very little written regarding what self-stimulation means to autists. However, studies by Sroufe, Steucher, and Stutzer (1973) provide empirical data that suggest how a psychotic child may use self-stimulation and how self-stimulation may be related to other autistic behaviors. They measured several relevant observable behaviors (e.g., stereotypic finger flicking, staring, aggression, individual play, active avoidance, certain emotional expressions) and simultaneously monitored the heart rate, respiration, muscle tension, and skin conductance of an autistic boy during a variety of activities over the course of 17 weeks, including 12 weeks of therapeutic educational treatment. In this way, they were able to observe the interrelationships among autistic self-stimulation and physiological responses indicating attention (e.g., heart rate deceleration), stress (e.g., heart rate and respiratory acceleration), and emotionality (e.g., muscle tone and skin conductance). Their studies clearly showed that the behavior of this autistic child "made sense." His overt behaviors (including self-stimulation and negativism) and physiological responses occurred in identifiable patterns and relationships to each other, and the patterns of behaviors and their relationships changed over the course of treatment. For this child, at least, self-stimulation seemed to serve different purposes at different times. When not engaged in any structured activities, he apparently used self-stimulation to avoid boredom (to boost arousal) or accompany hallucinations, but in demanding and emotionally arousing circumstances, he appeared to use self-stimulation to block out environmental input and release energy. Before treatment, self-stimulation occurred most frequently in structured situations and at the beginning of a task, whereas by the end of treatment, it had declined in overall frequency and tended to occur most often in unstructured settings and following task completion. These findings, Sroufe and his colleagues suspect, show that whereas before intervention, self-stimulation was associated primarily with boredom and stress, during intervention, it took on characteristics of expressions of joy and self-reinforcement for performance of appropriate tasks. These researchers also suggest that perhaps instead of trying to "stamp out" self-stimulation in autists, it would be better to try to change its form and function so that it is socially acceptable and does not interfere with learning.

More recently, Rincover, Newsom, Lovaas, and Koegel (1977) used various types of sensory stimulation (e.g., music, flickering light, windshield wiper) as reinforcement for a simple motor response. The type of sensory stimulation that served as an effective reinforcer was idiosyncratic for a particular child, and when small changes were made in the stimuli (to avoid satiation), the contingent stimulation could maintain a child's responding for a long period of time. Rincover et al. noted that the sensory stimuli appeared to function similarly to self-stimulation and could, perhaps, be used as an effective reinforcer in therapeutic work.

Relationship to other behaviors.   The research of Koegel and his associates (Koegel & Covert, 1972; Koegel, et al., 1974) has shown that self-stimulation is, at least as it is typically performed, inversely related to learning and appropriate play of autistic children. Koegel and Covert (1972) found that two particular autistic children could not learn even a simple experimental task as long as they were allowed to self-stimulate during training sessions. However, when self-stimulation was suppressed during training (by sharply saying "No!" and, if necessary, slapping the child's hand), the children quickly learned the task. For another child, Koegel and Covert found that the child could learn the task without suppression of self-stimulation, although self-stimulation and learning appeared to be incompatible. More recently, Koegel et al., (1974) showed that for two autistic children, appropriate spontaneous play with toys was inversely related to self-stimulation. The subjects were two children, one male and one female, exhibiting the self-stimulatory responses listed in Table 9-2. When these children were provided with several simple toys, they ignored them most of the time and instead spent nearly all their time engaged in self-stimulation (as shown for each subject during the baseline sessions in Figure 9-4). During sessions in which self-stimulation was suppressed (by sharply saying "No!" and briskly slapping or briefly holding and immobilizing the part of the child's body with which he or she was performing the response), appropriate play greatly increased. As shown in the second baseline phase for both subjects (Figure 9-4), appropriate play declined and self-stimulation resumed its prominence when suppression was no longer in effect.

The research data lead to the conclusion that for some (and perhaps most or all) autistically withdrawn children, self-stimulation is incompatible with learning and appropriate play. As long as there is no intervention in their self-stimulation, autistic children are not likely to learn desirable behaviors, and the more constant or pervasive their self-stimulation, the more likely that they will not learn.

Alternative means of control.   Intervention in self-stimulation does not, however, *necessarily* mean punishment or direct suppression. Des Lauriers and

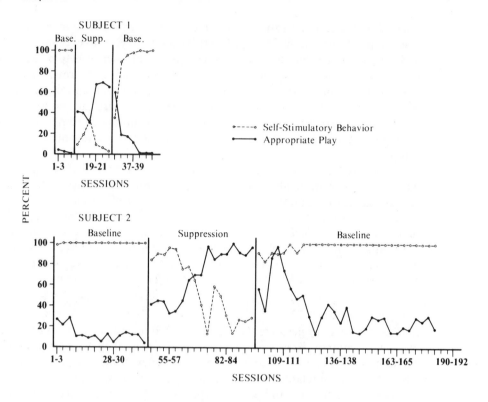

FIGURE 9-4   Percent of time-sample intervals in which self-stimulatory and appropriate play behaviors occurred during (a) baseline, (b) suppression of self-stimulation conditions, and (c) reversal.

Note. From "Increasing Spontaneous Play by Suppressing Self-stimulation in Autistic Children" by R. L. Koegel, P.B. Firestone, K. W. Kamme, and G. Dunlap, *Journal of Applied Behavior Analysis*, 1974, 7, 525. Copyright 1974 by Society for the Experimental Analysis of Behavior, Inc. Reprinted by permission.

Carlson (1969), Steucher (1972), and others describe treatment for autistic children that does not require direct suppression of self-stimulation. The alternatives to suppression may involve "entering into the child's world" and being in contact with him/her to the greatest extent possible. Attempts may be made to recreate for the autistic child many of the parent-child interactions experienced by the normal infant and to "seduce" him or her into interactive play, perhaps by imitation. In addition, opportunities to engage in self-stimulation may be made contingent on a short interval of appropriate behavior during a teaching session. In this way, self-stimulation is prevented from interfering with learning and is made to serve a therapeutic purpose.

Best method of direct control.   Assuming that self-stimulation is to be suppressed directly, there remains the question of the best method of suppression. Azrin and his colleagues (Azrin, Kaplan, & Foxx, 1973; Foxx & Azrin, 1973) explored new ways of reducing self-stimulation. Their techniques are referred to variously as *overcorrection* or *autism reversal*. They noted that self-stimulation has been suppressed through the use of punishment (for example, slaps, shock), medication (for example, Thorazine), and reinforcement for nonself-stimulatory behavior, but that in each case that method has been ineffective with some children, had only temporary effects, or required the use of very painful stimuli. Hence, they have sought a method that has general application, is quick and powerful in its effect, and involves a minimum of pain.

Overcorrection (sometimes called *positive practice* or *autism reversal*) is the technique of requiring the child who self-stimulates to practice a more correct mode of behavior under the direction of the teacher or therapist for a specific period of time. In a sense, it is requiring the child to "overcorrect" a behavioral error. For example, the child who self-stimulates by flapping hands or flicking fingers may be required, when observed performing these responses, to perform "functional" hand exercises that are hand movements different from those used in self-stimulation under the teacher's direction for 10 minutes. The child who mouths objects or hands may be required to brush his/her teeth and gums with an antiseptic solution for five minutes. Foxx and Azrin (1973) compared the overcorrection technique to other suppression procedures and found it to be superior in immediacy of effect, completeness, permanence of reduction of self-stimulation, and general applicability.

Overcorrection typically involves several components, one of which is a verbal warning to stop the self-stimulatory behavior before requiring the corrective movement. Wells, Forehand, and Hickey (1977) found that stern verbal warnings alone were effective in suppressing self-stimulation in two children. Use of the warnings did not result in increases in the appropriate play of either child, but positive practice overcorrection not only suppressed self-stimulation for both children but increased the appropriate play of one child.

To be maximally effective, overcorrection procedures may need to be implemented in the home as well as the classroom (Simpson & Swenson, 1980). Requiring the child to go through the positive practice routine can become extremely time consuming and difficult to implement. An alternative to overcorrection is contingent physical restraint—for example, holding the child's hands so that he or she cannot use them for self-stimulation. Shapiro, Barrett, and Ollendick (1980) found that physical restraint (holding the child's hands on the table for 30 seconds) was just as effective as positive practice overcorrection (moving the child's hands through an appropriate task for 30 seconds) in decreasing stereotypic mouthing behavior in three mentally retarded and severely disturbed children. Physical restraint was a less complex intervention and required less staff training than overcorrecton. The *best* method of control of self-stimulation varies for different children and must be determined on an individual basis.

Fantasy and delusions.   Self-stimulation, at least as it is practiced by most autistically withdrawn children, is an overt behavior that is relatively easy to detect and record objectively. Fantasy, on the other hand, is a private activity that must be *inferred* from what children do—how they behave, the pictures they draw, or what they say. Undeniably, fantasy is characteristic of emotional health and behavioral normality. However, when fantasy dominates an individual's thought and interferes with ongoing behavior and reality-oriented demands, it represents pathological withdrawal. Excessive, debilitating fantasy (perhaps an activity that could be considered covert or cognitive self-stimulation) is sometimes evident in the extremely withdrawn child. The case of Wanda in Chapter 1 illustrates fantasy that is debilitating. Some psychotic children are able to tell the difference between fantasy and reality. They may engage in wild fantasies during play, and therapists often attempt to use such fantasies to help children "work through emotional conflicts" (see Wundheiler, 1976).

Delusional thinking was illustrated in Chapter 3 in the case of Thomas. Although such cases are rare, children do sometimes become convinced of the reality of their fantasies or the delusions of other people (Simonds & Glenn, 1976).

Severely and profoundly disturbed children with high intelligence and verbal skills are relatively rare, but their cases have often provided grist for psychoanalytic interpreters of their behavior. Very little is known about how to control maladaptive fantasy or delusions of children. Conjecture about treatment is usually based on research of other verbal behavior in children and the psychotic speech, obsessions, and delusions of adults. It is highly probable that responding to the inappropriate fantasies of the psychotic child will serve merely to reinforce and perpetuate the problem (see O'Leary & Wilson, 1975).

IMMATURITY-INADEQUACY

The behavior of an immature child is similar to that of a younger child—the immature child is "babyish." Immaturity may range from minor and occasional discrepancies from developmental norms to profound and chronic delay in development. The child may be uneven in behavioral development, exhibit normal or even advanced progress in some areas of behavior and at the same time show retarded progress in others. For example, a child may be advanced beyond his/her years in the ability to master academic tasks and to relate socially to adults, but may be retarded in the skills required for adequate peer relationships, or vice versa.

Simply stated, inadequate behavior does not measure up to the demands of the child's social environment. In most cases, inadequacy and immaturity amount to the same thing. However, a child may be immature, yet his/her behavior may be adequate for the unusually low demands of the particular social environment. Conversely, a child may not be immature but nevertheless be inadequate because an unreasonable level of performance is expected. Thus, *immaturity* refers to behavior that falls below the norms of a large population or cultural group, whereas *inadequacy* is a term referring to the child's behavior as it measures up to the more narrowly defined norms of the immediate social context.

Social maturity or adequacy is most often judged informally. Typically, complaints that the child is immature or inadequate rest on, perhaps, a parent's or teacher's judgment that the child is behaving inappropriately for someone of his/her age. The judgment is usually based on subjective comparison between the child's behavior and that of the peer group. Such informal judgments are especially likely in the case of children whose immaturity or inadequacy is not a severe problem. In more severe cases, it is likely that the child's behavior will be rated on a checklist or compared formally to developmental norms. Children who are thought to be mentally retarded may, for example, be rated on the *Vineland Social Maturity Scale* (Doll, 1965) or the *AAMD Adaptive Behavior Scale* (Nihira,

Foster, Shellhaas, & Leland, 1974). Other behavior rating scales may also be used in the case of children with behavior disorders. However, in the final analysis it is most often clinical judgment regarding the child's behavior vis-à-vis the parents' and other adults' expectations that is the test. Once immature or inadequate behaviors are identified objectively, they can be measured by direct daily observation so that the problem and its resolution can be monitored precisely.

A child's immaturity or inadequacy does not preclude his/her exhibiting maladaptive behavior in other categories. For example, immature behavior may include distractibility, aggression, or withdrawal. Furthermore, the concept of immaturity is so broad that it can be applied to nearly all disordered or inappropriate behavior. The following discussion will be focused on behavior that is considered to be a problem *primarily* because it is age-inappropriate or inadequate for the situation.

Some mention of etiological considerations is necessary. The position taken here is that inadequate and immature behavior can be most profitably conceptualized as a learning deficiency. That is, the principles of social learning theory, though not sufficient to prove the etiology of all disordered behavior, provide the strongest empirical analysis of the problem and the most effective guide to remedial efforts. Therefore, assume throughout this chapter that behavioral difficulties represent learning failures. Difficulties included in this chapter as immature-inadequate are:

1. crying and tantrums
2. negativism
3. fear
4. regression
5. psychophysiological disorders
6. obsessions, compulsions, and rituals
7. sexual problems
8. social ineptitude
9. helplessness
10. academic failure

Crying and Tantrums

Crying and tantrums can be expected of normal children in the process of growing up. At what age and under what circumstances crying and tantrums should not occur are judgments that will vary from culture to culture and family to family. There are, nevertheless, rather obvious cases in which it would be easy to see that the crying or tantruming being exhibited by a child in a given situation is totally uncalled for. "Brats," or children who often engage in tantrums and other ploys designed to intimidate their caretakers and enforce their demands, are not difficult for most adults to recognize (cf. Bernal, Duryee, Pruett, & Burns, 1968). The frequent crying and tantruming of autistic children, often for no identifiable reason or in response to the slightest change in routine or failure to comply with their tyrannical demands, is a case in point. For example, consider the problem presented by an 8-year-old boy who had frequent hysterical fits of crying at school because he had lost a pencil, gotten too warm on the playground, heard the fire alarm, or had been disturbed by some other very minor incident (the case of Sammy described by Kaufhold & Kauffman in Worell & Nelson, 1974). Yet another case of inappropriate crying in a young child is described by Williams (1959; see discussion of this case in Chapter 4). In these instances, firm and consistent management must be demanded. The child has undoubtedly learned through long experience that his crying and tantrums will "pay off"—that others will eventually acquiesce to his/her wishes. The same behavioral principles discussed in Chapters 4, 7, and 8 apply here: make expectations for appropriate behavior clear, arrange neutral or undesirable consequences to follow inappropriate responses, and provide reinforcement for appropriate behavior. Consistent application of these principles tailored to the needs of the individual case will nearly always quickly resolve the problem. When the child learns that tantrums and crying will not coerce adults and that appropriate behavior will be rewarded, he/she will behave more maturely.

Negativism

Negativism—refusal to comply with reasonable requests or deliberate performance of the opposite of the behavior requested—is seen for a short period of time in most youngsters during the second or third year of life. When such oppositional behavior persists and is emitted frequently into or beyond the middle childhood years, there is rightful cause for concern regarding the child's maturity, for it is obvious that the child has learned only inappropriate tactics for manipulating adults. Negativism may be a prominent part of the behavioral repertoire of the aggressive child. It is also commonly seen in autistically withdrawn children. In fact, in some cases overcoming persistent negativism seems to be at the core of therapeutic teaching of the autistic child (cf. Des Lauriers & Carlson, 1969; Steucher, 1972). As in the case of crying and tantrums, firm and consistent management is required. This statement does not mean that one may ride roughshod over children or their feelings, but it does mean that to be therapeutic, the teacher or parent must not let the child be a tyrant, behaving in a way that is self-defeating or that tramples the rights of others. There is no reason to believe that children will give up their negativism because they are allowed in a permissive, accepting environment to coerce others or bully them into subservience as has been suggested by some proponents of psychoanalytic methods.

Fear

Fear of falling and of loud noises are present in the normal infant at birth, and fear of other stimuli (for example, strange persons, objects, situations) ordinarily develops during the first few months of life. These fears probably have survival value, and they are considered normal and adaptive, not deviant. As children grow into the middle childhood years, they typically develop additional fears, especially about imaginary creatures or events (Jersild & Holmes, 1935). Unless these fears become excessive or debilitative, preventing the child from engaging in normal social interaction, sleep, school attendance, or exploration of the environment, they are not considered maladaptive. Indeed, the child without any fears at all is not only highly unusual but also likely to be hurt or killed because of inappropriate brashness.

Fears appear to be learned in several different ways (see Johnson & Melamed, 1979; O'Leary & Wilson, 1975, pp. 64–69 for an excellent review of analyses of fear acquisition). Especially in infants and young children, it is possible for fear to be learned by classical or respondent conditioning. If an already fright-producing stimulus is paired with another object or event, that object or event may become something of which the child is afraid. In children who have acquired language skills, the comments, remonstrations, and other verbal communications of the parents (especially the mother) and other adults regarding objects, activities, places, persons, or situations may induce fearfulness. The nonverbal behavior of adults and other children may also have a powerful influence on the child's learning of fear. For example, if a child is overly fearful of dogs, the fear may have been acquired in any one or a combination of the following ways: (a) a dog may have frightened the child by barking or growling, jumping, knocking the child down, biting, and so on; (b) the parents or another person may have warned the child in an emotional way about the dangers of dogs or the child may have heard people speaking about the meanness and dangerousness of dogs; (c) the child may have observed parents, siblings, or other children (or seen individuals in movies or on TV) being attacked by or frightened by dogs.

Children's fears may be mild and short-lived enough so that they do not seriously interfere with social growth. When the child's activity is unnecessarily restricted by fear, however, intervention is called for. Extreme, irrational fear that is out of proportion to the reality of the situation and leads to automatic avoidance of the feared situation is often called a *phobia*. Regardless of how fears and phobias are acquired, social learning principles can be used to resolve the problem. Two approaches to reducing excessive fears have been found to be particularly successful: modeling and desensitization.

Bandura and his fellow investigators, as well as other psychologists, found modeling to be a particularly effective way of ridding children of inappropriate fears (Bandura, Grusec, & Menlove, 1967; Bandura & Menlove, 1968; Weissbrod & Bryan, 1973; see also Bandura, 1969; Kirkland & Thelen, 1977). These researchers have found that having fearful children watch movies in which other youngsters are having fun (having a party or playing games) while approaching the feared object without hesitation (for example, the youngsters in the movie may be handling dogs or snakes while playing) reduces fear in the observers and makes them more willing to approach the thing they fear. Having the phobic children watch several different peer models nonanxiously approach several different feared objects and showing films in which the actual feared object (rather than a replica) is displayed have been found to increase the effectiveness of the *vicarious extinction* (or modeling) method of fear reduction. Positive reinforcement of the fearful child's approach to the feared object could be expected to add to the fear-reducing effects of vicarious extinction.

Procedures variously referred to as *systematic densensitization*, *reciprocal inhibition*, and *counter-conditioning* also have been shown effective in lowering children's fears. The central feature of these procedures involves the gradual and repeated approach of the child to the feared stimuli (either in real life—*in vivo*—or in purposeful fantasy of them) while the child remains nonanxious and perhaps engaging in an activity that is incompatible with or inhibitory of anxiety (such as eating a favorite treat or relaxing comfortably in a chair). The *gradual* approach to the feared object, *repeated* exposure to it, and maintenance of a *nonanxious* state during exposure to it are thought to weaken the conditioned or learned *bond* between the object and the fear response it elicits (cf. Wolpe, 1958, 1975). By using desensitization techniques, a wide array of children's fears have been overcome, including fear of high buildings (Croghan & Musante, 1975), busses (Obler & Terwilliger, 1970), separation from mother (Montenegro, 1968), stage fright (Kondas, 1967), water (Pomerantz, Peterson, Marholin, & Stern, 1977), dogs, dark, and school (Lazarus & Abramovitz, 1962), and other phobias. In some cases, vicarious extinction (modeling) and *in vivo* desensitization have been used together to help children overcome fears (Gelfand, 1978; Johnson & Melamed, 1979). Several specific fears will now be discussed: school phobia, fear of talking (or elective mutism) and fear of being overweight.

School Phobia

Some children show a specific fear of going to school and are termed "school phobic" (School phobia should not be confused with truancy, failure to attend school, which is discussed in a following section of this chapter.). School phobic children typically exhibit indications of anxiety about attendance and may develop abdominal pain, nausea, or other physical complaints just before it is time to go to school in the morning. There are insufficient data to support a firm conclusion regarding the cause of school phobia, but it seems unlikely that the psychodynamic idea that school phobia represents anxiety about separation from the mother (cf. Eisenberg, 1958) is correct, since school phobia often does not develop until after the child has attended school (and has been separated from the mother) without problems for several years (cf. Leventhal & Sills, 1964). It seems more likely that school becomes a fear-inducing situation for children due to traumatic incidents that occur there or threatening and stressful demands for academic or social performance which the child does not feel he/she can meet. When school becomes threatening or aversive to the child, it may be expected that the child will seek refuge and protection at home (Yates, 1970).

Behavior principles have been used quite successfully to remediate the problem of school phobia (Allyon, Smith, & Rogers, 1970; Gelfand, 1978; Kennedy, 1965; Lazarus, Davison, & Polefka, 1965; Patterson, 1965a). The specific techniques employed have varied somewhat from case to case, but in general, the procedures have included one or more of the following:

1. desensitization of the child's fear through role playing or *in vivo* approximations of attending school for an entire day
2. reinforcement for attending school, even if for a brief period of time, and gradual lengthening of the time the child is required to stay in school
3. matter-of-fact parental statements that the child will go back to school and

avoidance of lengthy or emotional parental discussion regarding school attendance

4. removal of reinforcers for staying home (e.g., being allowed to watch television, play a favorite game, stay close to mother, or engage in other pleasurable activities)

Elective Mutism

As mentioned previously, the electively mute child speaks only to a certain individual or group of persons, refusing to talk to others. The electively mute child presents a puzzling behavior problem to teachers, for it is known that he understands how to speak but under certain circumstances simply does not. The term "elective" mutism seems to connote a conscious effort on the part of the child to remain silent. As Kratochwill, Brody, and Piersel (1979) point out, however, there are many different perspectives on this problem and many terms used to describe it. Sanok and Ascione (1979) suggest using the term "selective" mutism to indicate that the child is mute only under specific environmental circumstances.

Because the child does not need to *acquire* normal speech but merely to learn to use speech under ordinary circumstances, remediation of the difficulty is often considerably easier than overcoming difficulties presented by the mute or echolalic child. The electively mute child is, at least to some degree, socially withdrawn, although he or she may be withdrawn only from adults (cf. the case of Jim presented by Taylor in Worell & Nelson, 1974) or only from peers (cf. Griffith, Schnelle, McNees, Bissinger, & Huff, 1975). Elective mutism appears to be social withdrawal based on a rather specific fear of talking to certain individuals or groups of people.

As in the case of other fears, behavior principles have been used to resolve the problem of elective mutism (Sanok & Ascione, 1979). The techniques employed have involved a form of desensitization and reinforcement for gradual approximations of speaking freely to the person(s) in whose presence the child has been mute.

Anorexia Nervosa

As defined by Brady and Rieger (1975), "Anorexia nervosa is a rare disorder characterized by profound weight loss due to self-imposed restriction of food intake and often aggravated by excessive exercise, self-induced vomiting, and purgation" (p. 45). *Anorexia* (literally, *loss of appetite*) is a misnomer, for anorexics do not report absence of hunger, and the problem is clearly a *refusal* to eat. As in the case of self-injurious behavior, the victim often is a pitiable ruin. The description of an anorexic woman provided by Bachrach, Erwin, and Mohr (1965) reveals how far some will go in self-starvation:

> The physical examination revealed a creature so cachetic and shrunken about her skeleton as to give the appearance of a poorly preserved mummy suddenly stuck with the breath of life. Her pasty white skin was mottled a purple hue over her feet and stretched like so much heavy spider webbing about the bony prominence of her face. Edematous ankles and feet ballooned out grotesquely from the margins of her slippers. Cavernous ulcers opened up over the right buttocks, pubis, and back of the skull while small ulcers stood out over the knees, elbows, and ankles. Delicate silky threads of hair

hung lifelessly from her skull. Broken grey teeth peered out between thin, white lips through which there weakly issued forth a high pitched distant voice, remarkable for its lack of pressing concern and alarm, which to the passing observer might have seemed a bit incongruous.   (p. 154)

Not all anorexics become so corpse-like, but somewhere between 3 and 20% do die of self-starvation (Stunkard, 1972). Anorexics are usually girls (by a ratio of about 10 to 1) in the early adolescent to young adult age range.

Psychodynamic ideas regarding the causes of anorexia have already been commented upon (see Chapter 5). It has been more useful to analyze anorexia as a fear of getting fat by eating too much than as a fear of sexual maturity, pregnancy, aggression, and the like. Anorexics often express a fear of becoming overweight, and so working with the fear of getting fat does not require obtuse reference to hidden drives or impulses. Furthermore, proper eating is the behavior that will change an anorexic into a nonanorexic person, and eating or the resulting weight gain can be reinforced directly without reference to "underlying" emotional problems. The evidence is considerable that anorexics can be deconditioned to fear of fatness and induced to gain weight quickly by providing reinforcement for eating and weight gain (Azerad & Stafford, 1969; Blinder, Freeman, & Stunkard, 1970; Brady & Rieger, 1975; Hallsten, 1965; Kellerman, 1977b; Leitenberg, Agras, & Thompson, 1968; Scrignar, 1971). For example, Azerad and Stafford (1969) quickly increased a 13-year-old anorexic's weight by requiring her to earn points by eating specified foods and showing a weight gain each day. The points could be used to purchase desired items (for example, hair curlers, writing paper, stamps) and activities (for example, movies, trips). Other studies in which similar behavioral strategies were used have also yielded good results.

Developmental Regression

Some children seem to develop normally and then slide back into an immature form of behavior that is characteristic of an earlier developmental period. Such developmental regression can be very disconcerting to parents or teachers who know that the child has acquired the ability to behave more maturely but now acts in an inappropriate, infantile manner. The child may begin using "baby talk," crawling, eating with his/her fingers, whining, thumb sucking, or regressing in other ways. Regressive behavior ordinarily results in much attention for the child. Teachers, parents, and even other children often comment on the behavior, perhaps expressing dismay or disgust or giving the child reminders to "grow up." Mild and fleeting regressions are typically seen in children and adults, particularly under stressful conditions, and are no cause for alarm. However, if the regressive behavior is severe or persists over more than a short while, intervention may be required.

Unlike psychodynamic proponents, who believe that regression represents the child's unconscious attempts to deal with repressed instincts, proponents of social learning theory examine the environmental conditions that may serve to support regressive behavior. In many cases it has been found that when attention for regressive behavior is withdrawn and age-appropriate behavior is reinforced (perhaps only with attention), the child's behavior resumes its forward developmental course. Behavioral psychologists suggest a rearrangement of the social environment so that desirable behavior can be reinforced and regressive behavior can be ignored and not reinforced.

The classic report of Harris, Johnston, Kelly, & Wolf (1964) illustrates the behavioral strategy. A 3-year-old nursery school child spent a very high proportion of her time crawling or off her feet, typically engaged in isolate play. The strategy of the nursery school teachers was simply to ignore off-feet behavior and pay attention to the child when she was standing or walking. The rapid, powerful effect of adult social reinforcement was soon demonstrated, for the child reversed her regressive pattern of behavior and spent a high proportion of her time on her feet playing appropriately with other children. Reversal of the contingencies of reinforcement (return to the plan of adult attention for off-feet, then switching back again to attention for on-feet behavior) provided a demonstration of the causal relationship between adult attention and the child's behavior.

It must be recognized that when behavioral regression is severe or profound, when the young child reverts into a truly infant-like state and remains in that state, or when an older child loses developmental progress in many areas of behavior very rapidly, the problem takes on a far different character than that discussed to this point. Severe and profound developmental regression may be caused by brain damage. In extremely rare cases, profound regression may occur following a horrifying incident or for unknown reasons. When the child has become severely or profoundly regressed, he/she presents, for many practical purposes, a problem similar to that of the child whose development has never advanced beyond an early level.

Corbett, Harris, Taylor, and Trimble (1977) describe two cases in which children developed normally until late childhood or early adolescence and then deteriorated rapidly. They describe the developmental regression as "progressive disintegrative psychosis" because the children become progressively more psychotic until, finally, they function at a profoundly retarded level.

Psychophysiological Disorders

The term *psychophysiological* implies that mental states cause or aggravate physiological disorders (see chapters 3 and 5). Because there is so little reliable evidence that biological problems are in fact caused by mental or emotional disorders, the term *psychophysiological* has been used merely to indicate those problems subsumed under that heading in usual systems of classification.

Enuresis and Encopresis

Attitudes toward toileting.   Attitudes toward toileting vary widely between cultures and within social groups. In Western culture, toilet training is considered very important and is generally begun at a young age. Although the extreme practice of beginning toilet training in the first few weeks of life is ill-advised, behavioral research has shown that by 16 or 18 months of age, most children can be taught (see O'Leary & Wilson, 1975). When children continue to wet or soil themselves after the age of 5 or 6 years, they are typically considered to have a problem demanding intervention. Enuresis may be either diurnal (wetting during waking hours) or nocturnal (bedwetting). About twice as many boys as girls are enuretic, and 2% or 3% of children are enuretic at 14 years of age. At the time they begin first grade, approximately 13% to 20% of children are enuretic. Encopresis, or soiling, typically occurs during the day and is a rarer problem than enuresis.

It must be remembered that toilet training is usually a gradual process, and that stress and illness have an effect on bowel and bladder control. Thus, the younger the child and the more stressful the circumstances, the more one may expect accidents to occur. Enuresis and encopresis are not, however, matters involving infrequent accidents. The enuretic or encopretic child has a chronic problem in retaining urine or feces until it can be released in the toilet.

Theory.   As O'Leary and Wilson (1975), Bemporad (1978), and Sours (1978) point out, advice regarding the management of encopresis and enuresis varies. The psychoanalytic warning that such problems are only symptoms of underlying emotional conflicts which must be resolved are countered by the behavioral assertion that bladder and bowel habits may be conditioned without worry that the child's future emotional adjustment will be jeopardized. There is an absence of experimental data underlying the psychoanalytic suggestions that the enuretic is trying to cool his firey penis (most enuretics are boys), which has been condemned for its transgressions or is threatened by the superego; that enuresis is a form of direct sexual gratification; that enuresis is symbolic weeping through the bladder; or that the enuretic is urinating on the world in retailiation for mistreatment. Readily available from behavior therapists, however, are research data showing not only that young children can be toilet trained quickly and easily, but also that enuresis and encopresis can often be remedied effectively without undesirable side effects (see O'Leary & Wilson, 1975). In fact, Nordquist (1971), Baker (1969), and Baller (1975) present data suggesting that if there are side effects of the behavioral treatment of enuresis, the side effects are *good* and the child may adopt *other appropriate* behaviors.

Psychodynamic theory assumes that enuresis and encopresis are symptoms of underlying emotional conflicts usually involving the family. Whether or not one subscribes to psychodynamic ideas, it is obvious that if the family is inconsistent or unreasonable in toilet training, then family factors play an important role. Furthermore, it is easy to see how wetting and soiling could sour parent-child relationships regardless of the cause of the problem. Not many parents can face such problems with complete equanimity, and it is the rare child who is completely unaffected by adults' typical reactions to misplaced excrement. Thus the fact that negative feelings about the problem often run high in families of encopretic or enuretic children should be recognized. Treatment of such problems must be planned to avoid further anger of parents and abuse of the child.

Sours (1978) points out that enuresis is seldom the only problem of the child. The enuretic child is often involved in other difficulties (perhaps stealing, overeating, self-stimulation, and/or underachievement) as well.

Management of enuresis.   In a few cases of enuresis, there may be physical causes that can be corrected by surgery or medication. However, in the vast majority of cases there is no known anatomical defect, and medication is not particularly helpful. The most effective methods of treating enuresis derive from the assumption that the problem is a deficiency in habit training or practice. Since the late 1930s, a conditioning device has been available for behavior therapy with enuretics (Mowrer & Mowrer, 1938). The device consists of two metal foil sheets separated by an insulating pad, the foil sheets being connected electrically to a buzzer alarm. The foil sheets are placed under the child's bedsheet so that when the child begins to urinate (and the urine closes the electrical contact between the two sheets of foil) he/she is immediately awakened by the buzzer. The child then turns off the buzzer, gets out of bed with the help of the parents, goes to the bathroom to finish urinating and to clean up, returns to the bedroom to change the sheets, resets the alarm, and goes back to bed. A chart of the child's progress is kept, a gold star being earned for each dry night. This device and procedure (and similar ones—see Lovibond, 1963, 1964) have been used for 40 years with great success (cf. Taylor & Turner, 1975). Behavioral conditioning has been shown to be more effective than psychotheraphy (Deleon & Mandell, 1966) or drugs (Forrester, Stein, & Susser, 1964; Young, 1965) and also to remediate the problem without the "symptom substitution" or ill side-effects feared by psychodynamic therapists (Baker, 1969; Baller, 1975). Furthermore, research shows that methods based on conditioning principles are effective with both normal and developmentally delayed (retarded) children (Mahoney, Van Wagenen, & Meyerson, 1971). Starfield (1972) and Paschalis, Kimmel, and Kimmel (1972), working under the assumption that enuretics have higher rates of urination than normals and need practice in retention of urine, obtained good results using methods of direct bladder training. These researchers were able to effect a relatively high rate of cure of enuretics simply by giving children repeated practice in urine retention and in stopping and starting the flow of urine.

In recent years, Azrin, Sneed, and Foxx (1974) have found that a combination of teaching procedures can be used to cure most enuretic children almost immediately. They used the urine alarm system plus several additional teaching procedures:

1. training in urine retention
2. positive reinforcement for appropriate urination
3. training in rapid awakening
4. increased fluid intake (to provide more opportunities for learning trials)
5. practice in toileting
6. increased social motivation to be continent
7. reprimands for and self-correction of accidents (a type of positive practice overcorrection procedure in which the child must put on dry night clothes and change the bed linen before going back to bed).

Management of encopresis. Encopresis may involve either of two conditions: (a) prolonged retention of feces which causes constipation, compaction of feces, and eventual passage of small, hard feces or leakage of mucous around the compacted mass which is pressing against the anal sphincter; or (b) a chronically dilated anal sphincter that allows a constant fecal discharge. Psychodynamic interpretations place the blame for encopresis on problems of "the potting couple"—strained relationships between mother and child due to overly rigid or overly lax bowel training (Anthony, 1957). Medical causes or complications of encopresis include congenital defects of the anus or colon, spinal defects which prevent anal sphincter control, and acquired dysfunction of the colon or anal sphincter due to extreme chronic constipation. A learning theory view of encopresis suggests that inadequate habit training or conditioning is the essence of the problem in the absence of known medical causes.

Regardless of the origin of the problem, passage of feces or feces-laden mucous anywhere but in the toilet is, in Western culture, extremely unacceptable and stigmatizing. Once past infancy, the child who soils or plays with feces is revolting to peers and adults alike, and unless an effective intervention stops the encopretic behavior, the child will suffer social stigma in addition to any medical problems he/she may have. It is fortunate that encopresis is relatively rare, for the encopretic child is seriously handicapped in social relationships and may be rejected by the public schools. O'Leary and Wilson (1975) report the case of a girl born without a rectum who had corrective surgery but was still encopretic:

vignettes

1 During the first five years of Laura's life, she was diapered, but the parents became particularly concerned about her lack of bowel control when she was teased by playmates and friends in nursery and kindergarten school; the children made fun of her with phrases such as "Laura stinks!" In fact, after several weeks in a public school kindergarten she was asked to leave because of her soiling problem. (p. 125)

In many cases of encopresis there is indeed evidence of parent-child conflict over toilet training (though a psychodynamic interpretation is not necessary to explain the results). Sometimes the parents become abusive to the child because of the inappropriate defecation. It is common for the child to exhibit multiple problems. The classic case descriptions of Neale (1963) are illustrative. Neale describes the case of a boy (IQ = 80) whose parents smacked him and forced him, at the age of 3, to sit on the pot for long periods if he was incontinent of feces:

2 This was followed, as would be predicted from learning theory, by refusal to defaecate in the pot and by the age of five he would not enter a toilet unless accompanied and if he did so he would not defaecate there. He was constantly defaecating in his trousers by day or pyjamas by night and nowhere else . . . On commencing primary school (age 5) he showed so much aggressive behavior that the head teacher feared for the safety of other children. We have no data by which to determine if his hostility to other children was

in part determined by their dislike and scorn of his dirty conditions. (p. 142)

Another boy (age 9 years, 10 months; IQ = 112) is described as follows:

3 Constipation had been a great problem to mother as a girl and she was
very frightened of it developing in her son. It did. . . . Defaecation
appeared painful and in retrospect he said he was frightened to
defaecate because of the pain. In arguments with his mother one of
the threats the boy made was, "If I don't get my way, I won't go
to the bloody lavatory."
 He was first brought to a Child Guidance Clinic at the age of 6 because
of aggressive behavior, phobias and sex play, but defaulted after
a few visits. He was again referred at age 8 for the same troubles to
which scholastic retardation was now added.   (p. 144)

Behavior principles have been successful where the learning problem presented
by the child's encopresis is the acquisition of sphincter pressure or the release of
feces in the toilet (Conger, 1970; Edelman, 1971; Ferinden & Handel, 1970; Lal &
Lindsley, 1968; Neale, 1963; O'Leary & Wilson, 1975; Tomlinson, 1970). Even in
seemingly intransigent cases where psychodynamic therapy and medical treatment
failed, behavior modification—providing rewards for sphincter control or
producing feces in the pot, and, in some instances, mild punishment for
incontinence —has frequently been successful. In brief, encopretic behavior has
been shown repeatedly to be responsive to the systematic application of
consequences. For example, Conger (1970) found that a 9-year-old physically
healthy but encopretic boy quickly stopped soiling himself when his mother
changed her behavior instead of her son's dirty pants. The mother had been paying
solicitous attention to her son's accidents (attempting to reassure him) and helping
him change his pants. When she ignored his soiling and refused to change his pants
(removed social reinforcement for soiling) the problem was quickly resolved.
Edelman (1971) found that soiling and wetting of a 12-year-old girl could be
dramatically reduced (and apparently overcome) by requiring her to spend 30
minutes alone in her room contingent on her mother finding that her pants were
soiled and, in addition, by letting her avoid having to wash dishes by keeping her
pants clean. Ferinden and Handel (1970) found that a 7-year-old boy with a long
history of soiling himself several times a day in the classroom began soiling much
less and interacted more positively with his peers when the following procedure was
used: The boy brought a change of clothing to school; he was made responsible for
washing out his soiled clothing; he was asked to clean himself with strong soap and
cool water; he was required to stay after school to make up for time lost in cleaning
his clothes and himself. Blechman (1979) also reports successful intervention in
encopresis using behavior modification techniques.

Other Disorders

Other psychophysiological disorders (for instance, asthma, colitis) will not be discussed separately here because there is so little evidence regarding the psychological origin or behavioral treatment of these problems. The few available data do suggest, however, that a social learning analysis is most useful in nonmedical resolution of the difficulties involved (see Egan, 1978; Vandersall, 1978).

Obsession, Compulsions, and Rituals

Obsessions (repetitive, persistent, preoccupying thoughts about something), *compulsions* (repetitive, stereotyped acts that the individual feels he or she must do), and *rituals* (repetitive, stereotyped acts that are an invariable prelude, accompaniment, or coda to a specific event) of children have not been the topics of much behavioral research. Obsessive, compulsive, and ritualistic behaviors in children are described in considerable detail (cf. Easson, 1969; Rubin, 1962), and both descriptive and treatment literature are usually psychodynamic in orientation.

According to the psychodynamic viewpoint, these three behaviors are symptoms of anxiety regarding instinctual drives, and cannot be tampered with directly without risk of either throwing the child into a worse state (by leaving the child without adequate ego defenses) or hindering psychological growth (by stripping the child of budding ego strengths—cf. Easson, 1969).

The behavioral view of obsessive-compulsive and ritualistic behavior is quite different:

> In short, obsessive-compulsive behavior is a response to a situation that is evaluated by others as socially inadequate. The behavior may result from failure to learn a correct response or focusing on aspects of the situation other people deem unexpected and incorrect. The formulation of obsessive-compulsive behavior is identical to that given for phobic behavior; the difference is that in the obsessive behavior the targets to be changed are repetitious thoughts and acts, while in phobic reaction the target is avoidant behavior. (Ullmann & Krasner, 1969, p. 308)

Roper, Rachman, and Marks (1975) note that most obsessive-compulsive behavior involves phobias, and they have shown fear-reducing behavioral intervention to be successful in eliminating obsessions and compulsions in adults. Doleys and Slapion (1975), Kolvin (1967), and Lahey, McNees, and McNees (1973) employed behavior modification techniques to reduce compulsive behavior in children and adolescents.

The study of obsessive-compulsive and ritualistic behavior in children is complicated by its close relationship not only to phobic behavior but also to excessive self-stimulation and fantasy. It is apparent that obsession, fear, related fantasy or delusions, and compulsive rituals often are interconnected, especially in the severely or profoundly disturbed child. Together, these behavioral characteristics present a clear picture of the severely disturbed or psychotic child. The behavior management techniques effective for self-stimulation and phobic behavior, then, might be expected to be effective for obsessive-compulsive behavior. It is obvious that more experimental behavioral research is needed on this aspect of children's behavior disorders.

Sexual Problems

A wide variety of sexual behavior is of concern to parents, teachers, and other adults who manage children and youth. For example, promiscuous sexual conduct is often thought to connote moral misjudgment and promiscuity is often involved in delinquency. Dating and related heterosexual relationships are of great concern to teens and their adult caretakers. Exhibitionism, sadomasochism, incest, prostitution, fetishism, transvestism, and sexual relations involving children are not condoned by most citizens, and such behaviors typically earn those who practice them serious social penalties. Contemporary sexual freedom notwithstanding, American social mores do not condone all sex practices—some sexual behavior is clearly taboo. Here we will discuss only two specific types of conduct that reflect withdrawal, immaturity, or inadequacy as defined in this chapter. These are public masturbation and childhood gender problems.

Public masturbation. Auto-erotic activity *per se* is not maladaptive. But when carried to excess or done publicly, sexual self-stimulation is disordered behavior. In spite of the fact that many or most teachers have observed children masturbating publicly, very little research has been done on the problem, perhaps because masturbation has for so long been looked upon as evil. Rekers (1978) mentions only one report (a nonexperimental case study) in which public masturbation was modified using behavioral reinforcement and punishment techniques. In that case, the masturbation of an 11-year-old girl in the classroom was eliminated by using verbal reprimands for auto-erotic behavior and social reinforcement of attention to academic tasks and participation in classroom activities (Wagner, 1968). Cook, Altman, Shaw, and Blaylock (1978) were successful in reducing public masturbation by a 7-year-old severely retarded boy by squirting lemon juice in his mouth contingent on masturbation.

Childhood gender problems. Probably the most widely known work on childhood gender problems is that of Rekers and his research group at UCLA (see Rekers, 1977a, 1977b, 1978). Rekers (1977b) states that gender problems may involve excessive masculinity or excessive femininity in either boys or girls, but that research has dealt almost exclusively with only one type: extreme femininity in boys. What Rekers refers to as *gender behavior disturbance* involves for boys a preference for girls' clothing, actual or imagined use of cosmetics, and feminine gestures, mannerisms, vocal inflections, and speech content. It also involves preference for girls' play and girl playmates. Boys with *cross-gender identification* not only exhibit these characteristics but truly wish to be or to fantasize that they are girls. Rekers and his colleagues have identified specific sex-typed mannerisms and ways of scaling gender problems from profound to mild. The identification and assessment of gender disturbance requires careful psychological and physical examination, interviews with the child and his parents, and direct observation in different settings. The gender-disturbed child does not just occasionally exhibit the characteristics of the opposite sex but persistently shows a cross-gender behavior that his peers reject.

Rekers (1977b) notes that cross-gender behavior is not merely a problem of characteristics that result in rejection by peers:

The psychological maladjustment of the gender-disturbed child goes beyond mere social rejection from the peer group, because it involves the elements of unhappiness, obsessive-compulsive trends, isolation and withdrawal, negativistic behavior, detachment, inability to form close interpersonal peer relationships, and low self-esteem. . . . (p. 277)

Behavioral intervention in childhood gender problems shows considerable promise, but more longitudinal research is necessary in order to draw firm conclusions about its efficacy. Current treatment procedures include a wide array of behavior modification techniques, including the following: reinforcement (often at home and at school) for sex-appropriate mannerisms, dress, and play; self-observation, self-recording of behavior, and self-reinforcement; and instruction in boys' athletic activities (Rekers, 1977b, 1978).

Social Ineptitude

There are children who are not social isolates but who do not "fit in" well with their peers and are hampered by inadequate social sensitivity or ineptness in delicate social situations. For example, children whose previous social experience is at odds with the majority of their peers, adolescents making their first approaches to members of the opposite sex, and adolescents interviewing for their first jobs are often quite tactless or unskilled in the social graces demanded for acceptance. Some individuals have irritating personal habits that detract from their social adequacy. The results of such social ineptitude may be a negative self-image, anxiety, and eventually withdrawal.

Bungling social behaviors can often be eliminated or avoided by teaching the child to recognize important social cues and to respond appropriately to them. Group and individual counseling, showing the child videotaped replays of his own behavior, modeling appropriate behavior, and guided practice (or some combination of these strategies) have been used to teach these social skills (see Cullinan, Kauffman, & LaFleur, 1975; Kirkland & Thelen, 1977; Combs & Slaby, 1977; for reviews). A social learning view of the origin and remediation of children's interpersonal ineptness is clearly a functional view for the special educator, for it implies that direct instruction will be most effective.

Helplessness

One of the most important criteria for positive mental health in Western culture is independence. As long as mature people can take care of themselves, they are likely to be viewed as mentally competent. When people become unusually dependent upon others to guide their behavior, they are likely to be considered mentally retarded or mentally ill (excepting, of course, instances in which the individual is physically disabled). In fact, one of the first signs of mental illness is very often an inability to function in daily life without more than the usual amount of help from others. The child who cannot perform the mundane tasks of daily living or who cannot perform simple academic tasks without the constant help of the teacher is usually considered a candidate for special education. Helpless children may be considered retarded, immature, inadequate, or depressed, depending on the combined features of their behavioral characteristics. Helplessness may range from failure to acquire ordinary daily living skills (dressing, bathing, feeding, toileting and so on) at the normal age to failure to perform previously acquired complex skills such as academic tasks. The helpless child, then, may present a picture of delayed development or developmental regression. Especially in older children whose behavior previously has been considered normal, helplessness is often associated with depression and feelings of hopelessness, despair, worthlessness, and resignation.

Lack of Daily Living Skills

Severely and profoundly disturbed children often function at a retarded level in areas of basic self-care. It is not at all unusual for such children to need supervision and help in such basic tasks as dressing, feeding, bathing, finding their way from place to place, and so on. Typically, their lack of competence in these areas of development fits an overall pattern of delayed development that is characteristic of the severely retarded child. It is appropriate to teach self-help or daily living skills to these severely and profoundly disturbed children in much the same way one teaches such skills to the severely retarded (see Lent, 1975; Lent & McLean, 1976; Snell, 1981).

Learned Helplessness and Depression

Acquired helplessness in children may range from "anaclitic depression" (infants who are suddenly bereft of their mothers or are reared in an almost completely non-stimulating institutional environment) to the older child's lack of joy and interest in life. Spitz (1946) describes the crying, social withdrawal, rigidity of emotional expression, and susceptibility to disease and death of infants who at 6 to 8 months of age have lost their mothers or been extremely emotionally deprived. Older children occasionally become so depressed following a traumatic incident, or even after a more ordinary life event, that they become highly dependent, disinterested, pessimistic, or suicidal. Depression may be accompanied by anxiety and obsessive thoughts that are debilitating. Unhappiness, feelings of depression, lack of vibrancy, and inability to carry on the everyday activities of home and school are well-recognized aspects of emotional disturbance in school-age children (Bower, 1969). It is common for disturbed school children to express a lack of confidence in their ability to learn or to perform academic or social tasks for which they obviously have the capacity. Teachers frequently find that disturbed children refuse even to try—they are defeated in their own minds before they give themselves any opportunity for success.

Regarding the etiology of depression, it is evident that some cases of depression are *endogenous* (a response to some unknown genetic, biochemical, or other biological process). *Reactive* depression is a response to environmental events, such as death of a loved one, financial reverses, or academic failure (cf. Seligman, 1975, pp. 78–79.) In Freudian analyses, these feelings of inadequacy, helplessness, and depression emphasize the "turning inward" or "turning upon the self" of aggressive drive. As discussed previously, Freud's ideas are supported by practically nothing other than the ethereal statements of other psychoanalysts, and it is worth noting that helplessness and depression are characterized by an absence of aggression, competitiveness, and assertiveness (Seligman, 1975). A large amount of experimental data can be found, however, to support the notion that helplessness and reactive depression often result from an individual's experience in an inconsistent, unpredictable, uncontrollable environment, at least if the individual comes to *believe* that he/she has no control over life and his/her "fate" is unalterable (Seligman, 1969, 1973, 1975). Much research with animals and humans indicates that after exposure to experimental conditions in which they cannot escape from aversive stimulation, they tend to passively accept the painful stimuli they could now easily escape and tend to have difficulty learning that they can escape or avoid unpleasantness. Furthermore, helplessness appears to be closely related to the attitude that external factors (chance, fate, or someone else) rather than internal factors (individuals themselves) control success and reinforcement (see Dweck & Reppucci, 1973). Note that criticisms have been leveled at Seligman's research (Costello, 1978) and that alternative theories of depression have been proposed (Blaney, 1977). Seligman's ideas are presented here as one plausible explanation for depression and helplessness that has clear implications for educational intervention (Diener & Dweck, 1978).

Locus of control, the belief in internal or external determinants of behavior, usually is measured by a questionnaire containing such items as "Do you feel that when you do something wrong there's very little you can do to make it right?"; "Most of the time, do you feel that you can change what might happen tomorrow by what you do today?"; and "Do you believe that when bad things are going to happen, they just are going to happen no matter what you try to do to stop them?" (Nowicki & Stickland, 1973, pp. 150–151; see also Rotter, 1966). It is apparent that many helpless or depressed individuals, including low-achieving disturbed children, believe that they have little control over their lives (Finch, Pezzuti, & Nelson, 1975; Seligman, 1973, 1975). That is, depression and helplessness seem to be associated with an external rather than internal locus of control.

Seligman's (1975) hypotheses that helplessness is learned and that helplessness and depression are closely tied have profound implications for special educators. His ideas regarding the origins of learned helplessness point to alterable environmental factors: either a demoralizing set of unavoidable failure experiences or traumas over which individuals could not gain control regardless of their efforts; or, conversely, a "heavenly" string of successes in which good fortune has befallen the individual without any effort (or very little effort) or experiences of failure being required. Certainly, repeated failure can quickly demoralize children, but so can unwarranted "success." Seligman (1975) warns about children's too easy "accomplishments":

> Their parents and teachers, out of a misguided sense of kindness, made things much too easy for them. If a reading list was too long and the student protested, the teacher shortened it—rather than have the students put in extra hours of work. If the teenager was picked up for vandalism, the parents bailed him out—rather than have the child find out that his actions have serious consequences. Unless a young person confronts anxiety, boredom, pain, and trouble, and masters them by his actions, he will develop an impoverished sense of his own competence. Even at the hedonic level, creating shortcuts around difficulties for children is not kind—depression follows from helpless-

ness. At the level of ego strength and character, making the road too easy is a disaster.

A sense of worth, mastery, or self-esteem cannot be bestowed. It can only be earned. If it is given away, it ceases to be worth having, and it ceases to contribute to individual dignity. If we remove the obstacles, difficulties, anxiety, and competition from the lives of our young people, we may no longer see generations of young people who have a sense of dignity, power, and worth.   (pp. 158–159)

Seligman's (1975) suggested antidotes for reactive depression and helplessness are not only congruent with the recent research he reviews, but also are consonant with other research in special education (e.g., Haring & Phillips, 1962; Hewett, 1968). His work may be interpreted to suggest:

1. making the environment predictable and controllable by the child in most but not all respects
2. setting the expectation that the child will master most tasks
3. demonstrating and pointing out response-consequence relationships
4. choosing tasks at which the child can usually but not always be successful
5. requiring children to make initial responses if they will not make them on their own initiative

The properly designed childrearing and educational environments can, Seligman believes, not only cure depression but *immunize* children against helplessness.

Academic Failure

As we have already seen in Chapter 6, scholastic performance plays a great part in social adequacy. A behavioral analysis of the academic performance of children shows that many inadequacies assumed to be inherent in the child actually are instructional deficiencies in teachers. Thus, what is most needed by special educators who are confronted with academic failure in a disturbed child is a careful examination of instructional tactics, not a probe of the child's psyche. There is, nonetheless, a problem of behavioral inadequacy which is prepotent over the instructional competence of the teacher—failure to attend school.

Truancy

Although attendance at school will certainly not guarantee academic success, chronic unexcused absence virtually assures school failure. Traditional counselling of truants by attendance officers has not been remarkably successful. Copeland et al. (1974), MacDonald, Gallimore, and MacDonald (1970), and Tharp and Wetzel (1969) found that a behavior modification approach to the problem is effective. Copeland et al. found that truants from an elementary school improved their attendance when the school principal stopped by their classrooms to compliment them on their presence (see Chapter 6). Working with older children and adolescents, Tharp and Wetzel increased school attendance by making participation in certain events or interaction with certain individuals in the community contingent on attendance. The contingencies of reinforcement were often administered with the aid of "natural mediators," persons living in the community who could control the child's access to rewards and themselves be rewarding to the child. For example:

vignette

Case #98.   Cowboy Gaines operated a riding stable on the outskirts of the city. Cowboy and his plumpish, fortyish wife were warm, homespun people, and they enjoyed the role of counselors to mixed-up youths. Cowboy himself was full of rustic figures of speech, and he dispensed his rough and ready ranch philosophy generously. Cowboy and his wife, Irma, proved to be highly effective mediators.

Case #98 was an extraordinarily truant seventh grader who was powerfully attracted to animals, especially horses. There was no adult person with whom he had a positive relationship.

The Behavior Analyst asked Cowboy and Irma if they would help with Billy, and they at once agreed. The arrangement was simple: Billy could earn time at Cowboy's stables by staying in school. Billy was allowed to ride the horses in return for attending to minor chores when he was not riding.

Billy responded perfectly and thereafter never missed an hour of school. Cowboy and Irma had a little trouble with him at first because the undersized boy complained in smart-alec terms when he felt he wasn't getting enough riding. Cowboy gave him a few bits of rough advice and Irma was obliged to become a disciplinarian. Billy sulked and made plain his displeasure, but the horses and riding were too important to give up. (Tharp & Wetzel, 1969, pp. 95-96)

MacDonald et al. (1970) compared contingency "deals" similar to those employed by Tharp and Wetzel to more traditional attendance counselling and found the contingency arrangements to be superior in increasing attendance by ninth grade and tenth grade pupils and high school seniors.

SUMMARY

Withdrawn children exhibit behavioral excesses and deficiencies that prevent their development of positive social relationships with other people. Inadequate and immature children exhibit behavior that is appropriate only for children who are chronologically younger or that is not adequate for the demands of their social environment. Withdrawal may involve social isolation or autistic unrelatedness to people, including unresponsiveness to social stimuli, gaze aversion, muteness or other severe language deficiencies, or excessive self-stimulation and fantasy. Immaturity and inadequacy are often characterized by crying and tantrums, negativism, fearfulness, developmental regression, enuresis, encopresis, obsessive-compulsive and ritualistic behavior, sexual problems, social ineptitude, helplessness, or academic failure. The most useful and productive conceptualization of withdrawal, inadequacy, and immaturity is that such behavior disorders represent social learning failures. A social learning analysis suggests instructional methods that can be employed in order to teach children the skills required for social interaction, maturity, and adequacy.

chapter 10

Problems in Moral Development and Delinquency

Much of the disordered behavior discussed in Chapters 7, 8, and 9 carries with it a connotation of undesirability but not a connotation of moral reprehensibility. It should be clear that while moral development implies social development, not all aspects of social development carry moral implications. In this chapter, we turn our attention to behavior that is undesirable primarily because it offends standards of morality, often to such an extent that it is legally proscribed.

For the most part, morality has been thought of as a set of virtues such as honesty, self-sacrifice, temperance, friendliness, self-control, and so on rather than as a special case of social reasoning or behavior based on the concept of justice (Kohlberg, 1970). Both virtue and vice may be defined by legal standards or by community expectations. While the concept of justice is the foundation stone of the legal codes of Western civilization, communities may invoke social rules or moral ideology also derived from custom, tradition, convention, or religious teachings. Turiel (1975) argues that much of children's reasoning about social conventions (for instance, sexual conduct) is essentially different from moral reasoning. If Turiel's argument is accepted, then some of the material included in this chapter represents deficiencies in social-conventional reasoning or behavior and does not actually reflect *moral* development. *Moral* in this chapter includes a broad spectrum of social behavior, including social conventions that Turiel would not consider moral precepts. From whatever source the legal and community definition of *right* is derived, our concern in this chapter is with children's behavior that is considered to be morally "wrong" in the eyes of the child's social group or the law.

Since the last months of the Nixon administration, the American public has been acutely aware of the pervasiveness of moral dilemmas and moral failure in contemporary life. Although the Watergate scandal and subsequent disclosures regarding the activities of the FBI, CIA, and corporation executives undoubtedly increased the interest of the public in the topic of how people acquire and maintain moral standards, an upsurge of research into the development of conscience and moral values began in the mid 1950s. The early work of Hartshorne and May (1928–1930) on the moral conduct of children and Piaget's (1932) early observations of children's moral judgment are now examined and elaborated upon in considerable detail (cf. DePalma & Foley, 1975; Hoffman, 1970; Kohlberg, 1964). The findings of research over the years have been quite consistent on several points:

1. Children's moral judgment, their abilities to interpret and use rules in conflict situations and give reasons for moral actions, develops through stages, progressing from egocentric judgment based on the actual consequences of an act or the act per se to judgment based on highly abstract and universal ethical principles.

2. Children's moral behavior often does not match their moral judgment—they often *do* wrong even though they *know* what is right.

3. Children's moral behavior tends to be controlled at least as much by situational factors as by moral or character traits. Children are "honest" or "altruistic" at some times and in some situations but not in others.

4. The usual means of moral instruction or "character education" have little apparent effect on children's moral behavior.

Moral judgment and moral behavior may or may not have legal implications. Behavior that violates statutes is usually considered immoral (criminal or delinquent), and moral judgment is often called for when laws are created and enforced as well as when magistrates or court officials prescribe punishment for offenses. Thus, moral judgment and moral behavior are intimately related to the society's legal structure and system of justice. However, much moral behavior and judgment has no statutory basis, but rather derives from social interaction that is neither prescribed nor proscribed by law. Sharing and donating to charity are not prescribed by law, nor are miserliness and avarice proscribed. Many of the moral precepts of religions are completely unrelated to the laws of the state, a circumstance which itself reflects the concept of justice and moral judgment of the founders of democratic governments. The remainder of this chapter will be divided into two major sections: deficiencies in moral judgment and moral behavior having no statutory foundation, and juvenile delinquency (law-violating behavior).

MORAL JUDGMENT AND MORAL BEHAVIOR: EXTRALEGAL DEFICIENCIES IN DISTURBED CHILDREN

As mentioned previously, moral judgment and moral behavior are not synonymous. A child's ability to supply reasons for behaving in a certain way may be quite unrelated to her conduct. Exactly how cognitive development is related to the development of moral judgment is not known (cf. Keasey, 1975; Stephens, McLaughlin, Hunt, Mahoney, Kohlberg, Moore, & Aronfreed, 1974), but it is generally thought that children higher in intelligence, social class, and peer group status tend to be more advanced in both moral judgment and moral conduct. However, judgment and conduct have different paths of development.

> The picture of moral development emerging from the moral judgment findings contrast in several ways with the picture derived from the findings on moral conduct. Judgment does not appear to become "moral" until early adolescence, while "morality" of conduct appears to develop early. Individual differences in level of moral judgment are quite general and stable; morality of conduct is more specific to the situation and more unstable over time. Moral judgment appears to develop in the same direction regardless of social groups; moral conduct appears to develop in line with specific social class and peer-group norms. (Kohlberg, 1964, p. 408)

Because moral judgment and action appear in many ways to be independent phenomena (see also Santrock, 1975), each will be considered separately.

Deficiencies in Moral Judgment

The development of moral reasoning, attitudes, and emotions—a topic related to but not synonymous with the growth of conscience, character, superego, and guilt, remorse, or anxiety following transgression—has been a fundamental problem in social psychology. It is apparent that as children mature and fantasize or experience blame and punishment, they begin to internalize the standards of external authority. Through discipline, modeling, reasoning, and encouraging the child to "take the role of the other" in situations of moral conflict, parents, teachers, peers, and other socialization agents sensitize children to moral issues. A child's moral reasoning and sentiment are likely to be more advanced if the child is intelligent and has been provided with clear, consistent examples of moral reasoning and conduct.

Definition and Measurement

The developmental level of a child's moral reasoning or judgment of social conventions typically has been measured by means of an interview. The child is presented with a moral dilemma: Should a husband steal an expensive drug which he cannot otherwise obtain in order to save his wife's life? Should a doctor "mercy kill" a woman who requests him to kill her when she is fatally ill and in extreme pain? Or a dilemma is presented to the child by social convention: Is it right to call teachers by their first names? The child's responses are then subjectively analyzed according to the stage or level of reasoning represented (cf. Kohlberg, 1964; Turiel, 1975). The interview techniques and subjective scoring employed by Kohlberg and his colleagues are criticized by Kurtines and Grief (1974). More recently, Rest and his colleagues (cf. Rest, 1975; Rest, Cooper, Coder, Masanz, & Anderson, 1974) have devised an objective test of moral judgment, the *Defining Issues Test* (DIT). The DIT requires a child to read a hypothetical moral dilemma and then select from among 12 alternatives those statements that represent the most crucial issues in making a moral decision about the case.

Antecedents of Moral Judgment

Today probably the most popular theory of the development of moral thought is the Piagetian idea that moral judgment follows an invariable developmental sequence of stages (Kohlberg, 1964). The assumptions underlying Kohlberg's approach are questioned by Kurtines and Grief (1974). Sound empirical research indicates that social learning processes, especially modeling, guided practice, reasoning, punishment, and reinforcement, influence both moral judgment and moral behavior (Bandura & McDonald, 1963; Bryan, 1975a, b; Reid & Patterson, 1976; Scheiderer & O'Connor, 1973; Staub, 1975). As is the case with other facets of disordered behavior, a social learning perspective is undergirded by more reliable data and is more productive of effective interventions than are other viewpoints.

Moral Judgment of Children with Behavior Disorders

There are few, if any, research studies comparing the moral judgment of nondelinquent disturbed and normal children. Today one must be satisfied primarily with intuition and speculation based on research of other characteristics of disturbed children. Given that disturbed children tend to be developmentally behind normals in concepts of self (cf. Farnham-Diggory, 1966), academic achievement and intelligence (see Chapter 6), and other social skills (see chapters 7, 8, and 9), it would come as no surprise to find their moral judgment lagging behind that of their normal age mates. The knowledge that disturbed children frequently exhibit immoral and antisocial behavior also suggests, at least at first thought, that they are deficient in moral reasoning. However, the research findings on the relationship between moral judgment and behavior cast doubt on the assumption that disturbed behavior implies a lack of moral judgment or vice versa.

> In the absence of more data on the relation between antisocial behavior and moral judgment, it appears that a child's level of moral judgment may be constrained by his level of cognitive development. Judgmental level may, in turn, be a significant factor in determining what sort of socialization techniques a child is amenable to, but there is little to indicate that a child's behavior is very much constrained by the level of moral judgment he is capable of verbalizing. (Achenbach, 1974, p. 473)

Moral judgment may be neither a necessary nor a sufficient condition for moral behavior, but the absence of moral judgment may be used by social agents to absolve children of guilt for deeds that otherwise would be viewed as morally reprehensible. The ability to know right from wrong underlies the concepts of moral imperative, legal responsibility, and legal insanity.[35] Few adults or children will condemn an individual who behaves reprehensibly if it is clear that "he didn't know any better."

Deficiencies in Moral Behavior

It is quite obvious from the descriptive literature on children's behavior disorders that disturbed children (including those not categorized as delinquent) are prone to commit moral misdeeds. Stealing, lying, cheating, abusiveness, and other actions that violate principles of fairness and social justice are the rule, not the exception, with many disturbed children. Furthermore, disturbed youngsters are not noted as a group for their willingness to help others, cooperate, share, or exhibit other "prosocial" behaviors. There are, of course, those disturbed children who are obsessed with "goodness" and compulsively follow the dictates of their hypertrophied consciences, but they are a decided minority.

Definition and Measurement

As mentioned previously, there are differences of opinion regarding what behavior actually falls within the "moral" realm. As defined in this chapter, a behavior is moral or immoral depending on the value judgments of persons in the child's social group, whether or not those judgments involve the concept of justice. Thus, moral sanctions may be applied by primary social agents (for example, parents) to a Mormon child's drinking of an alcoholic beverage, an Old Order Mennonite child's wearing of jewelry, a Jewish child's eating of pork, and so on, as well as to any child's thievery. Ordinarily, moral behavior has been measured by counting *in situ* the frequency of immoral acts or by observing the child in experimental situations under laboratory conditions. For example, cheating may be measured in the natural environment of the classroom or in a laboratory experiment where opportunity to cheat is provided. In the case of "prosocial" moral behavior or altruism (such as sharing, helping, or donating), much the same measurement

---

[35] See the entries *McNaghten Rule and Durham Decision* in *A Psychiatric Glossary*, 2nd ed. (Washington, D.C.: American Psychiatric Association, 1964).

strategies have been used. Most of the literature regarding children's moral behavior (aside from the literature on delinquency) has involved data obtained under contrived laboratory conditions. For example, in research of altruism, children are typically given a task to perform, for which they receive "payment" of some sort, after which they are given an opportunity to donate part or all of their earnings to "poor" or "needy" children.

Origins of Deficiencies in Moral Behavior

The kinds of experience that lead to children's having little or no hesitation to engage in immoral conduct are rather well known. Overly harsh and restrictive or overly lax and uncaring parental discipline; neglect, cruelty, hostility, and disorganization in the family; reinforcement for moral transgression; parents, other family members, and associates with a history of immoral conduct or arrest— these bode ill for the child's moral behavior development. However, the interpretation of *how* such experiences produce a breakdown in moral conduct vary. Psychoanalytic theory posits deficient superego development or the erection of ego defenses to ward off panic, depression, emotional stupor, or diffuse guilt feelings (cf. Shields, 1962). Social learning theory asserts that moral conduct is learned through observation of models, reinforcement, punishment, and guided practice and that assertion is supported by experimental data (cf. Bandura, 1969; Bryan, 1975a, b; Reid & Patterson, 1976; Staub, 1975).

Moral Behavior Deficiencies of Disturbed Children

It has already been stated that disturbed children frequently behave in ways that offend their parents' or teachers' moral sensibilities. Relatively little is written about the nondelinquent (extralegal) moral behavior of disturbed children, especially prosocial moral deficiencies. In one of the very few studies of the prosocial behavior of disturbed children, Kauffman, Epstein, and Chlebnikow (1977) gave several disturbed children repeated opportunities over a period of weeks to perform a simple task and to earn pennies which they could keep or donate to "needy" children. The disturbed children were found to be less "altruistic" or willing to donate their earnings to someone less fortunate than themselves than were normal children. Although research data are few, it seems a reasonable assumption that disturbed children tend to be less self-denying, self-sacrificing, or altruistic than normal youngsters.

In an early case study, Wetzel (1966) found that he could modify the compulsive stealing of a disturbed boy by using behavior modification principles. Reid and his associates (Moore et al., 1979; Patterson, Reid, Jones, & Conger, 1975; Reid & Hendriks, 1973; Reid & Patterson, 1976) conducted systematic research into the characteristics and behavior modification of aggressive children who steal. Their subjects were "predelinquent" children referred to the Oregon Research Institute (ORI) for treatment of social aggression. About half of the children referred for aggression were also in trouble because of stealing. Reid and Hendriks (1973) found that children who stole exhibited a lower rate of positive-friendly behaviors at home than did nonstealers or normals. In turn, stealers also exhibited a higher rate of negative-coercive acts than normals. However, compared with aggressive children who did not steal, stealers showed a lower rate of negative-coercive acts. In all groups (normals, stealers, and nonstealers) the fathers interacted less than mothers with their families, but there were no significant differences in the interaction of fathers in the three groups. Mothers of stealers exhibited a lower rate of positive-friendly interaction than mothers of nonstealers or normals. The rate of negative-coercive acts by mothers of stealers fell between the rates for mothers of normals and mothers of nonstealers. To summarize, the following generalizations can be made:

1. Stealers exhibited lower rates of observable out-of-control (negative-coercive or antisocial) behavior than aggressive children who did not steal.
2. Families of stealers demonstrated lower rates of both positive-friendly and negative-coercive behaviors than families of aggressive children who did not steal.
3. The differences in positive-friendly and negative-coercive behavior rates were due almost completely to the mothers' behaviors.

Reid and Hendriks found also that the stealers did not respond as well as non-stealers to the usual social learning based treatment provided for aggressive children at ORI. Their speculation regarding this finding is based on the nature of the child's behavior and the nature of the family's social interaction. First, it appears that stealers may exhibit high rates of antisocial behavior only away from home or at home when observers are not present. It seems likely that many stealers confine their antisocial behavior to settings outside the home, punishing the community rather than their parents and leaving their parents with little motivation to work on the problem. Parents of stealers are notorious for putting the blame for the problem on someone else, or refusing to recognize the problem, and for failing to follow through on intervention plans (see Patterson et al., 1975; Reid & Patterson, 1976). Second, the families of stealers appear to be loosely structured and characterized by lack of parental supervision and a boring social climate (see Reid & Patterson, 1976). The stealer may, therefore, be motivated to seek stimulation and reinforcement outside the family.

In spite of the difficult and destructive family interaction patterns of stealers, successful behavioral interventions have been devised. As described by Patterson et al. (1975), the ORI antistealing program involves several essential components. Before the actual antistealing program can be instituted, it is necessary to resolve a fundamental problem—parental definition of stealing. Typically, parents of stealers are very hesitant to accuse the child of theft and take disciplinary action. Since it is very unlikely that they will observe the child in the act of taking something, the parents feel obliged to accept any explanation offered by the child for how something came into his/her possession. Many parents blandly accept the child's explanations that he/she found, borrowed, traded, won, or received as payment the stolen items. Frequently, when their child is accused by teachers, peers, or police, the parents of stealers argue that their child is being unjustly attacked by people who are prejudiced against him or her. By placing the blame on others, making it "their problem," the parents can avoid having to deal with the problem themselves. Even when the behavior in question occurs at home, however, stealing is often not adequately defined by parents. Some parents consider taking food from the refrigerator without specific permission as theft, while others may view all possessions of family members as common property. The value of the item taken is also an issue, for many parents of stealers cannot bring themselves to apply consequences for stealing something they consider to be worth very little.

As Patterson et al. (1975) point out, the first step in dealing with theft behavior is to recognize that the child in question is in difficulty because he/she (a) steals more than other children, (b) may steal valuable objects, and (c) has been labeled by others as a *thief*. The strategy must include steps to help the child stop being *accused* of theft and being viewed with suspicion—unless even the appearance of wrongdoing is avoided the child will not lose the stigma associated with the label "thief."

According to Patterson et al. (see also Reid & Patterson, 1976), the following strategy will help the family deal with theft:

1. Agree to define *stealing* as the child's possession of *anything* that does not belong to him/her or taking anything that he/she does not own.

2. Only the parents decide whether or not a theft has occurred. They may base their judgment either on their own observation or on the report of a reliable informant.

3. When it is determined that the child has stolen, the parents merely state that according to the rules, the child has taken the item in question and then apply the consequences. The parents must not shame or counsel the child at the time they discover the theft and apply the consequences, but they are encouraged to discuss the theft with him/her at another time.

4. Every instance of stealing must receive consequences.

5. Parents are advised to keep their eyes open and ask about "new property" rather than use detective tactics such as searching the child's room or clothing.

6. Consequences for stealing are either a specified interval of useful work or a period of "grounding" or restriction, with stealing of more expensive items receiving more severe consequences. Harsh consequences, such as humiliation or beating, are prohibited.

7. No positive reinforcement is given for periods of nonstealing, for it is impossible to know that successful covert stealing has not occurred.

8. The program should stay in effect at least six months following the last episode of stealing.

The findings of Reid and his co-workers, although not conclusive, support several tentative statements (Reid & Patterson, 1976). First, parents have a harder time recognizing stealing behavior than socially aggressive behavior. Second, stealing and social aggression can be modified in much the same way once parents adequately define the problem and apply appropriate consequences. Third, the parents of stealers are harder to motivate than the parents of aggressive children who do not steal. Fourth, children who steal are much more likely to become adjudicated delinquents than are aggressive children who do not steal (Moore et al., 1979).

Control of Moral Behavior: General Findings

At present, it appears that the predominant mode of moral training or character education is the use of punishment, threat of punishment, or rebuke. Although aversive consequences for misdeeds, for example, negative consequences for theft, may indeed be necessary components of moral remediation once moral misconduct has become established, a positive approach may be more effective to prevent the initial violation of moral standards. There is some evidence that *induction* (an explanation, reasoning, or love-oriented approach) is superior to *sensitization* (a punishing, power-assertive approach) in developing prosocial behavior, promoting desirable attitudes toward transgression, and controlling moral conduct for most children (see Hoffman, 1970; Leizer & Rogers, 1974; Bryan, 1975b). Goldiamond (1968) speculates that moral teaching can be made more effective by using positive reinforcement for "good" moral choices instead of punishment or threats for transgression.

> Laboratory research in behavior analysis suggests that we might turn our attention to the possibility of establishing moral and other discriminations without extinction and aversive control, but using errorless procedures that provide continual reinforcement. It may thereby be possible to program behavioral relations with the environment which are dictated by conscience, which are moral, and which are altruistic, but at the same time are spontaneous, existential and free, since they have been programmed without fear or threat. (p. 70)

Kohlberg (1970) views moral teaching as a cognitive-developmental process quite different from Goldiamond's reinforcement hypothesis.

> The first step in teaching virtue, then, is the Socratic step of creating dissatisfaction in the student about his present knowledge of the good. This we do experimentally by exposing the student to moral conflict situations for which his principles have no ready solution. Second, we expose him to disagreement and argument about these situations with his peers. Our Platonic view holds that if we inspire cognitive conflict in the student and point the way to the next step up the divided line, he will tend to see things previously invisible to him. (p. 82)

Further research will be necessary in order to discover the most effective means of moral education for normal children. Perhaps a rapprochement between the behavior analysis and cognitive-developmental approaches will be made in future years. Furthermore, it remains to be demonstrated that the techniques of moral education found effective for normal children will be applicable to remediation of the moral behavior deficiencies of disturbed youngsters. It may be the case that once moral judgment or moral behavior has gone awry, special techniques are required to rectify the problem.

JUVENILE DELINQUENCY

Nature and Scope of the Problem

Many of the aggressive and immoral acts already discussed in this chapter and Chapter 8 are characteristic of children considered to be delinquent. However, juvenile delinquents are often defined as children who have been apprehended by legal authorities because they are accused or suspected of committing illegal acts. Of course, many juveniles break the law and are not apprehended or even suspected (cf. Griffin & Griffin, 1978). Too, many juveniles are taken into custody or referred to a juvenile court with little or no evidence of their criminal offenses or with evidence only of quite vaguely defined problems such as "incorrigibility." The differences in the laws, law enforcement practices, and juvenile court procedures from one state and locality to another make reliable and meaningful statistics regarding juvenile delinquency difficult to obtain and even more difficult to interpret.[36] However, it is abundantly clear that serious crimes committed by persons under the age of 18 have increased at a tremendous rate within the past several decades; that girls are becoming involved in more serious and more aggressive crimes at an increasing rate; that juvenile crime is more frequent in inner-city and poverty areas than in other types of communities, and that in a given year approximately 3 percent of all American children are adjudicated (cf. Achenbach, 1974; Griffin & Griffin, 1978; Kirk, 1976).

There is no arguing with the facts—juvenile delinquency is increasing quantitatively and is becoming qualitatively more violent and destructive (Cohen, 1973). Davids and Falkof (1975) found evidence that over a period of 15 years, delinquents appear to become more jaded and less well adjusted psychologically and socially. In comparing the responses of delinquents in 1959 to those in 1974, they found that the more recent sample was more present oriented, less willing to delay gratification, and less concerned for others. In 1959, none of the delinquents mentioned drugs as something of interest, whereas in 1974 delinquents frequently mentioned wanting to buy drugs.

The range of offenses for which children under age 18 are arrested is illustrated by the categories listed in government crime reports:

1. Criminal homicide, including murder and manslaughter, both negligent and non-negligent
2. Forcible rape, prostitution, commercialized vice, and other sex offenses
3. Carrying concealed weapons or illegally possessing weapons
4. Aggravated assault, disorderly conduct, and other assaults
5. Robbery, burglary (breaking and entering), larceny, auto theft; buying, receiving or possessing stolen property

[36] Reports of national statistics can be obtained from the Federal Bureau of Investigation's *Uniform Crime Reports for the United States*, issued by the U.S. Department of Justice, and the U.S. Children's Bureau's *Juvenile Court Statistics*.

6. Forgery and counterfeiting

7. Fraud

8. Embezzlement

9. Gambling

10. Arson and vandalism

11. Violations of narcotic and liquor laws, including drunkenness and driving under the influence

12. Vagrancy, curfew, and loitering violations; runaways

13. Suspicion of illegal activity

The nature of the problem is not just the law-violating behavior of children but also the responses of adult authority to it. The typical measures of incarceration and punishment have been miserable failures in controlling delinquency. In short, the problem is one of a rising wave of criminality in children coupled with responses by adult authorities that tend to exacerbate rather than reduce the problem (Cohen, 1973). The scope of the problem is so great and so convoluted in its legal, moral, psychological, and sociological complexities that the reader is referred to volumes specifically on juvenile delinquency (see Cavan, 1975; Cavan & Ferdinand, 1975; Giallombardo, 1976; Gibbons, 1975; Griffin & Griffin, 1978; Kittrie, 1971). The following discussion on delinquency will examine these areas of interest:

1. definition and measurement

2. origins

3. moral judgment of delinquents

4. intervention

Definition and Measurement of Delinquents' Behavior

Quay (1975) points out that the label *delinquency* is a legal one. Delinquents may be expected to exhibit a variety of behaviors, all leading to adjudication even though the behaviors in question may involve quite different patterns of delinquent conduct. Indeed, factor-analytic studies of delinquent behavior have revealed several rather distinct personality patterns within the delinquent group. Citing a variety of studies of behavioral ratings and life history variables of delinquents, Quay (1975) describes four major clusters of behaviors (see Chapter 3 for a discussion of the four dimensions of behavior and table 3-1). The findings that the same dimensions apply to delinquent and nondelinquent populations argues for a commonality of causal factors and appropriate intervention techniques for the behavior of delinquent and nondelinquent groups. Quay (1975) suggests that delinquents will respond differently to a particular treatment method depending on the behavioral cluster most descriptive of their personality.

Achenbach notes that a syndrome characterized primarily by drug abuse should be added to Quay's behavioral clusters. He points out that drug abuse is found in delinquents comprising all of the groups described by Quay's behavioral dimensions. "No clear-cut personality constellations have been verified for LSD, amphetamine, and marijuana users, although they tend to be middle class" (Achenbach, 1974, p. 540). Adolescents who misuse alcohol, however, seem to be characterized by low self-esteem, high anxiety, and depression, and to have parents and associates who are heavy drinkers. Adolescent heroin users tend to come from poor inner-city neighborhoods, broken homes, and racial minority groups and to exhibit personality test responses indicative of immaturity, irresponsibility, insecurity, and egocentrism. Gorsuch and Butler (1976) review the literature on initial drug abuse and conclude that disruption of normal parent-child relationships, lack of involvement in organized groups, and few effective peer relationships may be predisposing factors. However, they point out that there are different paths leading to initial drug abuse, including positive experiences with drugs, parental modeling of illicit drug use, involvement with drug-abusing peers, and socialization to nontraditional (delinquent) norms. Wong (1979) suggests the possibility that special education populations may be particularly vulnerable to drug abuse and calls for more research on the relationship of drug abuse to handicaps.

The dimensional approach to categorizing delinquent behavior may indeed have utility in designing intervention strategies. However, precise behavioral definition and counting of the frequency of specific responses are important to the success and evaluation of behavioral interventions. Direct measurement and analysis of specific responses, as illustrated in chapters 7 and 8, for example, are valuable tools in the control of delinquent behavior.

Origins of Delinquency

Today there are several theories of delinquency. The most popular theories are those of Miller (1958), who hypothesizes that the lower-class culture is a generating milieu for gang delinquency, and Cohen (1955) and Cloward and Ohlin (1960), who believe that gang delinquencies might result from social structure and *anomie*.

Miller's idea is that the lower-class culture has a long tradition of behavior and values of its own and that life in lower-class society focuses on concerns that foster delinquent patterns. Six "focal concerns" of lower-class culture, according to Miller, are:

1. *Trouble*: emphasis on law-violating versus law-abiding behavior.
2. *Toughness*: physical prowess combined with "masculinity," lack of sentimentality, an exploitative attitude toward women (and, in the light of recent increases in female juvenile delinquency and the emphasis on women's rights, one might suspect an attitude of exploitation toward men on the part of females), and any other behavior that might be interpreted to show "weakness."
3. *Smartness*: the ability to "con," outwit, "take," or dupe others and to avoid being so "taken" by others.
4. *Excitement*: periods of intense excitement breaking an overall rhythm of boredom and routine.

5. *Fate*: the belief that luck rather than personal control or decision controls one's life.

6. *Autonomy*: the desire to be free from constraint and control by authority, mixed with the wish to be "cared for."

The lower-class adolescent can achieve status and a sense of "belonging" by exhibiting behavior in line with the focal concerns of his/her culture, by behaving as a delinquent.

The concept of anomie, or normlessness, has to do with the absence of norms for moral conduct among lower-class individuals who aspire to transcend class lines (that is, to achieve success according to American middle-class values) but are blocked in achieving material goals by legitimate means (Cohen, 1955). The lower-class person who cannot achieve middle-class status in an acceptable way may turn to delinquent (i.e., lawless or normless) means of acquiring materials goods and "the good life." Cloward and Ohlin (1960) hypothesize that out of the several types of delinquent subcultures—*criminal* (stealing for profit), *conflict* (seeking status through violence), or *retreatist* (taking drugs)—one subculture may develop as a substitute for the dominant culture that cannot be achieved by or has been rejected by lower-class youths.

Other theories of delinquency, including biological, sociological, and social learning formulations have been proposed over the years. There is no conclusive evidence supporting any theory of delinquency (cf. Achenbach, 1974; O'Leary & Wilson, 1975; Short, 1966), but there is a fair degree of knowledge regarding the kinds of experiences or social environments that are predictive of future delinquency (cf. Becker, 1964; Cohen, 1973; Glueck & Glueck, 1950, 1962, 1970; Gorsuch & Butler, 1976; Robins, West, & Herjanic, 1975; Stumphauser, Aiken, & Veloz, 1977; West, 1969). Factors predicting an increased chance that the child will exhibit delinquent behavior include:

1. low verbal intelligence
2. alcoholism and arrest record of the parents
3. reliance on welfare
4. erratic supervision and lax or inconsistent discipline by the parents
5. poor management of family income
6. crowded, disorderly, or broken home
7. indifference or hostility of parents and siblings toward the child

As has been discussed in previous chapters, antisocial behavior in combination with low academic achievement and low intelligence provide a very pessimistic outlook for the child; often the young child who is an antisocial academic failure turns out to be an antisocial delinquent youth and a criminal adult.

Growing up in a high delinquency area does not necessarily mean that the child will become delinquent (Dinitz, Scarpitti, & Reckless, 1962; Scarpitti, Murray, Dinitz, & Reckless, 1960). According to these studies, boys who were not likely to become delinquent saw themselves clearly as nondelinquents by the age 12, were "good citizens" and favorably inclined toward school (though not necessarily outstanding students), admitted to little delinquent behavior, had favorable attitudes toward police, felt their parents accepted them and used the right amount of discipline, avoided delinquent peers, and expected to finish high school.

Moral Judgment of Delinquents

Evidence linking delinquent behavior to deficiencies in moral judgment is slight. Ruma and Mosher (1967) found that delinquent boys apparently were not lacking in feelings of guilt or lacking a "conscience." Prentice (1972) found that he could improve the moral judgment of adolescent delinquent boys by providing appropriate live and symbolic models. However, the improvement in moral judgment did not result in a decrease in the number of delinquent offenses committed by his subjects during a nine month follow-up period. Jukovic and Prentice (1977) found that while psychopathic delinquents were lacking in moral judgment, neurotic and subcultural (socialized) delinquents were not. Even if the moral judgment of delinquents is defective compared to their nondelinquent peers, there appears to be no simple relationships between judgment and behavior. As Prentice (1972) comments:

> . . . many internal as well as external factors appear to influence whether or not delinquent fantasies or attitudes are translated into delinquent actions. Given this complexity, it would seem unduly optimistic to expect isomorphism between level of moral judgment alone and significant moral behaviors, especially in psychopathological cases. (p. 161)

Intervention in Delinquent Behavior

Special educational services for maladjusted and delinquent adolescents have lagged behind services for younger children. Furthermore, the programs that are available experience the same fate as their counterparts in previous generations. Consequently, the statistics regarding juvenile delinquency still contribute to the same dismal picture: rising rates of unemployment, welfare payments, juvenile crime, and recidivism (Nelson & Kauffman, 1977). Achenbach (1975) notes the recurrent pattern of failure to provide effective help for delinquent children.

> Again and again, those who would help children have been fired with enthusiasm for new paradigms. When these paradigms have won enough support to become institutionalized, they have failed to live up to the hopes they aroused. Subsequent disillusionment made them ripe for replacement by other, equally unsubstantiated paradigms. (p. 14)

The Juvenile Court System and the Rights of Children

Juvenile courts were instituted in the United States at the turn of the twentieth century for the purpose of offering more humane treatment of juvenile offenders than that provided by the nineteenth century "reform" schools. Juvenile court judges were empowered to use their discretion in determining the consequences of a child's misconduct, the idea being that the judge would consider the case carefully and then act as a "wise father" in its disposition. Although the intent of the juvenile court was good, the institution has become mired down in great numbers of cases, judges are often not "wise fathers," and the rights of children—if children are considered to have constitutional rights equal to those of all other citizens—have been abridged blatantly (Kittrie, 1971; Silberman, 1978). Consequently, the juvenile court system is now receiving close scrutiny and the question of the legal rights of children is receiving great attention. One of the central issues in the question of children's legal rights is the role of the family versus the role of the court. As articulated by Noah Weinstein, judge of the Circuit Court of St. Louis County:

> Implementing the concept that children are people with rights faces the dilemma that our social structure is based on the family; and the courts, and the community as well, are at the very least reluctant to take any action which they erroneously believe will undermine the family unit. It is this mistaken apprehension which causes the courts to disregard children's rights and to seek out a security blanket of vague parental fitness to avoid equal consideration of the protection of children.   (Kirk, 1976, p. 396)

The juvenile court is likely to remain an institution for some time to come, and in the light of evidence that a sizable proportion of children and youth will make court appearances during their school years, it would be profitable for educators to become familiar with how it works.[37] The issue of children's rights will undoubtedly increase in importance as children's advocates become more numerous and more vocal.

Alternative Interventions

That traditional institutionalization and probation are miserable failures insofar as rehabilitation and prevention are concerned is obvious from the high recidivism rates of delinquents who are incarcerated or placed on probation. Traditional counseling and psychotherapy do not produce consistent results. Attempts to establish therapeutic milieux and halfway houses to design differential treatment methods for delinquents with different behavioral or personality characteristics have been shown in some cases to be superior to traditional imprisonment or punishment (see Achenbach, 1974, for a review.) Behavior modification techniques have been used successfully with many delinquents (cf. Davidson & Seidman, 1974; Stephens, 1973; Stumphauser, 1971). A wide variety of specific techniques can be used, but contingency contracting (Tharp & Wetzel, 1969) and token reinforcement (e.g., Cohen & Filipczak, 1971; Phillips, Fixsen, Phillips, & Wolf, 1979; Phillips, Phillips, Fixsen, & Wolf, 1971) are the predominant means employed. The behavior modification strategy does not focus exclusively on the delinquent juvenile's illegal behavior but also includes concern for improvement of delinquents' attitudes and self-perceptions (e.g., Eitzen, 1975), mobilization of community resources (e.g., Marholin, Plienis, Harris & Marholin, 1975), and modification of encounters of delinquent youth with police officers (e.g., Werner, Minkin, Minkin, Fixsen,

---

[37] Kirk (1976) provides a concise and readable outline of the functions and operation of juvenile courts (see also Cavan & Ferdinand, 1975, chapters 18 and 19; Kittrie, 1971; Paulsen & Whitebread, 1974; Silberman, 1978).

Phillips, & Wolf, 1975). Currently, it appears that behavior modification techniques combined with a modification of community responsiveness to the problems of delinquents offers some reason for optimism regarding what *can* be done to control and prevent delinquency. The home-type setting called Achievement Place (Phillips et al., 1971) and the institutional program known as the CASE-II-MODEL project (Contingencies Applicable to Special Education—Motivationally Oriented Designs for an Ecology of Learning; Cohen & Filipczak, 1971), in which token reinforcement plays a prominent part, have been associated with particularly encouraging outcomes (see also Cohen, 1973). Caution is in order, however, for it is too early to judge the ultimate value of behavioral interventions. For example, Davidson and Wolfred (1977) reported that a behavior modification program that appeared to be highly successful in changing delinquents' behavior in a residential institution did not result in improved outcomes for discharged youths. As Achenbach notes:

> In order to identify what is good in a paradigm and to adapt it to real-world problems, we must be prepared to test it in a careful, objective fashion, shorn of its messianic pretensions. This requires forebearance and a long-term perspective in which the ultimate goal is to help promote children's development in ways that can be objectively validated rather than in ways that merely appeal to our own reformist whims. We need to temper our spirit of reform with an attitude of scientific skepticism and to build into our paradigims fundamental research and development components designed to insure that our enthusiasms are well founded.   (1975, p. 14)

SUMMARY

Moral judgment, the ability to apply concepts of justice to moral dilemmas, is different from *moral behavior*, actions consistent with moral principles. There is little evidence indicating that moral behavior is controlled by moral judgment or that disturbed children are deficient in moral judgment. Disturbed children clearly are deficient in moral behavior, although the parameters of moral behavior deficiencies in nondelinquent disturbed children have not been researched. The usual means of moral education—exhortation, punishment, or threats—are apparently of little value in improving or controlling moral behavior. Modeling has been found effective in improving moral judgment and behavior in some experimental settings. Behavior modification techniques have been effective in remediating some behavior problems associated with moral deficiencies, such as stealing.

When children's behavior violates the law, it is considered delinquent. Juvenile delinquency is a problem of illegal behavior and ineffective responses of adult authorities to it. Several types of delinquent behavior have been identified: unsocialized-psychopathic, neurotic-disturbed, socialized-subcultural, and inadequate-immature. While no theory of delinquency is supported by unassailable research evidence, it is clear that poor home conditions, parental delinquency, and inappropriate parental discipline contribute to the growth of delinquent conduct in children. Traditional forms of intervention fail to control delinquency. Research evidence does support a cautious optimism regarding the efficacy of behavior modification programs with juvenile delinquents.

part four

Implications for Special Education

chapter 11 _____

A Personal Statement

It is my purpose in this chapter to discuss what I consider to be some primary considerations in the articulation of an approach to educating children with behavior disorders, including definition and measurement of behavior; causal factors and the teacher's role; essential experiences of work, play, love, and fun; communication, directness, and honesty; modeling and self-control; and finally, a look at the past to predict the future.

Whereas in previous chapters I have concentrated my attention on the characteristics of disordered behavior in children, it is now time to examine the amelioration or resolution of behavior problems. Remember that my comments provide only a preface or a brief orientation to educational methodology, and that they are based primarily on the research findings in the first ten chapters.

DEFINITION AND MEASUREMENT OF BEHAVIOR

The problems of defining and classifying disturbed children certainly are not resolved, nor do the problems appear close to a truly satisfactory resolution. The intractibility of the problems of defining and classifying children do not, fortunately, preclude the useful definition and measurement of children's behavior. The teacher of disturbed children can define and measure precisely the behaviors of children that bring them into conflict with others. Indeed, the teacher who cannot or will not pinpoint and measure the relevant behaviors of the children he or she is teaching probably is not going to be very effective. As we have seen in previous chapters, disturbed children are considered to need help *primarily because they exhibit behavioral excesses or deficiencies*. Not to define precisely and to measure these behavioral excesses and deficiencies, then, is a fundamental error: It is akin to the malpractice of a nurse who decides not to measure vital signs (heart rate, respiration rate, temperature, and blood pressure), perhaps arguing that he/she is too busy, that subjective estimates of vital signs are quite adequate, that vital signs are only superficial estimates of the patient's health, or that vital signs do not signify the nature of the underlying pathology. The teaching profession is dedicated to the task of changing behavior—changing behavior demonstrably for the better. What can one say, then, of educational practice that does not include reliable and forthright measurement of the behavior change induced by the teacher's methodology? I believe this: *It is indefensible*.

The technology of behavioral definition and measurement is readily available to teachers (cf. Haring, Lovitt, Eaton, & Hansen, 1978; Haring & Schiefelbusch, 1976; Lovitt, 1977; White & Haring, 1976). With little effort, the teacher can learn behavior measurement techniques and teach them to children. When children know how to define and measure their own behavior and the responses of those with whom they live, two additional benefits accrue: The teacher is relieved of some of the mechanical aspects of teaching, and the children have an opportunity to gain an extra degree of control over their own environment.

My suggestion here is not that every behavior of every child should be measured, or that the teacher should become preoccupied with measurement to

the exclusion of other crucial concerns. If the most important behavioral characteristics of the child are not being monitored, however, it will be almost impossible for
the teacher to communicate anything of substance about the child's progress to
the child or to anyone else.

The importance of behavioral measurement is demonstrated so clearly and
frequently that one is prompted to ask why many teachers of disturbed children
still do not measure their pupils' behavior.[38] It seems likely that measurement has
been neglected for at least the following reasons:

1. There has been a strong bias among special educators toward theoretical
   models (for example, psychoanalysis) that do not include direct measurement of behavior and, in fact, include the presumption that measurable
   responses are an unimportant or superficial aspect of psychopathology.

2. Parents of disturbed children have placidly accepted less than adequate
   evidence of teachers' effectiveness as the best that the education profession
   can offer.

3. Many teachers are still uninformed of the value of direct measurement of
   behavior or are untutored in the appropriate methodology.

4. There are incompetent and negligent teachers.

5. Although measurement of behavior is invaluable for precise assessment of
   therapeutic effects, it is obvious that measurement often is not a pre-
   requisite for behavioral change.

6. Informal and subjective estimates of children's behavioral status including
   anecdotal records and statements such as "She is much improved this
   week" without any objective data to back up the claim, give the impression
   that more precise measurement is unnecessary.

Admittedly, there are qualitative or affective aspects of pupils' behavior and
teachers' methodology that cannot be measured directly, and these affective
variables may be extremely important. I do not mean to imply that one should
ignore everything that cannot be measured. But I do believe that it is unconscionable for a teacher of disturbed children *not* to ask "Exactly what is it this child
does or does not do that is causing a problem?" and then set about measuring the
behavior in question as objectively and precisely as possible. Without direct
measurement of behavior, the teacher runs the risk of being misled by subjective
impressions of the child's responses and the effects of instructional and behavior management techniques. It is not too much to ask that the teacher show objective and precise evidence of pupils' behavioral change as well as describe in more
subjective terms the quality of his or her relationship to children.

---

[38] By *measure* I mean observe directly and record the occurence of specific behaviors. Most teachers
could be said to measure behavior if standardized testing, anecdotal records, or subjective appraisal
were considered to constitute measurement. *Direct measurement* implies obtaining data such as those
plotted in Figures 7–2, 7–3, 8–3, 8–4, 9–1, and so on.

CAUSAL FACTORS AND THE ROLE OF THE TEACHER

The first or ultimate causes of behavior disorders almost always remain unknown. It is much more realistic and productive to consider *contributing factors* which may interact to cause disordered behavior. Contributing factors may be *predisposing* or *precipitating*—factors which increase the probability that a behavior disorder will occur under a given set of circumstances and factors that are responsible for triggering a maladaptive response, given a set of predisposing variables. An important task of the teacher is to identify the contributing factors that account for the child's current behavioral status.

The *focus* of the special educator's concern should be on those contributing factors *that can be altered by the teacher*. Factors over which the teacher has no control may indeed come into the picture in that they may determine how the child is approached initially. However, the teacher of disturbed children is called upon to begin working with children *after* behavior disorders have appeared. The special educator has two primary responsibilities: first, to make sure that he or she does no *further* disservice to the child; and second, to manipulate the child's present environment in order to cause more appropriate behavior to develop *in spite of* past and present circumstances that cannot be changed. The emphasis must be on the present and future, not the past, and on the classroom environment. It is certainly true that it may be profitable for teachers to extend their influence beyond the classroom, perhaps working with parents to improve the home environment or using community resources for the child's benefit. But talk of influence beyond the classroom, including such high-sounding phrases as *ecological management*, is patent nonsense until the teacher has demonstrated that he or she can make the *classroom* environment productive of improved behavior.

The stance of the special educator must be that behavior is lawful—that in the case of disordered behavior, enough of the controlling factors can be found and changed to produce a therapeutic result. The past cannot be changed by anyone, and many of the contributing factors operating in the present cannot be altered by the teacher. Educators must have faith that the proper classroom environment alone can make a difference in the child's life even if nothing else can be altered, and hope that more than the classroom environment can be changed.

WORK, PLAY, LOVE, AND FUN

It does not require great sagacity to see that disturbed children typically do not do productive work or know how to play, give and receive love, and have fun. Yet these four experiences—work, play, love, and fun—are near the essence of satisfying and meaningful existence. The education of disturbed children requires a curriculum that will allow these essential experiences to be brought into sharp focus. This fact does not mean that one must design a curriculum to teach such experiences directly. In fact, someone wishing to teach a child how to work, to play, to love, or to have fun must have a curriculum with a content of specific skills that are useful but that *in themselves* do not constitute essential life experiences. The vapid antics of "fun-seekers" and the desperate "play" of professional athletes illustrate the difficulty in apprehending fun and play through concentrated effort alone. The relations among events, the structure of experience as well as events themselves, teach one to work, play, love, and enjoy.

The teacher's primary task is to structure or order the environment for the child in such a way that work is accomplished, play is learned, love is felt, and fun is enjoyed—by the child and the teacher. Structure and order cannot be provided by allowing the child complete freedom to choose what to do. It must be recognized that disturbed children are in difficulty because they have made and continue to make unguided and unfortunate choices about how to conduct themselves. Value judgments must be made regarding what a child should learn. Hobbs (1974, p. 156) writes, "A child simply must know how to read, write, spell, and do arithmetic, and it is good for him to know how to hit a ball, to play a guitar, to scull a canoe, to lash a table, and to travel by bus across town." The teacher must have confidence in his/her own judgment about what is good for the child to learn and how it is good for the child to behave, or else there can be no effective structuring of the child's environment. Do not interpret this statement to mean that *every* skill learned by the child or *every* way of behaving should be determined by the teacher. Only a fool or a despot would try to process children into mindless conformity to ridiculous behavioral standards; but only a fool or a charlatan would fail to require of children a reasonable standard of conduct and learning that will allow them greater personal choice and fulfillment in a free society.

Granted that one must make value judgments and hard decisions regarding what disturbed children will be taught, there remain questions of how one can best order the environment to teach. There are two fundamental guiding principles for arranging the environment to teach effectively: choosing tasks that are appropriate for the child (tasks that are at the right level and at which the child can succeed), and arranging appropriate consequences for performance. Work, play, love and fun are not learned by failure, but by success and mastery. Pride, dignity, self-worth, and other attributes associated with mental health are not learned by having wishes immediately gratified, but by struggling to overcome difficulties, meeting requirements, and finding that one's own efforts will achieve desired goals.

Disturbed children cannot be depended upon to learn by some magical mysterious, internally guided process; their learning will be assured only by a skillful and sensitive adult who makes the expectations for their behavior appropriately difficult. Hobbs (1974) describes the appropriate level of expectation as the "Principle of Just Manageable Difficulties." The "J.M.D. Principle" is that people are best adjusted or in the most robust mental health when they choose for themselves problems or tasks that are just about, but not quite, insurmountable.

> Part of the art of choosing difficulties is to select those that are indeed just manageable. If the difficulties chosen are too easy, life is boring; if they are too hard, life is defeating. The trick is to choose trouble for oneself in the direction of what he would like to become at a level of difficulty close to the edge of his competence. When one achieves this fine tuning of his life, he will know zest and joy and deep fulfillment. (Hobbs, 1974, p. 165)

The teacher's task is at first to choose just manageable tasks *for* disturbed children, and then gradually to allow them to set their own goals as they become attuned to their true capabilities and desires.

There is ample evidence indicating that the order in which events are structured to occur will have a profound influence on children's learning—specifically, that making highly preferred events (e.g., play) contingent or dependent upon less preferred events (i.e., work) will improve the child's work performance (cf. Haring & Phillips, 1962; Hewett, 1968; Stevenson, 1972). The structure "work before play (or pay)" is a fundamental principle of behavior modification. An environment in which rewards and privileges (beyond those that are the right of everyone) are gratis is stultifying. "Earning your way," on the other hand, builds self-esteem. Rothman (1970), who worked with disturbed and delinquent girls in New York City, comments on the value of work and pay:

> If I had my way, all children in school would work and be paid for the work they do. If the work of children is to learn, then children should be paid for learning. Money is a powerful motivator. I daresay that truancy might decrease and that more children would learn, even those children who have been relegated to the substratum of the nonachiever, if they were paid for services rendered. Someday, I would like a fund to pay girls for increasing their reading and arithmetic skills. Supposing I could say to a girl, "You increased your reading from fourth grade to fifth. You have earned five dollars." How great! If only we could do it.   (p. 211)

It *can* be done, if not with money then with special privileges, goods, or services that are meaningful to the child. The fundamental principle underlying a token economy is payment of a fair wage for work. Rothman (1970) also notes one of the usual outcomes of work: "Pride—an essential personal ingredient. All the girls who work find it" (p. 232).

I will not be so presumptuous as to try to define *play*, *love*, or *fun*; a definition of *work*—purposeful and necessary expenditure of effort to achieve a desired goal —is daring enough. Suffice to say that for the emotionally healthy individual, work, play, love, and fun are inextricably intertwined and that for the emotionally disturbed person, they are unrelated or unattainable. When a child's behavior has become disordered, it appears that the most effective strategy for restoring a "vital balance" or "zest, joy, and deep fulfillment" is to provide appropriate work and consistent consequences for performance. Play, love, and fun are likely to follow the experience of having accomplished a valued task and earned a reward by one's own labor. To work is to build a sound basis for self-esteem.

COMMUNICATION, DIRECTNESS, AND HONESTY

Some advocates of a structured approach and some behavior modification enthusiasts give the impression that consistent consequences for behavior alone will be sufficient to bring about therapeutic change in disturbed children. There is more to teaching than just providing a structured relationship among events. The process by which the environment is arranged may be as important as the structure itself in determining the outcome for the child.

How one listens and talks to children will have an effect on their perceptions and their responses to other environmental events. For example, in describing the consequences of behavior, the teacher can emphasize either the positive or the negative aspects of an arrangement. For example, a teacher may say, "You may not go to recess until your math is finished." Another teacher might phrase it, "You may go to recess as soon as you finish your math." Whereas both teachers have described the response-consequence relationship, and both statements are equally correct, the second draws attention to the positive consequences of appropriate performance, and the first to the negative results of nonperformance. It is obvious that each statement affects the child differently. Nonverbal communication, too, is important and should be consistent with what is said in word. To be therapeutic, teachers must listen, talk, and act in ways that communicate respect, caring, and confidence both in themselves and in the children.

It does not follow that the teacher must always communicate approval or positive regard for the child's behavior. In fact, it will frequently be necessary for the teacher of disturbed children to communicate disapproval with great clarity. A disturbed child cannot be expected to learn to behave appropriately if all behavior is responded to with approval or equanimity. Candor, including honest appraisal of behavior when the child's actions are inappropriate, will serve the teacher of disturbed children well.

Communication is a two-way affair, and the teacher of disturbed children will not be successful unless he/she learns to listen skillfully to children, to watch their behavior with understanding, and to interpret accurately the relation between their verbal and nonverbal behavior. Children who do not believe they are being listened to will go to extreme lengths to make themselves understood, often getting themselves into additional trouble by their efforts to establish communication. Rothman (1970) provides exceptionally clear and refreshing examples of how a teacher can communicate with disturbed children.

Directness in talking to disturbed children will facilitate communication. There is a tendency on the part of many teachers and parents to be tentative, noncommittal, and obfuscatory in their conversations with disturbed children, perhaps out of fear of rejecting or being rejected by children, or perhaps due to the misguided notion that to help disturbed children one must never direct them. Disturbed children typically do not profit from being kept guessing about adults' wishes or intentions. A few children, in fact, will change their behavior for the better almost immediately if the teacher merely states clearly, forthrightly, and unequivocally how they are to behave. No advantage is gained by keeping one's hopes for a disturbed child's behavior a mystery, especially when the person most mystified is the child.

Honesty is a quality sure to be tested by disturbed children. Honesty is more than candor in expressing opinions and reporting facts accurately. The disturbed child will want to know whether or not the teacher is as good as his/her word. The teacher who makes idle threats or fails to deliver positive consequences as promised will surely run afoul of disturbed children.

MODELING AND SELF-CONTROL

There is overwhelming evidence that children learn much through observing the behavior of others (see Cullinan, Kauffman, & LaFleur, 1975). Teachers whose own behavior is not exemplary may corrupt children rather than help them regardless of the finesse of their other teaching strategies. To be blunt, teaching disturbed children is not an appropriate job for social misfits or those who are psychologically unstable. Imitation of the teacher should mean that the child is *improving*, not exhibiting maladaptive responses. Hobbs (1966) sums up the kind of model a teacher (in this example a teacher-counselor in Project Re-ED) should provide:

> But most of all a teacher-counselor is a decent adult; educated, well trained; able to give and receive affection, to live relaxed, and to be firm; a person with private resources for the nourishment and refreshment of his own life; not an itinerant worker but a professional through and through; a person with a sense of the significance of time, of the usefulness of today and the promise of tomorrow; a person of hope, quiet confidence, and joy; one who has committed himself to children and to the proposition that children who are emotionally disturbed can be helped by the process of re-education.   (pp. 1,106 –1,107)

One of the behavioral characteristics modeled by a teacher of disturbed children should be self-control. Not only should self-control be modeled, but it should be taught through direct instruction. To the extent possible, every child, disturbed children included, should exercise free choice and self-determination, for appropriate self-guidance is both inherent in the concept of individual rights and inimical to the loss of control that characterizes disordered behavior. This statement should not be misconstrued to mean that disturbed children should always be allowed to behave as they will without interference, or that the teacher is always wrong to require a child to behave willy-nilly. I am suggesting that children should be allowed to choose for themselves how they will behave *except* when they choose to behave in ways that are self-defeating or their choice clearly is not in their best interest. The teacher's role should be to structure the classroom environment so that the child is aware of options, can exercise choice in as many areas of behavior as possible, and is tutored in and rewarded for appropriate decisions. Cognitive behavior modification techniques, such as self-instruction, rehearsal, and guided practice, should be taught to the children to make them as self-sufficient as possible in controlling their own behavior. External control may be required at first to humanize the child, but the task of truly humanistic education is not completed until control is internalized to the greatest extent possible.

THE PAST

It is customary for a book to end with speculation about the future. I have chosen instead to comment on the past because I believe the best prediction of future developments is derived from an analysis of past events. In the past, there has been an ebb and flow of concern for the plight of disturbed children and periods of progress and regression in effective intervention in their lives. There has been enthusiasm for new methods and disillusionment when the "final solution" turned out to be less than final. A legal-bureaucratic approach to fulfilling society's obligation to the handicapped has been a failure in the past, and it shows no bright promise for the future (Kauffman, 1980; 1981; Sarason & Doris, 1979). Public Law 94-142 and its successors may set forth legal standards and promises, but standards and promises can easily be circumvented. More effective and humane education of disturbed children has always depended on the individual actions of competent, caring teachers, and this will be the case in the future regardless of legal mandates or prohibitions.

The issues today parallel those of the last century (Kauffman, 1976), though the *potential* for helping disturbed children today is greater than it was then because of our broader base of knowledge and experience. There is reason, then, for guarded optimism. Quick and easy cures are unlikely to be found, but as long as people care—and go beyond caring to search diligently for answers to the questions of how disturbed children came to be that way and how they can be helped to develop appropriate behavior—one can have confidence that periods of regression will be outweighed by periods of progress.

glossary

Adjustment Disorders Maladaptive reactions to an identifiable and stressful life event or circumstance; includes impairment of social/occupational functioning; maladaptive behavior is expected to change when stress is removed

Affective Disorders Disorders of affect or mood; a disorder of emotion that colors one's outlook on life, usually characterized by either elation or depression; may be episodic or chronic, manic or depressive

Amenorrhea Absence or suppression of menstruation; may result from emotional factors

Amnesia Chronic or severe inability to remember; loss of memory that is general or more than temporary

Anomie Normlessness, especially absence of norms for moral conduct among lower class persons who aspire to achieve a higher class status

Anorexia Nervosa Severe self-starvation and marked weight loss that may be life threatening; most often in adolescent girls

Anoxia Deprivation of oxygen for a long enough time to result in brain trauma

Anxiety Disorders Disorders in which anxiety is the primary feature; anxiety may be focused on specific situations, such as separation or social contact with strangers, or generalized and pervasive

Anxiety-Withdrawal *see* Personality Problem

Attentional Strategies The use of verbal labeling, rehearsal, self-instruction, or other techniques by a child in order to improve his ability to attend efficiently to appropriate stimuli

Athetoid Movement Involuntary, jerky, writhing movements, especially of the fingers and wrists, associated with athetoid cerebral palsy

Atypical Childhood Psychosis Profound disturbance in relations with other people accompanied by many bizarre behaviors; characteristics appear after 30 months but before 12 years of age

Autist One who is autistic *see* Autistic

Autistic; Autism A severe disturbance or psychosis of childhood characterized by extreme social isolation, bizarre behavior, and delayed development, usually beginning in the first 2½ years *see also* Childhood Psychosis, Psychosis

Behavior Modification Systematic control of environmental events, especially consequences, to produce specific changes in observable responses; may include reinforcement, punishment, modeling, self-instruction, desensitization, guided practice, or any other technique employed to teach or eliminate a particular response

293

Behavioral Model   Assumptions that behavior disorders are primarily a result of inappropriate learning and that the most effective preventative actions and therapeutic interventions will involve controlling the child's environment in order to teach appropriate behaviors

Biological Model   Assumptions that behavior disorders are primarily a result of dysfunction of the central nervous system due to brain lesions, neurochemical irregularities, or genetic defects and that the most effective preventative actions and therapeutic interventions will involve prevention or correction of such biological defects.

Brain Syndrome   *see* Organic Brain Syndrome

Bulimia   Binge eating; person is aware of problem and has fear of not being able to stop eating

Catharsis   Cleansing; in psychoanalytic theory, the notion that it is therapeutic to express one's feelings freely under certain conditions (e.g., that aggressive drive can be reduced by free expression of aggression in a safe way, such as hitting a punching bag or doll)

Cerebral Palsy   A developmental disability resulting from brain damage before, during, or soon after birth and having as a primary feature weakness or paralysis of the extremities; often accompanied by mental retardation, sensory deficiencies, and/or behavior disorders

Character Disorder   Acting-out, aggressive behavior with little or no indication of associated anxiety or guilt

Childhood Psychosis   Used to denote a wide range of severe and profound disorders of children, including autism, schizophrenia, and symbiotic psychosis

Choreoathetoid   Involuntary, purposeless, uncontrolled movement characteristic of some types of neurological disorder

Conceptual Model   A theory; in behavior disorders, a set of assumptions regarding the origins and nature of the problem and the nature of therapeutic mechanisms; a set of assumptions guiding research and practice

Conduct Disorder; Conduct Problem   Disorder characterized by acting out, aggressive, disruptive behavior

Contingency Contract   In behavior modification, a written agreement between a child and adult(s) specifying what the consequences will be for specific behavior

Countertheorists   *see* Humanistic Education

Desensitization; Systematic Desensitization   The elimination of fears or phobias by gradually subjecting the fearful individual to successively more anxiety-provoking stimuli (real or imagined) while the individual remains relaxed and free of fear

Developmental Deviations; Developmental Disorders   Behavior disorders apparently caused by failure of the child to develop at a normal rate or according to the usual sequence

Distractibility   Inability to direct and sustain attention to the appropriate or relevant stimuli in a given situation   *see also* Selective Attention

Down's Syndrome   A genetic defect in which the child is born with an extra chromosome (number 21 in the 22 pairs—hence, *trisomy 21*) in each cell; a syndrome associated with characteristic *mongoloid* facial features, mental retardation, and other congenital defects; also called *mongolism*

Dynamic Psychiatry   The study of emotional processes, mental mechanisms, and their origins; the study of evolution, progression, or regression in human behavior and its motivation; distinguished from descriptive psychiatry (in which the focus is on static clinical patterns, symptoms, and classification)

Echolalia   The parroting repetition of words or phrases either immediately after they are heard or later; usually observed only in psychotic, schizophrenic, or autistic children

Ecological Model   Assumptions that behavior disorders are primarily a result of flaws in a complex social system in which various elements of the system (e.g., child, school, family, church, community) are highly interdependent, and that the most effective preventative actions and therapeutic interventions will involve changes in the entire social system

Elective Mutism   Muteness of a child who is able to talk; the child chooses to be mute, usually except in the presence of mother or a few other select people

Electroencephalogram (EEG)   A graphic record of changes in the electrical potential of the brain; used in neurological and psychiatric research

Emotional Liability   Unstable or rapidly shifting emotional states

Encopresis   Incontinence of feces, which may consist of passing feces into the clothing or bed at regular intervals or leaking mucus and feces into the clothing or bed almost continuously

Endogenous Depression   Depression apparently precipitated by biological factors rather than adverse environmental circumstances

Enuresis   Incontinence of urine, which may be diurnal (wetting oneself during the day) or nocturnal (bedwetting)

Epilepsy   An abnormal electrical discharge in the brain which causes a seizure; a person is not considered to be an epileptic unless repeated seizures occur

Ethology   The scientific comparative study of animal and human behavior, especially the study of the development of human character

Follow-back Studies   Studies in which adults with a given disorder are "followed back" in an attempt to find the antecedents of their condition in their medical, educational, or social histories

Frustration-Aggression Hypothesis: The hypothesis that frustration always produces aggression and that aggression is always the result of frustration

Humanistic Education   Education suggested by "countertheorists" who call for radical school reform and/or greater self-determination by the child; education in which freedom, openness, innovation, self-direction, and self-evaluation by students and mutual sharing between students and teachers are practiced

Hyperactivity   A high level of motor activity accompanied by socially inappropriate behavior, often including conduct problems, distractibility, and impulsivity

Hyperkinesis   Excessive motor activity

Hyperkinetic; Hyperkinetic Impulse Disorder; Hyperkinetic Reaction; Hyperkinetic Syndrome   Characterized by excessive motor activity or hyperactivity

Hyperthyroidism   Enlargement and excessive secretion of hormones from the thyroid gland which may result in nervousness, weakness, and restless overactivity

Hypoglycemia   An abnormally low level of blood sugar which may produce behavioral symptoms such as irritability, fretfulness, confusion, negativism, or aggression; may be associated with diabetes

Hypoxia   A severly reduced supply of oxygen   *see* Anoxia

Immaturity Inadequacy   Disorder characterized by social incompetence, passivity, day-dreaming, and behavior typical of younger children

Impulsivity   The tendency to react quickly and inappropriately to a situation rather than to take the time to consider alternatives and to choose carefully

Induction Approach   The use of reasoning, explanation, modeling, and expressions of love and concern in discipline, especially in teaching or enforcing moral standards

Infantile Autism   *see* Autistic

Interactional-Transactional Model   Assumptions that behavior disorders are primarily a result of the mutual influence of the child and other persons on each other and that the most effective preventative actions and therapeutic interventions will involve changing the nature of the interactions and transactions between the child and other persons

Intervention   The method or strategy used in the treatment of a behavior disorder

Intrapsychic; Intrapsychic Causal Factors   Having to do with the mind; in the mind itself; conflict or disequilibrium between parts of the mind, in psychoanalytic theory the id, ego, and superego; especially conflict in the unconscious

Kanner's Syndrome   Early infantile autism (originally described by Leo Kanner in 1943), the primary symptoms of which are extreme isolation or aloneness from the first years of life and obsessive insistence on the preservation of sameness. Generally replaced by the terms *autism* and *childhood psychosis*   *see also* Autism

Lesch-Nyhan Syndrome   A severe neurologic disorder resulting from a genetically trans-mitted metabolic defect; symptoms first appear at about 6 months of age and children with the defect rarely live beyond their teens

Life Space Interview   A therapeutic way of talking with disturbed children about their be-havior; a set of techniques for managing behavior by means of therapeutic communi-cation

Locus of Control   The belief that one's behavior is under internal or external control; an in-dividual has an internal locus to the extent that he or she believes that they are respon-sible for their actions, an external locus to the extent that one believes chance or others' actions determine ones behavior

Megavitamin Therapy   The administration of extremely large doses of vitamins in the hope of improving or curing behavior disorders

Metachromatic Leukoencephalopathy   A genetic disease involving abnormal lipid (fat) metabolism and neurological degeneration; development is normal until the age of 2 or 3 years, when neurological symptoms appear; the disease is progressive, resulting in men-tal retardation and early death

Minimal Brain Dysfunction; Minimal Brain Damage   A term applied to children who ex-hibit behavioral characteristics (e.g., hyperactivity, distractibility) thought to be as-sociated with brain damage, in the absence of other evidence that their brains have been damaged

Minimal Cerebral Dysfunction   *see* Minimal Brain Dysfunction

Modeling   Providing an example which, it is hoped, the child will imitate; a behavior mod-ification technique in which a clear model of the desired behavior is provided (reinforce-ment is typically given for imitation of the model)

Mongolism; Mongoloid   *see* Down's Syndrome

Moral Therapy; Moral Treatment   Treatment provided in the late 18th and early 19th centuries, and characterized by humane and kindly care, therapeutic activity, and consistent consequences for behavior

Neurosis; Neurotic Behavior   Behavior disorder characterized by emotional conflict but not a loss of contact with reality   *see also* Personality Disorder

Operant Conditioning   Changing behavior by altering its consequences; altering the future probability of a response by providing reinforcement or punishment as a consequence

Organic Brain Syndrome; Organic Psychosis   Behavior disorder caused by damage to the brain

Organic Mental Disorders   Disorders of behavior caused by transient or permanent dysfunction of the brain, often due to anoxia, ingestion of drugs or other toxic substances, or injury of brain tissue

Organicity   Behavioral indications of brain damage or organic defects

Orthomolecular Therapy   The administration of chemical substances, vitamins, or drugs under the assumption that a basic chemical or molecular error that causes behavior disorders will be corrected

Overcorrection   A set of procedures designed to "overcorrect" behavioral errors; may be *positive practice* overcorrection (requiring the individual to practice a more adaptive or appropriate form of behavior) or *restitution* overcorrection (requiring the individual to restore the environment to a condition better than its status before the misbehavior occurred)

Overselective Attention   *see* Selective Attention

Permissive Approach to Education   Allowing the child to behave as she wishes within very broad or loosely defined limits under the assumptions that it is therapeutic to allow the child to "act out" her feelings (unless she endangers someone) and that the teacher must be permissive in order to build a sound relationship with the child; derived mostly from psychoanalytic theory

Personality Disorders   Deeply ingrained, inflexible, maladaptive patterns of relating to, perceiving, and thinking about the environment and oneself that impair adaptive functioning or cause subject distress

Personality Problem   Disorder characterized by neurotic behavior, depression, and withdrawal

Pervasive Developmental Disorder   Distortion of or lag in all or most areas of development, as in autism or other childhood psychosis

Phenomenological Model   Assumptions that behavior disorders are primarily a result of inadequate or distorted conscious experience of life events and that the most effective preventative actions and therapeutic interventions will involve helping individuals to examine their own conscious experience of the world

Phobia   An irrational and debilitating fear

Pica   Persistent eating of non-nutritional substances (e.g., paint, plaster, cloth)

Play Therapy   Therapeutic treatment in which the child's play is used as the theme for communication between therapist and child

Positive Practice   *see* Overcorrection

Postencephalitic Behavior Syndrome   Abnormal behavior following encephalitis (inflammation of the brain)

Premorbid; Premorbid Personality   The condition or personality characteristics predictive of later onset of illness or disorder

Primary Process Thinking   The psychoanalytic concept that disorganized or primitive thought or activity represents the direct expression of unconscious mental processes; distinguished from secondary process (rational, logical) thinking

Psychoanalytic Model   Assumptions that behavior disorders are primarily a result of unconscious conflicts and that the most effective preventative actions and therapeutic interventions will involve uncovering and understanding the child's unconscious motivations

Psychodynamic Model   *see* Psychoanalytic Model

Psychoeducational   An approach to education of disturbed children in which psychodynamic concepts such as unconscious motivation are taken into account but which focuses intervention on the "ego processes" by which the child gains insight into his behavior

Psychogenic Megacolon   Chronic severe constipation and an enlargement of the colon, thought to be of mental, psychological, or emotional origin

Psychoneurosis; Psychoneurotic   *see* Neurosis

Psychopath; Psychopathic   An individual who exhibits mostly amoral or antisocial behavior and is usually impulsive, irresponsible, and self-gratifying without consideration for others (also called *sociopath* or *sociopathic*)

Psychopathology   Mental illness; in psychiatry, the study of significant causes and development of mental illness; more generally, behavior disorder

Psychophysiological   Physical disorders thought to be caused by psychological (emotional) conflict

Psychosexual Disorders   Disorders involving sexual functioning or sex-typed behavior

Psychosis; Psychotic Behavior; Psychotic Reaction   Behavior disorder characterized by major departure from normal patterns of acting, thinking, and feeling

Psychosomatic; Psychosomaticization   *see* Psychophysiological

Psychotherapy   Any type of treatment relying primarily on verbal and nonverbal communication between patient and therapist rather than medical procedures; not typically defined to include behavior modification; typically administered by a psychiatrist or clinical psychologist

Punishment   Consequences which reduce the future probability of a behavior; may be *response cost* (i.e., removal of a valued object or commodity) or *aversive conditioning* (i.e., presentation of an aversive stimulus such as a slap or electric shock)

Reactive Depression   Depression apparently precipitated by a specific event; depression that is a reaction to adverse circumstances

Reactive Disorders   Behavior disorders apparently caused by reaction to stressful circumstances

Reciprocal Inhibition   *see* Desensitization

Reinforcement   Presenting or removing stimuli following a behavior in order to increase its future probability; *positive reinforcement* refers to presenting positive stimuli (rewards) and *negative reinforcement* refers to removing negative stimuli (punishers) contingent on a response; both positive and negative reinforcement increase the rate or strength of the response

Respondent Behavior A response that is elicited; reflexive behavior elicited automatically by presenting a stimulus (e.g., pupillary contraction elicited by shining a light in the eye)

Respondent Conditioning A process by which a previously neutral stimulus comes to elicit a respondent behavior after the neutral stimulus has been paired with the presentation of another stimulus (an unconditioned stimulus which "naturally" elicits a response) on one or more trials

Response Cost A punishment technique consisting of taking away a valued object or commodity contingent on a behavior; a fine; making an inappropriate response "cost" the misbehaving child something

Response Topography The particular movements that comprise a response; the way the response looks to an observer, as opposed to the effect of the response on the environment

Restitution *see* Overcorrection

Rumination (Mercyism) Regurgitation with loss of weight or failure to thrive

Salt Depletion An abnormally reduced level of chloride (salt) in the blood which may result in behavioral symptoms; in rapid depletion weakness, dizziness, stupor, and profuse perspiration may be manifestations; in protracted (long) depletion headaches, tremors, nervousness, apprehension, depression, and restlessness may be manifestations

Schizoaffective Disorders Depression or manic behavior lasting at least one week and being concurrent with psychotic behavior not consistent with a purely affective disorder

Schizoid; Schizophrenic Spectrum Behavior Behavior like that of schizophrenics but occurring in individuals not diagnosed as schizophrenic; schizophrenic-like behavior not as deviant as that typically seen in schizophrenia (*see* Schizophrenic)

Schizophrenia; Schizophrenic A psychotic disorder characterized by distortion of thinking, abnormal perception, and bizarre behavior and emotions

Schizophrenic Disorders *see* Schizophrenia

School Phobia Fear of going to school, usually accompanied by indications of anxiety about attendance such as abdominal pain, nausea, or other physical complaints just before leaving for school in the morning

Selective Attention The ability to direct and sustain one's attention to the appropriate and relevant stimuli in a given situation; disorders of selective attention include *underselective attention* (the inability to focus attention only on the relevant stimuli or to disregard irrelevant stimuli) and *overselective attention* (the inability to attend to all the relevant stimuli or the tendency to focus on a particular irrelevant stimulus)

Self-Instruction Telling oneself what to do or how to perform; a technique for teaching children self-control or how to improve their performance by talking to themselves about what they are doing

Self-Stimulation Any repetitive, stereotyped activity which seems only to provide sensory feedback

Sensitization Approach The use of harsh punishment, threats, and overpowering force in discipline, especially in teaching or enforcing moral standards

Social Learning Theory Assumptions that antecedent or setting events (e.g., models, instructions), consequences (rewards and punishments), *and* cognitive processes (perceiving, thinking, feeling) influence behavior; includes features of behavioral model or behavior modification with additional consideration of cognitive factors

Socialized Delinquency; Subcultural Delinquency   Delinquent behavior relfecting adaptation to environmental circumstances rather than behavior that is maladaptive in the child's everyday life

Sociological Model   Approximate equivalent of Ecological Model

Sociopath; Sociopathic   *see* Psychopath

Soft Neurological Signs   Behavioral indications such as incoordination, distractibility, impulsivity, perceptual problems, and certain patterns of nerve reflexes which may occur in individuals who are not brain damaged as well as those who are; signs that the individual *may* be brain damaged but that cannot be said to indicate the *certainty* of brain damage

Somatoform Disorders   Physical symptoms suggesting a physical disorder in the absence of demonstrable organic findings to explain the symptoms

Stereotype   A persistent repetition of speech or motor activity characteristics of psychosis

Strauss Syndrome   A group of behavioral characteristics including hyperactivity, distractibility, impulsivity, perceptual disturbances, no history of mental retardation in the family, and a medical history suggestive of brain damage; named after Alfred A. Strauss

Structured Approach to Education   Making the child's classroom environment highly predictable by providing clear directions for how she is to behave, firm expectations that she will behave as directed, and consistent consequences for her behavior, under the assumptions that the child lacks order and predictability in her everyday life and that she will learn self-control in a highly structured (predictable) environment; derived primarily from learning theory

Substance Use Disorders   Disorders involving the abuse of mood-altering substances (e.g., alcoholism or other drug abuse)

Systematic Desensitization   *see* Desensitization

Target Assessment   Definition and direct measurement (counting) of behaviors that are considered to be a problem (as opposed to administering psychological tests that are designed to measure behavioral traits or mental characteristics)

Tay-Sachs Disease   A genetic disease in which lipids (fats) accumulate in cells of the brain and nervous system and the myelin sheath of nerves is destroyed; symptoms first appear at 4–6 months of age when slow rate of development, irritability, and hypersensitivity to sound are noted; progressive deterioration, death usually occuring by the age of 3 or 4 years

Temperament   An inborn behavioral style including general level of activity, regularity or predictability, approach or withdrawal, adaptability, intensity of reaction, responsiveness, mood, distractibility, and persistence

Therapeutic Milieu   A total treatment setting that is therapeutic; a therapeutic environment including attention to the therapeutic value of both physical and social surroundings

Tic   Stereotyped movement disorder in which there is disregulation of gross motor movement; recurrent, involuntary, repetitive, rapid, purposeless movement; may be transient or chronic

Time Out   Technically, time out from positive reinforcement; an interval of time during which reinforcement (rewards) cannot be earned; in classroom practice, usually a brief period of social isolation during which the child cannot receive attention or earn rewards

Token Economy; Token Reinforcement; Token System A system of behavior modification in which tangible or "token" reinforcers such as points, plastic chips, metal washers, poker chips, or play money are given as rewards and later exchanged for "backup" reinforcers that have value in themselves (e.g., food, trinkets, play time, books); a miniature economic system used to foster desirable behavior

Tourette's Disorder Motor tics accompanied by multiple vocal tics, which are frequently obscene (coprolalic)

Underselective Attention *see* Selective Attention

Unsocialized Aggression Unbridled aggressive behavior characterized by hostility, impulsivity, and alienation from others

Vicarious Extinction Extinction of a fear response due to watching someone else engage in an anxiety-provoking activity without apparent fear; loss of fear (or other response) by observing the behavior of others

Vicarious Reinforcement Reinforcement obtained by watching someone else obtain reinforcers (rewards) for a particular response

references

Achenbach, T. M. *Developmental psychopathology*. New York: Ronald Press, 1974.

Achenbach, T. M. The historical context of treatment for delinquent and maladjusted children: Past, present, and future. *Behavioral Disorders*, 1975, *1* (1), 3–14.

Achenbach, T. M., & Edelbrock, C. S. The classification of child psychopathology: A review and analysis of empirical efforts. *Psychological Bulletin*, 1978, *85*, 1275–1301.

Ack, M. Some principles of education for the emotionally disturbed. In P. A. Gallagher & L. L. Edwards (Eds.), *Educating the emotionally disturbed: Theory to practice*. Lawrence, Kan.: University of Kansas, 1970.

Ackerson, L. *Children's behavior problems*. Chicago: University of Chicago Press, 1942.

Agras, W. S., Barlow, D. H., Chapin, H. N., Abel, G. G., & Leitenberg, H. Behavior modification of anorexia nervosa. *Archives of General Psychiatry*, 1974, *30*, 279–286.

Aichhorn, A. *Wayward youth*. New York: Viking Press, 1935.

Ainsworth, M. D. S. The development of infant-motor attachment. In B. M. Caldwell & H. N. Ricciuti (Eds.), *Review of child development research, Vol. 3*. Chicago: University of Chicago Press, 1973.

Ainsworth, M. D. S., & Bell, S. M. Infant crying and maternal responsiveness: A rejoinder to Gewirtz and Boyd. *Child Development*, 1977, *48*, 1208–1216

Alexander, F. G., & Selsnick, S. T. *The history of psychiatry: An evaluation of psychiatric thought from prehistoric times to the present*. New York: Harper & Row, 1966.

Allen, K. E., & Harris, F. R. Elimination of a child's excessive scratching by training the mother in reinforcement procedures. *Behavior Research and Therapy*, 1966, *4*, 79–84.

Allen, K. E., Hart, B. M., Buell, J. S., Harris, F. R., & Wolf, M. M. Effects of social reinforcement on isolate behavior of a nursery school child. *Child Development*, 1964, *35*, 511–518.

American Psychiatric Association. *Diagnostic and statistical manual of mental disorders* (2nd ed.). Washington, D. C.: Author, 1968.

American Psychiatric Association, *Diagnostic and statistical manual of mental disorders* (3rd edition). Washington, D. C.: Author, 1980.

Anthony, E. J. An experimental approach to the psychopathology of childhood: Encopresis. *British Journal of Medical Psychology*, 1957, *30*, 146–175.

Ashem, B., & Jones, M. D. Deleterious effects of chronic undernutrition on cognitive abilities. *Journal of Child Psychology and Psychiatry*, 1978, *19*, 23–31.

Atkeson, B. M., & Forehand, R. Home-based reinforcement programs designed to modify classroom behavior: A review and methodological evaluation. *Psychological Bulletin*, 1979, *86*, 1298–1308.

Augustine, G. J., & Levitan, H. Neurotransmitter release from a vertebrate neuromuscular synapse affected by a food dye. *Science*, 1980, *207*, 1489–1490.

Axline, V. *Play therapy*. Boston: Houghton Mifflin, 1947.

Ayllon, T., Layman, D., & Kandel, H. J. A behavioral-educational alternative to drug control of hyperactive children. *Journal of Applied Behavior Analysis*, 1975, *8*, 137–146.

Ayllon, T., & Roberts, M. D. Eliminating discipline problems by strengthening academic performance. *Journal of Applied Behavior Analysis*, 1974, *7*, 71–76.

Ayllon, T., & Rosenbaum, M. S. The behavioral treatment of disruption and hyperactivity in school settings. In B. B. Lahey & A. E. Kazdin (Eds.), *Advances in clinical child psychology*, Vol. 1. New York: Plenum, 1977.

Ayllon, T., Simon, S. J., & Wildman, R. W. Instructions and reinforcement in the elimination of encopresis: A case study. *Journal of Behavior Therapy and Experimental Psychiatry*, 1975, *6*, 235–238.

Ayllon, T., Smith, D., & Rogers, M. Behavioral management of school phobia. *Journal of Behavior Therapy and Experimental Psychiatry*, 1970, *1*, 125–128.

Azerad, J., & Stafford, R. L. Restoration of eating behavior in anorexia nervosa through operant conditioning and environmental manipulation. *Behaviour Research and Therapy*, 1969, *7*, 165–171.

Azrin, N. H., Gottlieb, L., Hughart, L., Wesolowski, M. D., & Rahn, T. Eliminating self-injurious behavior by educative procedures. *Behaviour Research and Therapy*, 1975, *13*, 101–111.

Azrin, N. H., Kaplan, S. J., & Foxx, R. M. Autism reversal: Eliminating stereotyped self-stimulation of retarded individuals. *American Journal of Mental Deficiency*, 1973, *78*, 241–248.

Azrin, N. H., & Powers, M. A. Eliminating classroom disturbances of emotionally disturbed children by positive practice procedures. *Behavior Therapy*, 1975, *6*, 525–534.

Azrin, N. H., Sneed, T. J., & Foxx, R. M. Dry-bed training: Rapid elimination of childhood enuresis. *Behaviour Research and Therapy*, 1974, *12*, 147–156.

Bach, R., & Moylan, J. J. Parents administer behavior therapy for inappropriate urination and encopresis: A case study. *Journal of Behavior Therapy and Experimental Psychiatry*, 1975, *6*, 239–241.

Bachman, J. A. Self-injurious behavior: A behavioral analysis. *Journal of Abnormal Psychology*, 1972, *80*, 211–224.

Bachrach, A. J., Erwin, W. J., & Mohr, J. P. The control of eating behavior in an anorexic by operant conditioning. In L. Ullmann & L. Krasner (Eds.), *Case studies in behavior modification*. New York: Holt, Rinehart, & Winston, 1965.

Baer, D. M. Let's take another look at punishment. *Psychology Today*, 1971, *5*(5), 32–37; 111.

Baker, B. L. Symptom treatment and symptom substitution in enuresis. *Journal of Abnormal Psychology*, 1969, *74*, 42–49.

Baker, E. M., & Stullken, E. H. American research studies concerning the "behavior" type of exceptional child. *Journal of Exceptional Children*, 1938, *4*, 36–45.

Bakwin, H., & Bakwin, R. M. *Behavior disorders in children* (4th ed.). Philadelphia: Saunders, 1972.

Baller, W. R. *Bed-wetting: Origins and treatment*. New York: Pergamon, 1975.

Balthazaar, E., & Stevens, H. *The emotionally disturbed mentally retarded*. Englewood Cliffs, N.J.: Prentice-Hall, 1975.

Bandura, A. *Principles of behavior modification*. New York: Holt, Rinehart, & Winston, 1969.

Bandura, A. *Aggression: A social learning analysis*. Englewood Cliffs, N. J.: Prentice-Hall, 1973.

Bandura, A. *Social learning theory*. Englewood Cliffs, N. J.: Prentice-Hall, 1977.

Bandura, A. The self system in reciprocal determinism. *American Psychologist*, 1978, *33*, 344–358.

Bandura, A., Grusec, J., & Menlove, F. Vicarious extinction of avoidance behavior. *Journal of Personality and Social Psychology*, 1967, *5*, 16–23.

Bandura, A., & McDonald, F. J. Influence of social reinforcement and the behavior of models in shaping children's moral judgments. *Journal of Abnormal and Social Psychology*, 1963, *67*, 274–281.

Bandura, A., & Menlove, F. Factors determining vicarious extinction of avoidance behavior through symbols modeling. *Journal of Personality and Social Psychology*, 1968, *8*, 99–108.

Bandura, A., & Walters, R. H. *Adolescent aggression*. New York: Ronald Press, 1959.

Bandura, A., & Walters, R. H. *Social learning and personality development*. New York: Holt, Rinehart, & Winston, 1963.

Barker, R. G. *Ecological psychology: Concepts and methods for studying the environment of human behavior*. Palo Alto, Calif.: Stanford University Press, 1968.

Barker, R. G., & Wright, H. F. Psychological ecology and the problem of psychosocial development. *Child Development*, 1949, *20*, 131–143.

Barker, R. G., & Wright, H. F. *Midwest and its children*. Evanston, Ill.: Row, Peterson, 1954.

Barrett, D. E. A naturalistic study of sex differences in children's aggression. *Merrill-Palmer Quarterly*, 1979, *25*, 193–203.

Bartak, L., & Rutter, M. Special educational treatment of autistic children: A comparative study—I.

Design of study and characteristics of units. *Journal of Child Psychology and Psychiatry*, 1973, *14*, 161–179.

Bateman, B., & Herr, C. Law and special education. In J. M. Kauffman & D. P. Hallahan (Eds.) *Handbook of special education*. Englewood Cliffs, N. J.: Prentice-Hall, 1981.

Bateson, P., Day, W. F., McClosky, H., Meehl, P. E., & Michael, J. Control and countercontrol: A panel discussion. In T. Thompson & W. S. Dockens (Eds.), *Applications of behavior modification*. New York: Academic Press, 1975.

Baumeister, A.A., & Baumeister, A. A. Suppression of repetitive self-injurious behavior by contingent inhalation of aromatic ammonia. *Journal of Autism and Childhood Schizophrenia*, 1978, *8*, 71–77.

Becker, W. C. Consequences of different kinds of parental discipline. In M. L. Hoffman & L. W. Hoffman (Eds.), *Review of child development research, Vol. 1*. New York: Russel Sage Foundation, 1964.

Beers, C. W. *A mind that found itself: An autobiography*. New York: Longmans, Green, 1980.

Bell, J. E. Impact of emphasis on family units. In H.E. Rie (Ed.), *Perspectives in child psychopathology*. Chicago: Aldine, 1971.

Bell, R. Q. A reinterpretation of the direction of effects in studies of socialization. *Psychological Review*, 1968, *75*, 81–95.

Bell, R. Q., & Harper, L. V. *Child effects on adults*. Hillsdale, N. J.: Lawrence Erlbaum, 1977.

Bell, S. M., & Ainsworth, M. D. S. Infant crying and maternal responsiveness. *Child Development*, 1972, *43*, 1171–1190.

Bemporad, J. R. Encopresis. In B. B. Wolman (Ed.), *Handbook of treatment of mental disorders in childhood and adolescence*. Englewood Cliffs, N. J.: Prentice-Hall, 1978.

Bender, L. Genesis of hostility in children. *American Journal of Psychiatry*, 1948, *105*, 241–245.

Bender, L. Childhood schizophrenia—Its recognition, description, and treatment. *American Journal of Orthopsychiatry*, 1956, *26*, 499–506.

Bender, L. The nature of childhood psychosis. In J. G. Howells (Ed.), *Modern perspectives in international child psychiatry*. New York: Brunner/Mazel, 1969.

Bergman, P., & Escalona, S. Unusual sensitivities in very young children. *Psychoanalytic study of the child*, 1949, 3–4, 333–352.

Berkowitz, B., & Graziano, A. Training parents as behavior therapists: A review. *Behaviour Research and Therapy*, 1972, *10*, 297–318.

Berkowitz, L. Control of aggression. In B.M. Caldwell & H.N. Ricciuti (Eds.), *Review of child development research* (Vol. 3). Chicago: University of Chicago Press, 1973.

Berkowitz, P. H., Pearl H. Berkowitz. In J. M. Kauffman & C. D. Lewis (Eds.), *Teaching children with behavior disorders: Personal perspectives*. Columbus, Ohio: Charles E. Merrill, 1974.

Berkowitz, P. H. Public schools in treatment centers: An evaluation. In P. H. Berkowitz & E. P. Rothman (Eds.), *Public education for disturbed children in New York City*. Springfield, Ill.: Charles C. Thomas, 1967.

Berkowitz, P. H., & Rothman, E. P. *The disturbed child: Recognition and psychoeducational therapy in the classroom*. New York: New York University Press, 1960.

Berkowitz, P. H., & Rothman, E. P. (Eds.), *Public education for disturbed children in New York City*. Springfield, Ill.: Charles C. Thomas, 1967. (a)

Berkowitz, P. H., & Rothman, E. P. Educating disturbed children in New York City: An historical overview. In P. H. Berkowitz & E. P. Rothman (Eds.), *Public education for disturbed children in New York City*. Springfield, Ill.: Charles C. Thomas, 1967. (b)

Bernal, M. E., Duryee, J. S., Pruett, H. L., & Burns, B. J. Behavior modification and the brat syndrome. *Journal of Consulting and Clinical Psychology*, 1968, *32*, 447–455.

Bettelheim, B. *Love is not enough*. New York: Macmillan, 1950.

Bettelheim, B. The decision to fail. *The School Review*, 1961, *69*, 389–412.

Bettelheim, B. *The empty fortress*. New York: Free Press, 1967.

Bettelheim, B. Listening to children. In P. A. Gallagher & L. L. Edwards (Eds.), *Educating the emotionally disturbed: Theory to practice*. Lawrence, Kan.: University of Kansas, 1970.

Bettelheim, B., & Sylvester, E. A therapeutic milieu. *American Journal of Orthopsychiatry*, 1948, *18*, 191–206.

Bijou, S. W., & Baer, D. M. *Child development, Vol. 1: A systematic and empirical theory.* New York: Appleton-Century-Crofts (Prentice-Hall), 1961.

Biller, H. B., & Davids, A. Parent-child relations, personality development, and psychopathology. In A. Davids (Ed.), *Issues in abnormal child psychology.* Monterey, Calif.: Brooks/Cole, 1973.

Bird, B. L., Russo, D. C., & Cataldo, M. F. Considerations in the analysis and treatment of dietary effects on behavior: A case study. *Journal of Autism and Childhood Schizophrenia,* 1977, *7,* 373–382.

Blaney, P. H. Contemporary theories of depression: Critique and comparison. *Journal of Abnormal Psychology,* 1977, *86,* 203–223.

Blanton, S. The function of the mental hygiene clinic in schools and colleges. *New Republic,* 1925, *122,* 93–101.

Blatt, B. Toward an understanding of people with special needs. In J. M. Kauffman & J. S. Payne (Eds.), *Mental retardation: Introduction and personal perspectives.* Columbus, Ohio: Charles E. Merrill, 1975.

Blatt, B., Kaplan, F. *Christmas in purgatory: A photographic essay on mental retardation.* Boston: Allyn & Bacon, 1966.

Blechman, E. A. Short- and long-term results of positive homebased treatment of childhood chronic constipation and encopresis. *Child Behavior Therapy,* 1979, *1,* 237–247.

Blinder, B. J., Freeman, D. M., & Stunkard, A. J. Behavior therapy of anorexia nervosa: Effectiveness of activity as a reinforcer for weight gain. *American Journal of Psychiatry,* 1970, *126,* 1093–1098.

Bockoven, J. S. Moral treatment in American psychiatry. *Journal of Nervous and Mental Disease,* 1956, *124,* 167–194, 292–321.

Bockoven, J. S. *Moral treatment in community mental health.* New York: Springer, 1972.

Bollea, G. Acute organic psychoses of childhood. In J. G. Howells (Ed.), *Modern perspectives in international child psychiatry.* New York: Brunner/Mazel, 1969.

Bornstein, M. R., Bellack, A. S., & Hersen, M. Social-skills training for unassertive children: A multiple-baseline analysis. *Journal of Applied Behavior Analysis,* 1977, *10,* 183–195.

Bornstein, P. H., & Quevillon, R. P. The effects of a self-instructional package on overactive preschool boys. *Journal of Applied Behavior Analysis,* 1976, *9,* 179–188.

Bortner, M., & Birch, H. G. Patterns of intellectual ability in emotionally disturbed and brain-damaged children. *Journal of Special Education,* 1969, *3,* 351–369.

Bower, E. M. *Early identification of emotionally handicapped children in school* (2nd ed.). Springfield, Ill.: Charles C. Thomas, 1969.

Bower, E. M., & Lambert, N. M. *A process for in-school screening of children with emotional handicaps.* Princeton, N.J.: Educational Testing Service, 1962.

Bower, E. M., Shellhammer, T. A., & Daily, J. M. School characteristics of male adolescents who later became schizophrenic. *American Journal of Orthopsychiatry,* 1960, *30,* 712–729.

Bower, K. B. Impulsivity and academic performance in learning and behavior disordered children. (Doctoral dissertation, University of Virginia, 1975). *Dissertation Abstracts International,* 367A. (University Microfilms No. 76–1071)

Brady, J. P., & Rieger, W. Behavioral treatment of anorexia nervosa. In T. Thompson & W. S. Dockens (Eds.), *Applications of behavior modification.* New York: Academic Press, 1975.

Braud, L., Lupin, M. N., & Braud, W. G. The use of electromyographic biofeedback in the control of hyperactivity. *Journal of Leaning Disabilities,* 1975, *8,* 420–425.

Bremner, R. H. (Ed.) *Children and youth in America: A documentary history. Vol. 1, 1600–1865.* Cambridge, Mass.: Harvard University Press, 1970.

Bremner, R. H. (Ed.) *Children and youth in America: A documentary history. Vol. 2: 1866–1932.* Cambridge, Mass.: Harvard University Press, 1971.

Brigham, A. Schools in lunatic asylums. *American Journal of Insanity,* 1845, *1,* 326–340.

Brigham, A. The moral treatment of insanity. *American Journal of Insanity,* 1847, *4,* 1–15.

Brigham, A. Schools and asylums for the idiotic and imbecile. *American Journal of Insanity,* 1848, *5,* 19–33.

Brown, R. T., & Quay, L. C. Reflection-impulsivity in normal and behavior-disordered children. *Journal of Abnormal Child Psychology,* 1977, *5,* 457–462.

Bryan, D. P., & Herjanic, B. Depression and suicide in handicapped adolescents and young adults. *Exceptional Education Quarterly*, 1980, *I*(2), 57–65.

Bryan, J. H. "You will be well advised to watch what we do instead of what we say." In D. J. DePalma & J. M. Foley (Eds.), *Moral development: Current theory and research*. Hillsdale, N.J.: Lawrence Erlbaum, 1975. (a)

Bryan, J. H. Children's cooperation and helping behaviors. In E. M. Hetherington (Ed.), *Review of child development research, Vol. 5*. Chicago: University of Chicago Press, 1975. (b)

Bryan, T. S. An observational analysis of classroom behaviors of children with learning disabilities. *Journal of Learning Disabilities*, 1974, *7*, 26–34.

Buehler, R. E., Patterson, G. R., & Furniss, J. M. The reinforcement of behavior in institutional settings. *Behaviour Research and Therapy*, 1966, *4*, 157–167.

Buell, J., Stoddard, P., Harris, F. R., & Baer, D. M. Collateral social development accompanying reinforcement of outdoor play in a preschool child. *Journal of Applied Behavior Analysis*, 1968, *1*, 167–174.

Burbach, H. J. Labelling: Sociological issues. In J. M. Kauffman & D. P. Hallahan (Eds.), *Handbook of special education*. Englewood Cliffs, N.J.: Prentice-Hall, 1981.

Burke, D. Countertheoretical interventions in emotional disturbance. In W. C. Rhodes & M. L. Tracy (Eds.), *A study of child variance, Vol. 2: Interventions*. Ann Arbor, Mich.: University of Michigan, 1972.

Byasee, J., & Murrell, S. Interaction patterns in families of autistic, disturbed, and normal children. *American Journal of Orthopsychiatry*, 1975, *45*, 473–478.

Campbell, M., & Small, A. M. Chemotherapy. In B. B. Wolman (Ed.), *Handbook of treatment of mental disorders in childhood and adolescence*. Englewood Cliffs, N.J.: Prentice-Hall, 1978.

Campbell, S. B. Cognitive styles and behavior problems of clinic boys. *Journal of Abnormal Child Psychology*, 1974, *2*, 307–312.

Campbell, S. B., & Paulauskas, S. Peer relations in hyperactive children. *Journal of Child Psychology and Psychiatry*, 1979, *20*, 233–246.

Campbell, S. B., Schleifer, M., & Weiss, G. Continuities in maternal reports and child behaviors over time in hyperactive and comparison groups. *Journal of Abnormal Child Psychology*, 1978, *6*, 33–45.

Cantor, P. C. Personality characteristics found among youthful female suicide attempters. *Journal of Abnormal Psychology*, 1976, *85*, 324–329.

Cantwell, D. P., Baker, L., & Rutter, M. Families of autistic and dysphasic children. II. Mothers' speech to the children. *Journal of Autism and Childhood Schizophrenia*, 1977, *7*, 313–327.

Caplan, R. B. *Psychiatry and the community in nineteenth century America*. New York: Basic Books, 1969.

Carlson, E. T., & Dain, N. The psychotherapy that was moral treatment. *American Journal of Psychiatry*, 1960, *117*, 519–524.

Carr, E. G. Teaching autistic children to use sign language: Some clinical research issues. *Journal of Autism and Developmental Disorders*, 1979, *9*, 345–359.

Carr, E. G., Binkoff, J. A., Kologinsky, E., & Eddy, M. Acquisition of sign language by autistic children. I: Expressive labelling. *Journal of Applied Behavior Analysis*, 1978, *11*, 489–501.

Carr, E. G., Newsom, C. D., & Binkoff, J. A. Stimulus control of self-destructive behavior in a psychotic child. *Journal of Abnormal Child Psychology*, 1976, *4*, 139–153.

Castells, S., Chakrabarti, C., Winsberg, B. G., Hurwic, M., Perel, J. M., & Nyhan, W. L. Effects of L-5-hydroxytryptophan on monoamine and amino acids turnover in the Lesch-Nyhan syndrome. *Journal of Autism and Developmental Disorders*, 1979, *9*, 95–103.

Cavan, R. S. (Ed.) *Readings in juvenile delinquency* (3rd ed.). New York: Lippincott, 1975.

Cavan, R. S., & Ferdinand, T. N. *Juvenile delinquency* (3rd ed.). New York: Lippincott, 1975.

Chapin, W. *Wasted*. New York: McGraw-Hill, 1972.

Chess, S., & Thomas, A. Temperamental individuality from childhood to adolescence. *Journal of the American Academy of Child Psychiatry*, 1977, *16*, 218–226.

Churchill, D. W. The relation of infantile autism and early childhood schizophrenia to developmental language disorders of childhood. *Journal of Autism and Childhood Schizophrenia*. 1972, *2*, 182–197.

Churchill, D. W. *Language of autistic children*. New York: Wiley, 1978.

Ciminero, A. R., & Drabman, R. S. Current developments in the behavioral assessment of children. In B. B. Lahey & A. E. Kazdin (Eds.), *Advances in clinical child psychology*, Vol. 1. New York: Plenum, 1977.

Clarke-Stewart, A. K. Interactions between mothers and their young children: Characteristics and consequences. *Monographs of the Society for Research in Child Development*, 1973, *38*, Nos. 6–7, Serial No. 153.

Clausen, J. A. Family structure, socialization, and personality. In L. W. Hoffman & M. L. Hoffman (Eds.), *Review of child development research. Vol. 2*. New York: Russel Sage Foundation, 1966.

Cloward, R., & Ohlin, L. *Delinquency and opportunity: A theory of delinquent gangs*. Glencoe, Ill.: Free Press, 1960.

Cobb, J. A. Relationship of discrete classroom behavior to fourth-grade academic achievement. *Journal of Educational Psychology*, 1972, *63*, 74–80.

Cohen, A. K. *Delinquent boys*. Glencoe, Ill.: Free Press, 1955.

Cohen, H. L. Behavior modification and socially deviant youth. In C. E. Thoresen (Ed.), *Behavior modification in education*. Chicago: University of Chicago Press, 1973.

Cohen, H. L., & Filipczak, J. *A new learning environment*. San Francisco: Jossey-Bass, 1971.

Colletti, G., & Harris, S. L. Behavior modification in the home: Siblings as behavior modifiers, parents as observers. *Journal of Abnormal Child Psychology*, 1977, *5*, 21–30.

Combs, M. L., & Slaby, D. A. Social-skills training with children. In B. B. Lahey & A. E. Kazdin (Eds.). *Advances in clinical child psychology*, Vol. 1. New York: Plenum, 1977.

Conger, J. C. The treatment of encopresis by the management of social consequences. *Behavior Therapy*, 1970, *1*, 386–390.

Conners, C. K. A teacher rating scale for use in drug studies with children. *American Journal of Psychiatry*, 1969, *126*, 152–156.

Conners, C. K. Rating scales for use in drug studies in children. *Psychopharmacology Bulletin*, Special Issue, Pharmacotherapy of Children, 1973, 24–84.

Conners, C. K., & Werry, J. S. Pharmacotherapy. In H. C. Quay & J. S. Werry (Eds.). *Psychopathological disorders of childhood*. (2nd ed.). New York: Wiley, 1979.

Cook, J. W., Altman, K., Shaw, J., & Blaylock, M. Use of contingent lemon juice to eliminate public masturbation by a severely retarded boy. *Behaviour Research and Therapy*, 1978, *16*, 131–134.

Cooper, B., & Shepherd, M. Epidemiology and abnormal psychology. In H. J. Eysenck (Ed.), *Handbook of abnormal psychology*. San Diego, CA: Robert R. Knapp, 1973.

Coopersmith, S. *The antecedents of self-esteem*. San Francisco: Freeman, 1967.

Copeland, A. D. *Testbook of adolescent psychopathology and treatment*. Springfield, Ill.: Charles C. Thomas, 1974.

Copeland, R. E., Brown, R. E., & Hall, R. V. The effects of principal-implemented techniques on the behavior of pupils. *Journal of Applied Behavior Analysis*, 1974, *7*, 77–86.

Corbett, J., Harris, R., Taylor, E., & Trimble, M. Progressive disintegrative psychosis of childhood. *Journal of Child Psychology and Psychiatry*, 1977, *18*, 211–219.

Corte, H. E., Wolf, M. M., & Locke, B. J. A comparison of procedures for eliminating self-injurious behavior of retarded adolescents. *Journal of Applied Behavior Analysis*, 1971, *4*, 201–213.

Costello, C. G. A critical review of Seligman's laboratory experiments on learned helplessness and depression in humans. *Journal of Abnormal Psychology*, 1978, *87*, 21–31.

Crandall, B. F. Genetic disorders in mental retardation. *Journal of the American Academy of Child Psychiatry*, 1977, *16*, 88–108.

Cravioto, J., & DeLicardie, E. R. Environmental and learning deprivation in children with learning disabilities. In W. M. Cruickshank & D. P. Hallahan (Eds.), *Perceptual and learning disabilities in children. Vol. 2. Research and theory*. Syracuse, N.Y.: Syracuse University Press, 1975.

Cravioto, J., Gaona, C. E., & Birch, H. G. Early malnutrition and auditory-visual integration in school-age children. *Journal of Special Education*, 1967, *2*, 75–91.

Creedon, M. P. Language development in nonverbal autistic children using a simultaneous communication system. Paper presented at the meeting of the Society for Research in Child Development, Philadelphia, March, 1973.

Crissey, M. S. Mental retardation: Past, present, and future. *American Psychologist*, 1975, *30*, 800–808.

Croghan, L., & Musante, G. J. The elimination of a boy's high building phobia by in vivo desensitization and game playing. *Journal of Behavior Therapy and Experimental Psychiatry*, 1975, *6*, 87–88.

Cromwell, R. L., Blashfield, R. K., & Strauss, J. S. Criteria for classification systems. In N. Hobbs (Ed.), *Issues in the classification of children, Vol. I.* San Francisco: Jossey-Bass, 1975.

Cruickshank, W. M. The learning environment. In W. M. Cruickshank & D. P. Hallahan (Eds.), *Perceptual and learning disabilities in children. Vol. 1. Psychoeducational practices.* Syracuse, N.Y.: Syracuse University Press, 1975.

Cruickshank, W. M., Bentzen, F., Ratzeburg, F., & Tannhauser, M. A. *A teaching method for brain-injured and hyperactive children.* Syracuse, N.Y.: Syracuse University Press, 1961.

Cruickshank, W. M., Paul, J. L., & Junkala, J. B. *Misfits in the public schools.* Syracuse, N.Y.: Syracuse University Press, 1969.

Crumley, F. E. Adolescent suicide attempts. *Journal of the American Medical Association*, 1979, *241*, 2404–2407.

Csapo, M. Peer models reverse the "one bad apple spoils the barrel" theory. *Teaching Exceptional Children*, 1972, *5*(1), 20–24.

Cullinan, D., & Epstein, M. H. Administrative definitions of behavior disorders: Status and directions. Paper presented at an Advanced Institute for Trainers of Teachers of Seriously Emotionally Disturbed Children and Youth, Charlottesville, Va., Feb. 23, 1979.

Cullinan, D. A., Kauffman, J. M., & LaFleur, N. K. Modeling: Research with implications for special education. *Journal of Special Education*, 1975, *9*, 209–221.

Dain, N., & Carlson, E. T. Milieu therapy in the nineteenth century: Patient care at the Friend's Asylum, Frankford, Pennsylvania, 1817–1861. *Journal of Nervous and Mental Disease*, 1960, *131*, 277–290.

Dancer, D. D., Braukmann, C. J., Schumaker, J. B., Kirigin, K. A., Willner, A. G., & Wolf, M. M. The training and validation of behavior observation and description skills. *Behavior Modification*, 1978, *2*, 113–134.

Daniels, L. Parental treatment of hyperactivity in a child with ulcerative colitis. *Journal of Behavior Therapy and Experimental Psychiatry*, 1973, *4*, 183–186.

Davids, A. Therapeutic approaches to children in residential treatment: Changes from the mid-1950s to the mid-1970s. *American Psychologist*, 1975, *30*, 809–814.

Davids, A., & Falkof, B. B. Juvenile delinquents then and now: Comparison of findings from 1959 to 1974. *Journal of Abnormal Psychology*, 1975, *84*, 161–164.

Davidson, W. S., & Seidman, E. Studies of behavior modification and juvenile delinquency: A review, methodological critique, and social perspective. *Psychological Bulletin*, 1974, *81*, 998–1011.

Davidson, W. S., & Wolfred, T. R. Evaluation of a community based behavior modification program for prevention of delinquency: The failure of a success. *Community Mental Health Journal*, 1977, *13*, 296–306.

deCatanzaro, D. A. Self-injurious behavior: A biological analysis. *Motivation and Emotion*, 1978, *2*, 45–65.

deCatanzaro, D. A., & Baldwin, G. Effective treatment of self-injurious behavior through a forced arm exercise. *American Journal of Mental Deficiency*, 1978, *82*, 433–439.

DeGiovanni, I. S., & Epstein, N. Unbinding assertion and aggression in research and clinical practice. *Behavior Modification*, 1978, *2*, 173–192.

Deleon, G., & Mandell, W. A comparison of conditioning and psychotherapy in the treatment of functional enuresis. *Journal of Clinical Psychology*, 1966, *22*, 326–330.

Delgado, J. M. R. *Physical control of the mind: Toward a psychocivilized society.* New York: Harper, 1969.

DeMyer, M. K. The nature of neuropsychological disability in autistic children. *Journal of Autism and Childhood Schizophrenia*, 1975, *5*, 109–128.

DeMyer, M. K., Barton, S., Alpern, G. D., Kimberlin, C., Allen, J., Young, E., & Steele, R. The measured intelligence of autistic children. *Journal of Autism and Childhood Schizophrenia*, 1974, *4*, 42–60.

DeMyer, M. K., Pontius, W., Norton, J. A., Barton, S., Allen, J., & Steele, R. Parental practices and innate activity in normal, autistic, and brain-damaged infants. *Journal of Autism and Childhood Schizophrenia*, 1972, *2*, 49–66.

Dennison, G. *The lives of children.* New York: Random House, 1969.

DePalma, D. J., & Foley, J. M. (Eds.) *Moral development: Current theory and research.* Hillsdale, N.J.: Lawrence, Erlbaum, 1975.

DesLauriers, A. M. *The experience of reality in childhood schizophrenia.* New York: International Universities Press, 1962.

DesLauriers, A. M. The cognitive-affective dilemma in ealy infantile autism: The case of Clarence. *Journal of Autism and Childhood Schizophrenia,* 1978, *8,* 219–229.

DesLauriers, A. M., & Carlson, C. F. *Your child is asleep: Early infantile autism.* Homewood, Ill.: Dorsey Press, 1969.

Despert, J. L. *The emotionally disturbed child—Then and now.* New York: Brunner, 1965.

DeStefano, M. A., Gesten, E. L., & Cowen, E. L. Teachers' views of the treatability of children's school adjustment problems. *Journal of Special Education,* 1977, *11,* 275–280.

Deutsch, A. *The shame of the states.* New York: Harcourt, Brace, & World, 1948.

Devany, J., Rincover, A., & Lovaas, O. I. Teaching speech to nonverbal children. In J. M. Kauffman & D. P. Hallahan (Eds.), *Handbook of special education.* Englewood Cliffs, N.J.: Prentice-Hall, 1981.

Diener, C. I., & Dweck, C. S. An analysis of learned helplessness: Continuous changes in performance, strategy, and achievement cognitions following failure. *Journal of Personality and Social Psychology,* 1978, *36,* 451–462.

Dinitz, S., Scarpitti, F. R., & Reckless, W. C. Delinquency vulnerability: A cross group and longitudinal analysis. *American Sociological Review,* 1962, *27,* 515–517.

Dokecki, P. R., Strain, B. A., Bernal, J. J., Brown, C. S., & Robinson, M. E. Low-income and minority groups. In N. Hobbs (Ed.), *Issues in the classification of children, Vol. I.* San Francisco: Jossey-Bass, 1975.

Doleys, D. M., & Slapion, M. J. The reduction of verbal repetitions by response cost controlled by a sibling. *Journal of Behavior Therapy and Experimental Psychiatry,* 1975, *6,* 61–63.

Doll, E. A. *Vineland Social Maturity Scale* (1965 ed.). Circle Pines, Minn.: American Guidance Service, 1965.

Doll, E. A. Trends and problems in the education of the mentally retarded: 1900–1940. *American Journal of Mental Deficiency,* 1967, *72,* 175–183.

Dollard, J., Doob, L. W., Miller, N. E., Mowrer, O. H., & Sears, R. R. *Frustration and aggression.* New Haven, Conn.: Yale University Press, 1939.

Dunn, L. M. Special education for the mildly retarded—Is much of it justifiable? *Exceptional Children,* 1968, *35,* 5–22.

Dutton, G. The growth pattern of psychotic boys. *British Journal of Psychiatry,* 1964, *110,* 101–103.

Dweck, C. S., & Reppucci, D. Learned helplessness and reinforcement responsibility in children. *Journal of Personality and Social Psychology,* 1973, *25,* 109–116.

Earls, F. The fathers (not the mothers): Their importance and influence with infants and young children. *Psychiatry,* 1976, *39,* 209–226.

Easson, W. M. *The severely disturbed adolescent.* New York: International Universities Press, 1969.

Edelman, R. I. Operant conditioning treatment of encopresis. *Journal of Behavior Therapy and Experimental Psychiatry,* 1971, *2,* 71–73.

Egan, J. Asthma: Psychological treatment. In B. B. Wolman (Ed.), *Handbook of treatment of mental disorders in childhood and adolescence.* Englewood Cliffs, N.J.: Prentice-Hall, 1978.

Eggers, C. Course and prognosis of childhood schizophrenia. *Journal of Autism and Childhood Schizophrenia.* 1978, *8,* 21–36.

Eiduson, B. T., Eiduson, S., & Geller, E. Biochemistry, genetics, and the nature-nurture problem. *American Psychologist,* 1962, *119,* 342–350.

Eisenberg, L. School phobia: A study in the communication of anxieties. *American Journal of Psychiatry,* 1958, *114,* 712–718.

Eisenberg, L. Child psychiatry: The past quarter century. *American Journal of Orthopsychiatry,* 1969, *39,* 389–401.

Eisenberg, L., & Kanner, L. Early infantile autism, 1943–55. *American Journal of Orthopsychiatry,* 1969, *39,* 389–401.

Eissler, K. R. *Searchlights on delinquency.* New York: International Universities Press, 1949.

Eitzen, D. S. The effects of behavior modification on the attitudes of delinquents. *Behaviour Research and Therapy,* 1975, *13,* 295–299.

Epstein, M. H., Cullinan, D., & Sabatino, D. A. State definitions of behavior disorders. *Journal of Special Education,* 1977, *11,* 417–425.

Epstein, M. H., Hallahan, D. P., & Kauffman, J. M. Implications of the reflectivity-impulsivity dimension for special education. *Journal of Special Education,* 1975, *9,* 11–25.

Eron, L. D., Huesmann, L. R., Lefkowitz, M. M., & Walder, L. O. How learning conditions in early childhood—including mass media—relate to aggression in late adolesence. *American Journal of Orthopsychiatry,* 1974, *44,* 412–423.

Esquirol,. E. Mental maladies: A treatise on insanity. Translated by E. K. Hunt. Philadelphia: Lea & Blanchard, 1845.

Etzel, B. C., & Gewirtz, J. L. Experimental modification of caretaker-maintained high-rate operant crying in a 6- and 20-week-old infant (*Infans tyrannotearus*): Extinction of crying with reinforcement of eye contact and smiling. *Journal of Experimental Child Psychology,* 1967, *5,* 303–317.

Evans, I. M., & Nelson, R. O. Assessment of child behavior problems. In A. R. Ciminero, K. S. Calhoun, & H. E. Adams (Eds.), *Handbook of behavioral assessment.* New York: Wiley, 1977.

Evers, W. L., & Schwarz, J. C. Modifying social withdrawal in preschoolers: The effects of filmed modeling and teacher praise. *Journal of Abnormal Child Psychology,* 1973, *1,* 248–256.

Eyde, D. R., & Fink, A. H. (Eds.) Bio-physiological issues in behavioral disorders. *Behavioral Disorders,* 1979, *5,* whole No. 1.

Fagen, S. A. Psychoeducaional management and self-control. In D. Cullinan & M. H. Epstein (Eds.), *Special education for adolescents: Issues and perspectives.* Columbus, Ohio: Charles E. Merrill, 1979.

Fagen, S. A., & Long, N. J. A psychoeducational curriculum approach to teaching self-control. *Behavioral Disorders,* 1979, *4,* 68–82.

Fagen, S. A., Long, N. J., & Stevens, D. J. *Teaching children self-control.* Columbus, Ohio: Charles E. Merrill, 1975.

Farnham-Diggory, S. Self, future, and time: A developmental study of the concepts of psychotic, brain-damaged, and normal children. *Monographs of the Society for Research in Child Development,* 1966, *31* (Whole No. 103).

Fedoravicius, A. S. The patient as shaper of required parental behaior: A case study. *Journal of Behavior Therapy and Experimental Psychiatry,* 1973, *4,* 395–396.

Fenichel, C. Psychoeducational approaches for seriously disturbed children in the classroom. In P. Knoblock (Ed.), *Intervention approaches in educating emotionally disturbed children.* Syracuse, N.Y.: Syracuse University Press, 1966.

Fenichel, C. Carl Fenichel. In J. M. Kauffman & C. D. Lewis (Eds.), *Teaching children with behavior disorders: Personal perspectives.* Columbus, Ohio: Charles E. Merrill, 1974.

Fenichel, C., Freedman, A. M., & Klapper, Z. A day school for schizophrenic children. *American Journal of Orthopsychiatry,* 1960, *30,* 130–143.

Ferinden, W., & Handel, D. V. Elimination of soiling behavior in an elementary school child. *Journal of School Psychology,* 1970, *8,* 207–269.

Fernald, W. E. The history of the treatment of the feebleminded. In I. C. Barrows (Ed.), *Proceedings of the National Conference of Charities and Correction.* Boston: G. Ellis, 1893.

Ferster, C. B. Positive reinforcement and behavioral deficits of autistic children. *Child Development,* 1961, *32,* 437–456.

Ferster, C. B. The autistic child. *Psychology Today,* 1968, *2*(6), 35–37; 61.

Feshbach, S. Aggression. In P. H. Mussen (Ed.), *Carmichael's manual of child psychology, Vol. II* (3rd ed.). New York: Wiley, 1970.

Feuerstein, M., Ward, M. M., & LeBaron, S. W. M. Neuropsychological and neurophysiological assessment of children with learning and behavior problems: A critical appraisal. In B. B. Lahey & A. E. Kazdin (Eds.), *Advances in child clinical psychology,* (Vol. 2). New York: Plenum, 1979.

Finch, A. J., Pezzuti, K. A., & Nelson, W. M. Locus of control and academic achievement in emotionally disturbed children. *Journal of Consulting and Clinical Psychology,* 1975, *43,* 103.

Finch, A. J., & Spirito, A. Use of cognitive training to train cognitive processes. *Exceptional Education Quarterly*, 1980, *1*(1), 31-39.

Finegold, B. F. *Why your child is hyperactive.* New York: Random House, 1975.

Finegold, B. F. Hyperkinesis and learning disabilities linked to the ingestion of artifical food colors and flavors. *Journal of Learning Disabilities*, 1976, *9*, 551-559.

Fish, B. Neurobiologic antecedents of schizophrenia in children. *Archives of General Psychiatry*, 1977, *34*, 1297-1313.

Fixsen, D. L., Phillips, E. L., & Wolf, M. M. Achievement place: Experiments in self-government with pre-delinquents. *Journal of Applied Behavior Analysis*, 1973, *6*, 31-47.

Folstein, S., & Rutter, M. Infantile autism: A genetic study of 21 twin pairs. *Journal of Child Psychology and Psychiatry*, 1977, *18*, 297-321.

Foltz, D. Judgment withheld on DSM-III, new child classification pushed. *APA Monitor*, 1980, *11*(1), 1, 33.

Forness, S. R., & MacMillan, D. L. The origins of behavior modification with exceptional children. *Exceptional Children*, 1970, *37*, 93-99.

Forrester, R. M., Stein, Z., & Susser, M. W. A trial of conditioning therapy in nocturnal enuresis. *Developmental Medicine and Child Neurology*, 1964, *6*, 158-166.

Foster, G. G., Ysseldyke, J. E., & Reese, J. H. "I wouldn't have seen it if I hadn't believed it." *Exceptional Children*, 1975, *41*, 469-473.

Foxx, R. M., & Azrin, N. H. Restitution: A method of eliminating aggressive-disruptive behavior of retarded and brain damaged patients. *Behaviour Research and Therapy*, 1972, *10*, 15-27.

Foxx, R. M., & Azrin, N. H. The elimination of autistic self-stimulatory behavior by overcorrection. *Journal of Applied Behavior Analysis*, 1973, *6*, 1-14.

Frankel, F., & Simmons, J. Q. Self-injurious behavior in schizophrenic and retarded children. *American Journal of Mental Deficiency*, 1976, *80*, 512-522.

Freedman, D. G. The impact of behavior genetics and ethology. In H. E. Rie (Ed.), *Perspectives in child psychopathology.* Chicago: Aldine, 1971.

Freeman, R. D. Special education and the electroencephalogram: Marriage of convenience. *Journal of Special Education*, 1967, *2*, 67-74.

Freud, A. *The ego and the mechanisms of defense.* New York: International Universities Press, 1946.

Freud, A. The relation between psychoanalysis and pedagogy. In N. J. Long, W. C. Morse, & R. G. Newman (Eds.), *Conflict in the classroom.* Belmont, Calif.: Wadsworth, 1965.

Friedrich, L. K., & Stein, A. H. Aggressive and prosocial television programs and the natural behavior of preschool children. *Monographs of the Society for Research in Child Development*, 1973, *38*(4, Serial No. 151).

Friedrich, L. K., & Stein, A. H. Prosocial television and young children: The effects of verbal labeling and role playing on learning and behavior. *Child Development*, 1975, *46*, 27-38.

Frostig, M. Marianne Frostig. In J. M. Kauffman & D. P. Hallahan (Eds.), *Teaching children with learning disabilities: Personal perspectives.* Columbus, Ohio: Charles E. Merrill, 1976.

Furman, W., Rahe, D. F., & Hartup, W. W. Rehabilitation of socially withdrawn preschool children through mixed-age and same-age socialization. *Child Development*, 1979, *50*, 915-922.

Gadow, K. *Children on medication: A primer for school personnel.* Reston, VA: Council for Exceptional Children, 1979.

Garmezy, N. Children at risk: The search for the antecedents of schizophrenia. Part I. Coceptual models and research methods. *Schizophrenia Bulletin*, Issue No. 8, Spring, 1974, 14-89.

Garn, S. M. Body size and its implications. In L. W. Hoffman & M. L. Hoffman (Eds.), *Review of child development research, Vol. 2.* New York: Russel Sage Foundation, 1966.

Gast, D. L., & Nelson, C. M. Legal and ethical considerations for the use of timeout in special education settings. *Journal of Special Education*, 1977, *11*, 457-467.

Gelfand, D. M. Social withdrawal and negative emotional states: Behavior therapy. In B. B. Wolman (Ed.), *Handbook of treatment of mental disorders in childhood and adolescence.* Englewood Cliffs, N.J.: Prentice-Hall, 1978.

George, C., & Main, M. Social interactions of young abused children: Approach, avoidance, and aggression. *Child Development*, 1979, *50*, 306-318.

Gesten, E. L., Scher, K., Cowen, E. L. Judged school problems and competencies of referred children with varying family background characteristics. *Journal of Abnormal Child Psychology*, 1978, *6*, 247–255.

Gewirtz, J. L., & Boyd, E. F. Does maternal responding imply reduced infant crying? A critique of the 1972 Bell and Ainsworth report. *Child Development*, 1977, *48*, 1200–1207. (a)

Gewirtz, J. L., & Boyd, E. F. In reply to the rejoinder to our critique of the 1972 Bell and Ainsworth report. *Child Development*, 1977, *48*, 1200–1207. (b)

Giallombardo, R. (Ed.) *Juvenile delinquency: A book of readings* (3rd ed.). New York: Wiley, 1976.

Gibbons, D. C. *Delinquent behavior* (2nd ed.). Englewood Cliffs, N.J.: Prentice-Hall, 1975.

Glavin, J. P., & DeGirolamo, G. Spelling errors of withdrawn and conduct problem children. *Journal of Special Education*, 1970, *4*, 199–204.

Glidewell, J. C. The child at school. In J. G. Howells (Ed.), *Modern perspectives in international child psychiatry*. New York: Brunner/Mazel, 1969.

Glidwell, J. C., Kantor, M. B., Smith, L. M., & Stringer, L. A. Socialization and social structure in the classroom. In L. W. Hoffman & M. L. Hoffman (Eds.), *Review of child development research*, *Vol. 2*. New York: Russel Sage Foundation, 1966.

Glidewell, J. C., & Swallow, C. S. The prevalence of maladjustment in elementary schools. Report prepared for the Joint Commission on the Mental Health of Children, University of Chicago, July 26, 1968.

Glueck, S., & Glueck, E. *Unraveling juvenile delinquency*. Cambridge, Mass.: Harvard University Press, 1950.

Glueck, S., & Glueck, E. *Family environment and delinquency*. Boston: Houghton Mifflin, 1962.

Glueck, S., & Glueck, E. *Toward a typology of juvenile offenders: Implications for therapy and prevention*. New York: Grune & Stratton, 1970.

Goldiamond, I. Moral behavior: A functional analysis. *Psychology Today*, 1968, *2*(4), 31–34; 70.

Goldfarb, W. *Childhood schizophrenia*. Cambridge, Mass.: Harvard University Press, 1961.

Goldstein, H. *The social learning curriculum*. Columbus, Ohio: Charles E. Merrill, 1974.

Goldstein, H., Arkell, C., Ashcroft, S. C., Hurley, O. L., & Lilly, M. S. Schools. In N. Hobbs (Ed.), *Issues in the classification of children, Vol. II*. San Francisco: Jossey-Bass, 1975.

Goldstein, M. J., & Rodnick, E. H. The family's contribution to the etiology of schizophrenia: Current status. *Schizophrenia Bulletin*, Issue No. 14, fall, 1975, 48–63.

Goodall, K. Shapers at work. *Psychology Today*, 1972, *6*(6), 53–63; 132–138.

Goodwin, S. E., & Mahoney, M. J. Modification of aggression through modeling: An experimental probe. *Journal of Behavior Therapy and Experimental Psychiatry*, 1975, *6*, 200–202.

Gorsuch, R. L., & Butler, M. C. Initial drug abuse: A review of predisposing social psychological factors. *Psychological Bulletin*, 1976, *83*, 120–137.

Gottman, J. The effects of a modeling film on social isolation in preschool children: A methodological investigation. *Journal of Abnormal Child Psychology*, 1977, *5*, 69–78.

Gottman, J., Gonso, J., & Schuler, P. Teaching social skills to isolated children. *Journal of Abnormal Child Psychology*, 1976, *4*, 179–197.

Gourlay, N. Heredity versus environment: An integrative analysis. *Psychological Bulletin*, 1979, *86*, 596–615.

Graham, P. J. Epidemiological studies. In H.C. Quay & J.S. Werry (Eds.), *Psychopathological disorders of childhood* (2nd ed.). New York: Wiley, 1979.

Graubard, P. S. The extent of academic retardation in a residential treatment center. *Journal of Educational Research*, 1964, *58*, 78–80.

Graubard, P. S. The relationship between academic achievement and behavior dimensions. *Exceptional Children*, 1971, *37*, 755–757.

Graubard, P. S. The use of indigenous grouping as the reinforcing agent in teaching disturbed delinquents to learn. In N.J. Long, W.C. Morse, & R.G. Newman (Eds.), *Conflict in the classroom* (3rd ed.). Belmont, Calif.: Wadsworth, 1976.

Graubard, P. S., Rosenberg, H., & Miller, M. Ecological approaches to social deviancy. In B.L. Hopkins & E. Ramp (Eds.), *A new direction for education: Behavior analysis 1971*. Lawrence, Kan.: Kansas University Department of Human Development, 1971.

Green, H. *I never promised you a rosegarden*. New York: Signet, 1964.

Griffin, B. S., & Griffin, C. T. *Juvenile delinquency in perspective*. New York: Harper & Row, 1978.

Griffith, E. E., Schnelle, J. F., McNees, M. P., Bissinger, C., & Huff, T. M. Elective mutism in a first grader: The remediation of a complex behavioral problem. *Journal of Abnormal Child Psychology*, 1975, *3*, 127–134.

Griffiths, W. *Behavior difficulties of children as perceived and judged by parents, teachers, and children themselves*. Minneapolis: University of Minnesota Press, 1952.

Grob, G. N. *Mental institutions in America: Social policy to 1875*. New York: Free Press, 1973.

Gronlund, N. E. *Sociometry in the classroom*. New York: Harper, 1959.

Grosenick, J. K., & Huntze, S. L. *National needs analysis in behavior disorders: A model for a comprehensive needs analysis in behavior disorders*. Department of Special Education, University of Missouri, Columbia, MO., December, 1979.

Grossman, H. *Teaching the emotionally disturbed: A casebook*. New York: Holt, Rinehart, & Winston, 1965.

Grossman, H. *Nine rotten lousy kids*. New York: Holt, Rinehart, & Winston, 1972.

Group for the Advancement of Psychiatry, Committee on Child Psychiatry. *Psychopathological disorders in childhood: Theoretical considerations and a proposed classification*. Volume VI, Report No. 62, June, 1966.

Gump, P. V. Ecological psychology and children. In E. M. Hetherington (Ed.), *Review of child development research, Vol. 5*. Chicago: University of Chicago Press, 1975.

Gunderson, J. G., Autry, J. H., Mosher, L. R., & Buchsbaum, S. Special report: Schizophrenic, 1974. *Schizophrenic Bulletin*, Issue No. 9., Summer, 1974.

Hagen, J. W., Huntsman, N. J. Selective attention in mental retardates. *Developmental Psychology*, 1971, *5*, 151–160.

Hagen, J. W., & Kail, R. V. The role of attention in perceptual and cognitive development. In W.M. Cruickshank & D. P. Hallahan (Eds.), *Perceptual and learning disabilities in children. Vol. 2. Research and theory*. Syracuse, N. Y.: Syracuse University Press, 1975.

Hagen, J. W., Meacham, J. A., & Mesibov, G. Verbal learning, rehearsal, and short-term memory. *Cognitive Psychology*, 1970, *1*, 47–58.

Haines, T. H. State laws relating to special classes and schools for mentally handicapped children in the public schools. *Mental Hygiene*, 1925, *9*, 545–551.

Hall, R. V., & Broden, M. Behavior changes in brain-injured children through social reinforcement. *Journal of Experimental Child Psychology*, 1967, *5*, 463–479.

Hall, R. V., Panyon, M., Rabon, D., & Broden, M. Instructing beginning teachers in reinforcement procedures which improve classroom control. *Journal of Applied Behavior Analysis*, 1968, *1*, 315–322.

Hallahan, D. P. Comparative research studies on the psychological characteristics of learning disabled children. In W. M. Cruickshank & D. P. Hallahan (Eds.), *Perceptual and learning disabilities in children. Vol. 1.: Psychoeducational practices*. Syracuse, N.Y.: Syracuse University Press, 1975. (a)

Hallahan, D. P. Distractibility in the learning disabled child. In W. M. Cruickshank & D. P. Hallahan (Eds.), *Perceptual and learning disabilities in children. Vol. 2: Research and theory*. Syracuse, N. Y.: Syracuse University Press, 1975. (b)

Hallahan, D. P., & Cruickshank, W. M. *Psychoeducational foundations of learning disabilities*. Englewood Cliffs, N. J.: Prentice-Hall, 1973.

Hallahan, D. P., & Kauffman, J. M. Research on the education of distractible and hyperactive children. In W. M. Cruickshank & D. P. Hallahan (Eds.), *Perceptual and learning disabilities in children. Vol. 2: Research and theory*. Syracuse, N.Y.: Syracuse University Press, 1975.

Hallahan, D. P., & Kauffman, J. M. *Introduction to learning disabilities: A psycho-behavioral approach*. Englewood Cliffs, N. J.: Prentice-Hall, 1976.

Hallahan, D. P., & Kauffman, J. M. Categories, labels, behavioral characteristics: ED, LD, and EMR reconsidered. *Journal of Special Education*, 1977, *11*, 139–149.

Hallahan, D. P., Kauffman, J. M., & Ball, D. W. Selective attention and cognitive tempo of low achieving and high achieving sixth grade males. *Perceptual and Motor Skills*, 1973, *36*, 579–583.

Hallahan, D. P., Kauffman, J. M., & Ball, D. W. Developmental trends in recall of central and incidental auditory material. *Journal of Experimental Child Psychology*, 1974, *17*, 409–421.

Hallahan, D. P., Lloyd, J., Kosiewicz, M. M., Kauffman, J. M., & Graves, A. W. Self-monitoring of attention as a treatment for a learning disabled boy's off-task behavior. *Learning Disabilities Quarterly*, 1979, *2*, 24–32.

Hallahan, D. P., Stainback, S., Ball, D. W., & Kauffman, J. M. Selective attention in cerebral palsied and normal children. *Journal of Abnormal Child Psychology*, 1973, *1*, 280–291.

Hallsten, E. A. Adolescent anorexia nervosa treated by desensitization. *Behaviour Research and Therapy*, 1965, *3*, 87–92.

Halmi, K. A. Anorexia nervosa: Demographic and clinical features in 94 cases. *Psychosomatic Medicine*, 1974, *36*, 18–26.

Hammond, W. A. *A treatise on insanity and its medical relations.* New York: Appleton, 1891.

Hanson, D. R., & Gottesman, I. I. The genetics, if any, of infantile autism and childhood schizophrenia. *Journal of Autism and Childhood Schizophrenia*, 1976, *6*, 209–234.

Hanson, D. R., Gottesman, I. I., & Meehl, P. E. Genetic theories and the validation of psychiatric diagnoses: Implications for the study of children of schizophrenics. *Journal of Abnormal Psychology*, 1977, *86*, 575–588.

Hare, E. H. Masturbatory insanity: The history of an idea. *Journal of Mental Science*, 1962, *108*, 1–25.

Haring, N. G. *Attending and responding.* San Rafael, Calif.: Dimensions, 1968.

Haring, N. G. Social and emotional behavior disorders. In N. G. Haring (Ed.), *Behavior of exceptional children: An introduction to special education.* Columbus, Ohio: Charles E. Merrill, 1974. (a)

Haring, N. G. Norris G. Haring. In J. M. Kauffman & C. D. Lewis (Eds.), *Teaching children with behavior disorders: Personal perspectives.* Columbus, Ohio: Charles E. Merrill, 1974. (b)

Haring, N. G., Lovitt, T. C., Eaton, M. D., & Hansen, C. L. *The fourth R: Research in the classroom.* Columbus, Ohio: Charles E. Merrill, 1978.

Haring, N. G., & Phillips, E. L. *Educating emotionally disturbed children.* New York: McGraw-Hill, 1962.

Haring, N. G., & Phillips, E. L. *Analysis and modification of classroom behavior.* Englewood Cliffs, N. J.: Prentice-Hall, 1972.

Haring, N. G., & Schiefelbusch, R. L. (Eds.), *Teaching special children.* New York: McGraw-Hill, 1976.

Haring, N. G., & Whelan, R. J. Experimental methods in education and management. In N. J. Long, W. C. Morse, & R. G. Newman (Eds.), *Conflict in the classroom.* Belmont, Calif.: Wadsworth, 1965.

Harley, J. P., Matthews, C. G., & Eichman, P. Synthetic food colors and hyperactivity in children: A double-blind challenge experiment. *Pediatrics*, 1978, *62*, 975–983.

Harms, E. *Origins of modern psychiatry.* Springfield, Ill.: Charles C. Thomas, 1967.

Harrington, M. *The other America: Poverty in the United States.* New York: Macmillan, 1962.

Harris, A. An empirical test of the situation specificity/consistency of aggressive behavior. *Child Behavior Therapy*, 1979, *1*, 257–270.

Harris, F. R., Johnston, M. K., Kelly, C. S., & Wolf, M. M. Effects of positive social reinforcement on regressed crawling of a nursery school child. *Journal of Educational Psychology*, 1964, *55*, 35–41.

Harris, S. L. DSM-III—Its implications for children. *Child Behavior Therapy*, 1979, *1*, 37–46.

Hart, B. M., Allen, K. E., Buell, J. S., Harris, F. R., & Wolf, M. M. Effects of social reinforcement on operant crying. *Journal of Experimental Child Psychology*, 1964, *1*, 145–153.

Hart, B. M., Reynolds, N. J., Baer, D. M., Brawley, E. R., & Harris, F. R. Effect of contingent and noncontingent social reinforcement on the cooperative play of a preschool child. *Journal of Applied Behavior Analysis*, 1968, *1*, 73–76.

Hartshorne, H., & May, M. A. *Studies in the nature of character: Vol. 1, studies in deceit; Vol. 2, studies in self-control; Vol. 3, studies in the organizaton of character.* New York: Macmillan, 1928–1930.

Hastings, J. E., & Barkley, R. A. A review of psychophysiological research with hyperkinetic children. *Journal of Abnormal Child Psychology*, 1978, *6*, 413–447.

Hay, L. A new school channel for helping the troubled child. *American Journal of Orthopsychiatry*, 1953, *23*, 678–683.

Hayman, M. The interrelations between mental defect and mental disorder. *Journal of Mental Science*, 1939, *85*, 1183–1193.

Healy, W. *The individual delinquent*. Boston: Little, Brown, 1915. (a)

Healy, W. *Mental conflicts and misconduct*. Boston: Little, Brown, 1915. (b)

Healy, W. *Reconstructing behavior in youth: A study of problem children in foster homes*. New York: Alfred A. Knopf, 1931.

Healy, W., & Bronner, A. F. *Delinquents and criminals: Their making and unmaking*. New York: Macmillan, 1926. (Reprinted by Patterson-Smith in 1969).

Henker, B., Whalen, C., & Hinshaw, S. The attributional contexts of cognitive training. *Exceptional Education Quarterly*, 1980, *1*(1), 17–30.

Henry, N. B. (Ed.) *The education of exceptional children*. Forty-ninth yearbook of the National Society for the Study of Education, Part II. Chicago: University of Chicago Press, 1950.

Hermelin, B., & Frith, U. Psychological studies of childhood autism: Can autistic children make sense of what they see and hear? *Journal of Special Education*, 1971, *5*, 107–117.

Herson, P. F. Biasing effects of diagnostic labels and sex of pupil on teachers' views of pupils' mental health. *Journal of Educational Psychology*, 1974, *66*, 117–122.

Hertzig, M. E., Bortner, M., & Birch, H. G. Neurologic findings in children educationally designated as "brain-damaged." *American Journal of Orthopsychiatry*, 1969, *39*, 437–445.

Herzog, E., & Sudia, C. E. Children in fatherless families. In B. M. Caldwell & H. N. Ricciuti (Eds.), *Review of child development research, Vol. 3*. Chicago: University of Chicago Press, 1973.

Heston, L. L. The genetics of schizophrenic and schizoid disease. *Science*, 1970, *167*, 249.

Hetherington, E. M., & Martin, B. Family interaction. In H. C. Quay & J. S. Werry (Eds.), *Psychopathological disorders of childhood* (2nd ed.). New York: Wiley, 1979.

Hewett, F. M. A hierarchy of educational tasks for children with learning disorders. *Exceptional Children*, 1964, *31*, 207–214. (a)

Hewett, F. M. Teaching reading to an autistic boy through operant conditioning. *The Reading Teacher*, 1964, *18*, 613–618. (b)

Hewett, F. M. Teaching speech to an autistic boy through operant conditioning. *American Journal of Orthopsychiatry*, 1965, *35*, 927–936.

Hewett, F. M. A hierarchy of competencies for teachers of emotionally handicapped children. *Exceptional Children*, 1966, *33*, 7–11.

Hewett, F. M. Educational engineering with emotionally disturbed children. *Exceptional Children*, 1967, *33*, 459–471.

Hewett, F. M. *The emotionally disturbed child in the classroom*. Boston: Allyn & Bacon, 1968.

Hewett, F. M. The Madison Plan really swings. *Today's Education*, 1970 (November), *59*, 15–17.

Hewett, F. M. Introduction to the behavior modification approach to special education: A shaping procedure. In N. J. Long, W. C. Morse, & R. G. Newman (Eds.), *Conflict in the classroom* (2nd ed.). Belmont, Calif.: Wadsworth, 1971.

Hewett, F. M. Frank M. Hewett. In J. M. Kauffman & C. D. Lewis (Eds.), *Teaching children with behavior disorders: Personal perspectives*. Columbus, Ohio: Charles E. Merrill, 1974.

Hewett, F. M., & Forness, S. R. *Education of exceptional learners*. Boston: Allyn & Bacon, 1974.

Hewitt, L. E., & Jenkins, R. L. *Fundamental patterns of maladjustment: The dynamics of their origin*. Springfield: State of Illinois, 1946.

Hingtgen, J. N., & Bryson, C. Q. Recent developments in the study of early childhood psychoses: Infantile autism, childhood schizophrenia, and related disorders. *Schizophrenia Bulletin*, 1972, Issue No. 5, 8–54.

Hirschberg, J. C. The role of education in the treatment of emotionally disturbed children through planned ego development. *American Journal of Orthopsychiatry*, 1953, *23*, 684–690.

Hobbs, N. How the Re-ED plan developed. In N. J. Long, W. C. Morse, & R. G. Newman (Eds.), *Conflict in the classroom*. Belmont, Calif.: Wadsworth, 1965.

Hobbs, N. Helping the disturbed child: Psychological and ecological strategies. *American Psychologist*, 1966, *21*, 1105–1115.

Hobbs, N. Re-education, reality, and responsibility. In J. W. Carter (Ed.), *Research contributions from psychology to community health*. New York: Behavioral Publications, 1968.

Hobbs, N. Nicholas Hobbs. In J. M. Kauffman & C. D. Lewis (Eds.), *Teaching children with behavior disorders: Personal perspectives*. Columbus, Ohio: Charles E. Merrill, 1974.

Hobbs, N. (Ed.), *Issues in the classification of children, Vols I and II*. San Francisco: Jossey-Bass, 1975. (a)

Hobbs, N. *The futures of children*. San Francisco: Jossey-Bass, 1975. (b)

Hoffman, E. The treatment of deviance by the educational system: History. In W. C. Rhodes & S. Head (Eds.), *A study of child variance, Vol. 3: Service delivery systems*. Ann Arbor, Mich.: University of Michigan, 1974.

Hoffman, E. The American public school and the deviant child: The origins of their involvement. *Journal of Special Education*, 1975, *9*, 415–423.

Hoffman, M. L. Moral development. In P. H. Mussen (Ed.), *Manual of child psychology, Vol. 2*. (3rd ed.). New York: Wiley, 1970.

Hollandsworth, J. G., Jr. Differentiating assertion and aggression: Some behavioral guidelines. *Behavior Therapy*, 1977, *8*, 347–352.

Hollister, W. G., & Goldston, S. E. *Considerations for planning classes for the emotionally handicapped*. Washington, D.C.: Council for Exceptional Children, 1962.

Howe, S. G. On training and educating idiots: The second annual report to the legislature of Massachusetts. *American Journal of Insanity*, 1851, *8*, 97–118.

Howe, S. G. Third and final report of the Experimental School for Teaching and Training Idiotic Children; also, the first report of the trustees of the Massachusetts School for Idiotic and Feebleminded Youth. *American Journal of Insanity*, 1852, *9*, 20–36.

Howells, J. G. (Ed.) *Modern perspectives in international child psychiatry*. New York: Brunner/Mazel, 1971.

Hoy, E., Weiss, G., Minde, K., & Cohen, N. The hyperactive child at adolescence: Cognitive, emotional, and social functioning. *Journal of Abnormal Child Psychology*, 1978, *6*, 311–324.

Hunter, R., & Macalpine, I. (Eds.), *Three hundred years of psychiatry, 1535–1860: A history in selected English texts*. London: Oxford University Press, 1963.

Hutt, C., & Hutt, S. J. Biological studies of autism. *Journal of Special Education*, 1969, *3*, 3–14.

Hutt, C., & Ounsted, C. The biological significance of gaze aversion with particular reference to the syndrome of infantile autism. *Behavioral Science*, 1966, *11*, 346–356.

Hymes, J. L. *Teacher listen: The children speak*. New York: State Charities Aid Association, 1949.

Itard, J. M. G. *The wild boy of Aveyron*. New York: Appleton-Century-Crofts (Prentice-Hall), 1962.

Jacob, R. G., O'Leary, K. D., & Rosenblad, C. Formal and informal classroom settings: Effects on hyperactivity. *Journal of Abnormal Child Psychology*, 1978, *6*, 47–59.

Jacob, T. Family interaction in disturbed and normal families: A methodological and substantive review. *Psychological Bulletin*, 1975, *82*, 33–65.

James, H. *Children in trouble: A national scandal*. Boston: The Christian Science Publishing Society, 1969.

Jarvis, E. On the supposed increase on insanity. *American Journal of Insanity*, 1852, *8*, 333–364.

Jerslid, A. T., & Holmes, F. B. Methods of overcoming children's fears. *Journal of Psychology*, 1935, *1*, 75–104.

Johnson, C., & Katz, R. Using parents as change agents for their children: A review. *Journal of Child Psychology and Psychiatry*, 1973, *14*, 181–200.

Johnson, J. L. Special education and the inner city: A challenge for the future or another means for cooling the mark out? *Journal of Special Education*, 1969, *3*, 241–251.

Johnson, J. L. Croton-on-campus: Experiment in the use of the behavioral sciences to educate black ghetto children. In N.J. Long, W.C. Morse, & R.G. Newman (Eds.), *Conflict in the classroom* (2nd ed.). Belmont, Calif.: Wadsworth, 1971.

Johnson, S. B., & Melamed, B. G. The assessment and treatment of children's fears. In B. B. Lahey & A. E. Kazdin (Eds.), *Advances in clinical child psychology*, Vol. 2. New York: Plenum, 1979.

Johnson, W. L., & Baumeister, A. A. Self-injurious behavior: A review and analysis of methodological details of published studies. *Behavior Modification*, 1978, *2*, 465–487.

Jukovic, G. J., & Prentice, N. M. Relation of moral and cognitive development to dimensions of juvenile delinquency. *Journal of Abnormal Psychology*, 1977, *86*, 414–420.

Kagan, J. Impulsive and refelctive children. In J. Krumboltz (Ed.), *Learning and the educational process*. Chicago: Rand McNally, 1965.

Kagan, J., Rosman, B., Day, D., Albert, J., & Phillips, W. Information processing in the child: Significance of analytic and reflective attitudes. *Psychological Monographs*, 1964, *78* (Whole No. 578).

Kandel, H. J., Ayllon, T., & Rosenbaum, M. S.Flooding or systematic exposure in the treatment of extreme social withdrawal in children. *Journal of Behavior Therapy and Experimental Psychiatry*, 1977, *8*, 75–81.

Kanfer, F. H., & Grimm, L. G. Behavioral analysis: Selecting target behaviors in the interview. *Behavior Modification*, 1977, *1*, 7–28.

Kanner, L. Autistic disturbances of affective contact. *Nervous Child*, 1943, *2*, 217–250.

Kanner, L. *Child psychiatry*. Springfield, Ill.: Charles C. Thomas, 1957.

Kanner, L. Child psychiatry: Retrospect and prospect. *American Journal of Psychiatry*, 1960, 117, 15–22.

Kanner, L. Emotionally disturbed children: A historical review. *Child Development*, 1962, *33*, 97–102.

Kanner, L. *History of the care and treatment of the mentally retarded*. Springfield, Ill.: Charles C. Thomas, 1964.

Kanner, L. The birth of early infantile autism. *Journal of Autism and Childhood Schizophrenia*, 1973, *3*, 93–95. (a)

Kanner, L. Historical perspective on development deviations. *Journal of Autism and Childhood Schizophrenia*, 1973, *3*, 187–198. (b)

Kanner, L. *Childhood psychosis: Initial studies and new insights*. Washington, D.C.: V.H. Winston, 1973. (c)

Kanner, L., Rodriguez, A., & Ashenden, B. How far can autistic children go in matters of social adaptation? *Journal of Autism and Childhood Schizophrenia*, 1972, *2*, 9–33.

Kaplan, B. (Ed.) *The inner world of mental illness*. New York: Harper & Row, 1964.

Kauffman, J. M. Conclusion: Issues. In J. M. Kauffman & C. D. Lewis (Eds.), *Teaching children with behavior disorders: Personal perspectives*. Columbus, Ohio: Charles E. Merrill, 1974. (a)

Kauffman, J. M. Severely emotionally disturbed. In N. G. Haring (Ed.), *Behavior of exceptional children: An introduction to special education*. Columbus, Ohio: Charles E. Merrill, 1974. (b)

Kauffman, J. M. Nineteenth century views of children's behavior disorders: Historical contributions and continuing issues. *Journal of Special Education*, 1976, *10*, 335–349.

Kauffman, J. M. An historical perspective on disordered behavior and an alternative conceptualization of exceptionality. Paper presented at an Advanced Institute for Trainers of Teachers of Seriously Emotionally Disturbed Children and Youth, Charlottesville, Va., Feb. 23, 1979.

Kauffman, J. M. Where special education for disturbed children is going: A personal view. *Exceptional Children*, 1980, *48*, 522–527.

Kauffman, J. M. Historical trends and contemporary issues in special education in the United States. In J. M. Kauffman & D. P. Hallahan (Eds.), *Handbook of special education*. Englewood Cliffs, N. J.: Prentice-Hall, 1981.

Kauffman, J. M., Boland, J., Hopkins, N., & Birnbrauer, J. S. *Managing and teaching the severely disturbed and retarded: A guide for teachers*. Columbus, Ohio: Special Press, 1980.

Kauffman, J. M., Cullinan, D. A., Scranton, T. R., & Wallace, G. An inexpensive device for programming ratio reinforcement. *Psychological Record*, 1972, *22*, 543–544.

Kauffman, J. M., Epstein, M. H., & Chlebnikow, B. Emotionally disturbed boys' work for self and others. *Child Study Journal*, 1977, *7*, 179–188.

Kauffman, J. M., & Hallahan, D. P. Control of rough physical behavior using novel contingencies and directive teaching. *Perceptual and Motor Skills*, 1973, *36*, 1225–1226.

Kauffman, J. M., & Hallahan, D. P. Learning disability and hyperactivity (with comments on minimal brain dysfunction). In B. B. Lahey & A. E. Kazdin (Eds.), *Advances in clinical child psychology*. New York: Plenum, 1979.

Kauffman, J. M., & Kneedler, R. D. Behavior disorders. In J. M. Kauffman & D. P. Hallahan (Eds.), *Handbook of special education*. Englewood Cliffs, N. J.: Prentice-Hall, 1981.

Kauffman, J. M., & Lewis, C. D. (Eds.), *Teaching children with behavior disorders: Personal perspectives*. Columbus, Ohio: Charles E. Merrill, 1974.

Kazdin, A. E. Assessing the clinical or applied importance of behavior change through social validation. *Behavior Modification*, 1977, *1*, 427–452.

Kazdin, A. E. *History of behavior modification: Experimental foundations of contemporary research.* Baltimore: University Park Press, 1978.

Kazdin, A. E. *Behavior modification in applied settings* (Rev. ed.). Homewood, Ill.: Dorsey Press, 1980.

Keasy, C. B. Implicators of cognitive development for moral reasoning. In D. J. DePalma & J. M. Foley (Eds.), *Moral development: Current theory and research.* Hillsdale, N. J.: Lawrence Erlbaum, 1975.

Keller, B. B., & Bell, R. Q. Child effects on adult's method of eliciting altruistic behavior. *Child Development*, 1979, *50*, 1004–1009.

Keller, M. F., & Carlson, P. M. The use of symbolic modeling to promote social skills in preschool children with low levels of social responsiveness. *Child Development*, 1974, *45*, 912–919.

Kellerman, J. Behavioral treatment of a boy with 47,XYY karyotype. *Journal of Nervous and Mental Disease*, 1977, *165*, 67–71. (a)

Kellerman, J. Anorexia nervosa: The efficacy of behavior therapy. *Journal of Behavior Therapy and Experimental Psychiatry*, 1977, *8*, 387–390. (b)

Kendall, P. C., & Finch, A. J. A cognitive-behavioral treatment for impulsivity: A group comparison study. *Journal of Consulting and Clinical Psychology*, 1978, *46*, 110–118.

Kendall, R., Hall, D., Hailey, A., & Babigan, H. The epidemiology of anorexia nervosa. *Psychological Medicine*, 1973, *3*, 200–203.

Kendon, A. Some functions of gaze-direction during social interaction. *Acta Psychologica*, 1967, *26*, 1–47.

Kennedy, W. A. School phobia: Rapid treatment of fifty cases. *Journal of Abnormal Psychology*, 1965, *70*, 285–289.

Keogh, B. K. Hyperactivity and learning disorders: Review and speculation. *Exceptional Children*, 1971, *38*, 101–109.

Keogh, B. K., & Becker, L. D. Early detection of learning problems: Questions, cautions, and guidelines. *Exceptional Children*, 1973, *40*, 5–11.

Kety, S. S. It's not all in your head. *Saturday Review*, Feb. 21, 1976, 28–32.

Kety, S. S. Disorders of the human brain. *Scientific American*, 1979, *241* (3), 202–214.

Key, E. *The century of the child.* New York: Putnam, 1909.

Kirby, F. D., & Shields, F. Modification of arithmetic response rate and attending behavior in a seventh-grade student. *Journal of Applied Behavior Analysis*, 1972, *5*, 79–84.

Kirk, S. A. *Educating exceptional children* (2nd ed.). Boston: Houghton-Mifflin, 1972.

Kirk, W. J. Juvenile justice and delinquency. *Phi Delta Kappan*, 1976, *57*, 395–398.

Kirkland, K. D., & Thelen, M. H. Uses of modeling in child treatment. In B. B. Lahey & A. E. Kazdin (Eds.), *Advances in clinical child psychology*, Vol. 1. New York: Plenum, 1977.

Kitano, H. L. Refusals and illegibilities in the spelling errors of maladjusted children. *Journal of Educational Psychology*, 1959, *50*, 129–131.

Kittrie, N. N. *The right to be different: Deviance and enforced therapy.* Baltimore: The Johns Hopkins Press, 1971.

Knapczyk, D. R. Diet control in the management of behavior disorders. *Behavioral Disorders*, 1979, *5*, 2–9.

Kneedler, R. D. The use of cognitive training to change social behaviors. *Exceptional Education Quarterly*, 1980, *1* (1), 65–73.

Knoblock, P. (Ed.) *Educational programming for emotionally disturbed children: The decade ahead.* Syracuse, N. Y.: Syracuse University Press, 1965.

Knoblock, P. (Ed.) *Intervention approaches in educating emotionally disturbed children.* Syracuse, N. Y.: Syracuse University Press, 1966.

Knoblock, P. A new humanism for special education: The concept of the open classroom for emotionally disturbed children. In P. A. Gallagher & L. L. Edwards (Eds.), *Educating the emotionally disturbed: Theory to practice.* Lawrence, Kan.: University of Kansas, 1970.

Knoblock, P. Open education for emotionally disturbed children. *Exceptional Children.* 1973, *39*, 358–365.

Knoblock, P. Educational alternatives for adolescents labeled emotionally disturbed. In D. Cullinan & M. H. Epstein (Eds.), *Special education for adolescents: Issues and perspectives.* Columbus, Ohio: Charles E. Merrill, 1979.

Knoblock, P., & Goldstein, A. *The lonely teacher.* Boston: Allyn & Bacon, 1971.

Knoblock, P., & Johnson, J. L. (Eds.) *The teaching-learning process in educating emotionally disturbed children.* Syracuse, N.Y.: Syracuse University Press, 1967.

Koegel, R. L., & Covert, A. The relationship of self-stimulation to learning in autistic children. *Journal of Applied Behavior Analysis,* 1972, *5,* 381–387.

Koegel, R. L., Firestone, P. B., Kramme, K. W., & Dunlap, G. Increasing spontaneous play by suppressing self-stimulation in autistic children. *Journal of Applied Behavior Analysis,* 1974, *7,* 521–528.

Koegel, R. L., & Rincover, A. Treatment of psychotic children in a classroom environment: 1. Learning in a large group. *Journal of Applied Behavior Analysis,* 1974, *7,* 45–59.

Koegel, R. L., & Wilhelm, H. Selective responding to multiple visual cues by autistic children. *Journal of Experimental Child Psychology,* 1973, *15,* 442–453.

Kohl, H. *The open classroom.* New York: Vintage, 1970.

Kohlberg, L. Development of moral character and moral ideology. In M. L. Hoffman & L. W. Hoffman (Eds.), *Review of child development research, Vol. 1.* New York: Russel Sage Foundation, 1964.

Kohlberg, L. Education for justice: A modern statement of the Platonic view. In *Moral education: Five lectures.* Cambridge, Mass.: Harvard University Press, 1970.

Kolstoe, O. P. Oliver P. Kolstoe: Secondary programs. In J. M. Kauffman & D. P. Hallahan (Eds.), *Mental retardation: Introduction and personal perspectives.* Columbus, Ohio: Charles E. Merrill, 1975.

Kolvin, I. "Aversive imagery" treatment in adolescents. *Behaviour Research and Therapy,* 1967, *5,* 245–248.

Kolvin, I. Studies of childhood psychoses: I. Diagnostic criteria and classification. *British Journal of Psychiatry,* 1971, *118,* 381–384.

Kondas, O. Reduction of examination anxiety and "stage fright" by group desensitization and relaxation. *Behaviour Research and Therapy,* 1967, *5,* 275–281.

Konstantareas, M. M., Webster, C. D., & Oxman, J. Manual language acquisition and its influence on other areas of functioning in four autistic and autistic-like children. *Journal of Child Psychology and Psychiatry,* 1979, *20,* 337–350.

Kornberg, L. *A class for disturbed children: A case study and its meaning for education.* New York: Teachers College Press, 1955.

Kornetsky, C. Minimal brain dysfunction and drugs. In W. M. Cruickshank & D. P. Hallahan (Eds.), *Perceptual and learning disabilities in children: Vol. 2. Research and theory.* Syracuse, N.Y.: Syracuse University Press, 1975.

Koupernik, C., MacKeith, R., & Francis-Williams, J. Neurological correlates of motor and perceptual development. In W. M. Cruickshank & D. P. Hallahan (Eds.), *Perceptual and learning disabilities in children. Vol. 2. Research and theory.* Syracuse, N.Y.: Syracuse University Press, 1975.

Kozloff, M. A. *Reaching the autistic child: A parent training program.* Champaign, Ill.: Research Press, 1973.

Kozol, J. *Death at an early age.* New York: Bantam, 1967.

Kozol, J. *Free schools.* Boston: Houghton Mifflin, 1972.

Kratochwill, T. R., Brody, G. H., & Piersel, W. C. Elective mutism in children. In B. B. Lahey & A. E. Kazdin (Eds.), *Advances in clinical child psychology,* Vol. 2. New York: Plenum, 1979.

Krugman, M. (chairman) Symposium, 1953: The education of emotionally disturbed children. *American Journal of Orthopsychiatry,* 1953, *23,* 667–731.

Kubany, E. S., Weiss, L. E., & Sloggett, B. B. The good behavior clock: A reinforcement/time-out procedure for reducing disruptive classroom behavior. *Journal of Behavior Therapy and Experimental Psychiatry,* 1971, *2,* 173–179.

Kurtines, W., & Grief, E. B. The development of moral thought: Review and evaluation of Kohlberg's approach. *Psychological Bulletin,* 1974, *81,* 453–470.

Lahey, B. B., McNees, M. P., & McNees, M. C. Control of an obscene "verbal tic" through timeout in an elementary school classroom. *Journal of Applied Behavior Analysis,* 1973, *6,* 101–104.

Lal, H., & Lindsley, O. R. Therapy of chronic constipation in a young child by rearranging social contingencies. *Behavior Research and Therapy*, 1968, *6*, 484–485.

Lamb, M. E. Father-infant and mother-infant interaction in the first year of life. *Child Development*, 1977, *48*, 167–181.

Lane, H. *The wild boy of Aveyron*. Cambridge, Mass.: Harvard University Press, 1976.

Lazarus, A. A., & Abramovitz, A. The use of "emotive imagery" in the treatment of children's phobias. *Journal of Mental Science*, 1962, *108*, 191–195.

Lazarus, A. A., Davison, G. C., & Polefka, D. A. Classical and operant factors in the treatment of a school phobia. *Journal of Abnormal Psychology*, 1965, *70*, 225–229.

Ledwidge, B. Cognitive-behavior modification: A step in the wrong direction? *Psychological Bulletin*, 1978, *85*, 353–375.

Lee, B. Curriculum design: The re-education approach. In N. J. Long, W. C. Morse, & R. G. Newman (Eds.), *Conflict in the classroom* (2nd ed.). Belmont, Calif.: Wadsworth, 1971.

Lefkowitz, M. M., Eron, L. D., Walder, L. O., & Huesmann, L. R. *Growing up to be violent: A longitudinal study of the development of aggression*. New York: Pergamon, 1977.

Leitenberg, H. (Ed.) *Handbook of behavior modification and behavior therapy*. Englewood Cliffs, N.J.: Prentice-Hall, 1976.

Leitenberg, H., Agras, W. S., & Thompson, L. E. A sequential analysis of the effect of selective positive reinforcement in modifying anorexia nervosa. *Behaviour Research and Therapy*, 1968, *6*, 211–218.

Leizer, J. I., & Rogers, R. W. Effects of method of discipline, timing of punishment, and timing of test on resistance to temptation. *Child Development*, 1974, *45*, 790–793.

Lennox, C., Callias, M., & Rutter, M. Cognitive characteristics of parents of autistic children. *Journal of Autism and Childhood Schizophrenia*, 1977, *7*, 243–261.

Lent, J. R. Teaching daily living skills. In J. M. Kauffman & J. S. Payne (Eds.), *Mental retardation: Introduction and personal perspectives*. Columbus, Ohio: Charles E. Merrill, 1975.

Lent, J. R., & McLean, B. M. The trainable retarded: The technology of teaching. In N. G. Haring & R. L. Schiefelbusch (Eds.), *Teaching special children*. New York: McGraw-Hill, 1976.

Leonard, G. *Education and ecstasy*. New York: Delacorte, 1968.

Levental, T., & Sills, M. Self-image in school phobia. *American Journal of Orthopsychiatry*, 1964, *34*, 685–695.

Levin, H. M., Guthrie, J. W., Kleindorfer, G. B., & Stout, R. T. School achievement and post-school success: a review. *Review of Educational Research*, 1971, *41*, 1–16.

Levine, M. Psychological testing of children. In L. W. Hoffman & M. L. Hoffman (Eds.), *Review of child development research*, Vol. 2. New York: Russel Sage Foundation, 1966.

Lewis, C. D. Introduction: Landmarks. In J. M. Kauffman & C. D. Lewis (Eds.), *Teaching children with behavior disorders: Personal perspectives*. Columbus, Ohio: Charles E. Merrill, 1974.

Lewis, M. The development of attention and perception in the infant and young child. In W. M. Cruickshank & D. P. Hallahan (Eds.), *Perceptual and learning disabilities in children. Vol. 2. Research and theory*. Syracuse, N.Y.: Syracuse University Press, 1975.

Linton, T. E. The European educateur program for disturbed children. *American Journal of Orthopsychiatry*, 1969, *39*, 125–133.

Linton, T. E. The European educateur model: An alternative and effective approach to the mental health of children. *Journal of Special Education*, 1970, *3*, 319–327.

Lippitt, R., & Gold, M. Classroom social structure as a mental health problem. *Journal of Social Issues*, 1959, *15*, 40–58.

Lipton, E. L., Steinschneider, A., & Richmond, J. B. Psychophysiological disorders in children. In L. W. Hoffman & M. L. Hoffman (Eds.), *Review of child development research, Vol. 2*. New York: Russel Sage Foundation, 1966.

Lloyd, J. Academic instruction and cognitive-behavior modification: The need for attack strategy training. *Exceptional Education Quarterly*, 1980, *1*(1), 53–63.

Lobitz, C. W., & Johnson, S. M. Parental manipulation of the behavior of normal and deviant children. *Child Development*, 1975, *46*, 719–726.

Loney, J. The intellectual functioning of hyperactive elementary school boys: A cross-sectional investigation. *American Journal of Orthopsychiatry*, 1974, *44*, 754–762.

Long, N. J. Nicholas J. Long. In J. M. Kauffman & C. D. Lewis (Eds.), *Teaching children with behavior disorders: Personal perspectives.* Columbus, Ohio: Charles E. Merrill, 1974.

Long, N. J., Morse, W. C., & Newman, R. G. (Eds.) *Conflict in the classroom.* Belmont, Calif.: Wadsworth, 1965. Second edition, 1971. Third edition, 1976. Fourth edition, 1979.

Long, N.J., & Newman, R. G. Managing surface behavior of children in school. In N. J. Long, W. C. Morse, & R. G. Newman (Eds.), *Conflict in the classroom.* Belmont, Calif.: Wadsworth, 1965.

Lovaas, O. I. A program for the establishment of speech in psychotic children. In J. K. Wing (Ed.), *Early childhood autism: Clinical, educational, and social aspects.* New York: Pergamon, 1966.

Lovaas, O. I. A behavior therapy approach to the treatment of childhood schizophrenia. In J. P. Hill (Ed.), *Minnesota symposia on child psychology.* Minneapolis: University of Minnesota Press, 1967.

Lovaas, O. I. *Behavior modification: Teaching language to psychotic children,* 45 min., 16 mm sound, color film. New York: Appleton-Century-Crofts (Prentice-Hall), 1969.

Lovaas, O. I. *The autistic child: Language development through behavior modification.* New York: Irvington, 1977.

Lovaas, O. I. Contrasting illness and behavioral models for the treatment of autistic children: A historical perspective. *Journal of Autism and Developmental Disorders,* 1979, *9,* 315–323.

Lovaas, O. I., Freitag, G., Gold, V. J., & Kassorla, I. C. Experimental studies in childhood schizophrenia: Analysis of self-destructive behavior. *Journal of Experimental Child Psychology,* 1965, *2,* 67–81.

Lovaas, O. I., & Koegel, R. L. Behavior therapy with autistic children. In C. Thoresen (Ed.), *Behavior modification in education.* Chicago: University of Chicago Press, 1973.

Lovaas, O. I., Koegel, R. L., & Schriebman, L. Stimulus overselectivity in autism: A review of research. *Psychological Bulletin,* 1979, *86,* 1236–1254.

Lovaas, O. I., Koegel, R. L., Simmons, J. Q., & Long, J. S. Some generalizations and follow-up measures on autistic children in behavior therapy. *Journal of Applied Behavior Analysis,* 1973, *6,* 131–166.

Lovaas, O. I., Schaeffer, B., & Simmons, J. Q. Building social behavior in autistic children by use of electric shock. *Journal of Experimental Research in Personality,* 1965, *1,* 99–109.

Lovaas, O. I., & Simmons, J. Q. Manipulation of self-destruction in three retarded children. *Journal of Applied Behavior Analysis,* 1969, *2,* 143–157.

Lovaas, O. I., Young, D. B., & Newsom, C. D. Childhood psychosis: Behavioral treatment. In B. B. Wolman (Ed.), *Handbook of treatment of mental disorders in childhood and adolescence.* Englewood Cliffs, N.J.: Prentice-Hall, 1978.

Love, L. R., & Kaswan, J. W. *Troubled children: Their families, schools, and treatments.* New York: Wiley, 1974.

Lovibond, S. H. The mechanism of conditioning treatment of enuresis. *Behaviour Research and Therapy,* 1963, *1,* 17–21.

Lovibond, S. H. *Conditioning and enuresis.* New York: Pergamon, 1964.

Lovitt, T. C. *In spite of my resistance—I've learned from children.* Columbus, Ohio: Charles E. Merrill, 1977.

Lovitt, T. C., & Curtiss, K. A. Effects of manipulating an antecedent event on mathematics response rate. *Journal of Applied Behavior Analysis,* 1968, *1,* 329–333.

Lovitt, T. C., & Smith, J. O. Effects of instructions on an individual's verbal behavior. *Exceptional Children,* 1972, *38,* 685–693.

Lubar, J. F., & Shouse, M. N. Use of biofeedback in the treatment of seizure disorders and hyperactivity. In B. B. Lahey & A. E. Kazdin (Eds.), *Advances in clinical child psychology,* Vol. 1. New York: Plenum, 1977.

Lyons, D. F., & Powers, V. Follow-up study of elementary school children exempted from Los Angeles City Schools during 1960–1961. *Exceptional Children,* 1963, *30,* 155–162.

McCaffrey, I., & Cumming, J. Persistence of emotional disturbances reported among second- and fourth-grade children. In H. Dupont (Ed.) *Educating emotionally disturbed children: Readings.* New York: Holt, Rinehart, & Winston, 1969.

McCarthy, J. M., & Paraskevopoulos, J. Behavior patterns of learning disabled, emotionally disturbed, and average children. *Exceptional Children,* 1969, *36,* 69–74.

McClearn, G. E. Genetics and behavior development. In M. L. Hoffman & L. W. Hoffman (Eds.), *Review of child development research, Vol. 1.* New York: Russel Sage Foundation, 1964.

McClung, M. S. Lawyers, courts, and educational policy: The real case of minimal competency testing —A response to Getz and Glass. *High School Journal*, 1979, *62*, 243–251.

McCord, W., McCord, J., & Zola, I. K. *Origins of crime.* New York: Columbia University Press, 1959.

McKinney, J. D., & Haskins, R. Cognitive training and the development of problem solving strategies. *Exceptional Education Quarterly*, 1980, *1*(1), 41–51.

McKinney, J. D., Mason, J., Perkerson, K., & Clifford, M. Relationship between classroom behavior and academic achievement. *Journal of Educaional Psychology*, 1975, *67*, 198–203.

McMahon, R. C. Genetic etiology in the hyperactive child syndrome: A critical review. *American Journal of Orthopsychiatry*, 1980, *50*, 145–150.

Maccoby, E. E. Selective auditory attention in children. In L. P. Lippsitt & C. C. Spiker (Eds.), *Advances in child development and behavior.* New York: Academic Press, 1967.

MacDonald, W. S., Gallimore, R., & MacDonald, G. Contingency counseling by school personnel: An economical model of intervention. *Journal of Applied Behavior Analysis*, 1970, *3*, 175–182.

Macfarlane, J., Allen, L., & Honzik, M. *A developmental study of the behavior problems of normal children between 21 months and 14 years.* Berkeley: University of California Press, 1955.

Mackie, R. P., Kvaraceus, W. C., & Williams, H. M. *Teachers of children who are socially and emotionally maladjusted.* Washington, D. C.: Office of Education, U. S. Department of Health, Education and Welfare, 1957.

MacMillan, D. L., Forness, S. R., & Trumbull, B. M. The role of punishment in the classroom. *Exceptional Children*, 1973, *40*, 85–96.

MacMillan, M. B. Extra-scientific influences in the history of childhood psychopathology. *American Journal of Psychiatry*, 1960, *116*, 1091–1096.

Maes, W. R. The identification of emotionally disturbed elementary school children. *Exceptional Children*, 1966, *32*, 607–609.

Magliocca, L. A., & Stephens, T. M. Child identification or child inventory? A critique of the federal design of child identification systems implemented under P.L. 94–142. *Journal of Special Education*, 1980, *14*, 23–36.

Mahler, M. S. On child psychosis and schizophrenia. *Psychoanalytic Study of the Child*, 1952, *7*, 286–305.

Mahoney, K., Van Wagenen, R. K., & Meyerson, L. Toilet training of normal and retarded children. *Journal of Applied Behavior Analysis*, 1971, *4*, 173–181.

Mahoney, M. J. *Cognition and behavior modification.* Cambridge, Mass.: Ballinger, 1974.

Mahoney, M. J., & Kazdin, A. E. Cognitive-behavior modification: Misconceptions and premature evacuation. *Psychological Bulletin*, 1979, *86*, 1044–1049.

Maloney, D. M., Fixsen, D. C., & Maloney, K. B. Antisocial behavior: Behavior modification. In B. B. Wolman (Ed.), *Handbook of treatment of mental disorders in childhood and adolescence.* Englewood Cliffs, N. J.: Prentice-Hall, 1978.

Mann, L. *On the trail of process: A historical perspective on cognitive processes and their training.* New York: Grune & Stratton, 1979.

Marholin, D., Plienis, A. J., Harris, S. D., & Marholin, B. L. Mobilization of the community through a behavioral approach: A school program for adjudicated females. *Criminal Justice and Behavior*, 1975, *2*, 130–145.

Marlowe, R. H., Madsen, C. H., Bowen, C. E., Reardon, R. C., & Logue, P. E. Severe classroom behavior problems: Teachers or counsellors. *Journal of Applied Behavior Analysis*, 1978, *11*, 53–66.

Martin, B. Parent-child relations. In F. D. Horowitz (Ed.), *Review of child development research, Vol. 4.* Chicago: University of Chicago Press, 1975.

Martin, E. W. Individualism and behaviorism as future trends in educating handicapped children. *Exceptional Children*, 1972, *38*, 517–525.

Martin, G. L., & Powers, R. B. Attention span: An operant conditioning analysis. *Exceptional Children*, 1967, *33*, 565–570.

Martin, R. Legal issues in special education. In D. Cullinan & M. H. Epstein (Eds.), *Special education for adolescents: Issues and perspectives.* Columbus, Ohio: Charles E. Merrill, 1979.

Martin, R. Legal issues in assessment. *Exceptional Education Quarterly*, 1980, *1*(3), 13–19.

Maslow, A. *Toward a psychology of being.* New York: Van Nostrand, 1962.

Maslow, A. Some educational implications of the humanistic psychologies. *Harvard Educational Review*, 1968, *38*, 385–696.

Maudsley, H. *The pathology of the mind.* New York: Appleton, 1880.

Maurer, A. Peek-a-boo: An entry into the world of the autistic child. *Journal of Special Education*, 1969, *3*, 309–312.

Mayhew, G., & Harris, F. Decreasing self-injurious behavior: Punishment with citric acid and reinforcement of alternative behavior. *Behavior Modification*, 1979, *3*, 322–336.

Mayo, T. *Elements of the pathology of the human mind.* Philadelphia: A. Waldie, 1839.

Meichenbaum, D. *Cognitive-behavior modification: An integrative approach.* New York: Plenum, 1977.

Meichenbaum, D. Teaching children self-control. In B.B. Lahey & A.E. Kazdin (Eds.), *Advances in clinical child psychology*, Vol. 2. New York: Plenum, 1979.

Meichenbaum, D. Cognitive-behavior modification: A promise yet unfulfilled. *Exceptional Education Quarterly*, 1980, *1*(1), 83–88.

Meichenbaum, D. H., Bowers, K. S., & Ross, R. R. A behavioral analysis of teacher expectancy effect. *Journal of Personality and Social Psychology*, 1969, *13*, 306–316.

Meichenbaum, D. H., & Goodman, J. Reflection-impulsivity and verbal control of motor behavior. *Child Development*, 1969, *40*, 785–797.

Meichenbaum, D. H., & Goodman, J. Training impulsive children to talk to themselves. *Journal of Abnormal Psychology*, 1971, *77*, 115–126.

Menninger, K. *The vital balance.* New York: Viking Press, 1963.

Menolascino, F. J. Primitive, atypical, and abnormal-psychotic behavior in institutionalized mentally retarded children. *Journal of Autism and Childhood Schizophrenia*, 1972, *3*, 1, 49–64.

Messer, S. B., & Brodzinsky, D. M. The relation of conceptual tempo to aggression and its control. *Child Development*, 1979, *50*, 758–766.

Miller, W. B. Lower class culture as a generating milieu of gang delinquency. *Journal of Social Issues*, 1958, *14*, 5–19.

Minde, K., Lewin, D., Weiss, G., Lavigueur, H., Douglas, V., & Sykes, E.   The hyperactive child in elementary school: A 5 year, controlled, followup. *Exceptional Children*, 1971, *38*, 215–221.

Mischel, W.   Toward a cognitive social learning reconceptualization of personality. *Psychological Review*, 1973, *80*, 252–283.

Mischel, W. Introduction to personality (2nd ed.). New York: Holt, Rinehart, & Winston, 1976.

Mishler, E. G., & Waxler, N. E. *Interaction in families: An experimental study of family processes in schizophrenia.* New York: Wiley, 1968.

Money, J. Behavior genetics: Principles, methods, and examples from XO, XXY, and XYY syndromes. *Seminars in Psychiatry*, 1970, *2*, 11–29.

Montagu, M. F. A. (Ed.) *Man and aggression.* New York: Oxford University Press, 1968.

Montenegro, H. Severe separation anxiety in two preschool children: Successfully treated by reciprocal inhibition. *Journal of Child Psychology and Psychiatry*, 1968, *9*, 93–103.

Moore, D. R., Chamberlain, P., & Mukai, L. H. Children at risk for delinquency: A follow-up comparison of aggressive children and children who steal. *Journal of Abnormal Child Psychology*, 1979, *7*, 345–355.

Morena, D. A., & Litrownik, A. J. Self-concept in educable mentally retarded and emotionally handicapped children: Relationship between behavioral and self-report indices and an attempt at modification. *Journal of Abnormal Child Psychology*, 1974, *2*, 281–292.

Morse, W. C. The development of a mental hygiene milieu in a camp program for disturbed boys. *American Journal of Orthopsychiatry*, 1953, *23*, 826–833.

Morse, W. C. Intervention techniques for the classroom teacher. In P. Knoblock (Ed.), *Educational programming for emotionally disturbed children: The decade ahead.* Syracuse, N.Y.: Syracuse University, 1965. (a)

Morse, W. C., The crisis teacher. In N. J. Long, W. C. Morse, & R. G. Newman (Eds.), *Conflict in the classroom.* Belmont, Calif.: Wadsworth, 1965. (b)

Morse, W. C. The crisis or helping teacher. In N. J. Long, W. C. Morse, & R. G. Newman (Eds.), *Conflict in the classroom* (2nd ed.). Belmont, Calif.: Wadsworth, 1971. (a)

Morse, W. C. Crisis intervention in school mental health and special classes for the disturbed. In N. J. Long, W.C. Morse, & R.G. Newman (Eds.), *Conflict in the classroom* (2nd ed.). Belmont, Calif.: Wadsworth, 1971. (b)

Morse, W. C. William C. Morse. In J. M. Kauffman & C.D. Lewis (Eds.), *Teaching children with behavior disorders: Personal perspectives.* Columbus, Ohio: Charles E. Merrill, 1974.

Morse, W. C., Cutler, R. L., & Fink, A. H. *Public school classes for the emotionally handicapped: A research analysis.* Washington, D.C.: Council for Exceptional Children, 1964.

Morse, W. C., & Wineman, D. Group interviewing in a camp for disturbed boys. In N. J. Long, W. C. Morse, & R. G. Newman (Eds.), *Conflict in the classroom.* Belmont, Calif.: Wadsworth, 1965.

Motto, J. J., & Wilkins, G. S. Educational achievement of institutionalized emotionally disturbed children. *Journal of Educational Research*, 1968, *61*, 218–221.

Moustakas, C. E. *Children in play therapy.* New York: McGraw-Hill, 1953.

Mowrer, O. H., & Mowrer, W. M. Enuresis: A method for its study and treatment. *American Journal of Orthopsychiatry*, 1938, *8*, 436–459.

Mulhern, R. K., & Passman, R. H. The child's behavioral pattern as a determinant of maternal punitiveness. *Child Development*, 1979, *50*, 815–820.

Neale, D. H. Behavior therapy and encopresis in children. *Behaviour Research and Therapy*, 1963, *1*, 139–149.

Neill, A. S. *Summerhill.* New York: Hart, 1960.

Nelson, C. M. Techniques for screening conduct disturbed children. *Exceptional Children*, 1971, *37*, 501–507.

Nelson, C. M. Classroom management. In J. M. Kauffman & D. P. Hallahan (Eds.), *Handbook of special education.* Englewood Cliffs, N. J.: Prentice-Hall, 1981.

Nelson, C. M., & Kauffman, J. M. Educational programming for secondary school age delinquent and maladjusted pupils. *Behavioral Disorders*, 1977, *2*, 102–113.

Ney, P. G., Palvesky, A. E., & Markeley, J. Relative effectiveness of operant conditioning and play therapy in childhood autism. *Journal of Autism and Childhood Schizophrenia*, 1971. *1*, 337–349.

Nielsen, J., Christensen, K. R., Friedrich, U., Zeuthen, E., & Ostergaard, O. Childhood of males with the XYY syndrome. *Journal of Autism and Childhood Schizophrenia*, 1973, *3*, 5–26.

Nihira, K., Foster, R., Shellhaas, M., & Leland, H. *AAMD Adaptive Behavior Scale* (1974 revision). Washington, D. C.: American Association on Mental Deficiency, 1974.

Nordquist, V. M. The modification of a child's enuresis: Some response-response relationships. *Journal of Applied Behavior Analysis*, 1971, *4*, 241–247.

Nowicki, S. J., & Strickland, B. R. A locus of control scale for children. *Journal of Consulting and Clinical Psychology*, 1974, *40*, 148–154.

Nyhan, W. L. Behavior in the Lesch-Nyhan syndrome. *Journal of Autism and Childhood Schizophrenia*, 1976, *6*, 235–252.

O'Banion, D., Armstrong, B., Cummings, R. A., & Stange, J. Disruptive behavior: A dietary approach. *Journal of Autism and Childhood Schizoprenia*, 1978, *8*, 325–337.

Obler, M., & Terwilliger, R. F. Pilot study of the effectiveness of systematic desensitization with neurologically impaired children with phobic disorders. *Journal of Clinical and Consulting Psychology*, 1970, *34*, 314–318.

O'Connor, R. D. Modification of social withdrawal through symbolic modeling. *Journal of Applied Behavior Analysis*, 1969, *2*, 15–22.

O'Connor, R. D. Relative efficacy of modeling, shaping, and the combined procedures for modification of social withdrawal. *Journal of Abnormal Psychology*, 1972, *79*, 327–334.

O'Dell, S. Training parents in behavior modification: A review. *Psychological Bulletin*, 1974, *81*, 418–433.

Offord, D. R., Abrams, N., Allen, N., & Proushinsky, M. Broken homes, parental psychiatric illness, and female delinquency. *American Journal of Orthopsychiatry*, 1979, *49*, 252–264.

Ojemann, R. H. Investigations on the effects of teaching as understanding and appreciation of behavior dynamics. In G. Caplan (Ed.), *Prevention of mental disorders in children.* New York: Basic Books, 1961.

O'Leary, K. D., & Johnson, S. B. Psychological assessment. In H.C. Quay & J.S. Werry (Eds.), *Psychopathological disorders of childhood* (2nd ed.). New York: Wiley, 1979.

O'Leary, K. D., & Wilson, G. T. *Behavior therapy: Application and outcome*. Englewood Cliffs, N. J.: Prentice-Hall, 1975.

O'Leary, S. G. A response to cognitive training. *Exceptional Education Quarterly*, 1980, 1(1), 89–94.

O'Leary, S. G., & Dubey, D. R. Applications of self-control procedures by children: A review. *Journal of Applied Behavior Analysis*, 1979, *12*, 449–465.

Olweus, D. Stability of aggressive reaction patterns in males: A review. *Psychological Bulletin*, 1979, *86*, 852–875.

Ornitz, E. M. The modulation of sensory input and motor output in autistic children. *Journal of Autism and Childhood Schizophrenia*, 1974, *4*, 197–215.

Palkes, H., & Stewart, M. Intellectual ability and performance of hyperactive children. *American Journal of Orthopsychiatry*, 1972, *42*, 35–39.

Palkes, H., Stewart, M., & Freedman, J. Improvement in maze performance of hyperactive boys as a function of verbal training procedures. *Journal of Special Education*, 1971, *5*, 337–342.

Palkes, H., Stewart, M., & Kahana, M. Porteus maze performance of hyperactive boys after training in self-directed verbal commands. *Child Development*, 1968, *39*, 817–826.

Park, C. C. *The seige*. Boston: Little, Brown, 1972.

Parke, R. D., & Collmer, C. W. Child abuse: An interdisciplinary analysis. In E.M. Hetherington (Ed.), *Review of child development research*, Vol. 5. Chicago: University of Chicago Press, 1975.

Parkinson, J. Observations on the excessive indulgence of children, particularly intended to show its injurious effects on their health, and the difficulties it occasions in their treatment during sickness. London: Symonds, et al., 1807. In R. Hunter & I. Macalpine (Eds.), *Three hundred years of psychiatry, 1835-1860*. London: Oxford University Press, 1963.

Parsley, N. J., & Rabinowitz, F. M. Crying in the first year: An operant interpretation of the Bell and Ainsworth (1972) findings. *Child Study Journal*, 1975, *5*, 83–89.

Parsons, J. A. The reciprocal modification of arithmetic behavior and program development. In G. Semb (Ed.), *Behavior analysis and education—1972*. Lawrence, Kan.: Kansas University Department of Human Development, 1972.

Paschalis, A., Kimmel, H. D., & Kimmel, E. Further study of diurnal instrumental conditioning in the treatment of enuresis nocturna. *Journal of Behavior Therapy and Experimental Psychiatry*, 1972, *3*, 253–256.

Patterson, G. R. A learning theory approach to the treatment of the school phobic child. In L. P. Ullmann & L. Krasner (Eds.), *Case studies in behavior modification*. New York: Holt, Rinehart, & Winston, 1965. (a)

Patterson, G. R. An application of conditioning techniques to the control of a hyperactive child. In L. P. Ullmann & L. Krasner (Eds.), *Case studies in behavior modification*. New York: Holt, Rinehart, & Winston, 1965. (b)

Patterson, G. R. *Families*. Champaign, Ill.: Research Press, 1971.

Patterson, G. R. Reprogramming the families of aggressive boys. In C. Thoresen (Ed.), *Behavior modification in education*. Seventy-second yearbook of the National Society for the Study of Education, Part I. Chicago: University of Chicago Press, 1973.

Patterson, G. R. The aggressive child: Victim or architect of a coercive system? In L. A. Hamerlynck, L. C. Handy, & E. J. Mash (Eds.), *Behavior modification and families*. New York: Brunner Mazell, 1975.

Patterson, G. R., & Cobb, J. A. A dyadic analysis of "aggressive" behaviors. In J. P. Hill (Ed.), *Minnesota symposia on child psychology* (Vol. 5). Minneapolis: University of Minnesota Press, 1971.

Patterson, G. R., Cobb, J. A., & Ray, R. S. Direct intervention in the classroom: A set of procedures for the aggressive child. In F. W. Clark, D. R. Evans, & L. A. Hammerlynck (Eds.), *Implementing behavioral programs in schools and clinics*. Champaign, Ill.: Research Press, 1972.

Patterson, G. R., & Fleischman, M. J. Maintenance of treatment effects: Some considerations concerning family systems and follow-up data. *Behavior Therapy*, 1979, *10*, 168–185.

Patterson, G. R., Littman, R. A., & Bricker, W. A. Assertive behavior in children: A step toward a theory of aggression. *Monographs of the Society for Research in Child Development*, 1967, 32(5, 1–43, Serial No. 113).

Patterson, G. R., & Reid, J. B. Reciprocity and coercion: Two facets of social systems. In C. Neuringer & J. L. Michael (Eds.), *Behavior modification in clinical psychology*. New York: Appleton-Century-Crofts (Prentice-Hall), 1970.

Patterson, G. R., Reid, J. B., Jones, R. R., & Conger, R. E. *A social learning approach to family intervention: Vol. 1 Families with aggressive children*. Eugene, Ore.: Castalia, 1975.

Paulsen, M. G., & Whitebread, C. H. *Juvenile law and procedure*. Reno, Nev.: National Council of Juvenile Court Judges, 1974.

Payne, J. S., Kauffman, J. M., Patton, J. R., Brown, G. B., & DeMott, R. M. *Exceptional children in focus* (2nd ed.). Columbus, Ohio: Charles E. Merrill, 1979.

Pearson, G. H. J. *Psychoanalysis and the education of the child*. New York: Norton, 1954.

Phillips, E. L. Problems in educating emotionally disturbed children. In N. G. Haring & R. L. Schiefelbusch (Eds.), *Methods in special education*. New York: McGraw-Hill, 1967.

Phillips, E. L., Fixsen, D. L., Phillips, E. A., & Wolf, M. M. The teaching family model: A comprehensive approach to residential treatment of youth. In D. Cullinan & M. H. Epstein (Eds.), *Special education for adolescents: Issues and perspectives*. Columbus, Ohio: Charles E. Merrill, 1979.

Phillips, E. L., & Haring, N. G. Results from special techniques for teaching emotionally disturbed children. *Exceptional Children*, 1959, *26*, 64–67.

Phillips, E. L., Phillips, E. A., Fixsen, D. L., & Wolf, M. M. Achievement place: Modification of the behaviors of predelinquent boys within a token economy. *Journal of Applied Behavior Analysis*, 1971, *4*, 45–59.

Phillips, L., Draguns, J. G., & Bartlett, D. P. Classification of behavior disorders. In N. Hobbs (Ed.), *Issues in the classification of children, Vol. I*. San Francisco: Jossey-Bass, 1975.

Piaget, J. *The moral judgment of the child*. New York: Free Press, 1932.

Pick, A. D., Christy, M. D., & Frankel, G. W. A developmental study of visual selective attention. *Journal of Experimental Child Psychology*, 1972, *14*, 165–175.

Polirstok, S. R., & Greer, R. D. Remediation of mutually aversive interactions between a problem student and four teachers by training the student in reinforcement techniques. *Journal of Applied Behavior Analysis*, 1977, *10*, 707–716.

Polsgrove, L. Self-control: Methods for child training. *Behavioral Disorders*, 1979, *4*, 116–130.

Pomerantz, P. B., Peterson, N. T., Marholin, D., & Stern, S. The *in vivo* elimination of a child's water phobia by a paraprofessional at home. *Journal of Behavior Therapy and Experimental Psychiatry*, 1977, *8*, 417–421.

Potter, H. W. Schizophrenia in children. *American Journal of Psychiatry*, 1933, *89*, 1253–1270.

Prentice, N. M. The influence of live and symbolic modeling on prompting moral judgment of adolescent delinquents. *Journal of Abnormal Psychology*, 1972, *80*, 157–161.

Prescott, D. A. *Emotions and the education process*. Washington, D. C.: American Council on Education, 1954.

Purcell, K. Distinctions between subgroups of asthmatic children: Parental reactions to experimental separation. *Journal of Abnormal Child Psychology*, 1973, *1*, 2–15.

Purcell, K., Brady, K., Chai, H., Muser, J., Molk, L., Gordon, N., & Means, J. The effect on asthma in children of experimental separation from the family. *Psychosomatic Medicine*, 1969, *31*, 144–164.

Pusser, H. E., & McCandless, B. R. Socialization dimensions among inner-city five-year-olds and later school success: A follow-up. *Journal of Educational Psychology*, 1974, *66*, 285–290.

Quay, H. C. Classification in the treatment of delinquency and antisocial behavior. In N. Hobbs (Ed.), *Issues in the classification of children, Vol. I*. San Francisco: Jossey-Bass, 1975.

Quay, H. C. Measuring dimensions of deviant behavior: The Behavior Problem Checklist. *Journal of Abnormal Child Psychology*, 1977, *5*, 277–289.

Quay, H. C. Classification. In H. C. Quay & J. S. Werry (Eds.), *Psychopathological disorders of childhood* (2nd ed.). New York: Wiley, 1979.

Quay, H. C., Morse, W. C., & Cutler, R. L. Personality patterns of pupils in special classes for the emotionally disturbed. *Exceptional Children*, 1966, *32*, 297–301.

Quay, H. C., & Peterson, D. R. Manual for the Behavior Problem Checklist. Mimeographed, University of Illinois, 1967.

Quilitch, H. R., & Risley, T. R. The effects of play materials on social play. *Journal of Applied Behavior Analysis*, 1973, *6*, 573–578.

Ragland, E. U., Kerr, M. M., & Strain, P. S. Behavior of withdrawn autistic children: Effects of peer social initiations. *Behavior Modification*, 1978, *2*, 565–578.

Ramey, C. T., Stedman, D. J., Borders-Patterson, A., & Mengel, W. Predicting school failure from information available at birth. *American Journal of Mental Deficiency*, 1978, *82*, 525–534.

Rank, B. Adaptation of the psychoanalytic techniques for the treatment of young children with atypical development. *American Journal of Orthopsychiatry*, 1949, *19*, 130–139.

Rappaport, M. M., & Rappaport, H. The other half of the expectancy equation: Pygmalion. *Journal of Education Psychology*, 1975, *67*, 531–536.

Rappaport, S. R. Sheldon R. Rappaport. In J. M. Kauffman & D. P. Hallahan (Eds.), *Teaching children with leaning disabilities: Personal perspectives*. Columbus, Ohio: Charles E. Merrill, 1976.

Ray, I. Observations of the principle hospitals for the insane, in Great Britain, France, and Germany. *American Journal of Insanity*, 1846, *2*, 289–390.

Redl, F. The concept of the life space interview. *American Journal of Orthopsychiatry*, 1959, *29*, 1–18. (a)

Redl, F. The concept of a therapeutic milieu. *American Journal of Orthopsychiatry*, 1959, *29*, 721–734. (b)

Redl, F. Designing a therapeutic classroom environment for disturbed children: The milieu approach. In P. Knoblock (Ed.), *Intervention approaches in educating emotionally disturbed children*. Syracuse, N.Y.: Syracuse University Press, 1966.

Redl, F., & Wattenberg, W. W. *Mental hygiene in teaching*. New York: Harcourt, Brace, and World, 1951.

Redl, F., & Wineman, D. *Children who hate*. New York: Free Press, 1951.

Redl, F., & Wineman, D. *Controls from within*. New York: Free Press, 1952.

Reed, E. W. Genetic anomalies in development. In F. D. Horowitz (Ed.), *Review of child development research, Vol. 4*. Chicago: University of Chicago Press, 1975.

Rees, T. P. Back to moral treatment and community care. *Journal of Mental Science*, 1957, *103*, 303–313.

Reid, J. B., & Hendricks, A. F. C. J. Preliminary analysis of the effectiveness of direct home intervention for the treatment of predelinquent boys who steal. In L. A. Hammerlynck, L. C. Handy, & E. J. Mash (Eds.), *Behavior change: Methodology, concepts, and practice*. Champaign, Ill.: Research Press, 1973.

Reid, J. B., & Patterson, G. R. The modification of aggression and stealing behavior of boys in the home setting. In A. Bandura & E. Ribes (Eds.), *Behavior modification: Experimental analyses of aggression and delinquency*. Hillsdale, N.J.: Lawrence Erlbaum, 1976.

Rekers, G. A. Atypical gender development and prosocial behavior. *Journal of Applied Behavior Analysis*, 1977, *10*, 559–571. (a)

Rekers, G. A. Assessment and treatment of childhood gender problems. In B. B. Lahey & A. E. Kazdin (Eds.), *Advances in clinical child psychology*, Vol. 1. New York: Plenum, 1977. (b)

Rekers, G. A. Sexual problems: Behavior modification. In B. B. Wolman (Ed.), *Handbook of treatment of mental disorders in childhood and adolescence*. Englewood Cliffs, N.J.: Prentice-Hall, 1978.

Resnick, L. B. The future of IQ testing in education. *Intelligence*, 1979, *3*, 241–253.

Rest, J. R. Recent research on an objective test of moral judgment: How the important issues of a moral dilemma are defined. In D. J. DePalma & J. M. Foley (Eds.), *Moral development: Current theory and research*. Hillsdale, N.J.: Lawrence Erlbaum, 1975.

Rest, J. R., Cooper, D., Coder, R., Masanz, J., & Anderson, D. Judging the important issues in moral dilemmas—an objective measure of development. *Developmental Psychology*, 1974, *10*, 491–501.

Restak, R. José Delgado: Exploring inner space. *Saturday Review*, August 9, 1975, 21–25.

Reynolds, B. S., Newsom, C. D., & Lovaas, O. I. Auditory overselectivity in autistic children. *Journal of Abnormal Child Psychology*, 1974, *2*, 253–263.

Rhodes, W. C. Curriculum and disordered behavior. *Exceptional Children*, 1963, *30*, 61–66.

Rhodes, W. C. Institutionalized displacement and the disturbing child. In P. Knoblock (Ed.), *Educational programming for emotionally disturbed children: The decade ahead*. Syracuse, N.Y.: Syracuse University, 1965.

Rhodes, W. C. The disturbing child. A problem of ecological management. *Exceptional Children*, 1967, *33*, 449–455.

Rhodes, W. C. A community participation analysis of emotional disturbance. *Exceptional Children*, 1970, *37*, 309–314.

Rhodes, W. C., & Head, S. (Eds.), *A study of child variance, Vol. 3: Service delivery systems*. Ann Arbor, Mich.: University of Michigan, 1974.

Rhodes, W. C., & Paul, J. L. *Emotionally disturbed and deviant children: New views and approaches*. Englewood Cliffs, N.J.: Prentice-Hall, 1978.

Rhodes, W. C., & Tracy, M. L. (Eds.), *A study of child variance, Vol. 1: Theories*. Ann Arbor, Mich.: University of Michigan, 1972. (a)

Rhodes, W. C., & Tracy, M. L. (Eds.), *A study of child variance, Vol. 2: Interventions*. Ann Arbor, Mich.: University of Michigan, 1972. (b)

Rie, H. E. Historical perspective of concepts of child psychopathology. In H. E. Rie (Ed.), *Perspectives in child psychopathology*. Chicago: Aldine Atherton, 1971.

Rieth, H. J., Polsgrove, L., McLeskey, K. P., & Anderson, R. The use of self-recording to increase the arithmetic performance of severely behaviorally disordered students. In R. B. Rutherford & A. G. Prieto (Eds.), *Monograph in Behavioral Disorders*. Reston, VA: Council for Exceptional Children, 1978.

Rimland, B. *Infantile autism*. New York: Appleton-Century-Crofts (Prentice-Hall), 1964.

Rincover, A. Variables affecting stimulus-fading and discriminative responding in psychotic children. *Journal of Abnormal Child Psychology*, 1978, *87*, 541–553.

Rincover, A., & Koegel, R. L. Research on the education of autistic children: Recent advances and future directions. In B. B. Lahey & A. E. Kazdin (Eds.), *Advances in clinical child psychology*, Vol. 1. New York: Plenum, 1977.

Rincover, A., Newsom, C. D., Lovaas, O. I., & Koegel, R. L. Some motivational properties of sensory stimulation in psychotic children. *Journal of Experimental Child Psychology*, 1977, *24*, 312–323.

Risley, T. R. The effects and side-effects of punishing the autistic behaviors of a deviant child. *Journal of Applied Behavior Analysis*, 1968, *1*, 21–34.

Risley, T. R., & Baer, D. M. Operant behavior modification: The deliberate development of behavior. In B. M. Caldwell & H. N. Ricciuti (Eds.), *Review of child development research, Vol. 3*. Chicago: University of Chicago Press, 1973.

Risley, T. R., & Wolf, M. M. Establishing functional speech in echolalic children. *Behaviour Research and Therapy*, 1967, *5*, 73–88.

Ritvo, E. R. Biochemical studies of children with the syndromes of autism, childhood schizophrenia, and related developmental disabilities: A review. *Journal of Child Psychology and Psychiatry*, 1977, *18*, 373–379.

Robin, A. L., Armel, S., & O'Leary, K. D. The effects of self-instruction on writing deficiencies. *Behavior Therapy*, 1975, *6*, 178–187.

Robins, L. N. *Deviant children grown up*. Baltimore: Williams & Wilkins, 1966.

Robins, L. N. Antisocial behavior disturbances of childhood: Prevalence, prognosis, and prospects. In E. J. Anthony & C. Koupernik (Eds.), *The child in his family: Children at psychiatric risk*. New York: Wiley, 1974.

Robins, L. N. Follow-up studies. In H. C. Quay & J. S. Werry (Eds.), *Psychopathological disorders of childhood* (2nd ed.). New York: Wiley, 1979.

Robins, L. N., West, P., & Herjanic, B. Arrests and delinquency in two generations: A study of urban families and their children. *Journal of Child Psychology and Psychiatry*, 1975, *16*, 125–140.

Robinson, F. J., & Vitale, L. J. Children with circumscribed interest pattens. *American Journal of Orthopsychiatry*, 1954, *24*, 755–766.

Rogers, C. *Freedom to learn*. Columbus, Ohio: Charles E. Merrill, 1969.

Roos, P. Parents and families of the retarded. In J. M. Kauffman & J. S. Payne (Eds.), *Mental retardation: Introduction and personal perspectives*. Columbus, Ohio: Charles E. Merrill, 1975.

Roper, G., Rachman, S., & Marks, I. Passive and participant modeling in exposure treatment of obsessive-compulsive neurotics. *Behaviour Research and Therapy*, 1975, *13*, 271–279.

Rose, T. The functional relationship between artificial food colors and hyperactivity. *Journal of Applied Behavior Analysis*, 1978, *11*, 439–446.

Rosenbaum, A., O'Leary, K. D., & Jacob, R. G. Behavioral intervention with hyperactive children:

Group consequences as a supplement to individual contingencies. *Behavior Therapy*, 1975, *6*, 315–323.

Rosenbaum, M.S., & Drabman, R.S.   Self-control training in the classroom: A review and critique. *Journal of Applied Behavior Analysis*, 1979, *12*, 467–485.

Rosenberg, H. E., & Graubard, P. S. Peer use of behavior modification. *Focus on Exceptional Children*, 1975, *7*(6), 1–10.

Rosenthal, R., & Jacobson, L. *Pygmalion in the classroom.* New York: Holt, Rinehart, & Winston, 1968.

Ross, A. O. *Psychological disorders of children.* New York: McGraw-Hill, 1974.

Ross, A. O. *Psychological aspects of learning disabilities and reading disorders.* New York: McGraw-Hill, 1976.

Ross, D. M., & Ross, S. A. *Hyperactivity: Research, theory, action.* New York: Wiley, 1976.

Rothman, D. *The discovery of the asylum: Social order and disorder in the new republic.* Boston: Little, Brown, 1971.

Rothman, E. P. The Livingston School: A day school for disturbed girls. In P. H. Berkowitz & E. P. Rothman (Eds.), *Public education for disturbed children in New York City.* Springfield, Ill.: Charles C. Thomas, 1967.

Rothman, E. P. *The angel inside went sour.* New York: David McKay, 1970.

Rothman, E. P. Esther P. Rothman. In J. M. Kauffman & C. D. Lewis (Eds.), *Teaching children with behavior disorders: Personal perspectives.* Columbus, Ohio: Charles E. Merrill, 1974.

Rothman, E. P., & Berkowitz, P. H. The concept of clinical teaching. In P. H. Berkowitz & E. P. Rothman (Eds.), *Public education for disturbed children in New York City.* Springfield, Ill.: Charles C. Thomas, 1967. (a)

Rothman, E. P., & Berkowitz, P. H. Some aspects of reading disability. In P. H. Berkowitz & E. P. Rothman (Eds.), *Public education for disturbed children in New York City.* Springfield, Ill.: Charles C. Thomas, 1967. (b)

Rothman, E. P., & Berkowitz, P. H. The clinical school—A paradigm. In P. H. Berkowitz & E. P. Rothman (Eds.), *Public education for disturbed children in New York City.* Springfield, Ill.: Charles C. Thomas, 1967. (c)

Rotter, J. B. Generalized expectancies for internal versus external control of reinforcement. *Psychological Monographs*, 1966, *80* (Whole No. 609), 1–28.

Rubenstein, E. A. Childhood mental disease in America. *American Journal of Orthopsychiatry*, 1948, *18*, 314–321.

Rubin, R., & Balow, B. Learning and behavior disorders: A longitudinal study. *Exceptional Children*, 1971, *38*, 293–299.

Rubin, R. A., & Balow, B. Prevalence of teacher identified behavior problems: A longitudinal study. *Exceptional Children*, 1978, *45*, 102–111.

Rubin, T. I. *Jordi, Lisa, and David.* New York: Macmillan, 1962.

Ruma, E. H., & Mosher, D. L. Relationship between moral judgment and guilt in delinquent boys. *Journal of Abnormal Psychology*, 1967, *72*, 122–127.

Rutter, M. Childhood schizophrenia reconsidered. *Journal of Autism and Childhood Schizophrenia*, 1972, *2*, 315–337.

Rutter, M. Maternal deprivation, 1972–1978. New findings, new concepts, new approaches. *Child Development*, 1979, *50*, 283–305.

Rutter, M., & Bartak, L. Causes of infantile autism: Some considerations from recent research. *Journal of Autism and Childhood Schizophrenia*, 1971, *1*, 20–32.

Rutter, M., & Bartak, L. Special educational treatment of autistic children: A comparative study—II. Follow-up findings and implications for services. *Journal of Child Psychology and Psychiatry*, 1973, *14*, 241–270.

Rutter, M., Graham, P., & Yule, W. *A neuropsychiatric study in childhood.* Philadelphia: Lippincott, 1970.

Rutter, M., Tizard, J., Yule, W., Graham, P., & Whitmore, K. Isle of Wight studies, 1964–1974. *Psychological Medicine.* 1976, *6*, 313–332.

Sameroff, A. J., & Chandler, M. J. Reproductive risk and the continuum of caretaking casualty. In F. D. Horowitz (Ed.), *Review of child development research, Vol. 4.* Chicago: University of Chicago Press, 1975.

Samuels, S. J., & Turnure, J. E. Attention and reading achievement in first-grade boys and girls. *Journal of Educational Psychology,* 1974, *66,* 29–32.

Sanok, R. L., & Ascione, F. R. Behavioral interventions for childhood elective mutism: An evaluative review. *Child Behavior Therapy,* 1979, *1,* 49–68.

Santrock, J. W. Moral structure: The interrelations of moral behavior, moral judgment, and moral affect. *Journal of Genetic Psychology,* 1975, *127,* 201–213.

Sarason, S. B., & Doris, J. *Educational handicap, public policy, and social history: A broadened perspective on mental retardation.* New York: Macmillan, 1979.

Savage, G. H. *Insanity and allied neuroses: Practical and clinical.* London: Cassell, 1891.

Scarpitti, F. R., Murray, E., Dinitz, S., & Reckless, W. C. The "good" boy in a high delinquency area: Four years later. *American Sociological Review,* 1960, *25,* 555–558.

Scarr-Salapatek, S. Genetics and the development of intelligence. In F.D. Horowitz (Ed.), *Review of child development research, Vol. 4.* Chicago: University of Chicago Press, 1975.

Schaefer, E. S. Development of adaptive behavior: Conceptual models and family correlates. In M. Begab, H. Garber, & H. C. Haywood (Eds.), *Prevention of retarded development in psychosocially disadvantaged children.* Baltimore: University Park Press, in press.

Schaeffer, H. H. Self-injurious behavior: Shaping "head banging" in monkeys. *Journal of Applied Behavior Analysis,* 1970, *3,* 111–116.

Scharfman, M. A. Psychoanalytic treatment. In B. B. Wolman (Ed.), *Handbook of treatment of mental disorders in childhood and adolescence.* Englewood Cliffs, N. J.: Prentice-Hall, 1978.

Scheiderer, E. G., & O'Connor, R. D. Effects of modeling and expectancy of reward on cheating behavior. *Journal of Abnormal Child Psychology,* 1973, *1,* 257–266.

Schiefelbusch, R. L., Ruder, K. F., & Bricker, W. A. Training strategies for language-deficient children: An overview. In N. G. Haring & R. L. Schiefelbusch (Eds.), *Teaching special children.* New York: McGraw-Hill, 1976.

Schopler, E., & Reichler, R. J. Parents as cotherapists in the treatment of psychotic children. *Journal of Autism and Childhood Schizophrenia,* 1971, *1,* 87–102.

Schreibman, L. Effects of within-stimulus and extra-stimulus prompting on discrimination learning in autistic children. *Journal of Applied Behavior Analysis,* 1975, *8,* 91–112.

Schreibman, L., & Lovaas, O. I. Overselective response to social stimuli by autistic children. *Journal of Abnormal Child Psychology,* 1973, *1,* 152–168.

Schulman, J. L., Stevens, T. M., & Kupst, M. J. The biomotometer: A new device for the measurement and remediation of hyperactivity. *Child Development,* 1977, *48,* 1152–1154.

Schulman, J. L., Stevens, T. M., Suran, B. G., Kupst, M. J., & Naughton, M. J. Modification of activity level through biofeedback and operant conditioning. *Journal of Applied Behavior Analysis,* 1978, *11,* 145–152.

Schultz, E. W., Heuchert, C. M., & Stampf, S. W. *Pain and joy in school.* Champaign, Ill.: Research Press, 1973.

Schultz, E. W., Hirshoren, A., Manton, A. B., & Henderson, R. A. Special education for the emotionally disturbed. *Exceptional Children,* 1971, *38,* 313–319.

Scrignar, C. B. Food as the reinforcer in the outpatient treatment of anorexia nervosa. *Journal of Behavior Therapy and Experimental Psychiatry,* 1971, *1,* 31–36.

Seguin, E. *Idiocy and its treatment by the physiological method.* New York: Brandow, 1866.

Seligman, M. E. P. For helplessness: Can we immunize the weak. *Psychology Today,* 1969, *3*(1), 42–44.

Seligman, M. E. P. The fall into helplessness. *Psychology Today,* 1973, *7*(1), 43–49.

Seligman, M. E. P. *Helplessness.* San Francisco: Freeman, 1975.

Senn, M. J., & Solnit, A. J. *Problems in Child Behavior and Development.* Philadelphia: Lee & Febiger, 1968.

Shapiro, E. S., Barrett, R. P., & Ollendick, T. H. A comparison of physical restraint and positive practice overcorrection in treating stereotypic behavior. *Behavior Therapy,* 1980, *11,* 227–233.

Sheldon, W. H. Constitutional psychiatry. In T. Millon (Ed.), *Theories of psychopathology.* Philadelphia: Saunders, 1967.

Sheldon, W. H., Hartl, E. M., & McDermott, E. *Varieties of delinquent youth: An introduction to constitutional psychiatry.* New York: Harper, 1949.

Sherman, H., & Farina, A. Social inadequacy of parents and children. *Journal of Abnormal Psychology,* 1974, *83,* 327-330.

Sherman, J. A., & Bushell, D. Behavior modification as a educational technique. In F. D. Horowitz (Ed.), *Review of child development research, Vol. 4.* Chicago: University of Chicago Press, 1975.

Shields, R. W. *A cure of delinquents: The treatment of maladjustment.* New York: International Universities Press, 1962.

Short, J. F. Juvenile delinquency: The sociocultural context. In L. W. Hoffman & M. L. Hoffman (Eds.), *Review of child development research, Vol. 2.* New York: Russel Sage Foundation, 1966.

Silberberg, N. E., & Silberberg, M. C. School achievement and delinquency. *Review of Educational Research,* 1971, *41,* 17-32.

Silberman, C. E. *Criminal violence, criminal justice.* New York: Random House, 1978.

Simonds, J. F., & Glenn, T. Folie a deux in a child. *Journal of Autism and Childhood Schizophrenia,* 1976, *6,* 61-73.

Simpson, R. L., & Swenson, C. R. The effects and side-effects of an overcorrection procedure applied by parents of severely emotionally disturbed children in a home environment. *Behavioral Disorders,* 1980, *5,* 79-85.

Skinner, B. F. *Science and human behavior.* New York: Free Press, 1953.

Slavson, S. R. *Re-educating the delinquent through group and community participation.* New York: Harper, 1954.

Smith, J. O. Criminality and mental retardation. *Trainig School Bulletin,* 1962, *59,* 74-80.

Snell, M. E. Daily living skills. In J. M. Kauffman & D. P. Hallahan (Eds.), *Handbook of special education.* Englewood Cliffs, N. J.: Prentice-Hall, 1981.

Sours, J. A. Enuresis. In B. B. Wolman (Ed.), *Handbook of treatment of mental disorders in childhood and adolescence.* Englewood Cliffs, N. J.: Prentice-Hall, 1978.

Spergel, S. M. Induced vomiting treatment of acute compulsive vomiting. *Journal of Behavior Therapy and Experimental Psychiatry,* 1975, *6,* 85-86.

Spitz, R. Anaclitic depression. *The psychoanalytic study of the child,* 1946, *2,* 313-342.

Spivack, G., & Shure, M. B. *Social adjustment of young children:* A cognitive approach to solving real-life problems. San Francisco: Jossey-Bass, 1974.

Spivack, G., & Swift, M. S. The Devereux Elementary School Behavior Rating Scales: A study of the nature and organization of achievement related disturbed classroom behavior. *Journal of Special Education,* 1966, *1,* 71-90.

Spivack, G., & Swift, M. The Hahnemann High School Behavior (HHSB) Rating Scale. *Journal of Abnormal Child Psychology,* 1977, *5,* 299-307.

Sprague, R., & Ullmann, R. Psychoactive drugs and child management. In J. M. Kauffman & D.P. Hallahan (Eds.), *Handbook of special education.* Englewood Cliffs, N. J.: Prentice-Hall, 1981.

Sroufe, L. A. Drug treatment of children with behavior problems. In F. D. Horowitz (Ed.), *Review of child development research, Vol. 4.* Chicago: University of Chicago Press, 1975.

Sroufe, L. A., Sonies, B. C., West, W. D., & Wright, F. S. Anticipatory heart rate deceleration and reaction time in children with and without referral for learning disability. *Child Development,* 1973, *44,* 267-273.

Sroufe, L. A., Steucher, H. U., & Stutzer, W. The functional significance of autistic behaviors for the psychotic child. *Journal of Abnormal Child Psychology,* 1973, *1,* 225-240.

Starfield, B. Enuresis: Its pathogenesis and management. *Clinical Pediatrics,* 1972, *11,* 343-394.

Staub, E. To rear a prosocial child: Reasoning, learning by doing, and learning by teaching others. In D. J. DePalma & J.M. Foley (Eds.), *Moral development: Current theory and research.* Hillsdale, N. J.: Lawrence Erlbaum, 1975.

Steen, P. L., & Zuriff, G. E. The use of relaxation in the treatment of self-injurious behavior. *Journal of Behavior Therapy and Experimental Psychiatry,* 1977, *8,* 447-448.

Stein, A. H., & Friedrich, L. K. Impact of television on children and youth. In E.M. Hetherington (Ed.), *Review of child development research, Vol. 5.* Chicago: University of Chicago Press, 1975.

Stephens, B., McLaughlin, J. A., Hunt, J. McV., Mahoney, E. J., Kohlberg, J., Moore, G., & Aronfreed, J. Symposium: Developmental gains in the reasoning, moral judgment, and moral conduct of retarded and nonretarded persons. *American Journal of Mental Deficiency*, 1974, *79*, 113–161.

Stephens, T. M. Using reinforcement and social modeling with delinquent youth. *Review of Educational Research*, 1973, *43*, 323–340.

Steucher, U. *Tommy: A treatment study of an autistic child.* Washington, D.C.: Council for Exceptional Children, 1972.

Stevenson, H. W. *Children's learning.* New York: Appleton-Century-Crofts (Prentice-Hall), 1972.

Stewart, M. A. Hyperactive children. *Scientific American*, 1970, *222*(4), 94–98.

Stewart, M. A., Pitts, F. N., Craig, A. G., & Dieruf, W. The hyperactive child syndrome. *American Journal of Orthopsychiatry*, 1966, *36*, 861–867.

Stone, F., & Rowley, V. N. Educational disability in emotionally disturbed children. *Exceptional Children*, 1964, *30*, 423–426.

Strain, P. S. An experimental analysis of peer social initiations on the behavior of withdrawn preschool children: Some training and generalization effects. *Journal of Abnormal Child Psychology*, 1977, *5*, 445–455.

Strain, P. S. (Ed.) *Classroom peers as agents of behavioral change.* New York: Academic Press, in press.

Strain, P. S., Shores, R. E., & Kerr, M. M. Direct and "spillover" effects of social reinforcement on the social interaction of behaviorally handicapped preschool children. *Journal of Applied Behavior Analysis*, 1976, *9*, 31–40.

Strain, P. S., Shores, R. E., & Timm, M. A. Effects of peer social initiations on the behavior of withdrawn preschool children. *Journal of Applied Behavior Analysis*, 1977, *10*, 289–298.

Strain, P. S., & Timm, M. A. An experimental analysis of social interaction between a behaviorally disordered preschool child and her classroom peers. *Journal of Applied Behavior Analysis*, 1974, *7*, 583–590.

Strauss, A. A., & Kephart, N. C. *Psychopathology and education of the brain-injured child, Vol. 2: Progress in theory and clinic.* New York: Gruen & Stratton, 1955.

Strauss, A. A., & Lehtinen, L. E. *Psychopathology and education of the brain-injured child.* New York: Grune & Stratton, 1947.

Stribling, F. T. Physician and superintendent's report. In *Annual Reports of the Court of Directors of the Western Lunatic Asylum to the Legislature of Virginia.* Richmond, Va.: Shepherd & Conlin, 1842.

Strider, F. D., & Strider, M. A. Current applications of biofeedback technology to the problems of children and youth. *Behavioral Disorders*, 1979, *5*, 53–59.

Stullken, E. H. Special schools and classes for the socially maladjusted. In N.B. Henry (Ed.), *The education of exceptional children.* Forth-ninth Yearbook of the National Society for the Study of Education, Part II. Chicago: University of Chicago Press, 1950.

Stumphauser, J. S. Modifying delinquent behavior: Beginnings and current practices. *Adolescence*, 1971, *11*, 13–28.

Stumphauser, J. S., Aiken, T. W., & Veloz, E. V. East side story: Behavioral analysis of a high juvenile crime community. *Behavioral Disorders*, 1977, *2*, 76–84.

Stunkard, A. New therapies for eating disorders. *Archives of General Psychiatry*, 1972, *26*, 391–398.

Stutte, H., & Dauner, I. Systematized delusions in early life schizophrenia. *Journal of Autism and Childhood Schizophrenia*, 1971, *1*, 411–420.

Sulzer-Azaroff, B., & Mayer, G. R. *Applying behavior-analysis procedures with children and youth.* Holt, Rinehart, & Winston, 1977.

Swanson, J. M., & Kinsbourne, M. Food dyes impair performance of hyperactive children on a laboratory learning test. *Science*, 1980, *207*, 1485–1487.

Swap, S. Disturbing classroom behaviors: A developmental and ecological view. *Exceptional Children*, 1974, *41*, 163–172.

Swap, S. The ecological model of emotional disturbance in children: A status report and proposed synthesis. *Behavioral Disorders*, 1978, *3*, 186–196.

Swift, M. S., & Spivack, G. The assessment of achievement related classroom behavior: Normative, reliability, and validity data. *Journal of Special Education*, 1968, *2*, 137–153.

Swift, M. S., & Spivack, G. Achievement related classroom behavior of secondary school normal and disturbed students. *Exceptional Children*, 1969, *35*, 677–684. (a)

Swift, M. S., & Spivack, G. Clarifying the relationship between academic success and overt classroom behavior. *Exceptional Children*, 1969, *36*, 99–104. (b)

Swift, M. S., & Spivack, G. Academic success and classroom behavior in secondary schools. *Exceptional Children*, 1973, *39*, 392–399.

Szasz, T. S. The myth of mental illness. *American Psychologist*, 1960, *15*, 113–118.

Tamkin, A. S. A survey of educational disability in emotionally disturbed children. *Journal of Educational Research*, 1960, *53*, 313–315.

Tarver, S. G., Hallahan, D. P., Kauffman, J. M., & Ball, D. W. Verbal rehearsal and selective attention in children with learning disabilities: A developmental lag. *Journal of Experimental Child Psychology*, 1976, *22*, 375–385.

Tate, B.G., & Baroff, G.S. Aversive control of self-injurious behavior in a psychotic boy. *Behavior Research and Therapy*, 1966, *4*, 281–287.

Taylor, E. Food additives, allergy, and hyperkinesis. *Journal of Child Psychology and Psychiatry*, 1979, *20*, 357–363.

Taylor, P. D., & Turner, R. K. A clinical trial of continuous, intermittent, and overlearning 'bell and pad' treatments for nocturnal enuresis. *Behavior Research and Therapy*, 1975, *13*, 281–293.

Tedeschi, J. T., Smith, R. B., & Brown, R. C. A reinterpretation of research on aggression. *Psychological Bulletin*, 1974, *81*, 540–562.

Tharp, R. G., & Wetzel, R. J. *Behavior modification in the natural environment*. New York: Academic Press, 1969.

Theander, S. Anorexia nervosa: A psychiatric investigation of 94 female patients. *Acta Psychiatrica Scandinavia*, 1970, Suppl. 214.

Thomas, A. Impact of interest in early individual differences. In H. E. Rie (Ed.), *Perspectives in child psychopathology*. Chicago: Aldine, 1971.

Thomas, A., & Chess, S. A longitudinal study of three brain damaged children. *Archives of General Psychiatry*, 1975, *32*, 457–462.

Thomas, A., Chess, S., & Birch, H. G. *Temperament and behavior disorders in children*. New York: New York University Press, 1968.

Thomas, M. H., Horton, R. W., Lippincott, E. C., & Drabman, R. S. Desensitization to portrayals of real-life aggression as a function of exposure to television violence. *Journal of Personality and Social Psychology*, 1977, *35*, 450–458.

Thoresen, C. (Ed.) *Behavior modification in education*. Seventy-second Yearbook of the National Society for the Study of Education, Part I. Chicago: University of Chicago Press, 1973.

Tobin, D. D. Overcoming crude behavior in a "600" school. In N. J. Long, W. C. Morse, & R. G. Newman (Eds.), *Conflict in the classroom* (2nd ed.). Belmont, Calif.: Wadsworth, 1971.

Tomlinson, J. R. Bowel retention. *Journal of Behavior Therapy and Experimental Psychiatry*, 1970, *1*, 83–85.

Trieschman, A. E., Whittaker, J. K., & Brendtro, L. K. *The other 23 hours*. Chicago: Aldine, 1969.

Trippe, M. J. Love of life, love of truth, love of others. Presidential address, Annual meeting of the Council for Children with Behavioral Disorders, Gary, Indiana, April, 1970.

Turiel, E. The development of social concepts: Mores, customs, and conventions. In D. J. DePalma & J. M. Foley (Eds.), *Moral development: Current theory and research*. Hillsdale, N. J.: Lawrence Erlbaum, 1975.

Turnbull, A. P., & Turnbull, H. R. (Eds.) *Parents speak out*. Columbus, Ohio: Charles E. Merrill, 1978.

Ullmann, L. P., & Krasner, L. *A psychological approach to abnormal behavior*. Englewood Cliffs, N.J.: Prentice-Hall, 1969.

Vandersall, T. A. Ulcerative colitis. In B.B. Wolman (Ed.), *Handbook of treatment of mental disorders in childhood and adolescence.* Englewood Cliffs, N. J.: Prentice-Hall, 1978.

Varni, J. W., & Henker, B. A self-regulation approach to the treatment of three hyperactive boys. *Child Behavior Therapy*, 1979, *1*, 171–192.

Verghese, A., Large, P., & Chiu, E. Relationship between body build and mental illness. *British Journal of Psychiatry*, 1978, *132*, 12–15.

Verhaaren, P. & Connor, F.P.   Physical disabilities. In J.M. Kauffman & D.P. Hallahan (Eds.), *Handbook of Special Education.* Englewood Cliffs, N. J.: Prentice-Hall, 1981.

Von Isser, A., Quay, H. C., & Love, C. T. Interrelationships among three measures of deviant behavior. *Exceptional Children*, 1980, *46*, 272–276.

Wagner, M. K. A case of public masturbation treated by operant conditioning. *Journal of Child Psychology and Psychiatry*, 1968, *9*, 61–65.

Wahler, R. G. Child-child interaction in a free-field setting: Some experimental analyses. *Journal of Experimental Child Psychology*, 1967, *5*, 278–293.

Wahler, R. G., Winkle, G. H., Peterson, R. F., & Morrison, D. C. Mothers as behavior therapists for their own children. *Behavior Research and Therapy*, 1965, *3*, 113–124.

Walk, A. The pre-history of child psychiatry. *British Journal of Psychiatry*, 1964, *110*, 754–767.

Walker, H. M., Greenwood, C. R., Hops, H., & Todd, N. M. Differential effects of reinforcing topographic components of social interaction: Analysis and direct replication. *Behavior Modification*, 1979, *3*, 291–321.

Wallace, B. R. Negativism in verbal and nonverbal responses of autistic children. *Journal of Abnormal Psychology*, 1975, *84*, 138–143.

Wallace, G., & Kauffman, J. M. *Teaching children with learning problems* (2nd ed.). Columbus, Ohio: Charles E. Merrill, 1978.

Watt, N. F., Stolorow, R. D., Lubensky, A. W., & McClelland, D. C. School adjustment and behavior of children hospitalized for schizophrenia as adults. *American Journal of Orthopsychiatry*, 1970, *40*, 637–657.

Webster, D. R., & Azrin, N. H. Required relaxation: A method of inhibiting agitative-disruptive behavior of retardates. *Behavior Reserch and Therapy*, 1972, *11*, 67–78.

Wechsler, J. A.   *In a darkness.* New York: Norton, 1972.

Weinstein, L. Project Re-ED schools for emotionally disturbed children: Effectiveness as viewed by referring agencies, parents, and teachers. *Exceptional Children*, 1969, *35*, 703–711.

Weiss, B., Williams, J. H., Margen, S., Abrams, B., Cann, B., Citron, L. J., Cox, C., McKibben, J., Ogar, D., & Schulz, S. Behavioral responses to artificial food colors. *Science*, 1980, *207*, 1487–1489.

Weiss, G., Minde, K., Werry, J. S., Douglas, V., & Nemeth, E. Studies on the hyperactive child: VIII. Five-year follow-up. *Archives of General Psychiatry*, 1971, *24*, 409–414.

Weissbrod, C. S., & Bryan, J. H. Filmed treatment as an effective fear-reduction technique. *Journal of Abnormal Child Psychology*, 1973, *1*, 196–201.

Wells, K. C., Forehand, R., & Hickey, K. Effects of a verbal warning and overcorrection on stereotyped and appropriate behaviors. *Journal of Abnormal Child Psychology*, 1977, *5*, 387–403.

Wender, P. H. *Minimal brain dysfunction in children.* New York: Wiley, 1971.

Werner, J. S., Minkin, N., Minkin, B. L., Fixsen, D. L., Phillips, E. L., & Wolk, M. M. "Intervention Package": An analysis to prepare juvenile delinquents for encounters with police officers. *Criminal Justice and Behavior*, 1975, *2*, 55–84.

Werry, J. S. The childhood psychoses. In H. C. Quay & J. S. Werry (Eds.), *Psychopathological disorders of childhood* (2nd ed.). New York: Wiley, 1979. (a)

Werry, J. S. Organic factors. In H. C. Quay & J. S. Werry (Eds.), *Psychopathological disorders of childhood* (2nd ed.). New York: Wiley, 1979. (b)

Werry, J. S. Psychosomatic disorders, psychogenic symptoms, and hospitalization. In H. C. Quay & J.S. Werry (Eds.), *Psychopathological disorders of childhood* (2nd ed.). New York: Wiley, 1979. (c)

West, C. Lectures on the diseases of infancy and childhood. London: Longman, et al., 1848. In R. Hunter & I. Macalpine (Eds.), *Three hundred years of psychiatry, 1535–1860.* London: Oxford University Press, 1963.

West, D. J. *Present conduct and future delinquency.* New York: International Universities Press, 1969.

Wetzel, R. Use of behavioral techniques in a case of compulsive stealing. *Journal of Consulting Psychology*, 1966, *30*, 367–374.

Whalen, C. K., Collins, B. E., Henker, B., Alkus, S. R., Adams, D., & Stapp, J. Behavior observations of hyperactive children and methylphenidate (Ritalin) effects in systematically structured classroom environments: Now you see them, now you don't. *Journal of Pediatric Psychology*, 1978, *3*, 177–187.

Whelan, R. J. Educating emotionally disturbed children: Reflections upon educational methods and therapeutic processes. *Forum for Residential Therapy*, 1963, *1*, 9–14.

Whelan, R. J. The relevance of behavior modification procedures for teachers of emotionally disturbed children. In P. Knoblock (Ed.), *Intervention approaches in educating emotionally disturbed children*. Syracuse, N. Y.: Syracuse University Press, 1966.

Whelan, R. J. Richard J. Whelan. In J. M. Kauffman & C. D. Lewis (Eds.), *Teaching children with behavior disorders: Personal perspectives*. Columbus, Ohio: Charles E. Merrill, 1974.

Whelan, R. J., & Gallagher, P. A. Effective teaching of children with behavior disorders. In N. G. Haring & A. H. Hayden (Eds.), *The improvement of instruction*. Seattle: Special Child Publications, 1972.

Whelan, R. J., & Haring, N. J. Modification and maintenance of behavior through systematic application of consequences. *Exceptional Children*, 1966, *32*, 281–289.

White, L. Organic factors and psychophysiology in childhood schizophrenia. *Psychological Bulletin*, 1974, *81*, 238–255.

White, M. A., & Charry, J. B. (Eds.), *School disorder, intelligence, and social class*. New York: Teachers College Press, 1966.

White, O. R., & Haring, N. G. *Exceptional teaching: A multimedia program* (text, 8mm filmloops and cassettes, video cassette, and 16 mm film). Columbus, Ohio: Charles E. Merrill, 1976.

Wickman, E. K. *Children's behavior and teachers' attitudes*. New York: The Commonwealth Fund, Division of Publications, 1929.

Williams, C. D. The elimination of tantrum behavior by extinction procedures. *Journal of Abnormal and Social Psychology*, 1959, *59*, 269.

Williams, J. S. Aspects of dependence—independence conflict in children with asthma. *Journal of Child Psychology and Psychiatry*, 1975, *16*, 199–218.

Wing, J. K. Diagnosis, epidemiology, aetiology. In J. K. Wing (Ed.), *Early childhood autism: Clinical, educational, and social aspects*. New York: Pergamon, 1966.

Wing, L. *Autistic children: A guide for parents and professionals*. New York: Brunner/Mazel, 1972.

Wolf, M. M., Risley, T. R., & Mees, H. Application of operant conditioning techniques to the behavior problems of an autistic child. *Behaviour Research and Therapy*, 1964, *3*, 305–312.

Wolpe, J. *Psychotherapy by reciprocal inhibition*. Stanford, Calif.: Stanford University Press, 1958.

Wolpe, J. Laboratory-derived clinical methods of deconditioning anxiety. In T. Thompson & W. S. Dockens (Eds.), *Applications of behavior modification*. New York: Academic Press, 1975.

Wong, M. R. Drug abuse and prevention in the special education students. In D. Cullinan & M. H. Epstein (Eds.), *Special education for adolescents: Issues and perspectives*. Columbus, Ohio: Charles E. Merrill, 1979.

Wood, F., & Lakin, C. Defining emotionally disturbed/behavior disordered populations for research purposes. Paper presented at an Advanced Institute for Trainers of Teachers of Seriously Emotionally Disturbed Children and Youth. Charlottesville, Va., Feb 23, 1979.

Worell, J., & Nelson, C. M. *Managing instructional problems: A case study workbook*. New York: McGraw-Hill, 1974.

Wright, W. G. The Bellevue Psychiatric Hospital School. In P.H. Berkowitz & E.P. Rothman (Eds.), *Public education for disturbed children in New York City*. Springfield, Ill.: Charles C. Thomas, 1967.

Wundheiler, L. N. "Liberty Boy": The play of a schizophrenic child. *Journal of the American Academy of Child Psychiatry*, 1976, *15*, 475–490.

Yablonsky, L. *The violent gang*. New York: Macmillan, 1962.

Yarrow, L. J. Separation from parents during early childhood. In M. L. Hoffman & L. W. Hoffman (Eds.), *Review of child development research, Vol. 1*. New York: Russel Sage Foundation, 1964.

Yates, A. *Behavior therapy*. New York: Wiley, 1970.

Young, G. C. Conditioning treatment of enuresis. *Developmental Medicine and Child Neurology*, 1965, *7*, 557–562.

Ysseldyke, J. E., & Foster, G. G. Bias in teachers' observations of emotionally disturbed and learning disabled children. *Exceptional Children*, 1978, *44*, 613–615.

Zentall, S. S. Optimal stimulation as a theoretical basis of hyperactivity. *American Journal of Orthopsychiatry*, 1975, *45*, 547–563.

Zentall, S. S. Effects of environmental stimulation on behavior as a function of type of behavior disorder. *Behavioral Disorders*, 1979, *5*, 19–29.

Zimmerman, J., & Zimmerman, E. The alteration of behavior in a special classroom stituation. *Journal of the Experimental Analysis of Behavior*, 1962, *5*, 59–60.

index _____

about the author

James M. Kauffman received his undergraduate degree in elementary education from Goshen College in 1962 and his M.Ed. in elementary education from Washburn University in 1966. He was a classroom teacher for several years before undertaking graduate work at the University of Kansas, where he received his Ed.D. degree in special education in 1969. He taught regular and special education classes in public schools in Indiana and Kansas and also was a teacher of severely emotionally disturbed children at Southard School, Children's Division of the Menninger Clinic in Topeka. Dr. Kauffman is currently professor and chair of the Department of Special Education, University of Virginia, where he has been a faculty member since 1970. He is the author or coauthor of numerous articles and books in special education. His wife, Myrna, is a nurse. He has a son, Tim and a daughter, Melissa, who are teenagers.

For readers of

Characteristics of Children's Behavior Disorders
Second Edition